The First World War as a Clash of Cultures

Studies in German Literature, Linguistics, and Culture

The First World War
as a Clash of Cultures

Edited by
Fred Bridgham

CAMDEN HOUSE

First published 2006
by Camden House

Camden House is an imprint of Boydell & Brewer Inc.
668 Mt. Hope Avenue, Rochester, NY 14620, USA
www.camden-house.com
and of Boydell & Brewer Limited
PO Box 9, Woodbridge, Suffolk IP12 3DF, UK
www.boydellandbrewer.com

ISBN: 1–57113–340–2

Library of Congress Cataloging-in-Publication Data

The First World War as a clash of cultures / edited by Fred Bridgham.
        p. cm. — (Studies in German literature, linguistics, and culture)
Includes bibliographical references and index.
ISBN 1–57113–340–2 (hardcover: alk. paper)
    1. German literature — 20th century — History and criticism.
2. English literature — 20th century — History and criticism.
3. German literature — Themes, motives.   4. English literature —
Themes, motives. 5. World War, 1914–1918 — Germany — Literature
and the war.   6. World War, 1914–1918 — Great Britain — Literature
and the war.   7. Germany — Civilization — 20th century.   8. Great
Britain — Civilization — 20th century.   9. Literature, Comparative—
German and English.   10. Literature, Comparative — English and
German.   I. Bridgham, Frederick George Thomas, 1943–   II. Series:
Studies in German literature, linguistics, and culture (Unnumbered)

PT405.F495 2006
820.9'358—dc22
                                                    2006009905

A catalogue record for this title is available from the British Library.

This publication is printed on acid-free paper.
Printed in the United States of America.

Contents

Writers

Thinkers

Academics

Acknowledgments

I WISH TO EXPRESS my particular thanks to Helena Ragg-Kirkby, indispensable fellow coordinator of the international "Peacemakers and Warmongers" conference held at the University of Leeds in April 2002.

The present volume brings together newly edited versions of selected papers delivered on that occasion, with an additional invited contribution on popular fiction. Earlier versions of some have already appeared in journals, and acknowledgment is gratefully made to: *Modern Language Review* (Martin), *Comparative Literature* (Cornils), *Neophilologus* (Manz), and *Krieg und Literatur/War and Literature* (Klein).

Thanks are also due to the Austrian Cultural Forum, and to the German Department and the School of Modern Languages and Cultures at the University of Leeds for their generous subventions. An MA course on Anglo-German Cultural Relations, taught in the German Department over many years, provided much of the stimulus for the Peacemakers and Warmongers conference as also for this book.

Iain Boyd Whyte and Imanuel Geiss read and helpfully commented on drafts of the introduction. Translations from the German, when not otherwise attributed, are by Richard Byrn who also assumed much of the responsibility for editing and deserves special mention for his unstinting guidance and support.

F. B.
Leeds, March 2006

Introduction

Fred Bridgham

Fighting a Philosophy

As THE FIRST WORLD WAR recedes from living memory, our fascination with what George F. Kennan called "the seminal catastrophe of mankind" in the twentieth century remains undimmed. Perceptions shaped by vivid accounts of the war's genesis and unfolding, from Liddell Hart's *The Real War* (1930)[1] and A. J. P. Taylor's *The Struggle for Mastery in Europe 1848–1918* (1952)[2] to Barbara W. Tuchman's *August 1914* (1962) and Laurence Lafore's *The Long Fuse* (1965), likewise endure in the English-speaking world, amplified a further forty years on, though scarcely displaced, by Hew Strachan's monumental *The First World War* (vol. 1, 2001), and reinforced by a straightforwardly nostalgic appetite for commemorations and military histories, memoirs, and literary reconstructions.

In sharp contrast, Germany over the same period has had to come to terms with her troubled past in a difficult process of self-scrutiny. Fritz Fischer's pioneering work on Germany's war aims, *Griff nach der Weltmacht* (1961), was followed more contentiously in *Krieg der Illusionen* (1969) by even more minutely detailed evidence. Drawing on all currently available documents of the erstwhile belligerents assembled by Imanuel Geiss in *Julikrise und Kriegsausbruch 1914* (2 vols., 1963/1964), Fischer made a formidable case that Germany had been actively planning war with expansionist aims against France and Russia from 1912, gambling on British neutrality. This compelled most German historians, and in their wake prominent politicians and the reading public, to revise the comfortable belief that — in the Great War at least — all the powers were equally guilty. Specifically, they had to scrap the myth of the war as Germany's purely "defensive" response to Entente "encirclement."

More radically still, it was argued that Germany's disastrous fluctuation between power vacuum and power center led with tragic inevitability from her belated unification in 1871 to a major European war caused primarily by aggressive German *Weltpolitik* nearly half a century later (Geiss, *Der lange Weg in die Katastrophe*, 1990).[3] For remaining adherents of what had been an unbroken conservative and nationalist historical tradition, the suggestion that the same dynamic led inexorably from the impotence of Weimar to Hitler's even more catastrophic response to "the German Question" was anathema. Fischer's last book, *Hitler war kein Betriebsunfall* (1992) answered a (seemingly exculpatory) attempt to relativize the uniqueness of Nazi crimes by comparing them with those of Communist totalitarianism (*Historikerstreit*, 1986). A decade later, however, even "ordinary" Germans stood controversially accused of helping perpetrate the Holocaust in Daniel Goldhagen's *Hitler's Willing Executioners* (1996), with the so-called "Jewish Problem" retrospectively linked to the "German Question" as a cultural legacy of the decades before the Great War.[4] Celebrations marking the foundation of Prussia prompted equally heated exchanges on the role of "Prussian militarism" in Germany's disastrous past, while the continuing debate since reunification in 1991 over a return to "normality" and an appropriate role for Germany on the world stage still triggers memories of her abortive first attempt at global politics a century ago.

If the "Fischer school" effected a sea change in German historiography, a paradigm shift of comparable magnitude has now taken place, according to the venerable Wolfgang Mommsen. *Kultur* is the new key to international historical writing on the First World War.[5] Put even more pointedly by Niall Ferguson, "It is often asserted that the First World War was caused by culture."[6] By this is meant a clash of ostensibly antagonistic social attitudes and intellectual traditions along a cultural front no less entrenched than the Western fighting front. After hostilities began, G. K. Chesterton observed that "Culture is already almost beginning to be spelt with a k,"[7] but the perception had long taken root in Germany that their profound and soulful *Kultur* was encircled by the empty rationalism of French "civilization," the godless materialism of the Anglo-Saxons, and the "barbarism" of Russia. What came to be known in Germany as the "Ideas of 1914" had little to do with England's "golden summer of 1914," perceived in retrospect to have been the epitome of irretrievably lost innocence.[8] Rather they were a rejection of "the Ideas of 1789" — those universalist aspirations associated with the French Revolution, which in Germany today take the form of a pragmatic "constitutional patriotism."[9] German hopes for world-power status, and perhaps for global domination, were inextricably tied instead to a quasi-religious belief[10] in the benefits her unique culture could bestow, or impose, on the world.

The story is indeed broadly familiar, not least from individual chapters in Paul M. Kennedy's magisterial account of *The Rise of the Anglo-German Antagonism, 1860–1914* (1980). Other "cultural" studies have made their mark, such as John Mander's *Our German Cousins* (1974) and Peter Firchow's *The Death of the German Cousin: Variations on a Literary Stereotype, 1890–1920* (1986). Focusing on the war itself and its aftermath there is Paul Fussell's moving evocation of *The Great War and Modern Memory* (1977), Peter Buitenhuis's *The Great War of Words: Literature as Propaganda, 1914–18 and After* (1987),[11] and Stuart Wallace's *War and the Image of Germany: British Academics, 1914–1918* (1988). Popular literature of the prewar period has been examined by I. F. Clarke in *Voices Prophesying War* (1966) and illustrated with over fifty extracts from "fictions and fantasies of the War-to-come" in *The Tale of the Next Great War, 1871–1914* (1995) and *The Great War with Germany, 1890–1914* (1997).

The reassessments and new perspectives offered by the present volume supplement these studies and fall into three categories, often linked. First, the mainly popular literature in both English and German reflecting growing tensions between Germany and her imperial rival, often dramatizing the perceived threat of invasion, though also featuring intermarriage as a way of effecting reconciliation at a personal level. Then the ideas that informed or misinformed public debate and subsequently wartime propaganda, preeminently "Nietzscheanism" and Social Darwinism, with advocates and opponents on both sides. Finally, the role of scholars in conveying both cultural distinction and cultural distinctiveness across national, and after August 1914, enemy, frontiers.

It is indisputable that the period in question was a golden age in the cultural lives of each of the main combatant countries. They all experienced "the shock of the new," that sequence of "isms," by turn bewildering, exasperating, and exhilarating, that bridged the war years and cumulatively constitutes Modernism. At the same time, the aesthetic practice of the most prominent literary figures drawn into the conflict was broadly traditional and accessible. "Today in Britain most schoolchildren learn about the war through its literary legacy," Strachan surmises,[12] doubtless with the war poets in mind. The German equivalent is somewhat different, for the essentially German phenomenon of Expressionism predates the war by several years, and it is the premonitory apocalyptic visions of a Georg Heym (d. 1912) or the anguished exaltation of a Georg Trakl (d. 1914)[13] that have survived, rather than most of the war poetry itself. August Stramm's meticulous minimalism, written from the Eastern Front, is a memorable exception. Though few major writers remained *au-dessus de la mêlée*,[14] Germany's best-known poets — Rilke, George, and Hofmannsthal — stayed relatively aloof. Ferguson's assertion that "among the most haunting condemnations of the war in German poetry are Rilke's *Duino Elegies*" is simply wrong.[15] Nor is there a war poet "Robert" Owen (Mommsen),[16] or a manifesto entitled "An der Kulturwelt" (*sic*, Strachan).[17]

Historians' incursions into "culture" sometimes run "the risk of being mown down in inter-disciplinary no man's land," as Ferguson disarmingly puts it. They also bear out the truth of his own observation (to which the above, in their aims, are all honorable exceptions) that "most historians still tend to study the war from the vantage point of a single nation-state."[18] Too often the stereotypical distortions of the prewar years have been simply perpetuated as a sort of "reception history" in later accounts. Harold James admits as much in his survey of the period.[19] His view that "Treitschke, Richard Wagner and Friedrich Nietzsche represented an unholy trinity of intellectual anti-liberalism" is at least arguable, even though the antimodernist(!), anti-Semitic Wagner on view here is not one of the usual contenders (see Bridgham on *Bernhardi*, chapter 7 in this volume). But to say that for Thomas Mann in the 1910s "Nietzsche stood for a truly German synthesis of Weimar and Potsdam, culture and military heroism"[20] travesties both Thomas Mann's position[21] and Nietzsche's, and appears to endorse the clichéd notion of a Hegelian synthesis of opposites as something peculiarly German. E. M. Forster is a more reliable guide to the incompatibility of "Weimar and Potsdam" in *Howards End*, and the famous maxim of that novel, "only connect," in full awareness of the cultural differences, is a healthier guiding precept, both for analysis of the regrettable Anglo-German schism he had in mind in 1910 and for the historically-informed cultural criticism offered by this volume.

A decade was to elapse before survivors were ready to record, and readers to relive, the horrors of trench warfare in the memoirs of Robert Graves or Siegfried Sassoon or Edmund Blunden. Even then, they were often filtered through theatrical imagery and irony, or on the stage itself and "with all the great words cancelled out" for that generation (D. H. Lawrence), as in R. C. Sherriff's *Journey's End* (1928). Ernst Jünger's more immediate response, exalting the warrior's austere and mystical destiny as forged in the crucible of war, *In Stahlgewittern* (1920), could not be more different — as indeed were the German trenches: up to thirty feet deep, fully-equipped refuges from the "storm of steel" he so realistically describes.[22] But Erich Maria Remarque's *Im Westen nichts Neues* (1928) quickly translated into that universal anthem for doomed youth, the nightmarish "Gothic fantasia"[23] *All Quiet on the Western Front*. Graves left England, assuredly in the knowledge that it was not to be *Goodbye to All That* after all, and that the Great War had not been Wells's *War that Will End War* (1914). He had seen signs, however, that one particular cycle appeared to have come full circle, and that the Anglo-German antagonism had given way to an "almost obsessional" respect among ex-soldiers for "the most efficient fighting-man in Europe," and the conviction of some that "we had been fighting on the wrong side." Blunden, he tells us, used to vow "No more wars for me at any price! Except against the French."[24] This reversion to traditional affinities and enmities, however premature, takes us back to the beginning of the story half a century earlier.

Novelists in Both Camps

"Almost before the smoke had settled at Sedan, English writers began to construct pessimistic scenarios of further German conquests" (Iain Boyd Whyte on *Popular Fiction*, chapter 1). The astonishing success of the first such (initially anonymous) admonitory tract, Lieutenant-Colonel, later General, Sir George Tomkyns Chesney's *The Battle of Dorking* (1871), exposing English unpreparedness and incompetence when confronted with German military efficiency on Box Hill, and further humiliation following the enemy's "rough and boorish but not uncivil" occupation of Surbiton drawing rooms, unleashed a flood of invasion stories and novels. Not all agreed with Chesney that England was truly ripe for a fall, "wilfully blind" with "only ourselves to blame," "like the foolish virgins in the parable."[25] There were also outraged refutations and mocking travesties, but most preached the urgent need for increased military expenditure and conscription, a campaign finally given respectable if unofficial form as the National Service League under military hero Lord Roberts. A resurgent France ("France was different," Chesney had written, "rich soil . . . no colonies to lose (*sic*) . . . they rose again")[26] soon emerged as the likely foe after Tel-el-Kabir, the Franco-Russian alliance, and Fashoda. As the Kaiser's saber-rattling and "gift of the gaffe"[27] became more pronounced, however, especially from the Anglo-French agreement of 1904 onwards, the focus shifted inexorably to the threat from Germany.

After the bungled Jameson Raid in 1896, Alfred Harmsworth's newly launched *Daily Mail*, catering for a greatly expanded reading public, had responded to Wilhelm's provocative congratulatory telegram to Transvaal's President Kruger with inflammatory anti-German rhetoric. Britain's sharp diplomatic response in turn helped exacerbate the Anglophobia of Pan-Germans and nationalist intellectuals. Tentative operational planning against Britain "marks the first time that part of the German 'Official Mind' began to see the British as potential enemies, rather than as uncertain friends or devious neutrals."[28] "My own view," Harmsworth confided in 1900, "is that the Germans are being led definitely and irrevocably to make war on the rest of Europe, and we will have to take part in it."[29] German popular opinion was being similarly inflamed, and the Boer War novel — notably Karl Bleibtreu's *Bur und Lord* (1900) — was "invented as a vehicle for displaying the callousness of the English and the inherent nobility of the 'Teutonic' Boers"[30] — war, as it were, by proxy. In a letter penned to his uncle, the Prince of Wales, when England was faring badly in the Second Boer War, the Kaiser recommended that she accept defeat "quietly and with chivalrous acknowledgment of her opponent," just as she had "in the great Cricket Match between England and Australia" a year earlier.[31]

The sly allusion to the English mania for sport introduces a recurrent stereotype, but one that lends itself to good comic effect in the right hands. P. G. Wodehouse describes an August Bank Holiday on which England finds itself "not merely beneath the heel of the invader. It was beneath the heels of nine invaders. There was barely standing-room." News that the Germans had landed in Essex warrants the briefest notice below the banner headline "Surrey Doing Badly." Since his grown-up fellow countrymen dwell moodily on "the fact that this counter-attraction was bound to hit first-class cricket," it is left to the Boy Scout hero of *The Swoop! or How Clarence Saved England* (1909), true to his creed, to outwit the invaders, baffled as they are by the philistine Londoners' approval of the bombardment of the Albert Hall and burning of the Royal Academy as "a great comfort to all," and too intimidated by their supercilious stares to be able to comply with the Kaiser's telegrammed instructions: "At once mailed fist display. On get or out get — WILHELM."[32] Though not quite yet in top mid-season form (Jeeves, one of popular literature's supermen, did not appear until 1925,[33] when he pronounced Nietzsche "fundamentally unsound"), Wodehouse's levity "was as little appreciated in 1909 as it was in 1941,"[34] and signally failed to stem the rising tide of Germanophobia.

A more sardonically subversive observer of Edwardian society, H. H. Monro ("Saki"), paints an all too plausible picture of London under the Hohenzollerns in *When William Came* (1913), its occupation effortlessly achieved by clever German exploitation of native materialistic opportunism, the hedonistic frivolity of its social elite, and its already cosmopolitan musical and theatrical tastes. "The King across the water" was once a potent rallying cry, but not an emperor in Delhi, whither his Conservative supporters have largely followed him. Labour "are almost in as bad odour as the Liberals, because of having hobnobbed too effusively and ostentatiously with the German democratic parties on the eve of the war, exploiting an evangel of universal brotherhood which did not blunt a single Teuton bayonet when the hour came." Assimilation beckons, however, as the golf links and the hunting field are beginning to get back their votaries and "there is the alchemy of Sport and the Drama to bring men of different races amicably together. One or two sportsmanlike Germans in a London football team will do more to break down racial antagonism than anything that Governments or Councils can effect."

Saki's satire and shrewd psychological predictions are tempered by an elegiac tone and a predisposition for "overripe prose."[35] In a rousing finale at the projected Imperial Triumph in Hyde Park, with the yellow newspaper placards "announcing to an indifferent public the fate of Essex wickets," "Emperor and Princes, Generals and guards, sat stiffly in their saddles, and waited. And waited. . . ." But the Boy Scouts — object of their anxious suspense and symbol of the younger generation "whose hostility must be disarmed" if the German occupation is to be consolidated — fail to appear.[36] Long before fathers actually sent sons to war,[37] the "generation gap" was becoming one of the most resonant topoi of all in European literature.

The plucky, though preposterously implausible, heroine of William Le Queux's exceptionally bad novel *Spies of the Kaiser* (1909) is more skeptical of Baden-Powell's methods. "Instead of teaching boys to scout and instructing young men in the use of popguns, we should strike first," she declares — against a vast organization of German undercover agents plotting sabotage on the long-awaited day of reckoning.[38] This was a follow-up to *The Invasion of 1910*, a sensational success when serialized in the *Daily Mail* (1906), though of no greater literary merit. "Operations will shortly commence with the landing of the German forces on the Suffolk coast," *Gaumont* announced when it started filming in 1912 (the film, *If England Were Invaded*, was released from censorship in September 1914). With seven more novels to his questionable credit in 1907, six in 1908, and five in 1909, its author at least cannot be accused of short-changing Harmsworth (now Lord Northcliffe), his sponsor, but as Nicholas Hiley observes, their "overblown style is impervious to ridicule." Nonetheless, there is no denying Le Queux's influence, for the Committee of Imperial Defence set up a special bureau (MO5, the forerunner of MI5) to investigate Le Queux's fictional spy network. And the boundary between fact and fantasy became increasingly blurred when responses inspired by Le Queux to advertisements in the *Weekly News* ("Foreign Spies in Britain — £10 Given for Information — Have You Seen a Spy?") were passed on to the bureau, then back to Le Queux "to supplement his investigations."[39] Asquith, to his credit, remained "entirely unconvinced" by the "desperate concern" of Maurice Hankey, Secretary to the CID, about the "25,000 able-bodied Germans and Austrians still at large in London." But it is not clear whether another Committee member was being sarcastic or not when he asked if MO5 felt any alarm "regarding the large number of German waiters in this country."[40]

Only one of the "invasion novels" has truly stayed the course while its imitations have been all but forgotten, and that is *The Riddle of the Sands* (1903). In this ever-popular yarn, an intrepid young yachtsman discovers and foils plans to tow a German army in barges under cover of fog across to England's east coast from the tide-bound inlets behind the Frisian Islands. Its author, Erskine Childers, fully deserves his legendary aura, having progressed from Tory imperialist and Boer War veteran to Liberal

enthusiast for military reform, gun-running Home-Ruler, diehard opponent of the Irish Treaty, and executed martyr. De Valera made this
"prince of men" Minister of Propaganda, while his more suspicious deputy Arthur Griffiths accused Childers of causing one war with *The Riddle
of the Sands* and wanting to start another.[41] The same Churchill who as
First Lord of the Admiralty had employed him in 1914 for his expert
yachtsman's knowledge of the North German coast condemned him in
1922 as a "mischief-making murderous renegade."[42] Yet, in reality, the
novel had been a salutary "wake up to those Admiralty chaps," who did
then act to make good the deficiencies identified by its hero: "Chatham,
our only eastern base — no North Sea base or squadron — they'd land at
one of those God-forsaken flats off the Crouch and Blackwater."[43] Chesney had already warned against naval overstretch: "the best part of the
fleet had been decoyed down to the Dardanelles, and what remained of
the Channel squadron was looking after Fenian filibusters off the west of
Ireland."[44] When Churchill gave orders, therefore, on July 26, 1914 and
without Cabinet approval, for the Fleet not to disperse after manoeuvres
off Portland, but to sail for its war base at Scapa Flow, the legacy of
Childer's admonitory novel was palpable.[45]

While even Le Queux's *Invasion of 1910* found an eager readership in
its 1907 German translation, helped, perhaps, by omission of the final
German defeat,[46] the invasion novel scarcely reflected either the realistic
aspirations or the fears of German readers.[47] Since her colonial rivalry with
Britain focused rather on that "place in the sun" from which she felt un-
justly excluded, the most successful German novel of the kind, *1906 —
Der Zusammenbruch der alten Welt* (1906; English translation as *Armageddon 190–*, 1907) by Ferdinand Grautoff ("Seestern"), is instead a convincing vision of global struggle. In a canny prediction of future power
configurations, only the neutral Americans and Russians emerge as real
winners. According to several of these fantasies, only England and Germany combined, the "Teutonic" races, might resist the growing strength
of the USA. In one such fantasy, Lieutenant Eberhard von Mantey is
commissioned in 1897 to plot the dispatch of a huge fleet across the At-
lantic against the north-eastern seaboard. After US victory in the Spanish-
American war with the enviable acquisitions of Cuba, the Philippines,
Puerto Rico, and parts of Samoa and Hawaii, a revised German plan tar-
gets New York: "The greatest panic would break out in New York over
fears of bombardment . . . Two or three battalions of infantry and one
battalion of sappers should be sufficient." Abandoned only in 1906, these
long-standing plans are to be found not in a novel, however, but among
documents in a record office in Freiburg. Their author, as recently revealed in *Die Zeit*, was the Kaiser.[48] Even Childers's hero in 1903 can
scarcely have guessed at this further objective of German sea-power:

"It's a new thing with them, but it's going strong, and that Emperor of theirs is running it for all it's worth. He's a splendid chap, and anyone can see he's right. They've no colonies to speak of, and *must* have them, like us."[49]

Though both the naval arms race and the new aeronautical technologies — from Zeppelins to the spaceships of H. G. Wells and Lasswitz[50] — figure prominently in the invasion fictions of the day (Wells has the Germans wiping out New York from a fleet of airships in *The War in the Air*, 1908),[51] in the event the war at sea and in the air turned out to be sideshows. Few foresaw with the clarity of Lord Kitchener — a prognosis met with almost total disbelief — that "we must be prepared to put armies of millions in the field and maintain them for several years" — the time required to build up from barely seven to the seventy divisions needed to match the Continental armies.[52]

At the other end of the spectrum from such still unimagined horrors there were writers who, like E. M. Forster, countered the "life in which telegrams and anger count" with the conviction "that personal relations are the real life."[53] The "mixed-marriage" novel, often based on first-hand experience, provided an outlet for more nuanced comparisons, as in the case of Katherine Mansfield's cousin, the Gräfin von Arnim, better known as the author of *Elisabeth and her German Garden*, perhaps, than for other such reworkings of her own and similar predicaments as *Fräulein Schmidt and Mr. Anstruther*. Forster of course, who had tutored the Gräfin von Arnim's children in Pomerania, furnishes the best-known example with the Schlegel-Wilcox marriage in *Howards End* (1910), but Whyte also analyses lesser-known variations on the theme, notably by I. A. R. Wylie and Sybil Spottiswoode, in which "neither side is granted an absolute monopoly of virtue" and "the possibility of reconciliation is held open to the very end." His conclusion, however, is all too predictable: "While it is certain that the invasion novels (a strictly male preserve on both sides) actually encouraged the war psychosis on both sides of the Channel, there is little evidence that the novels of reconciliation had any effect as an antidote."[54]

Among the intriguing cultural insights they nevertheless afford are the conflicting national perspectives on, for example, German officialdom and English businessmen, or anti-Semitism (the much-hated Kipling, according to one character, is really a Jew called Cohen),[55] or "the confrontation of 'Händler und Helden,' of English luxury versus Prussian austerity, being fought out on the vestimentary front."[56] Or, most tellingly, the military caste and its conception of honor, reflecting the widely reported Zabern incident of 1913, which split even the *Reichstag* into pro- and anti-military camps.[57] Thus a Spottiswoode heroine's explanation of the *Ehrenkodex* elicits only an English yawn, while a Wylie heroine's wastrel brother is contemptuously told by the insulted German officer whose challenge he has rejected: "No; you go to law and take money for your injured honour. . . . That is the revenge of shopkeepers — not of gentlemen."[58] So dueling, already a topic of fascination to Mark Twain in Heidelberg (*A Tramp Abroad*, 1878), makes a return to English literature, pinpointing national stereotypes for good measure,[59] not long after its more deadly dissection at the hands of Fontane (*Effi Briest*, 1895) and Schnitzler, who was himself cashiered for "violating the professional honour of an officer," in *Leutnant Gustl* (1900). Converted into the philosophical terms which all but Oxford's neo-Hegelians would have found simply contradictory, a review of Rudolf Strass's *Seine englische Frau* (1913) describes the "Leben in freiem Gehorsam gegen die Vorgesetzten" (life in freely chosen obedience to one's superiors) awaiting the hero on his return from England to a naval career in Germany, where he will be "free to obey his superiors."[60]

D. H. Lawrence

One "mixed-marriage" novel, told with all the uninhibited gusto of a raw first draft (abandoned in 1922), deserves the special attention it receives here from Helena Ragg-Kirkby, for *Mr Noon* contains a lightly disguised record of D. H. Lawrence's experiences after his elopement to Germany in 1912 with Frieda Weekley, cousin of Germany's ace pilot, "the Red Baron" Manfred von Richthofen. The protagonist of the first part is plucked out of claustrophobic English insularity and set down in "High Germany" (the "gentle reader," so incessantly buttonholed and berated, is told not to get in a stew "because you don't know what Bavaria is doing in connection with such a disreputable land as Germany"). There he is soon entranced by "the vast patchwork of Europe. The glamorous vast multiplicity" spread before his mind's eye, which "seemed to break his soul like a chrysalis into new life . . . he became unEnglished." We are offered a kaleidoscope of all things German that Lawrence had imbibed as a languages student in Nottingham, then with and through Frieda and her family (notably sister Else, the intellectual of the family, and their mother Anna, Lawrence's "liebe Schwiegermutter" [dear mother-in-law]),[61] crowned by a set piece on the "militaristic insolence and parvenu imperialism" of Metz (or "Detsch," as the key strategic stronghold is called in the novel).

But this is offset by a Nietzschean determination to live dangerously (his alter ego's name is itself a Zarathustrian echo: "Noon is Now. That is, he is at his zenith") — in Life ("We are not so keen on peace . . . Let us have continual risk") as in Love ("what was the good of love that wasn't a fight! What was the good of anything that wasn't a fight!").[62] So no "reconciliation," any more than there is ever an easy synthesis of sexual pairings in his novels — rather a healthy dialectic clash. And the man who "would like to kill a million Germans — two million"[63] is also the one whose "chief grief is for Germany . . . a young and adorable country — adolescent — with the faults of adolescence."[64] "The war," he wrote in 1915, "is one bout in the terrific, horrible labour, our civilisation labouring in child-birth, and unable to bring forth."[65] Firchow nicely catches the paradox of this Lawrentian metaphysics: "Though he consistently opposed the war as the culmination of mechanized mass man, he just as consistently desired that culmination as the simultaneous destruction of mass man and the harbinger of a new man"[66] — a complex response then, which sees Englishman and German as parts of a common, currently debased humanity, and a far cry from the "deeply reactionary convictions, sometimes translated into fascist practice"[67] of which Lawrence often stands accused.

Carl Sternheim

Carl Sternheim was more unambiguously averse to any notion of the "spiritual necessity" of war, especially after Germany invaded Belgium, where he had his family home and where (like Lawrence in Metz) he was briefly arrested on suspicion of spying. However, Germany's most popular dramatist of the day shared Lawrence's reputation as a "progressive" in sexual matters and experienced similar problems with the censor over such increasingly untimely comic deflations of "the heroic life of the bourgeoisie" as *Die Hose* (1911, *Knickers*). His focus, like Lawrence's, on unconstrained individual self-fulfilment meant that personal ecstasy might take the form of a prostitute's piety touching off, and itself being kindled by, a policeman's blind Kaiser-worship (as in *Busekow*, 1913, published, tellingly, in the leading anti-war journal *Die Weißen Blätter*). Sternheim's survival strategy during the war years involved sheltering behind translations, mainly from the French (which did not help), but his 1914 adaptation of Klinger's drama *Das leidende Weib*, finally released for public performance (and flopping) in 1916, is an altogether more significant *drame à clef*. Its initial suppression by the Berlin censor, "in der Rücksicht auf die gegenwärtige große Zeit" (bearing in mind the great times we are living through), unwittingly — one presumes — parrots the title of Karl Kraus's famous attack on the manipulation of public opinion by the press and its generation of false heroic consciousness: "In These Great Times, which I knew when they were *this* small. . . ."[68]

As Rhys Williams explains in chapter 3, "if the *Liebestod* coincides with a *Heldentod*, the reader (and the censor) might be unaware of the difference" in this tale of an ambassador, his wife, and her lover, which both reflects Sternheim's affair with Mechtilde von Lichnowsky and, more importantly implies a defense of Prince Lichnowsky's despairing attempts as German Ambassador in London to avert war. When made the scape-goat for having allegedly misled the German Foreign Office into believing that violation of Belgian neutrality would not cause Britain to declare war, Lichnowsky published a spirited defense as *Meine Londoner Mission, 1912–1914* (1916). Four million copies of this memorandum were dis-tributed in the trenches and on the home front in March 1918 as *My Mis-sion to London 1912–1914*; it was also known as *Germany's War Guilt* for its account of how Germany had pushed Austria to take a hard line against Serbia in order to provoke Russia, and for its defense of Grey's efforts to secure a peaceful solution. It thus reinforced British propa-ganda's own attacks on what Lichnowsky pilloried as "the spirit of Treitschke and Bernhardi."[69]

The Belgian connection provides another curiosity of literary history in that Germany's most prominent poet of the younger generation, Gottfried Benn, having himself scandalized bourgeois sentiment with *Morgue* in 1912, was part of Sternheim's circle in Brussels (as an army doctor he officiated at the execution of Nurse Edith Cavell in 1915). While neither found the times propitious for their primary vocation and genre, Benn's "Rönne" *Novellen* from these years rank with Sternheim's *Busekow* and *Napoleon* as the most interesting though still little known examples of anti-ideological, proto-Existentialist, "Expressionist" prose. Both suffered a nervous collapse and "repatriation" to their less than ap-preciative fatherland.

H. G. Wells and Kurd Laßwitz

The last two literary works under discussion both appeared in 1897. As Ingo Cornils observes below, they turn the tables on English and Ger-mans alike, for it is their turn to be colonized. As the narrator of H. G. Wells's sensational *The War of the Worlds*[70] tells us, the landing of the Martian invaders in Weybridge "did not make the sensation an ultimatum to Germany would have done." But the march of hundred-foot-high tri-pod "ironclads" on London deploying heat rays and poisonous black clouds[71] soon demonstrates in more extreme form the small advance in military technology which had decided the issue at Sedan, and threatened to do so again as the naval arms race got under way.[72] Even more pre-scient, indeed influential, was Kurd Laßwitz's *Auf zwei Planeten*, which carried on the cover of an American edition in 1971 a testimonial from Wernher von Braun: "I shall never forget how I devoured this novel with curiosity and excitement as a young man . . ."[73] — inspiration, no doubt, for the US moon-shots and doughnut-shaped space-stations he helped design (even the word *Raumbahnhof* is a Laßwitz coinage), not to men-tion Hitler's V1 and V2 rockets.[74]

But the weapons technology that the Martians are obliged to employ as reluctant colonizers after first confronting English insolence at sea, then German military arrogance (most memorably, an airborne magnet that disarms the Kaiser's entire army in one fell swoop), is neither the distinguishing, nor indeed the most distinguished, feature of Laßwitz's 800-page epic. Nor is the enormously detailed scientific explanation of how these lords of the solar system have harnessed gravitational and solar energy after emancipating themselves from agricultural "idiocy" à la Marx and millennia-long Luddite civil wars, culminating in the founding of the Martian federation and what they take to be "the end of history."[75] Rather it is their superior ethical culture, the benefits and obligations of which,[76] along with their know-how, they had hoped to trade for earth's underdeveloped resources (for their planet lacks water — hence those newly observed "canals").[77]

What makes the book still readable, however, and even topical as an allegory, is the symbiotic process whereby Martian public opinion is gradually contaminated by its colonial adventure and the prevailing military culture of its "protectorate," while enlightened representatives of earth's *Kulturvölker* educate their fellow men towards emancipation through solidarity under the banner of "Martianness but without the Martians."[78] Laßwitz's pedagogical purpose recalls Voltaire's *Micromégas* on human hubris vis-à-vis visitors from space, or *Zadig* on tolerance. But beyond the social program of the Enlightenment, his Martian culture is essentially a realization of Kantian ethics, Goethe's doctrine of personality, and Schiller's of "aesthetic education," their shared central tenet, and Laßwitz's, being the inviolability of individual moral autonomy[79] — or to put it plainly, as one of his characters does: "Das sind allein die Gentlemen"[80] (they alone are the gentlemen). Appropriately, the possibility of reconciliation between these two great "Kulturplaneten"[81] is signaled, if not yet sealed, by a daring interplanetary "mixed marriage."

Wells's tale is altogether more pessimistic, reflecting his then current despair of man's evolutionary potential, or even survival, had not his Martians fortuitously succumbed to earthly bacteria.[82] His narrator concludes that mankind must "be prepared" for the next earth-shot from Mars. But *The War of the Worlds* and *When the Sleeper Wakes*, which followed in 1899, disclose the unmistakable impact of a philosophy as far removed from Baden-Powell as it is from Weimar humanism or German idealism.[83] In 1896, the first Nietzsche translations appeared — of *Zur Genealogie der Moral* and *Also sprach Zarathustra*. Though Wells initially disparaged "the Gospel of Nietzsche" as "the glorification of a sort of rampant egotism,"[84] it actually chimes with his most enduring convictions and themes, not least the gulf between Nietzsche's "sick animal, man" and the exceptional individual, and the moral relativism allegedly justified by that disparity. Patrick Bridgwater tells us that Nietzsche features in some twenty of the fifty-seven books Wells published by 1917.[85] Over the decades, "one constant factor in his political philosophy was Nietzschean elitism," which outlasted his faith in evolutionism or eugenics or Fabianism.[86] As early as 1906 Shaw told Wells: "From your Martians to your Samurai, what have you been preaching all your life but the Superman?"[87]

Yet the loathsome, blood-sucking Martians in *The War of the Worlds*, however technically advanced, are simply monsters calculated to make the reader's flesh creep, not the *Übermenschen* of Nietzsche's New Aristocracy.[88] It is rather the artilleryman whom the narrator meets on Putney Hill (inserted only in the book, a year after serialization) through whom Wells speaks, outlining his plans to propagate a new breed of "able-bodied, clean-minded men" with the appropriate women: "Cities, nations, civilization, progress — it's all over. That game's up. We're beat." A new beginning means life in the sewers, the accumulation of knowledge, the acquisition of Martian technology, the invasion of Mars — for perhaps the future of life lies there: "All those damn little clerks that used to live down *that* way — they'd be no good. They haven't any spirit in them — no proud dreams and no proud lusts; and a man who hasn't one or the other — Lord! what is he but funk and precautions? . . . Lives insured and a bit invested for fear of accidents. And on Sundays — fear of the hereafter. As if hell was built for rabbits." Such creatures "ought to die," the artilleryman concludes, and John Carey discerns the "exultation in death that sweeps through *The War of the Worlds*" and many other novels by Wells.[89] True, the narrator finally feels "a traitor to my wife and to my kind" and resolves "to leave this strange undisciplined dreamer of great things," though not before himself dismissing a passing curate as "one of those weak creatures full of a shifty cunning — who face neither God nor man, who face not even themselves, void of pride, timorous, anaemic, hateful souls." Thus spake Nietzsche of the *ressentiment* of the herd, and Wells followed suit.[90]

Carey also suggests, however, that "the avowed Nietzscheans in Wells's fiction . . . are always preposterous," partly because "the poetry of the suburbs was in his blood" as well, and the "cult of the open road," the draper's assistant on his bicycle, the aspirations of Mr Polly and Kipps, Mr Lewisham and Mr Britling — all of which showed Wells at his most humane. One might add that for a German equivalent to the anti-urban idyll of a Wells or a Jerome K. Jerome or a Chesterton (a consistent opponent of Nietzsche),[91] one looks not to the Zarathustrian figure "6,000 feet above man and time" in self-imposed Alpine exile, but to the *Wandervögel*, hiking through undulating forests and singing around campfires, with the occasional un-English admixture of nudity, vegetarianism and sun-worship.[92] And yet, even before such "little lives" fell victim in the war to "blood and iron, flagwagging Teutonic Kiplingism"[93] and the "Tribal Gods" Britannia and Germania (as illustrated in Wells's own great pedagogical project, *The Outline of History*, 1920), he began to lose sight of them as "system replaced freedom as his ruling principle" — those scientific utopias and dreams of a world republic that were equally un-Nietzschean and equally doomed.[94] Wells's Nietzscheanism was no less idiosyncratic than Shaw's or Lawrence's, but there is clearly some truth in Bridgwater's contention that "Nietzsche was the guru of the late Victorian/Edwardian age just as Wells was himself the guru of the following, Georgian, era."[95]

Thinkers and Agitators

Nietzsche

Few gurus can be as readily identified as Nietzsche was, indeed still is, with a cluster of words or phrases that serve as shorthand pointers to the major concerns of their philosophy. It was these rhetorical flourishes and lurid metaphors that largely accounted for his demonization in the decade before the war, when the sorry state of Nietzsche translations[96] meant that potential readers, stimulated by the introductory essays of a Shaw or a Havelock Ellis in the 1890s, now encountered mostly hostile synopses instead. Yet it is not the devil that lies in the detail of Nietzsche's writing, but its saving grace. The "will to power," a concept highlighted and politically contextualized by the eponymous book, controversially edited by his sister, seemed to advocate the value-free German *Machtpolitik* that Nietzsche consistently deplored. In the minds of English armchair warriors, the quite distinct, indeed contrary, notions of the "blond beast" and the "superman" fused, then became synonymous with the arrogant blond Prussian soldier — to Nietzsche, a contemptible automaton. The exhortation to "live dangerously" and glory in strength and beauty was perceived as a pagan attack on Christianity, a religion that does not hold with a view of life needing justification as a purely "aesthetic phenomenon." The moral free-for-all that follows if "God is dead" appeared to presage nihilism and the collapse of civilization into moral anarchy, rather than constitute a challenge to create meaning and live up to an ethic of the utmost strenuousness.

It is unlikely that the man in the street was aware of such nuanced distinctions, still less that, outside philosophical circles, "Hegel's state rather than Nietzsche's 'blond beast' was at the centre of attention."[97] In a Piccadilly bookseller's window, to take an often-cited example, the newly completed eighteen-volume Nietzsche in English was promoted as the key to "The Euro-Nietzschean war. Read the Devil in order to fight him the better."[98] Its editor Oscar Levy used the *New Age*, "house journal of the British Nietzscheans,"[99] to counter the loathing with which even "British opinion-formers were crediting Nietzsche with . . . shaping the principles, policies and prejudices of an entire nation."[100] The mainly avant-garde champions of the now notorious German thinker were no match for press propaganda against "supermania." Even *The Times* ascribed the sack of Louvain to latter-day Huns and Vandals, atavistic reincarnations of their marauding ancestors acting out the more recent intellectual atrocities perpetrated by Treitschke, Bernhardi, and Nietzsche. Consequently, Germany's "national conscience has undergone the change of moral values which Nietzsche desired."[101] True here to its sobriquet "The Thunderer," the newspaper's reputation is at least partially redeemed by the eloquent defense of Nietzsche that appeared in the *Times Literary Supplement* on October 1, 1914. With this voice in the wilderness, Nicholas Martin concludes his examination of how and why the Nietzsche who so detested virulent nationalism could become the legendary "execrable "Neetch."[102]

It is instructive to cite, almost at random, an instance of the use to which the more authentic Nietzsche could be put in Germany.[103] In a 1906 glossary, the entry under *Deutschland, Deutschland über alles* first cites several sources for Hoffmann von Fallersleben's famous 1841 "Lied der Deutschen." They all make it clear that it is *not* merely a case of "my country, right or wrong," but of potential world domination: a 1684 treatise after the Turks had been finally repelled, "Österreich über alles, wann es nur will" (Austria over all, if she but desire it); a whole journal in 1800 entitled "Teutschland über alles, wenn es nur will" (Germany over all, if she but desire it); a lament for the non-restoration of the Reich at the Congress of Vienna in 1815, "Deutschland über alle, wenn es einig ist und sein will" (Germany over everybody, if she is united and desires to be); and a further exhortation to political as well as new-found Protestant unity in 1817, "Preußen über alles, wenn es will" (Prussia over all, if it so wills). Nietzsche then leads for the opposition with multiple entries decrying this "blödsinnigste Parole, die je gegeben worden ist" (daftest slogan that ever existed) as "a pain in the ear," one we are "not stupid enough" to fall for.[104]

William James

Of course, Nietzsche's quarrel was with the Second Reich; he was not against war *per se*. "War is the *strong* life; it is life *in extremis*"; "our ancestors have bred pugnacity into our bone and marrow, and thousands of years of peace won't breed it out of us." The sentiments are Nietzschean, but these are quotations from a famous lecture entitled "The Moral Equivalent of War," delivered at Stanford University in 1906 by William James, like Nietzsche a philosopher-psychologist and no less of a guru.[105]

Indeed, the already influential perception of Jamesian pragmatism as the subordination of absolute truth to the relativism of power-based practicality and willed expediency led some to regard Nietzsche as "a Pragmatist in everything but name."[106] Though finally confessing "I devoutly believe in the reign of peace and in the gradual advent of some sort of socialistic equilibrium," James nevertheless insists that "pacifists ought to enter more deeply into the aesthetical and ethical point of view of their opponents," and gives a brilliant demonstration of doing just that. Since our volume turns next to Bernhardi, whose *Germany and the Next War* (1912) was peremptorily dismissed by most British commentators as "moral insanity," it is enlightening to see how a peacemaker and pragmatist like James attempts to find common ground with those who regarded war as a "biological necessity."

The classic statement of power politics, as reported by Thucydides, is the Athenians' explanation to the ex-Spartan inhabitants of Melos in the Peloponnesian war that their policy of strict neutrality is irrelevant, for "the powerful exact what they can and the weak grant what they must"; nor can an appeal to the gods prevent war or the Melians' enslavement, for "of the gods we believe and of men we know that, by a law of their nature, wherever they can rule they will." James cites America's "squalid" war with Spain in 1898 as a contemporary instance. (The lesson was soon to be learnt again by Belgium in August 1914.) He concedes that, today, "pure loot and mastery seem no longer morally allowable motives, and pretexts must be found for attributing them solely to the enemy." But reflective apologists for war "refuse to admit for a moment that war may be a transitory phenomenon in social evolution. The notion of a sheep's paradise like that revolts, they say, our higher imagination. Where then would be the steeps of life? If war ever stopped, we should have to re-invent it, on this view, to redeem life from flat degeneration." They hold its horrors to be "a cheap price to pay for rescue from the only alternative supposed, of a world of clerks and teachers . . . of "consumers' leagues" and "associated charities," of industrialism unlimited, and feminism unabashed."

Since "mankind was nursed in pain and fear" (James quoting Simon Patten), "a permanently successful peace-economy cannot be a simple pleasure-economy" (James *in propria persona*) and "martial virtues must be the enduring cement; intrepidity, contempt of softness . . ."; "militarism is the great preserver of our ideals of hardihood, and human life with no use for hardihood would be contemptible." This does not entail the inevitability of war, however, and "the fatalistic view of the war function is to me nonsense." And so he finally proposes a "moral equivalent of war" — the conscription of the young in "the immemorial human warfare against nature." But perhaps lest this Peace Corps or compulsory gap-year solution seem rather a let-down, he leaves the last word to H. G. Wells, who, "as usual, sees the centre of the situation" and who proceeds to compare, unfavorably, "the progress of civil conveniences which has been left almost entirely to the trader, to the progress in military apparatus during the last few decades." Wells, James concludes, "thinks that the conceptions of order and discipline, the tradition of service and devotion, of physical fitness, unstinted exertion, and universal responsibility, which universal military duty is now teaching European nations, will remain a permanent acquisition when the last ammunition has been used in the fireworks that celebrate the final peace. I believe as he does." Lords Roberts and Baden-Powell would doubtless have agreed.

This remarkable lecture was published four years later, in 1910, the same year in which General von Bernhardi was writing *Deutschland und der nächste Krieg* (1912) and Norman Angell (Ralph Lane) published his less accurate prediction, *The Great Illusion*. The 1914 *Times* editorial evoking Huns and Vandals, cited above, was also entitled "The Great Illusion," a debunking reference to Angell's cult book that had convinced all "Angellites" at least, notably Viscount Esher, that the growing economic interdependence of nations meant that war, or at any rate a protracted war, was impossible.[107] Literally, war did not pay.[108] Chapter titles in Bernhardi's equally influential book — "The Right to Make War," "The Duty to Make War," "World Power or Downfall" — point, instead, towards the inexorable certainty of war. Though not blind to economic self-interest, Bernhardi seems to be one of those militarist authors James has in mind when he says they "take a highly mystical view of their subject, and regard war as a biological or sociological necessity . . . in short, a permanent human *obligation*."[109] And James goes on to quote, first General Homer Lea's assertion, in *The Valor of Ignorance*, that "nations are never stationary — they must necessarily expand or shrink"; then S. R. Steinmetz's belief in *Philosophie des Krieges* that "die Weltgeschichte ist das Weltgericht," (the history of the world is its own doom) and that martial victory in this "ordeal instituted by God" necessarily ensues from "a totality of virtues — fidelity, cohesiveness, tenacity, heroism, conscience, education, inventiveness, economy, wealth, physical health and vigor." All of this pre-empts (or echoes) Bernhardi's argument. James attempts, if not exactly a reconciliation of the war party and the peace party, at least a sympathetic exploration of the "higher aspects" of the militaristic mind-set.

Though James does not mention Nietzsche here, he had done so in his Gifford Lectures, delivered at Edinburgh in 1901–2 and published as *The Varieties of Religious Experience*. "The most inimical critic of the saintly impulses whom I know is Nietzsche. He contrasts them with the worldly passions as we find these embodied in the predaceous military character, altogether to the advantage of the latter. . . . For Nietzsche the saint represents little but sneakingness and slavishness. He is the sophisticated invalid, the degenerate *par excellence*, the man of insufficient vitality. His prevalence would put the human type in danger." This is illustrated by a long passage from *The Genealogy of Morals*, which James glosses: "Poor Nietzsche's antipathy is itself sickly enough, but we all know what he means, and he expresses well the clash between the two ideals. The carnivorous-minded "strong man," the adult male and cannibal, can see nothing but moldiness and morbidity in the saint's gentleness and self-severity, and regards him with pure loathing."[110] James's sharp though not entirely accurate or sympathetic vignette of Nietzsche's typology ("the predaceous military character," "carnivorous," and "cannibal" are rather more reminiscent of Wells's early fictions) is interestingly at variance with those "higher aspects of military sentiment" thought principled, even honorable, in the "Moral Equivalent of War" lecture.

Bernhardi

Interesting because James's apportioning of respect seems to run counter both to Thomas Mann's "bemused contempt" that Nietzsche and Bernhardi could be named in one breath,[111] and to the emergence of Bernhardi as "the favorite whipping-boy of British propaganda."[112] Orage, too, plays down Nietzsche's influence on German public opinion compared with that of "journalists like Bernhardi."[113] But others were more willing to give Bernhardi his due — Professor J. A. Cramb, for instance, ghostwriter to Lord Roberts and author of *Germany and England* (1914), "a reply to Bernhardi" that vied in popularity with *Germany and the Next War* itself.[114] Cecil Chesterton somewhat caustically called Cramb's book "a whole-hearted welcome to Bernhardi, an enthusiastic endorsement of Bernhardi, an embracing of Bernhardi's big boots."[115] One reviewer in the *New Age* thought Cramb's interpretation of Bernhardi rightly restored to contemporary politics "the historical spirit, that sense of fatality that has been almost forgotten since Napoleon died." Another applauded Bernhardi for emphasizing the "evil effects of pacifism on the average State." A third exonerated Treitschke and Bernhardi as well as Nietzsche, while mocking "bellicose pacifists" such as Angell, whose new book, *Prussianism and its Destruction* (1915), overrated the power of ideas by arguing that "the war is the result of a philosophy propagated in Germany by a handful of professors and literary men."[116] And a fourth pointed to homegrown warmongering in 1909, well before Bernhardi's book: "The moment England and Germany begin to overcome their mutual jealousies, those crazy politicians Mr. Maxse and Mr. Robert Blatchford stir up blood with their renewed chatter about 'The Coming War with Germany.'"[117]

The present reevaluation traces Bernhardi's repeated invocations of, and thus manifest proximity to, those key Nietzschean concepts of the will and its relationship to power. Consequently, it cannot accept Hinton Thomas's view that Nietzsche's "association with Bernhardi stemmed only from an out-of-context quotation from Nietzsche with which he prefaced his book. Apart from that, it had as good as nothing to do with Nietzsche."[118] The continuation of this exoneration of Nietzsche (also, seemingly, of Bernhardi) shows just how confusing attributions of influence can be: "The hero of *Deutschland und der nächste Krieg* is not Nietzsche but Kant."[119] And the concluding step is even more surprising: "It is from Kant that Bernhardi derives the notion of subordinating individual happiness to the needs of the state, and the justification of universal individual military service."[120] Even Hegel, whom one might indeed connect with such thoughts (though no more concerned with "happiness" than Kant, or indeed Nietzsche),[121] appears only once in Bernhardi's book.[122] Kant receives credit for his categorical imperative, but is otherwise only mentioned as "der alternde Kant" — Kant in his dotage — who first promulgated in 1795 "that now ubiquitous dream of eternal peace, the anaemia afflicting most *Kulturvölker*."[123] One is reminded of Thomas Mann in 1914 — at the "low point of his career as a critical intellectual"[124] — equating Bismarck's *Realpolitik* with Kant's practical reason and "leaving all scepticism far behind" to conclude that "the categorical imperative is German." And it is Mann, not Bernhardi, who describes Kant and Nietzsche as "the moralists of German 'militarism' who demonstrate that German soldiery is a moral soldiery."[125]

The odium that attached to Bernhardi and from which he still suffers is most directly linked to the line of thought he pursues from Heraclitus's maxim that "war is the father of all things," to the conviction, supposedly confirmed by Darwin, that "war is a biological necessity."[126] But he never argued, as Wells did, that "man is a biological catastrophe."[127] Wells proposed multiple solutions in book after book for the elimination of the mass of "low-grade humanity" (of which selective breeding is by far the mildest, pending the availability of genetic engineering to complete the job more efficiently).[128] Bernhardi advocated not only universal conscription at a time when the German High Command still believed that urban recruitment spelt socialist danger, but also universal education, arguing that German qualitative superiority alone, with ever greater individual responsibility devolving upon the common soldier, would offset the quantitative advantage of Russia and France.[129] When so many, from the Kaiser and Moltke downwards, believed in the inevitability and imminence of war and in the need to prepare for it, the question of the degree to which Bernhardi was a conduit for widely-held views, rather than merely part of the "lunatic fringe," deserves revisiting.

The Evolutionary Debate

Certainly, the "struggle for existence," described in *The Origin of Species* (1859) as the engine of evolutionary progress, was all too readily equated with Bernhardi's "biological necessity of war." This "Darwinism 'made in Germany,'" as some called it, was as hotly denied by mainly, though not exclusively, British representatives of "peace biology,"[130] who could point to Darwin's own view, in *The Descent of Man* (1871), of war as a genetic disaster, and to his theistic belief in the evolution of a "higher morality" synonymous with the cosmopolitan Kant's categorical imperative rather than "the survival of the fittest." Herbert Spencer, who coined this latter term, became foremost among proponents of an inherent upward progression of mankind. Why, then, did Spencer become the "social Darwinist" bogeyman in Germany that Nietzsche and Bernhardi were in England?

In his investigation of "Darwinism and National Identity," Gregory Moore builds here on his pioneering study of the pre- and post-Darwinian evolutionary debates to which Nietzsche was both heir and contributor.[131] He concludes that this was "a war not just between competing conceptions of culture, but also of competing conceptions of nature." What was hardest to accept in the supposedly blind and random operations of natural selection was that the ubiquitous conflict was entirely without purpose. Hence the urgent attempts, including Darwin's own, to reconcile evolutionary theory with a Victorian belief in progress, with traditional ethics that did not entail a transvaluation of values, and even with the Christian supposition of providential design.[132]

From a German perspective, however, mere adaptation to environmental pressure seemed rather to characterize the mechanistic workings of brutal *Manchestertum*, epitomized by Spencer's argument that warlike societies such as Prussia and Russia were being superseded through a process of natural evolution by liberal, industrial ones based on free trade. Further sanctioned by Mill's Utilitarianism — the greatest happiness of the greatest number — and in truth closer to Lamarck than to Darwin, Spencer's dream of future contentment became Nietzsche's nightmare — "that there is an evolution of the whole of humanity, that is nonsense, and not even desirable."[133] Just as intolerable was the thought that the exceptional individual too was a random product of Darwinian adaptation and self-preservation, rather than an active agent impelled by the will to transcend itself.

So Nietzsche effectively bases his "will to power" on "an amalgam of a number of competing, non-Darwinian theories: Nägeli's perfection principle, Roux's concept of inner struggle, and Rolph's principle of insatiability."[134] He is best situated within the tradition of Romantic *Natur-*

philosophie, in which a holistic unfolding of life's creative energies is paramount; his rejection of Darwinism is a defense of vitalistic "Lebenswerte" against materialistic "Nutzwerte," a reenactment even of Goethe's opposition to mechanistic Newtonism. And as Moore demonstrates, Nietzsche's is just one voice among many in Germany — Scheler, Uexküll, Joël, Hartmann — who continue the debate on evolutionism into the twentieth century. Many of them — from Haeckel, Darwinism's main popularizer, who thought it an objective foundation for nationalism,[135] through to Sombart with his anti-Spencerian "Händler und Helden" polemic — made explicit the supposed political consequences in the war of ideas.

Academia

Alexander Tille

A century after the Scottish Enlightenment imported Kant's philosophy into Britain, the "furious Nietzschean" Alexander Tille spent the 1890s rousing the curiosity of his Glasgow students (and some of her citizens, through the Glasgow Goethe Society he founded) for the latest trends in German thinking. He edited and helped translate the first edition of Nietzsche in English, and traced the ostensible link to Darwin in his book on "evolutionary ethics," *Von Darwin bis Nietzsche: Ein Buch Entwicklungsethik* (1895). At the same time he was, by his own account, the first to bring Kipling to the attention of German readers and to help generate their interest in Stevenson and Wordsworth. But though a prolific popularizer of both cultures, Tille was "a social Darwinist of the most radical and brutal kind."[136] For instance, he took issue with Nietzsche "for thinking too little about racial struggle between competing elements in society, and he disliked Nietzsche's preoccupation with a dominating 'aristocratic' caste."[137]

For Tille, too, the Boer War was the crucial turning point in relations between Britain and Germany, *and* between him and the 500 Glasgow students who attacked him during a lecture after he had published comments in Germany disparaging British soldiers trying to impose "the universal happiness of democratic liberalism" on "a handful of Dutchmen with Mausers" in "a war of aggression."[138] Tille also drew criticism from Orage (who was perhaps challenging his claim to be the major mediator of Nietzsche in Britain)[139] over his introduction to Thomas Common's translation of *Zarathustra*: "One would suppose from the tone of it that the Professor [*sic* — Tille only became a full-time lecturer in his last year] was introducing a learned dunce to an audience of dons . . . there is nothing to indicate the meaning or value of the colossal poem that *Zarathustra* really is."[140]

On his return to Germany, Tille helped reinforce stereotypes of "perfidious Albion" as "a nation of traders" in his deeply Anglophobic book *Aus Englands Flegeljahren* (1900) — an allusion to the awkward adolescent, or even loutish, phase in a country's evolution. But however chastening his experience in Glasgow, it is rather the case, as Stefan Manz shows in his study of the limits of intercultural transfer, that "his social Darwinist world view provided a pseudo-scientific justification for the social stratification and evils of Wilhelmine capitalist society."[141] No wonder Germany's foremost suffragette, Helene Stöcker, who was in thrall to Nietzsche while also sharing some of Tille's emancipatory social Darwinist ideas, soon distanced herself — also emotionally — from the man who believed "bloody war inevitable to decide who is top dog, Germany or Great Britain."[142]

Kuno Meyer

Tille's forecast in 1900, "We will surely thrash this British highhandedness out of them, but it will take quite a thrashing before they learn their lesson," seemed less far-fetched in the days before the German advance was checked on the Marne in late August 1914, when Kuno Meyer relished the fact that "the English have taken such a licking."[143] This from a man whose twenty-seven ostensibly happy, well-integrated years at Liverpool University, latterly as its eminent Professor of Celtic, had only come to an end on his appointment in 1911 to the prestigious Chair of Celtic in Berlin, betokens an even more intriguing case history. Celtic is indeed the key, for as Andreas Huether explains below, the German linguistic scholars so highly respected by Irish cultural nationalists in the 1890s and 1900s were not necessarily immune — or averse — to mobilization in the service of Irish political nationalism when the time came. Leaked letters on the weakness of British defenses against invasion and on the questionable loyalty of Irish prisoners of war in Germany, whom Roger Casement was currently trying to recruit to fight against Britain, and even research trips to the Aran Islands retrospectively deemed suspect, all account for Liverpool University's decision to deprive Meyer of his honorary professorship.[144]

The other factor was of course German patriotism. In Berlin, Meyer became immersed in the Pan-German circles of which his brother was a prominent member. Another, even closer to the Kaiser, was Theodor Schiemann, who had published articles by Casement in German in the *Preußische Jahrbücher*,[145] and now encouraged Meyer to agitate among Irish-Americans on his forthcoming lecture tour. This he duly did, while Moltke, no less, arranged for him to brief the Kaiser on the value of the Irish to the German war effort. Within two weeks of the sinking of the *Lusitania* in 1915, Meyer reported that American outrage had died down, and that Germany should continue its U-boat attacks with full vigor. But unrestricted submarine warfare was the second great German miscalculation, ensuring the eventual loss of American neutrality, and thus the war, as surely as the invasion of neutral Belgium had ended any possibility of British neutrality.[146] According to the diaries of Kurt Riezler, secretary to Chancellor Bethmann Hollweg, who opposed Admiral Tirpitz's policy, it was accepted by the great mass of the public with uncritical enthusiasm, and "stirred neither moral doubts nor political misgivings." The wonder weapon of the submarine unleashed "an orgy of uncontrolled indulgence in power that makes men drunk. . . . As one listens to the tumult, it appears that the English are just about right when they say the Germans are mad."[147]

His longstanding English friendships notwithstanding, Meyer's social background and his double roles as *Professor* and *Reserveleutnant* meant that he instinctively, and it would seem enthusiastically, aligned with those who "spoke with an almost unanimous voice politically and became a self-perpetuating interest group."[148] When Ulrich von Wilamowitz-Moellendorff, doyen of classical philology and likewise in close contact with British academia, drew up his "Manifesto of the Intellectuals" in October 1914, the original ninety-three signatories to this *Aufruf an die Kulturwelt* grew within a fortnight to over four thousand — virtually the whole of the professoriate. Encapsulating the "Ideas of 1914" to which academics of every stripe literally, if not always wholeheartedly, subscribed (including Max Weber and Albert Einstein)[149] and to which the present volume is largely devoted, this manifesto was widely disseminated in translation and did much to fix a belief in Germany's intransigent ambitions.[150] Essentially, Germany's actions were perceived to belie the claim that she was truly mindful of "the legacy of a Goethe, a Beethoven, and a Kant," which her intellectual luminaries insisted she was both defending and propagating. Then again, neither Goethe et al, nor Goethe Societies, were of much help to those German academics who, unlike Tille and Meyer, remained in Britain and who publicly proclaimed their total support for the British cause.[151] Their generally shabby treatment at the hands of Vice-Chancellors and Heads of College is the sorry if perhaps inevitable story of a "broken fellowship."[152]

Austrian Anglists

Since there were no "enemy aliens" among Germany's thirty-two and Austria's six professors of *Anglistik* (native-speaking English *lektors* having also returned home at the onset of hostilities), internal strife of this kind within this particular "self-perpetuating interest group" was unknown. Austria is the main focus of Holger Klein's extensive research, which concludes our volume. Austria's academics, outside their actual scholarship, were not always above the initial nationalistic fervor — the *Rektor* of Innsbruck, for instance, addressing members of the university as "Kommilitonen!" in its original sense of "comrades-in-arms." But Austria's traditional friendship with Britain, unscarred by half a century of Prussian militarism and rivalry, meant that, in the hate campaign against all things German, she was "perhaps just trailing along as the arch-fiend's ally."[153]

Two Austrians moved to chairs of *Anglistik* in Germany and became involved in "the Professors' War,"[154] — one arguing that the diabolical English government had caused the war to divert attention from the explosive situation in Ireland and "die tollen Wahlweiber" (crazy suffragettes); the other enlisting Byron to attack English rapacity, puritanical hypocrisy, and plutocracy.[155] But only a single Austrian *Anglist* (who later moved into the orbit of National Socialism) joined the fray within Austria itself. The syllabus remained virtually unchanged (while staff and student numbers of course fell, as in all the countries at war), and the content of her academic journals likewise remained resolutely *au-dessus de la mêlée* (though the main journal aimed at schoolteachers did not).[156] Klein finds it reassuring that — against received opinion — German-language English studies periodicals in both Germany and Austria, as well as the august *Jahrbuch der Shakespeare-Gesellschaft,*[157] save for a very few items, simply do not mention the war.

Continued adherence to the cause of British culture, at least, was certainly made easier by the fact that the German-speaking world had long appropriated Shakespeare. The *Shakespeare-Gesellschaft*, representing scholars of English in Germany and Austria, had celebrated its fiftieth anniversary, fittingly in Weimar, in April 1914. It may have been the case that the nationalistically-tinged personality of its wartime president, the Austrian Alois Brandl (Kuno Meyer's colleague in Berlin), subsequently helped "draw the *Shakespeare-Gesellschaft* more deeply into the struggle, albeit only at the margins of its activities." But his Graz colleague Albert Eichler, his own bellicose inclinations notwithstanding, devoted his wartime scholarly efforts to attacking only the Austrian *Shakespeare-Bacon Gesellschaft* over Bacon's putative authorship of the Bard's works — his *Antibaconianus* a suitably Swiftian response to, or sublimation of, events.[158]

Shakespeare, Shaw, Karl Kraus, et al.

Shakespeare was of course too important to be left to the professors, and the common claim that his plays were more widely known in Germany, and their meaning (notably in the Schlegel-Tieck translation, among the many available) better understood than were the originals by modern Englishmen, is not implausible. In the years spanning the war, performances of this indispensable cornerstone of theatrical life, from Aachen to

Zürich, averaged around a thousand a year. *A Midsummer Night's Dream* led the field in 1913, *Twelfth Night* in 1914, *The Merchant of Venice* in 1915, *Hamlet* in 1916, *As You Like It* in 1917, 1918, and 1919. The popularity of the comedies is easy to understand. "Relevance" was scarcely yet the overriding criterion it became under the Nazis, when Goebbels belatedly banned Schiller's *Wilhelm Tell* lest the wrong moral be drawn. But with *Hamlet* it is tempting to recall Ferdinand Freiligrath's famous exhortation to Germany to avenge her entombed liberty in 1844, "Deutschland ist Hamlet," anticipating Germany's indecision in 1848, if not the coming of Bismarck's Fortinbras in 1864–71 and the shriller voices proclaiming the "Ideas of 1914."[159] Germany was indeed no longer Hamlet. *The Merchant of Venice*, too, must have seemed an apt choice in 1915 to those who had read Sombart's tract of that year drawing the starkest contrast between mercantile Englishmen and heroic Germans.

So unfailingly does *Händler und Helden* pinpoint the respective "philosophies" for which and against which each side is fighting, that Karl Kraus plays numerous variations on the phrase in *Die letzten Tage der Menschheit* (1915–19, published 1921), most memorably in the exchanges between the *Optimist* ("Sie sind Händler" [they are merchants]) and the *Nörgler* or *Cynic* — Kraus himself — ("Wir sind Helden" [we are heroes]).[160] Almost all the issues explored in the present volume are at least touched on in Kraus's uniquely entertaining yet forensically lethal investigation of the "war of words" and the reality it camouflaged. No British or German dramatist created, in order to expose to ridicule, such a multitude of voices (his own, distinctively Austrian, voice was also impressively deployed in public Shakespeare readings).

Only Shaw comes close in his skewering of humbug. Indeed, Kraus fell silent for most of the duration of the war after his initial broadside, *In dieser grossen Zeit*, whereas Shaw's jocular Irish tones continued to rile and often enrage almost everyone throughout "these great times" — not least the literary establishment enlisted to provide propaganda — whether he was speaking through his *dramatis personae* or, no less dialectically, in his often reprinted polemic, *Common Sense about the War*.[161] Kipling and Chesney and Wells[162] are incriminated as much as the Dreadnought builders; the 1839 treaty guaranteeing Belgian neutrality is declared obsolete; the war is really about power, specifically the balance of power, hypocritically disguised by Britain's governing "Junker" class. Noel Annan nicely catches the typical Shavian paradox: "The Kaiser was as much within his rights to declare war as Britain was right to resist him; Germany must be smashed but those who did the smashing were either criminals or rascals."[163] So while supporting the declaration of war, Shaw now (infamously, indeed unforgivably for some) advised soldiers on both sides to shoot their officers and go home. "The nation's leading gadfly"[164] targeted sacred cows to more provocative effect than had Wodehouse, "English literature's performing flea"[165] in his lighthearted parody of the invasion novel, though in the same year Shaw too had enjoyed mocking the militaristic-cum-imperialistic trappings of invasion hysteria in *Press Cuttings*.[166] His extensive if esoteric foreword to Thomas Common's pioneering Nietzsche anthology and his own *Man and Superman* aligned him with fellow-celebrants of what Samuel Butler had dubbed "the life force," such as D. H. Lawrence. But where "Lawrence did not, like Brooke and the others, welcome the Great War as purification,"[167] in *Heartbreak House* Shaw, his common sense notwithstanding, showed he was not immune to the exhilaration of violence: a Zeppelin raid to sweep away the contemptible materialism of a doomed civilization.[168]

Little wonder that A. J. P. Taylor cites Shaw as his unsurpassed stylistic mentor, or that Karl Kraus inspired Niall Ferguson's early fascination with the war.[169] Only connect a little further, and Taylor, on a visit to "that profound entertainment, *Oh! What a Lovely War*" finds the cast reading *The First World War: An Illustrated History*, delighted that he had "confirmed the version of the war they were putting on the stage"[170] Such are the symbiotic liaisons we encounter at every turn in the following pages between imaginative premonitions or reconstructions of the great event and the historical accounts they variously feed and utilize. "The war of words" here unfolded focuses largely on the transitional period before the Babel of voices polarizes into full-blown propaganda, or relative innocence into embittered experience. Still, the viewpoints of contributors as well as the subjects of their enquiry are consistently dual-perspective or bipolar (though not on that account two-dimensional). The leading and lesser lights under scrutiny all refract facets of a vast Anglo-German kaleidoscope and illuminate the same global issues that still inescapably concern us today.

It is fitting that Nietzsche looms large, for his doctrine of "eternal recurrence" insists on the perennial nature of the challenge, while his was the power-based philosophy that many thought they were fighting. The similar and linked uses and abuses of Darwinism receive long-overdue attention. We take stock of Thomas Mann's tortured apologia for a "defensive holy war" (the aggressive pursuit of which is in turn the butt of Kraus's satire),[171] but also of the very different "higher military mindset" of a Bernhardi preaching pre-emptive war (dismissed by Mann as fatuous jingoism). The more personal or domestic reverberations of this clash of cultures are pinpointed by neglected writers of the period (Karl Bleibtreu, I. A. R. Wylie, Sybil Spottiswoode), or in forgotten works by famous writers (Lawrence, Wodehouse, Saki), or projected into a virtually unknown but certainly more sophisticated science fiction than Wells's (Kurd Lasswitz), or dramatized in coded form fully deciphered here for the first time (Carl Sternheim). Those who have provided essays on the dilemmas of half-forgotten scholars caught up in conflicting loyalties, and soon in the heat of the intellectual cross-fire (Alexander Tille, Kuno Meyer, Alois Brandl et al), write with long experience of the tragic potential in such dual existences, happily remote a century on.

Lying beyond our scope, however, is the far from universal continuity of thought between the Second and the Third Reich (or in Britain, the growing polarity between Pacifism and "Vansittartism" in the 1920s and 1930s). Where Thomas Mann famously changed his mind, Werner Sombart infamously did not. Yet Kraus somehow neglected to pick up on one of Sombart's thought-provoking observations: Matthew Arnold had once complained that England was an intellectually impoverished country. Herbert Spencer, *the* English philosopher of the day, had then allegedly observed, as proof that Englishmen's belief in ideas is greater than that of the Germans, that Berlin itself, the very headquarters of German intellect ("das Hauptquartier des Geistes"), took its light supply from the English "Continental Gas Company."[172] Sombart naturally ridicules Spencer's assumption that such practical applications count as "ideas" at all, but one is left wondering — if a final flippancy is permitted — whether Lord Grey knew exactly why the lamps were going out all over Europe.

Notes

[1] A second, enlarged edition of Liddell Hart's work, with the new title *A History of the World War, 1914–1918*, was first published in 1934.

[2] Also, of course, Taylor's hugely popular *Illustrated History of the First World War* (1963) and *War by Timetable: How the First World War Began* (1969).

[3] Imanuel Geiss, *Der lange Weg in die Katastrophe: Die Vorgeschichte des Ersten Weltkrieges, 1815–1914* (Munich/Zurich: Piper, 1990), esp. 23–24, 54, 123.

[4] However, reviewing Michael Howard's *The First World War* (Oxford: Oxford UP, 2002), John Keegan notes: "In contradiction of the Goldhagen thesis of innate German anti-Semitism, the occupiers [i.e. German forces in Eastern Europe during the Great War] gave orders for the Jews to be treated with privilege, because their widespread knowledge of German, even if only through Yiddish, made them useful servants of *Ober Ost*." Perhaps they behaved better than in the West "because they had empire-building ambitions and did not wish to alienate future subjects" (*Times Literary Supplement*, April 12, 2002, 26).

[5] "In den letzten Jahren hat sich in der internationalen Geschichtsschreibung ein signifikanter Paradigmawandel vollzogen [*pace* Thomas Kuhn]. 'Kultur' ist zu einem maßgebenden Leitbegriff der gegenwärtigen Geschichtswissenschaft geworden" (In the past few years a major change has taken place in the way international history is written [*pace* Thomas Kuhn]: "culture" has become a determi-

native norm in the present-day study of history): Wolfgang J. Mommsen, *Bürgerliche Kultur und politische Ordnung* (Frankfurt: Fischer, 2000), 7.

[6] Niall Ferguson, *The Pity of War* (Harmondsworth, UK: Penguin, 1998), 1.

[7] G. K. Chesterton, *The Crimes of England* (London: Palmer & Hayward, 1915), 32.

[8] See Paul Fussell, *The Great War and Modern Memory* (Oxford: Oxford UP, 1975), 24.

[9] *Verfassungspatriotismus* — a concept coined by Dolf Sternberger and championed by Jürgen Habermas.

[10] See Hew Strachan, *The First World War*, vol. 1 (Oxford: Oxford UP, 2001), 1114–39: "holy war" rhetoric; the war as the coming of the Holy Ghost "like a mighty, rushing wind" (1116); the war as a continuation of Bismarck's anti-Catholic *Kulturkampf* (1117).

[11] Finding Buitenhuis's book very useful as a source of information, but that he moralizes too readily, Dominic Hibberd also regrets that he is content "to stay within the Anglophone world. There is a great need for comparative studies" (*Times Literary Supplement*, July 28, 1989).

[12] Strachan, *First World War* 1: xv.

[13] In early October 1914 Trakl actually experienced the battlefield of Grodek in Galicia as a medical orderly; it is the subject of his last poem.

[14] This was Romain Rolland's stance, "above the fray," and the title of his famous book of essays (1915) on "the war delirium of German intellectuals," which helped spark the "unpolitical" jingoism Thomas Mann poured into *Betrachtungen eines Unpolitischen*. See T. J. Reed, *Thomas Mann and the Uses of Tradition* (Oxford: Oxford UP, 1974), 189–90.

[15] Nor, while we're at it, is Expressionism a *fin-de-siècle* phenomenon, nor Zuckmayer one of the main war poets (Ferguson, *Pity of War*, 1998, 449, xxvi). Rilke did write a series of five "War Hymns" in August 1914, but they *celebrated* the sudden "authoritative" appearance of the God of War, the intoxication of a communal mission, and even the naturalness of the "human harvest" about to begin. He then had second thoughts and retreated into some of the most remarkable linguistic contortionism in the language. See R. M. Rilke, *Sämtliche Werke*, vol. 2 (Frankfurt: Insel, 1963), 86–92.

[16] Mommsen, *Bürgerliche Kultur*, 207.

[17] Strachan, *First World War* 1:1122. *An die Kulturwelt* is discussed below.

[18] Ferguson, *Pity of War*, xxv.

[19] "The figure depicted in this chapter ['Incomplete Nation-State: Wotan and Fafner'] is in many ways less the 'real' Nietzsche than Nietzsche as interpreted, and misinterpreted, by Germans at the turn of the century" (Harold James, *A German Identity, 1770–1990* [London: Weidenfeld & Nicolson, 1989], 92).

[20] James, *A German Identity*, 100.

[21] For Mann's stance in the war years, however, see my further comments in this introduction; also Nicholas Martin, "Nietzsche as Hate-Figure in Britain's Great War: "The Execrable Neech," chapter 5 in this volume.

[22] See Fussell, *Great War*, 44–45.

[23] See Fussell, *Great War*, chap. 6, "Theater of War," for the differing styles of remembrance.

[24] Robert Graves, *Goodbye to All That* (1929; repr. Harmondsworth, UK: Penguin, 1982), 240.

[25] Sir George Tomkyns Chesney, *The Battle of Dorking* (Edinburgh: Blackwood & Sons, 1871), 59, 3, 31.

[26] Chesney, *Battle of Dorking*, 62–63.

[27] I. F. Clarke, *The Great War with Germany, 1890–1914* (Liverpool: Liverpool UP, 1997), 16.

[28] Paul M. Kennedy, *The Rise of the Anglo-German Antagonism, 1860–1914* (London: George Allen & Unwin, 1980), 221.

[29] Cate Haste, *Keep the Home Fires Burning* (London: Allen Lane, 1977), 8 n. 1.

[30] See Iain Boyd Whyte, "Anglo-German Conflict in Popular Fiction, 1870–1914," chapter 1 in this volume.

[31] James D. Coldham, *German Cricket: A Brief History* (London: privately printed, 1983), 1.

[32] P. G. Wodehouse, *The Swoop! or How Clarence Saved England* (London: Alston Rivers, 1909), 47, 50, 51, 55.

[33] In Wodehouse's *Carry On Jeeves*.

[34] See Whyte, "Popular Fiction."

[35] Thus Samuel Hynes, who talks rather censoriously of Saki's celebration of "values that in their more attractive form we call patriotic; but as Saki represented them they emerge more often as militaristic, arrogant and xenophobic — the values that made the empire and at the same time made England's enemies" (*The Edwardian Turn of Mind* [Princeton: Princeton UP, 1968], 51, n. 64, cited by Whyte, "Popular Fiction").

[36] *When William Came* (1913), in *The Complete Stories of Saki* (Ware: Wordsworth Editions, 1993), 501, 499, 500, 513, 572, 571.

[37] The over-age Saki was an exception — shot by a sniper in 1916; his last words were "Put that bloody cigarette out!"

[38] William Le Queux, *Spies of the Kaiser: Plotting the Downfall of England* (1909; repr., London: Frank Cass, 1996), 94–95.

[39] See Nicholas Hiley's introduction to Le Queux, *Spies*, vii–xxi. Ironically, there were no such German military agents in Britain (though a handful of naval agents employed to monitor changes in the dockyards), while Colonel (later General Sir) Henry Wilson had from 1909 been leading secret reconnaissance tours of the Franco-Belgian border on a bicycle in preparation for the BEF's anticipated (though not yet "committed," as Hiley points out in his introduction to *Spies*, xix) entry into neutral Belgium (see esp. Barbara W. Tuchman, *August 1914* [London: Constable, 1962], 59, 63).

[40] Hiley, introduction to *Spies*, xviii.

[41] See Geoffrey Household, foreword to Erskine Childers, *The Riddle of the Sands* (Harmondsworth, UK: Penguin, 1978), 14–15.

[42] Speech at Dundee, see Claud Cockburn, *Bestseller: The Books That Everyone Read, 1900–1939* (Harmondsworth, UK: Penguin, 1975), 86.

[43] Childers, *Riddle of the Sands*, 312.

[44] Chesney, *Battle of Dorking*, 10.

[45] See Tuchman, *August 1914*, 98–99.

[46] Clarke, *The Great War with Germany*, 17.

[47] Though military strategists such as Bernhardi certainly foresaw at least a naval blockade of Germany in wartime. See Fred Bridgham, "Bernhardi and 'The Ideas of 1914,'" chapter 7 in this volume.

[48] *Die Zeit*, May 8, 2002. John Röhl, interviewed in the *Daily Telegraph* (May 9, 2002), commented that the outline of the plans had been known to scholars for some time, adding: "This is typical of the unpredictability of the Kaiser and shows his worldwide ambition to make Germany into a superpower. It was a crazy idea."

[49] Childers, *Riddle of the Sands*, 101.

[50] See Ingo Cornils, "The Martians Are Coming! War, Peace, Love, and Reflection in H. G. Wells's *The War of the Worlds* and Kurd Lasswitz's *Auf zwei Planeten*," chap. 4 in this volume.

[51] H. G. Wells, *The War in the Air and Other Forebodings* (1908: repr., London: T. Fisher Unwin, 1926), chap. 6: "How War came to New York."

[52] See Tuchman, *August 1914*, 193.

[53] E. M. Forster, *Howards End* (Harmondsworth, UK: Penguin, 1973), 41.

[54] See Whyte, "Popular Fiction."

[55] In Bleibtreu's *Bur und Lord*, cited by Whyte. In starkest contrast, Kipling was deemed too extreme to contribute to the war effort, and Grey threatened to resign as Foreign Secretary when he heard Kipling might be sent on an American lecture tour in 1914 (Dominic Hibberd, *Times Literary Supplement*, July 28, 1989).

[56] See Whyte, *Popular Fiction*.

[57] See Agatha Ramm, *Germany, 1789–1919* (London: Methuen, 1967), 429.

[58] See Whyte, "Popular Fiction."

[59] For Bleibtreu's memorable caricature of such stereotypes in *Deutschland und England*, see Whyte, "Popular Fiction."

[60] See Whyte, "Popular Fiction."

[61] See Martin Green, *The von Richthofen Sisters* (New York: Basic Books, 1974), *passim*, and Peter E. Firchow, *The Death of the German Cousin: Variations on a Literary Stereotype, 1890–1920* (London: Associated University Presses, 1986), 150–56.

[62] D. H. Lawrence, *Mr Noon* (London: Grafton Books, 1986), 124, 134–35, 201–2, 124, 192, 220.

[63] Letter to Lady Ottoline Morrell, May 1915. See Firchow, *Death of the German Cousin*, 152, and Helena Ragg-Kirkby, "Perversion and Pestilence: D. H. Lawrence and the Germans," chap. 2 in this volume.

[64] August 1914. See Harry T. Moore, *The Priest of Love: A Life of D H Lawrence* (Harmondsworth, UK: Penguin, 1980), 266, and Ragg-Kirkby, "Lawrence."

[65] In the essay "The Crown," Oct–Nov 1915. See Firchow, *Death of the German Cousin*, 149.

[66] See Firchow, *Death of the German Cousin*, 211, n. 45.

[67] Thus Eric Hobsbawm, *Age of Extremes* (London: Abacus, 1995), 186.

[68] See Rhys Williams, "'*Und muß ich von Dante schweigen, zieht Italien gegen uns?*' Carl Sternheim's Opposition to the First World War," chap. 3 in this volume, and Edward Timms, *Karl Kraus, Apocalyptic Satirist* (New Haven and London: Yale UP, 1986), 273–80.

[69] See Reed, *Mann and the Uses of Tradition*, 212–13 for Thomas Mann's tortuous argument resisting the memorandum. For Bernhardi's argument that Belgium as a colonial power did not have any right to neutrality, see Bridgham, "Bernhardi."

[70] H. G. Wells, *The War of the Worlds* (serialized 1897, book 1898) (London: Heinemann, 1968), 25.

[71] Wells, *War of the Worlds*, 61, 69, 81.

[72] More significant than the relative strength of the dreadnoughts was German appreciation of the potentialities of the heavy howitzer and the machine gun, which gave them a significant advantage in the opening phase of the war. See Liddell Hart, *A History of the World War, 1914–1918*, 54.

[73] Kurd Laßwitz, *Auf zwei Planeten* (1897), ed. Rudi Schweikert (Munich: Wilhelm Heyne, 1998), 545. See also Wernher von Braun and Willy Ley, *Die Eroberung des Weltraums* (Frankfurt am Main/Hamburg: Fischer, 1958), 71–75.

[74] See Schweikert's commentary in *Auf zwei Planeten*, 886; also 9 and 848. Similarly, Leo Szilard, who worked on the development of the atom bomb, said he took the idea of indefinite chain reaction from Wells's *The World Set Free* (1914). See Norman & Jean MacKenzie, *The Time Traveller: The Life of H. G. Wells* (London: Weidenfeld & Nicolson, 1973), 298, cited in *The Intellectuals and the Masses: Pride and Prejudice among the Literary Intelligentsia, 1880–1939*, by John Carey (London: Faber & Faber, 1992), 133.

[75] Laßwitz, *Zwischen zwei Welten*, "Herren des Sonnensystems" (Lords of the Solar System), 393; gravitational and solar energy, *passim*; "Steine in Brot verwandelten . . . von dem niedrigen Standpunkt des Ackerbaues emanzipiert" (stones turned into bread . . . emancipated from low-status land-cultivation), 393; civil wars, 406; "Beruf der Nume, die Menschheit von ihrer Geschichte zu erlösen" (the Martians' vocation to redeem mankind from its history), 635.

[76] "Aufgaben der Kultur," "Kulturarbeit," Laßwitz, *Zwischen zwei Welten*, 252, 264.

[77] Laßwitz, *Zwischen zwei Welten*, 105–6.

[78] "Numenheit ohne Nume!," Laßwitz, *Zwischen zwei Welten*, 719.

[79] E.g. "Wenn aber nicht Ihr individueller Wille, sondern Ihr sittlicher Wille im Spiel ist, Ihre freie Selbstbestimmung der Persönlichkeit . . . dann gibt es keine Macht, die Sie hindern kann . . ." (If, however, your individual will is not active but your moral will is, your freedom to develop your own personality, . . . then there exists no power that can prevent you; Laßwitz, *Auf zwei Planeten*, 242; similarly 267). See also Schweikert's commentary, ibid., 977.

[80] Laßwitz, *Auf zwei Planeten*, 722.

[81] "cultural planets" (Laßwitz, *Auf zwei Planeten*, 255).

[82] His key 1894 essay "The Extinction of Man" was reprinted in *Certain Personal Matters* (1898); see Patrick Bridgwater, *H. G. Wells and Nietzsche* (London: H. G. Wells Society Occasional Papers, Nr. 3, 1980), 26.

[83] Witness Wells's mockery of R. B. Haldane as the "luminously incomprehensible" Lord Chancellor in *Bealby* and "a fluent Hegelian. He spent his holidays, it was understood, in the Absolute — at any rate in Germany"; cited by Bridgwater, *Wells and Nietzsche*, 2. A Hegelian philosopher whose "spiritual home was Germany" (ibid., 5), Haldane was also the "Liberal Imperialist" Secretary of War in 1914. His talks with the Kaiser, Bethmann, and Tirpitz in Berlin in 1912 were, in Tuchman's words, "the last Anglo-German attempt to find a common ground of understanding and it failed." Haldane declared himself convinced "that once the German war party had got into the saddle, it would be war not merely for the overthrow of France or Russia but for the domination of the world" (Tuchman, *August 1914*, 62). He was later Lord Chancellor in the first Labour administration.

[84] Wells's first reference to Nietzsche, in an article entitled "Human Evolution. III — Mr. Wells Replies" (April, 1897), quoted in Bridgwater, *Wells and Nietzsche*, 12.

[85] Bridgwater, *Wells and Nietzsche*, 4.

[86] Bridgwater, *Wells and Nietzsche*, 25.

[87] Bernard Shaw, *Collected Letters, 1898–1910*, 649 — quoted in Bridgwater, *Wells and Nietzsche*, 4.

[88] Bridgwater's observation that "they come from 'beyond good and evil,' and live by power" is scarcely sufficient qualification for Superman status. Shaw may have been thinking rather of Wells's musings on "Intelligence on Mars" (in *The Saturday Review*, April 4, 1896), for which Wells later acknowledged his indebtedness to Percival Lowell's *Mars* (1896); see Bridgwater, *Wells and Nietzsche*, 13. Here Carey seems closer to the mark: that the Martians "are another version of Wells's nightmare crabs" (Carey, *Intellectuals and the Masses*, 131; for further examples of crabs, 128–29, and especially, for their sexual symbolism, 143).

[89] H. G. Wells, *The War of the Worlds* (1898; repr., London: Heinemann, 1968), 122–23, 141–42. This final injunction, Carey notes, "is just what Wells recommends three years later in *Anticipations*, and the tame, inert types the artilleryman condemns resemble the suburban lower-middle classes, lacking in ideas and initiatives, who are excluded from Wells's Utopias" (*Intellectuals and the Masses*, 131). Wells is naturally a prime target for Carey's polemic (the chapter is entitled:

"H. G. Wells Getting Rid of People"), as is Nietzsche *passim*, and the evidence assembled by Carey makes a powerful case, though a highly selective one with more than a whiff of *trahison des clercs* about it — Noel Annan, for instance, calls it a "diatribe" by "a master at fouling his own nest," and, incidentally, defends Nietzsche against Carey: see Annan, *The Dons* (London: Harper Collins, 1999), 290.

[90] Wells, *War of the Worlds*, 105, 141. The narrator's rejection of the Artilleryman — he leaves him "to his drink and gluttony" (129) — seems unbalanced after such an otherwise sympathetically drawn portrait. Bergonzi says there is no doubt that it is Wells himself speaking, but that he "redresses the balance" by making the narrator soon see the Artilleryman as a "complete idler" (Bernard Bergonzi, *The Early H. G. Wells: A Study of the Scientific Romances*, [Manchester: Manchester UP, 1961], 138). Wells had perhaps read Max Nordau's distorted depiction of Nietzsche's "degeneracy" in *Entartung* (trans. as *Degeneration*, 1895 — see Bridgwater, *Wells and Nietzsche*, 6), a "pathography" which Shaw felt compelled to "demolish" in 1908 — see Diane Milburn, *The "Deutschlandbild" of A. R. Orage and the "New Age" Circle* (Frankfurt am Main: Peter Lang, 1996), 49.

[91] Milburn, *"Deutschlandbild" of A. R. Orage*, 39.

[92] Nietzsche, however, and specifically Zarathustra's teachings, did enter the Youth Movement with the advent in 1913 of the *Freideutsche Jugend* — a more intellectually adventurous and cosmopolitan alternative to the *Wandervogel* movement founded at the turn of the century, which had become increasingly susceptible to *völkisch* sentiments: see Walter Laqueur, *Young Germany: A History of the German Youth Movement* (London: Routledge and Paul, 1962), 8–9; also R. Hinton Thomas, *Nietzsche in German Politics and Society, 1890–1918* (Manchester: Manchester UP, 1983), 96–111.

[93] Wells, on August 4, 1914 — see Tuchman, *August 1914*, 305.

[94] Carey, *Intellectuals and the Masses*, 136–47.

[95] Bridgwater, *Wells and Nietzsche*, 1. Although interest in Nietzsche intensified on the outbreak of war, when Wells's fascination also revived, the postwar climate was clearly less favorable.

[96] See for example Milburn, *"Deutschlandbild" of A. R. Orage*, 38–41.

[97] Stuart Wallace, *War and the Image of Germany* (Edinburgh: John Donald, 1988), 48–49.

[98] Wallace, *War and the Image of Germany*, 50; see also R. Hinton Thomas, *Nietzsche in German Politics*, 128, and Martin, *Nietzsche*, below.

[99] A. R. Orage had set out in 1903 to "reduce Leeds to Nietzscheism" (Holbrook Jackson) after reading Thomas Common's translation of *Also sprach Zarathustra* (1896), before editing the *New Age* from 1907 and 1922, initially under Shaw's patronage — see Patrick Bridgwater, "English Writers and Nietzsche," in *Nietzsche: Imagery and Thought*, ed. Malcolm Pasley (London: 1978), 225. By 1908 the *New Age* vied with the *Spectator* at around 20,000 copies. Orage's two volumes, *Friedrich Nietzsche: The Dionysian Spirit of the Age* (1906) and *Nietzsche in Outline and Aphorism* (1907) were both well received — see Milburn, *"Deutschlandbild" of A. R. Orage*, 22, 23, 25, 28; also Martin, "Nietzsche."

[100] Martin, "Nietzsche."

[101] August 29 and September 2, 1914; see Martin, "Nietzsche."

[102] The ironic phrase is Wyndham Lewis's; see Martin, "Nietzsche."

[103] Hinton Thomas, *Nietzsche in German Politics*, provides a brief but useful overview of such topics as "Social Democracy and Nietzsche," "Anarchism and Nietzsche," "The Feminist Movement and Nietzsche," "Social Darwinism and Nietzsche."

[104] "'Deutschland, Deutschland über Alles' klingt mir schmerzlich in den Ohren"; "Für das Prinzip 'Deutschland, Deutschland über Alles' oder für das deutsche Reich uns zu begeistern, sind wir nicht dumm genug" (ca. 1884; It's a painful experience, hearing the words "Deutschland, Deutschland über Alles"; we're not so stupid as to be enthusiastic about the principle "Deutschland, Deutschland über Alles" or about the German *Reich*; Otto Ladendorf, *Historisches Schlagwörterbuch* [Straßburg and Berlin: Karl J. Trübner, 1906], 56–57).

[105] William James, *The Moral Equivalent of War*, available at: http://www.constitution.org/wj/meow.htm.

[106] L. T. Hobhouse, for instance, a leading "Norman Angellite," lamenting that the younger generation had "come in large measure to believe in violence, and in impulse, emotion or instinct," singled out for blame "the Pragmatists, like the American William James, Bergson and especially Nietzsche, 'a Pragmatist in everything but name'" (Wallace, *War and the Image of Germany*, 48).

[107] "Norman Angell and his friends in the hastily formed Neutrality League described Germany in their manifesto as 'wedged in between hostile States, highly civilised, with a culture that has contributed greatly in the past to western civilisation, racially allied to ourselves and with moral ideals largely resembling our own'" (Kennedy, *Rise of the Anglo-German Antagonism*, 459). Esher was the King's friend and adviser as well as chairman of the War Committee charged with reshaping the army after the Boer War (Tuchman, *August 1914*, 21).

[108] Strachan, *First World War* 1:134–35; cf. Wallace, *War and the Image of Germany*, 15–16; Kennedy, *Rise of the Anglo-German Antagonism*, 452; Tuchman, *August 1914*, 21–22, 122–23.

[109] Cf. Bernhardi, "denn der Krieg ist in erster Linie eine *biologische Notwendigkeit*" (for, above all else, war is a *biological necessity*) — *Deutschland und der nächste Krieg*, 11. It seems likely that James had read Bernhardi's *Cavalry in Future Wars* (1906), a forerunner of *Deutschland und der nächste Krieg*; see Bridgham, "Bernhardi."

[110] William James, *The Varieties of Religious Experience* (1902; repr., London: Longmans, Green, 1912), 371–73. The Nietzsche passage is from *Zur Genealogie der Moral, Dritte Abhandlung*, paragraph 14, beginning "The sick are the greatest danger for the well" and advocating a cordon sanitaire between the two. "Poor Nietzsche . . . sickly" is perhaps more an allusion to Nietzsche's own suffering and recent death than to the passage, which shows Nietzsche at his most memorably scintillating. "All too often," however, "his predilection for the rhetoric of health and sickness has been portrayed as an idiosyncratic response to, and preoccupation

with, his own well-documented medical crises" (Gregory Moore, *Nietzsche, Biology and Metaphor* [Cambridge: Cambridge UP, 2002], 1).

[111] See Martin, "Nietzsche"; also Hinton Thomas, *Nietzsche in German Politics*, 128.

[112] Buitenhuis, *The Great War of Words*, 31.

[113] See Milburn, *"Deutschlandbild" of A. R. Orage*, 150.

[114] *Germany and England* ran through eight reprints between June and September 1914 — see M. E. Humble, "The Breakdown of a Consensus: British Writers and Anglo-German Relations, 1900–1920," *Journal of European Studies* (March 1977): 45; the "popular edition" of *Germany and the Next War* (1914) ran to six reprints — see Bridgham, "Bernhardi"; also Milburn, *"Deutschlandbild" of A. R. Orage*, 148–49; and Wallace, *War and the Image of Germany*, 68–69.

[115] Cecil Chesterton, *The Prussian Hath Said in His Heart* (London, 1914), 85, cited by Milburn, *"Deutschlandbild" of A. R. Orage*, 148–49.

[116] Milburn, *"Deutschlandbild" of A. R. Orage*, 85, 148–51.

[117] Leo Maxse was editor of the stridently anti-German *National Review*. In 1909, Robert Blatchford, editor of the Socialist *Clarion*, had written six scaremongering articles for the *Daily Mail* prophesying war — see Milburn, *"Deutschlandbild" of A. R. Orage*, 48.

[118] Hinton Thomas, *Nietzsche in German Politics and Society*, 128–29. The motto is "Der Krieg und der Mut haben mehr große Dinge getan als die Nächstenliebe" (War and courage have brought about more great things than loving thy neighbor). It continues: "Nicht euer Mitleiden, sondern eure Tapferkeit rettete bisher die Verunglückten. Was ist gut? fragt ihr. Tapfer sein ist gut." (*Also sprach Zarathustra*, 1:10; It has always been your courage, not your compassion, which saved life's hapless wretches. What is good? you ask. Courage is good). See Martin's essay on Nietzsche in this volume also for a somewhat differently weighted reading of Bernhardi.

[119] Hinton Thomas, *Nietzsche in German Politics and Society*. Support for this is found in John Dewey's *German Philosophy and Politics* (1915) — another pragmatist's reading of idealism.

[120] The intervening step spans a veritable abyss: "Prussia inaugurated the concept of duty and moral duty is Kant's key concept." For Nietzsche's advocacy of compulsory military service as an antidote to the decadent "softness" of democratic societies, see Moore, *Nietzsche, Biology and Metaphor*, 131.

[121] "Man does not seek happiness," says Nietzsche, "only the Englishman does" ("der Mensch strebt *nicht* nach Glück, nur der Engländer tut das"; *Götzendämmerung*, "Sprüche und Pfeile," 12), though it is the teleological "seeking" rather than incidental momentary pleasure he has in his sights. See also Moore, *Nietzsche, Biology and Metaphor*, 66–67, 74–75.

[122] And then only indirectly, via Kuno Fischer's book on Hegel (see Bernhardi, *Deutschland und der nächste Krieg*, 21).

[123] Bernhardi, *Deutschland und der nächste Krieg*, 54, 9, 11. "Wie eine Bleisucht hat das Friedensverlangen die meisten Kulturvölker befallen." One version of the "two Germanies" thesis sees Kant as the personification of "the cerebral, spiritual

and reasoned Germany; Hegel the materialist, militarist, and nationalist," and "a German people (presumably Kantian) being guided, gulled, and misled by a German leadership (presumably Hegelian)" — Strachan, *First World War*, 1:1121. Treitschke also attacked theories of "eternal peace," though omitting to mention their most famous German advocate: see Klaus Schröter, *Literatur und Zeitgeschichte* (Mainz: v. Hase und Koehler, 1970), 59–60; also Reed, *Mann and the Uses of Tradition*, 216, n. 70.

[124] Reed, *Mann and the Uses of Tradition*, 179.

[125] "Bismarcks Positivismus, seine 'Realpolitik,' sein Reichsgebilde — das korrespondiert auf tiefe und charakteristische Art mit Kants praktischer Vernunft im Gegensatz zur 'reinen,' — deutsch ist der kategorische Imperativ jenseits der abgründigsten Skepsis." Kant and Nietzsche are "die Moralisten des deutschen 'Militarismus,' — ja, sie zeigen, daß das deutsche Soldatentum ein Soldatentum aus Moralität ist." (Bismarck's positivism, his *Realpolitik*, his construction of the *Reich* — these correspond in a deep and characteristic way to Kant's practical reason as distinct from his "pure" reason; the categorical imperative is German above and beyond the most profound skepticism. Kant and Nietzsche provide the moral justification for German militarism, indeed they demonstrate that German soldierliness has its roots in morality; quoted by Reed, *Mann and the Uses of Tradition*, 189).

[126] Bernhardi, *Deutschland und der nächste Krieg*, 11–12.

[127] H. G. Wells, *Apropos of Dolores* (London: Jonathan Cape, 1938), 6.

[128] See Carey, *Intellectuals and the Masses*, 120–25.

[129] Bernhardi draws hope from Japan's victory over the "fast erdrückende Übermacht" (almost suffocating superiority) of Russia. Germany's aim must be, "das geistige und sittliche Niveau der Mannschaften zu heben" (to raise the men's spiritual and moral niveau) through progressive individuation à la Nietzsche (*Deutschland und der nächste Krieg*, 194–95, 203, 236). Somewhat ironically, this specialization was effected only in the reduced, post-Versailles army.

[130] See D. P. Crook, *Darwinism, War and History: The Debate over the Biology of War from "The Origin of Species" to the First World War* (Cambridge: Cambridge UP, 1994); also Gregory Moore, "Darwinism and National Identity, 1870–1918," chapter 6 in this volume.

[131] Gregory Moore, *Nietzsche, Biology and Metaphor* (Cambridge: Cambridge UP, 2002).

[132] Moore, *Nietzsche, Biology and Metaphor*, 27, 34, 30. Cf. "anthropomorphic and voluntarist descriptions of natural selection litter the pages of *The Origin of Species*" (ibid., 7).

[133] Moore, *Nietzsche, Biology, and Metaphor*, 34.

[134] Moore, *Nietzsche, Biology and Metaphor*, 63, 46, 55. While Nietzsche does develop Roux's militaristic metaphors (ibid., 38), he does not appear to have made any connection between Rolph's "unersättliche Aneignung" (insatiable appropriation) and Bismarck's famous claim that newly unified Germany was a "satiated" nation. Similarly, "according to his biologism, moral and physiological

'breeding' amount essentially to the same thing. Nowhere, as his eugenicist interpreters often complained, does he even hint at the biological measures necessary to realise his goal" (ibid., 162–63).

[135] Moore, *Nietzsche, Biology and Metaphor*, 2.

[136] See Alfred Kelly, *The Descent of Darwin: The Popularization of Darwin in Germany* (Chapel Hill: U of North Carolina P, 1981), 107; compare Hinton Thomas, *Nietzsche in German Politics*, 113. A characteristic example of Tille's "dehumanizing brutality" (Kelly, *Descent of Darwin*, 107) is his suggestion that London's East End served a useful function in purging society of its useless elements — see Manz, *Tille*, below.

[137] Thus Hinton Thomas, *Nietzsche in German Politics*, 114, drawing on the memoir of Tille's brother, Armin Tille, *Ein Kämpferleben: Alexander Tille 1866–1912* (Gotha: 1916).

[138] Extracts from Tille's article in Berlin's *Die Woche* were leaked to the *Glasgow Herald* by an enterprising Glaswegian student on his gap year — see Stefan Manz, "Peacemaker and Warmonger: Alexander Tille and the Limits of Anglo-German Intercultural Transfer," chap. 8 in this volume.

[139] Hinton Thomas, *Nietzsche in German Politics*, 113; Steven E. Aschheim, *The Nietzsche Legacy in Germany, 1890–1990* (Berkeley: U of California P, 1992), 123.

[140] In the *New Age*, June 20, 1908 — see Milburn, *"Deutschlandbild" of A. R. Orage*, 40.

[141] Chap. 8 in this volume.

[142] Alexander Tille, *Aus Englands Flegeljahren* (Dresden and Leipzig: Reißner, 1901); for Helene Stöcker, see R. J. Evans, *The Feminist Movement in Germany* (London and Beverly Hills: 1976), and Hinton Thomas, *Nietzsche in German Politics*, 91–92.

[143] Tille, *Flegeljahre*, 46: "Daß wir dem Briten diese Geringschätzung noch austreiben werden, steht ebenso fest, wie daß es noch manchen Hieb brauchen wird, bis sie ausgetrieben ist" (It is as certain that we shall drive this sense of superiority out of the British as it is that the process of so doing will require many a blow). See also Meyer, in an unpublished letter quoted by Huether: "Aber am meisten freue ich mich doch, daß die Engländer solche Hiebe bekommen haben" (But most of all, I guess, I'm delighted the English have taken such a licking; Andreas Huether, "*In Politik verschieden, in Freundschaft wie immer*': The German Celtic Scholar Kuno Meyer and the First World War," chap. 9 in this volume.

[144] See Wallace, *War and the Image of Germany*, 40. Cf. Childers's post-*Riddle* Irish sympathies and activities, such as gun-running à la Casement.

[145] See Andreas Huether, "Kuno Meyer"; and for Casement's *Gesammelte Schriften: Irland, Deutschland und die Freiheit der Meere*, see Holger Klein, "Austrian (and Some German) Scholars of English and the First World War," chap. 10 in this volume. Schiemann advocated "ein frischer, fröhlicher Krieg" (a jolly good war) as the best defense against democracy and socialism; see B. von Bülow, *Denkwürdigkeiten*, vol. 2 (Berlin, Ullstein, 1930), 81.

[146] To cite a single example of the latter point: Wilhelm Dibelius's famous stock-taking in 1924 of Germany's struggle "wider einen Feind, den es nicht kannte" (against an enemy it didn't know) begins with "einem Kanzler, der es für möglich hielt, den Krieg mit England zu vermeiden, auch wenn wir durch Belgien marschierten" (a Chancellor who thought it possible to avoid war with England, even if we marched through Belgium; *England*, 2 vols. [Stuttgart, Leipzig, and Berlin: Deutsche Verlags-Anstalt, 1922], xi). Dibelius's book, as Klein remarks below, was for many years a standard work on British civilization.

[147] Kurt Riezler, *Tagebücher, Aufsätze, Dokumente*, ed. Karl Dietrich Erdmann (Göttingen: 1972), 335 (February 22, 1916), quoted by Gordon A. Craig in *Germany, 1866–1945* (Oxford: Oxford UP, 1981), 369–70.

[148] See Huether, "Kuno Meyer."

[149] See below for the alternative manifesto to which Weber and Einstein lent their names in 1915.

[150] See Fischer, *Griff nach der Weltmacht*, 132–33; Wallace, *War and the Image of Germany*, 32–35.

[151] See Klein, "Austrian and German Scholars."

[152] The apt title of Wallace's first chapter. Wallace relates many instances, none more poignant than that of Albert-Wilhelm Schüddekopf, first Professor of German at the University of Leeds (Wallace, *War and the Image of Germany*, 163–64).

[153] See Klein, "Austrian and German Scholars" in this volume. Klein adds much new material that broadly endorses Klaus Schwabe's heavily documented study of German academics during the war, *Wissenschaft und Kriegsmoral*.

[154] See Peter Firchow, "Shakespeare, Goethe, and the War of the Professors, 1914–1919," in *Intimate Enemies: English and German Literary Reactions to the Great War, 1914–1918*, ed. F. K. Stanzel and M. Löschnigg (Heidelberg: Winter, 1993), 465–92; also Klein, "Austrian and German Scholars."

[155] Klein, "Austrian and German Scholars."

[156] Klein, "Austrian and German Scholars."

[157] In "Shakespeare, Goethe, and the War of the Professors, 1914–1919" Firchow examines entries from the war-year volumes of the Proceedings of the *Shakespeare-Gesellschaft*. See also Klein, "Austrian and German Scholars."

[158] See Klein, "Austrian and German Scholars."

[159] To develop the analogy with which Gordon Craig begins his *History of Germany 1866–1945*, vii.

[160] Act 1, scene 29. "Der Nörgler" is usually rendered as The Grumbler, though neither that nor "Carper," nor "Moaner," catch his bitingly satirical and often cynical tone (there is, admittedly, another "Zyniker" in the enormous cast of characters). In the same scene: Germany's "Platz an der Sonne"; misuse of Nietzsche's "Wille zur Macht"; U-Boats and the *Lusitania*; "deutsche Krieg-führung barbarisch? — deutsche Friedensführung barbarisch"; "das Volk der Dichter und Denker" or "das Volk der Richter und Henker"? Kantian idealism

versus "means and ends" pragmatism — the commercial impulse behind the war: "Lebensmittel" (groceries) not "Lebenszweck" (the purpose of life) — found already in *Die Fackel* of December 5, 1914. See also act 2, 10, 26, 29.

[161] For a good summary, see Buitenhuis, *The Great War of Words*, 32–36.

[162] He might have added Robert Blatchford, whose bellicose "chatter about 'The Coming War with Germany'" predated Bernhardi's famous book by three years. Noel Annan notes that "Blatchford, the old socialist, denounced him [Shaw] as a renegade Irish alien betraying England." See Annan, *Our Age* (London: Weidenfeld and Nicolson, 1990), 98.

[163] Annan, *Our Age*, 98.

[164] Stanley Weintraub, *Journey to Heartbreak: The Crucible Years of Bernard Shaw, 1914–1918* (New York: Weybright & Talley, 1971), 229, quoted in Buitenhuis, *The Great War of Words*, 36.

[165] Sean O'Casey's later description of P. G. Wodehouse was gratefully accepted by Wodehouse as a title for his autobiographies.

[166] See: "G. B. Shaw ist einer der wenigen, die sich von der allgemeinen Invasions-hysterie nicht anstecken lassen. In seiner Groteske *Press Cuttings* (1909) macht er sich lustig über die Eiferer im Lager der Imperialisten und Militaristen" (G. B. Shaw is one of the few who avoided catching the general infection of invasion hysteria. In his scornful *Press Cuttings* (1909) he mocks the agitators in the imperialist and militarist camp; Horst Oppel, *Englisch-deutsche Literaturbeziehungen II* [Berlin: Erich Schmidt Verlag, 1971], 80).

[167] Annan, *Our Age*, 85.

[168] See Buitenhuis, *The Great War of Words*, 36.

[169] A. J. P. Taylor, *A Personal History* (London: Hamish Hamilton, 1983), 59: "I fell under the spell of his style and have remained so. [What] I picked up from Shaw leads to other writers — Ibsen, Nietzsche, Samuel Butler." He acknowledges a similar debt to Wells, not the novels but his *Outline of History*, from which he learnt "perhaps more than from all other books" (Ferguson, *Pity of War*, xxiii–xxiv).

[170] Ferguson, *Pity of War*, 243.

[171] The catch phrase on which he plays numerous variations is "Wir führen einen heiligen Verteidigungskrieg."

[172] Werner Sombart, *Händler und Helden* (Munich and Leipzig: Duncker & Humblot, 1915), 10–11.

Writers

1: Anglo-German Conflict in Popular Fiction, 1870–1914

Iain Boyd Whyte

Introduction

THE OUTBREAK OF THE First World War was marked not only by the booming of cannons across Europe, but also by the frantic scratchings of pens and the clattering of typewriters, as the literati of the combatant nations set about damning their adversaries. Big guns were also wheeled out for this battle. A statement supporting the war "against the rule of 'Blood and Iron'" was published in *The Times* on September 18, 1914 and signed by fifty-three writers. The signatories included H. G. Wells, Thomas Hardy, Arthur Quiller-Couch, John Masefield, Arnold Bennett, Gilbert Murray, Rudyard Kipling and Arthur Conan Doyle. The counterblast to this and similar attacks by various groups of British writers and academics was not long in coming. On October 4 the *Aufruf an die Kulturwelt* was published in ten languages and signed by a distinguished collection of German cultural luminaries. The *Aufruf* rejected the charges of militarism and barbarism leveled by the British critics, insisted that: "Ohne den deutschen Militarismus wäre die deutsche Kultur längst vom Erdboden getilgt," and concluded:

> "Glaubt uns! Glaubt, daß wir diesen Kampf zu Ende kämpfen werden als ein Kulturvolk, dem das Vermächtnis eines Goethe, eines Beethoven, eines Kant ebenso heilig ist wie sein Herd und seine Scholle" (But for German willingness to fight, German culture would have been wiped off the earth long ago. . . . Believe us! Believe us when we say that we will fight this battle to the end as a cultured people for whom the legacy of a Goethe, a Beethoven and a Kant is as precious as our very hearths and homes).[1]

This reassurance was followed by a long list of names, a veritable Who's Who of contemporary German science, arts and letters, including Max Planck and Wilhelm Röntgen, Peter Behrens, Max Reinhardt, Siegfried Wagner, Engelbert Humperdinck, Felix Weingartner, and Max Liebermann. Among the writers and poets who had signed the *Aufruf* were

Richard Dehmel, Herbert Eulenberg, Ludwig Fulda, Gerhart and Carl Hauptmann, Hermann Sudermann, and Richard Voß. From the torrents of spleen and abuse that were poured out on both sides of the North Sea in the early months of the war, clear stereotypes emerged as expressions of the mutual antagonism of the two nations.

In Britain the Liberal conscience demanded an intellectual and ethical justification for the war, a reason to abandon the traditional Liberal tenets of non-intervention and pacifism. The diplomatic conflict had to be presented as a moral crusade that would not only free the German nation from its own internal oppressors but would also end all wars. As early as August 7, 1914, only three days after the outbreak of war, H. G. Wells set the pattern with an article in the *Daily Chronicle*:

> Every sword that is drawn against Germany is a sword drawn for peace. That trampling, drilling foolery in the heart of Europe that has arrested civilization and darkened the hopes of mankind for forty years, German Imperialism, German militarism, has struck its inevitable blow. The victory of Germany will mean the permanent enthronement of the War God over all human affairs. The defeat of Germany may open the way to disarmament and peace throughout the earth. To those who love peace there can be no other hope in the present conflict than the defeat, the utter discrediting of the German legend, the ending for good and all of the blood and iron superstition of Krupp, flag-waging Teutonic Kiplingism, and all the criminal sham efficiency that centres on Berlin. Never was war so righteous as war against Germany now.[2]

Wells expanded on his theme in a further piece entitled "The War of the Mind," published in *The Nation* on August 29.

> "All the realities of this war," he wrote, "are things of the mind. This is a conflict of cultures and nothing else in the world. . . . We fight not to destroy a nation but a nest of evil ideas. We fight because a whole nation has become obsessed by pride, by the cant of cynicism and the vanity of violence, by the evil suggestion of such third-rate writers as Gobineau and Houston Stewart Chamberlain, that they were a people of peculiar excellence destined to dominate the earth, by the base offer of advantage in cunning and treachery held out by such men as Delbruck [*sic*] and Bernhardi, by the theatricalism of the Kaiser and by two stirring songs about Deutschland and the Rhine. [. . .] On the back of it all, spurring it on, are the idea-mongers, the base-spirited writing men, pretentious little professors in frocks, scribbling colonels."[3]

Wells was willingly joined in his crusade by other liberal writers, and, naturally enough, by the Conservative polemicists who had long thrived on the diet of distrust and disinformation served up by Lord Northcliffe's

Daily Mail and *Observer*, and by the other influential conservative papers like *The Morning Post*, *The Daily Express*, *The National Review*, and *The Daily Telegraph*.

The years 1914 and 1915 saw a flurry of publishing activity by respected academics and writers, all intent on proving the maliciousness of the German national character. The *Oxford Pamphlets* led the way, with over thirty titles by the end of 1914, including "Might is Right" and "Nietzsche and Treitschke: The Worship of Power in Modern Germany" by Ernest Barker. Barker was a member of the Faculty of Modern History at Oxford and had changed his name from Otto Julius Eltzbacher. The vigor with which he denounced the country of his birth was matched by another emigré, Ford Madox Hueffer. In two articles on "High Germany," published in *The Saturday Review* in the autumn of 1911, Hueffer had taken a passionately pro-German position, which even saw the town of Giessen as an ideal social and intellectual community, as *utopia*.[4] This infatuation ended with the outbreak of war, and in 1915 Hueffer published two powerful attacks on Germany, *When Blood is Their Argument* and *Between St Dennis and St George*, described by a recent critic as the only two books from the mass of propaganda literature published between 1914 and 1919 that deserve to survive.[5] Hueffer's principal theme was the military ambitions of the German state. As he insisted in *Between St Dennis and St George*:

> The impression remains with me that, whereas every German serious writer takes the possibility of war as one of the resources of the German Empire, I have never read one single word in German which advocated peace as a constant and indestructible factor in the world. The philosophy of the State, whether the State be regarded merely as an ideal or whether that ideal be the present German Empire — philosophizing, then, about the State is an occupation to which every German writer devotes a large portion of his energies. Whether it be historians like Ranke, Mommsen, and Treitschke, or whether it be eminent investigators into every other branch of human material or mental activity, such as Professors Eucken, Oncken, von Wagner, von List, or whether it be the great who are great for quite other reasons — whether it be Wagner, Nietzsche, Kant, or Hegel — every one of these Teutonically eminent has accepted war as part of a theory of State about which they find it necessary to write.[6]

The same names and similar arguments recur throughout this genre, the literary propaganda tract. According to Cecil Chesterton, the Germans after Bismarck "were bitten with the new Superman idea, and were conscious of no facts save their own evident superiority to the rest of mankind. They had no idea of a policy save to 'hack their way through,' to destroy nation after nation until Prussia alone was left erect."[7] Similarly,

John Cowper Powys in his reply to Professor Münsterberg insisted that: "Massive, patient and efficient though the German intellect is, it would be a vast calamity to the world if this culture, so arrogant, so unsympathetic, were thrust upon us by the drill-sergeant and the machine";[8] while Arnold Bennett, in a very weak essay on liberty, insisted: "It is the intolerable arrogance of Germany, and nothing else, that has brought into existence the coalition against the Teuton Empires, and the remarkable character of the coalition is yet a further proof of the tremendous resentment which that arrogance has aroused."[9] In these and countless similar tracts a recurring image of Germany was proposed, the image of an autocratic and militaristic state, with expansionist aims, a blinkered and vainglorious intelligentsia tending towards mysticism, monism, nihilism and other anti-Christian tendencies, and a passion for efficiency, organization, and bureaucracy that dominated its civil and industrial life.

The German *Literaten* and academics were not slow to respond to the challenge, and produced their own tracts in defence of the moral rectitude of Germany and the duplicity of perfidious Albion. Once again, a few examples can be used to depict the favored stereotypes. The first must, of course, be Ernst Lissauer's celebrated "Haßgesang gegen England," for which Lissauer was awarded the *Roter Adlerorden* by the Kaiser himself. As Stefan Zweig recalled in *Die Welt von Gestern*:

> Man druckte das Gedicht in allen Zeitungen nach, die Lehrer lasen es in den Schulen den Kindern vor, die Offiziere traten vor die Front und rezitierten es den Soldaten, bis jeder die Haßlitanei auswendig konnte.[10]

> [The poem was published in every newspaper, schoolteachers read it out to their children, officers strode up to the front and recited it to their men until everybody knew the litany of hatred off by heart.]

The success of the poem in Germany provoked a leader in *The Times*, while Sir James Barrie's riposte, entitled "Der Tag," was performed in the London Colosseum and featured a debate between the Kaiser, the German Chancellor, and the "Spirit of Culture." The "Haßgesang" itself is remarkable only for its venom:

> Was schiert uns Russe und Franzos'!
> Schuß wider Schuß und Stoß um Stoß!
> Wir lieben sie nicht,
> Wir hassen sie nicht.
> Wir schützen Weichsel und Maasgaupaß,
> Wir haben nur einen einzigen Haß,
> Wir lieben vereint, wir hassen vereint,
> Wir haben nur einen einzigen Feind:
>
> Denn ihr alle wißt, denn ihr alle wißt,
> Er sitzt geduckt hinter der grauen Flut,

Voll Neid, voll Wut, voll Schläue, voll List,
Durch Wasser getrennt, die sind dicker als Blut.
Wir wollen treten in ein Gericht,
Einen Schwur zu schwören, Gesicht in Gesicht,
Einen Schwur von Erz, den verbläst kein Wind.
Einen Schwur für Kind und für Kindeskind,
Vernehmt das Wort, sagt noch das Wort,
Es wälze sich durch ganz Deutschland fort:
Wir wollen nicht lassen von unserm Haß,
wir haben alle nur einen Haß,
Wir lieben vereint, wir hassen vereint,
Wir haben alle nur einen Feind:
    England.

In der Bordkajüte, im Feiersaal,
Saßen Schiffsoffiziere beim Liebesmahl, —
Wie ein Säbelhieb, wie ein Segelschwung,
Einer riß grüßend empor den Trunk,
Knapp hinknallend wie Ruderschlag,
Drei Worte sprach er: "Auf den Tag!"
Wem galt das Glas?
Sie hatten alle nur einen Haß.
Wer war gemeint?
Sie hatten alle nur einen Feind:
    England.

Nimm du die Völker der Erde in Sold,
Baue Wälle aus Barren von Gold,
Bedecke die Meerflut mit Bug bei Bug,
Du rechnetest klug, doch nicht klug genug.
Was schiert uns Russe und Franzos'!
Schuß wider Schuß und Stoß um Stoß!
Wir kämpfen den Kampf mit Bronze und Stahl,
Und schließen Frieden irgend einmal,
Dich werden wir hassen mit langem Haß,
Wir werden nicht lassen von unserm Haß,
Haß zu Wasser und Haß zu Land,
Haß des Hauptes und Haß der Hand,
Haß der Hämmer und Haß der Kronen,
Drosselnder Haß von siebzig Millionen,
Sie lieben vereint, sie hassen vereint,
Sie alle haben nur einen Feind:
    England.[11]

[We don't give a damn for Russians or Frenchmen! Bullet for bullet, bayonet for bayonet! We do not love them, we do not hate them. We defend the Vistula and the Maas Gau Pass. There's only one thing we hate. United we love, united we hate, we have only a single enemy. For you all know him, all of you know him — he cowers behind the grey flood-tide, filled with envy, with rage, with trickery, with cunning. We are separated by waters thicker than blood. We will take our case to the court, to swear an oath, face to face, an oath of steel that no wind will blow away; an oath for our children and our children's children. Hear the word, speak out the word, let it roll onwards through the whole of Germany. We will not let up on our hatred; all of us hate but one thing only. United we love, united we hate, we all have a single enemy: England.

In ships' cabins and in their mess-rooms naval officers sat down to their banquet. — Like the slash of a sabre or the swing of a sail, one of them rose to toast a greeting, echoing sharply like the slap of an oar. He spoke these words: "To the Day of Reckoning!" Whom was he toasting? All of them hated one thing only. Who were they thinking of? All of them had but a single enemy: England.

Take all the earth's peoples into your pay, build up walls with bars of gold, cover the oceans with ship after ship; cleverly you calculated, but not clever enough. We don't give a damn for Russians or Frenchmen! Bullet for bullet, bayonet for bayonet! We fight the battle with bronze and steel, and some day we'll agree the peace. — You we shall hate with enduring hatred. We won't let up on our hatred. Hate at sea and hate on land, hate of the head and hate of the hand, hate of the hammer and hate of the crown, a throttling hatred, seventy million strong. United they love, united they hate. All of them have but a single enemy: England.]

Here, in repetitious verse, were the bones of Miquel's *Sammlungspolitik*, of the need of the German nation to abandon what Max Weber had called its "soft eudaemonism" and take up the struggle for world power: in other words, to confront the English.

While Lissauer's repetitious verse sketched the general mood of Anglophobia, more exact reasons for this phobia can be adduced from the rash of pamphlets and essays that followed the declaration of war. Lengthy articles, the German equivalent to the *Oxford Pamphlets*, were published in three volumes under the title *Deutsche Reden in schwerer Zeit*, with contributions from such leading academics as Hans Delbrück, Adolf von Harnack, Franz von Liszt, Friedrich Meinecke and Ernst Troeltsch.[12] The *Literaten* were also active, and a succinct synopsis of the reasons for hating the English was offered by Richard Dehmel in a letter "An meine Kinder," published in October 1914:

Man redet ja viel von englischer Kultur; besonders unsere ästhetischen Snobs, die sich als Dandys ausspielen wollen. Aber das ist sehr bezeichnend für diese Kultur; wenn man sie nämlich genauer ansieht, entpuppt sie sich bloß als Nerven- und Muskeldressur, als Sport, Komfort und Tipptoppdreß, als gute Haltung in allen Lebenslagen.

[Much indeed is said about English culture, particularly by our aesthetic snobs who fancy themselves as dandies. But that is exactly what this culture is about: examine it closely, and it's nothing more than smart posture, sport, fine clothes and comfort, good tone in every situation.]

When it came to high culture, the picture, said Dehmel, was quite different:

Dies Volk hat keinen einzigen Musiker auch nur zweiten Ranges hervorgebracht, keinen Maler ganz ersten Ranges, keinen Plastiker von Belang, keinen bedeutenden Architekten, hat seine Paar Dichter schlecht behandelt bis über ihren Tod hinaus, und seinen Philosophen mangelt der Sinn für das, was höher ist als alle Vernunft. [. . .] Fischblütig ist dieses Inselvolk, klug, umsichtig, gewandt, verschwiegen und von unersättlicher Beutegier; alle warmblütigen Tugenden läßt es mit heuchlerischem Gleichmut verkümmern. Rücksichtslose Gewinnsucht ist die Triebfeder seiner ganzen Politik.[13]

[This culture has not produced one musician of note, not even of the second rank, not a single first-rate painter, no sculptor worth mentioning, not one significant architect. They maltreat their few poets even after death, and their philosophers lack all instinct for that which passeth understanding. . . . Cold as fish are these island-folk: cunning, circumspect, conspiratorial, smart, and possessed of an insatiable appetite for booty. With hypocritical indifference they permit all warm-blooded virtues to decay. The sole motive of their policies is an uncompromising desire for profit.]

The picture of a cold, calculating culture, devoid of spiritual and artistic qualities, was one developed on a larger scale by Werner Sombart in his comparison of the English and German national characters, published in 1915 under the title *Händler und Helden: Patriotische Besinnungen*. In Sombart's very reductionist thesis, which exactly mirrored that of Wells, Chesterton et al, the war was not merely a political conflict but a greater struggle between two opposing worldviews. "Was im Kampfe steht, sind der Händler und der Held, sind händlerische und heldische Weltanschauung und dementsprechende Kultur" (The confrontation is between merchant and hero, between a mercantile and a heroic view of life and the culture that matches it).[14] According to Sombart:

Die Tugenden aber des Helden sind die entgegengesetzten des
Händlers: sie sind alle positiv, Leben gebend und weckend, es sind
"schenkende Tugenden": Opfermut, Treue, Arglosigkeit, Ehrfurcht,
Tapferkeit, Frömmigkeit, Gehorsam, Güte. Es sind kriegerische
Tugenden, Tugenden, die ihre volle Entfaltung im Kriege und durch
den Krieg erleben.[15]

[But a hero's virtues are the opposite of a merchant's: they are all
positive, life-enhancing; they are "gift-bringing virtues": self-
sacrifice, loyalty, innocence, respect, bravery, piety, obedience, kind-
ness. These are warlike virtues — virtues which blossom most fully in
and through war.]

The pantheon of German greats was ransacked to support this thesis, with
quotations from Frederick the Great, Goethe, Fichte, and Nietzsche.
Unlike the more discerning English polemicists, who tended to dissociate
Nietzsche from "Prussianism,"[16] Sombart felt he was "heimatberechtigt in
Potsdam und Weimar"[17] (he belonged equally to Potsdam and Weimar),
and quoted Nietzsche's attacks on Anglo-Saxon democracy and utilitarianism. The philosopher's contempt was mild, however, compared to that
of Sombart, who painted a bleak picture of the mercantile mentality:

Die Grundlage alles Engländertums ist ja wohl die unermeßlich
geistige Beschränktheit dieses Volkes, ist seine Unfähigkeit, sich auch
nur um Handbreit über die greifbare und alltägliche "Wirklichkeit"
zu erheben. (9).

[Fundamental to all Englishness is assuredly this people's limitless
spiritual poverty, their inability to rise even one hand's breadth
above tangible, everyday "reality."]

Devoid of any higher intellectual ideals, the English, said Sombart, were
concerned only to increase their wealth and physical comfort, at the expense, if necessary, of other races and continents:

Ich verstehe unter Händlergeist diejenige Weltauffassung, die an das
Leben mit der Frage herantritt: was kannst Du Leben mir geben; die
also das ganze Dasein des einzelnen auf Erden als eine Summe von
Handelsgeschäften ansieht. (14).

[By mercantile spirit I mean the attitude of mind which approaches
life asking: what can you give me, Life? — in other words, the attitude which sees an individual's whole life on earth as the sum of
business opportunities.]

The inevitable result of this parasitic Weltanschauung was the ideology of
"Komfortismus," defined by Sombart as:

nicht eine äußere Gestaltungsform des Daseins, sondern eine bestimmte Art und Weise der Bewertung der Lebensformen. . . . Wer das bequeme und behagliche Leben hochschätzt, muß notwendig auch den materiellen Gütern eine hohe Bedeutung beimessen, und wer das tut, muß im Reichtum an materiellen Gütern ebenfalls einen großen Wert erblicken. Womit dann also die Umkehrung aller Werte erreicht wäre, die, wenn sie zu einer allgemeinen Erscheinung im Volke wird, verheerende Wirkung anrichten wird. (102–3).

[not an external shaping of existence but a particular manner of evaluating life-forms. . . . The man who places high value on comfort and convenience is bound to give high importance to material goods, and the man who does that is also bound to regard the wealth of material goods as the measure of value. Therewith the reversal of all values is achieved, which, if it becomes widespread amongst the people, will have dreadful consequences.]

Sport — "der Zwillingsbruder des Komfort" (103) (twin brother of comfort) — was a particularly enticing manifestation of this ideology, and Sombart advised that tennis, football, cricket, and the like should be left, "neidlos" (without envy), to the English. Indeed, the true mission of the German nation had been clarified by the outbreak of war:

Damit sind aber die Richtlinien aller Erziehung uns vorgezeichnet. Deren Aufgabe kann nur diese sein: deutsche Helden zu erziehen. Heldische Männer und heldische Frauen. (120).

[But therein we perceive the guidelines for all education. Its task can only be this: to educate German heroes. Heroic men and heroic women.]

This selfless and profoundly antimodernist German hero was set by Sombart and his fellow polemicists against a stereotyped Englishman who was arrogant, egoistic and acquisitive, morally dishonest and intellectually superficial, with an obsession for material possessions and physical comfort matched only by his infatuation with sport. To match the one-dimensional image of militaristic Prussia favored in 1914 by the British, here was the complementary stereotype of "perfides Albion."

While concerted Germanophobia was a comparatively recent development in Britain, and had only flourished after the German victory over France in 1870, the Anglophobia of Sombart and his contemporaries drew on a longer tradition of distrust that went back to Hegel and Nietzsche, Heine and Fontane. Tellingly, Fontane's diaries from 1852, in which he criticized the materialism and cant of his English hosts, were published in the summer of 1914 in *Die Neue Rundschau*. As the editor explained, the diaries were worthy of publication:

Nicht nur wegen der Person seines Autors, sondern weil es die
Erfahrungen eines Deutschen in England vor zwei Menschenaltern
in einer heute beinah aktuell gewordenen Form schildert.[18]

[Not just because they are by this particular author, but because they
depict the experiences of a German in England two generations ago
in a form which corresponds almost exactly to circumstances today.]

While the older prejudices were of interest only to an educated public,
with access to languages and the prospect of travel, the mutual antagonism of 1914 was a mass emotion, reacting against a crude and simple
stereotype. Significantly, the polemics of 1914 were aimed directly at
these one-dimensional stereotypes, rather than at a whole nation. Sir Edward Grey insisted that the war was simply a war against German militarism and not against the German nation or against German culture, both
of which should be freed from the fetters of militarism, and Cecil Chesterton even managed to praise the non-Prussian Germans as "a people rather
kindly and rather dreamy."[19] A similar process also operated in reverse. As
the Hamburg academic Wilhelm Dibelius was at pains to point out:

Wogegen wir jetzt kämpfen, ist nicht das große England, das wir
lieben und schätzen gelernt haben, sondern das kleine England des
nationalen Hochmutes, des niedrigen Krämergeistes und der
puritanischen Heuchelei.[20]

[What we are fighting against now is not that great England which
we love and have learnt to admire, but that petty England of national
arrogance, mean-spirited commercialism and puritanical hypocrisy.]

In preparing the ground for the mass acceptance of these very simple
propositions, the popular fiction of the previous two decades made a significant contribution.

The Invasion Fear in Britain

In the best study of fictional prophesies of war, I. F. Clarke notes:

During the ten years before the First World War the growing antagonism between Britain and Germany was responsible for the
largest and most sustained development of the most alarmist and
aggressive stories of future warfare ever seen at any time in European
history.[21]

The first forecasts of an Anglo-German confrontation were penned, however, much earlier. Almost before the smoke had settled at Sedan, British
writers began to construct pessimistic scenarios of further German conquests, with Britain rather than France as the victim. The prototype inva-

sion story was submitted to *Blackwood's Magazine* in January 1871, only days after the new German Reich had hailed its first Emperor at a ceremony in the Galerie des Glaces in Versailles: it had been written by Lieutenant-Colonel Sir George Tomkyns Chesney and was entitled *The Battle of Dorking*. Using a device later adopted by William Morris in *News from Nowhere*, Chesney framed his narrative as the recollections of an old man, telling his grandchildren fifty years on of the great invasion that had taken place during his youth. The purpose of the tale was immediately clear in the old man's introductory comments:

> 'Tis sad work turning back to that bitter page in our history, but you may perhaps take profit in your new homes from the lesson it teaches. For us in England it came too late.[22]

With its fleet scattered across the oceans, from the West Indies to the China Sea, and the remaining ships rendered impotent by secret weapons, the English were in no position to halt the advance of the German army. On the ridge that runs from Guildford to Dorking, the English volunteer regiments, equipped more for a reenactment of Waterloo than for modern warfare, proved to be no match for the more disciplined German forces. The moral was drawn in the old soldier's closing lines: "The rich were idle and luxurious, the poor grudged the cost of defence. . . . Truly the nation was ripe for a fall."[23] *The Battle of Dorking* was reprinted as a sixpenny pamphlet in June 1871 and sold over 80,000 copies in a month. With its mixture of technical know-how, strong narrative, and a willingness to criticize the military authorities at home, Chesney's book established the model for the flood of admonitory tracts that appeared in the 1870s on the theme of English unpreparedness, carrying such names as *The Second Armada* (1871), *The Siege of London* (1871), *The Invasion of 1883* (1876), and *Fifty Years Hence* (1877). There was also a flourishing industry in composing refutations of the Dorking scare, usually with cosily absurd titles, doubtless conceived to reassure a nervous readership: Charles Stone's *What Happened after the Battle of Dorking; or, The Victory of Tunbridge Wells*, and Lt.-Col. William Hunter's *Army Speech by an Old Harrovian Dedicated to Those Who Have Been Frightened by the Battle of Dorking*, both from 1871, were typical of the genre.

Col. Hunter and his fellow optimists were unable to stem the tide of alarm, however, and the production of scaremongering literature continued vigorously throughout the 1880s and 1890s. Although Chesney had chosen the Germans as the enemy at Dorking, little of this literature was specifically anti-German. Rather, the vaunted efficiency and modernity of the German army was used merely as a yardstick against which to measure the inefficiency of the British military. At this point, of course, the German fleet was still in its infancy and offered no possible threat to the British fleet, unless one was prepared to believe Chesney's infelicitous device of secret naval weaponry. Indeed, the proposal in the early 1880s to build a channel tunnel spawned a second wave of invasion fiction, with France favored as the likely aggressor. Once the market for scare stories had been established, the hack writers and malcontents responded enthusiastically to successive political crises, and the worsening relations between Britain and France after the Battle of Tel-el-Kabir in 1882, the Franco-Russian alliance of 1894, and the Fashoda incident of 1898 all promoted new variations on the war-scare theme.

It was only during the Transvaal Crisis that the Germans began to emerge as enemy number one. The telegram that Kaiser Wilhelm II sent to President Kruger on January 3, 1896, congratulating him on his success in repelling the Jameson Raid and maintaining the peace of the country against attack from without, was widely condemned in the British press, where it was seen as proof of a conspiracy between Kruger and the German government. As *The Times* noted:

> There is grave reason to suspect that hostile designs against this country have been in contemplation for a long time; and that the Transvaal was deliberately selected as the spot at which a blow might advantageously be struck.[24]

The popular press, led by Alfred Harmsworth's *Daily Mail*, was less restrained, and the consequence of the press campaign was an upsurge of intense anti-German feeling, with public demonstrations and smashed windows in German-owned shops. The Transvaal crisis marked the beginning of a mutual antipathy between the two nations that extended beyond diplomatic circles to affect the wider population. It was an antipathy that was to be nourished by the cheap popular press, which was developing in both countries in the 1890s. A typical example was the *Daily Mail*, which was launched in 1896 and immediately adopted a provocative stance on the German question. In 1897 it commissioned George Warrington Steevens to write sixteen essays on life in Germany, which were published under the subtle title "Under the Iron Heel." Three years later Harmsworth confided to R. D. Blumenfield, editor of the *Daily Express*, "My own view is that the Germans are being led definitely and irrevocably to make war on the rest of Europe, and we will have to take part in it."[25] Fueled by the popular press, and given added authority by Lord Roberts and the National Service League, the conviction that a war against Germany was unavoidable stimulated a new crop of war prophecies in the early years of the new century.

Some were remarkably good, most notably Erskine Childers's *The Riddle of the Sands*, published in 1903. While Chesney had employed a fifty-year time shift to create a fictional context for what he was proposing as a real threat to national security, Childers favored the more straight-forward strategy of insisting that the story was true, merely the names altered. His preface concluded with the injunction: "Remember, also, that these persons are living now in the midst of us."[26] While the main protagonists were reputedly real, they conveniently corresponded to stereotyped Englishmen and Germans. Carruthers, the gilded youth from the Foreign Office, only accepts the invitation to go sailing in the Baltic since the demands of his work had caused him to miss the round of country house parties in July and August. His foppish expectations, which very much correspond to the popular German picture at the time of an English snob, are rudely shattered on meeting his host, Davies, at Flensburg: "Even in the dim gaslight he clashed on my notions of a yachtsman — no cool white ducks or neat blue serge; and where was the snowy-crowned yachting cap, that precious charm that so easily converts a landsman into a dashing mariner?" (12). Davies, replete in an old Norfolk jacket, muddy brown shoes and grey flannel trousers, is portrayed as a brilliant sailor who had nevertheless been rejected by the Royal Navy, and as a patriot with an insight into German strategic intentions superior to that of Carruthers, the career diplomat. Davies's enemy, Dollmann, is a former Royal Navy officer who is now working for the German Navy, preparing for an invasion of England. Far from the crass jingoism of 1914, Davies sees the rivalry between the two nations as healthy and inevitable, the German ascendancy as a challenge rather than a threat. As he explains to Carruthers, in terms that would not have offended the German Navy League:

> Here's this huge empire, stretching half over central Europe — an empire growing like wildfire, I believe, in people, and wealth and everything. They've licked the French and the Austrians, and are the greatest military power in Europe. I wish I knew more about all that, but what I'm concerned with is their sea-power. It's a new thing with them, but it's going strong, and that Emperor of theirs is running for it for all it's worth. He's a splendid chap, and anyone can see he's right. They've got no colonies to speak of, and must have them, like us. They can't get them and keep them and they can't protect their huge commerce without naval strength. The command of the sea is *the* thing nowadays, isn't it? (71–72)

In contrast, the British are painted by Davies as apathetic in defence of their sea power: "We've been safe so long, and grown so rich, that we've forgotten what we owe it [the sea]" (89). As a result, Britain, says Davies, is quite unprepared for a German invasion: "We don't look her way. We have no naval base in the North Sea, and no North Sea Fleet. Our best battleships are too deep in draught for North Sea work. And, to crown all, we were asses enough to give her Heligoland, which commands her

North Sea coast" (91). After a series of well-described adventures among the Frisian Islands, the two Englishmen uncover the German strategy. Carruthers records:

> I was assisting at an experimental rehearsal of a great scene, to be enacted, perhaps in the near future — a scene when multitudes of seagoing lighters, carrying full loads of soldiers, not half-loads of coal, should issue simultaneously, in seven ordered fleets, from seven shallow outlets, and, under escort of the Imperial Navy, traverse the North Sea and throw themselves bodily upon English shores (266).

In an epilogue Childers concluded that Germany was "pre-eminently fitted to undertake an invasion of Great Britain" (281) and the British Navy ill-prepared to stop her. This revelation was greedily snapped up by the reading public, with the result that *The Riddle of the Sands* ran to three print-runs in 1903, two in 1904 and 1905, and was reprinted again in 1907, 1908, 1910, 1913, and 1915. It then lay quiet until 1927 but enjoyed a predictable revival in the 1930s and 1940s, reaching twenty-three impressions by 1946. Part of Childers's success, like that of Chesney, must be attributable to the timing of his warning, at a point when home defence was a matter of considerable concern. Indeed, Childers's postscript, written in March 1903, when the book was already in press, praised the decision to site a new North Sea base at Rosyth, and to create a North Sea fleet. He noted, however, that "its ships are not modern, or in the least capable of meeting the principal German squadrons under the circumstances proposed above" (289).

Childers's admonishing pen was directed throughout at the British authorities, rather than at German militarism. Indeed, Germany's "peculiar genius for organization" (281) is the subject of constant praise, as is the Kaiser, admired by Davies as "a man . . . who doesn't wait to be kicked, but works like a nigger for his country and sees ahead" (89). Only in the matter of Dollmann's daughter, the romantic interest written in at the insistence of the publisher, did Childers lapse into theories of racial type or superiority. The self-mocking tone with which Childers described Carruthers's first meeting with the English-born Fräulein Dollmann was clearly intended to distance the author from his more xenophobic contemporaries: "Two honest English eyes were looking up into mine; an honest English hand. Is this insular nonsense? Perhaps so, but I stick to it — a brown, firm hand — no, not so very small, my sentimental reader — was clasping mine" (165).

While Childers' text merits close attention, the other vastly successful invasion novel of the period, William Le Queux's *The Invasion of 1910*, can be treated more briskly. It was conceived by Harmsworth in 1905 (by then ennobled as Lord Northcliffe) as a part of his campaign for national conscription — the theme of the closing remarks in *The Riddle of the Sands*,[27] and first published in serial form in 1906. Although Le Queux was the nominal author, the exact details of the invasion had been worked out by Lord Roberts and H. W. Wilson, the *Daily Mail's* naval affairs correspondent. The invasion route proposed by the experts had had to be amended, however, for commercial reasons, and Northcliffe directed his authors to march the German army through every decent-sized town, and "not to keep to remote, one-eyed villages where there was no possibility of large *Daily Mail* sales."[28] Although it ended in a British victory, the message of Le Queux's book was profoundly negative. A disadvantageous peace was concluded by a weak government that had abandoned aristocratic principles for vulgar populism:

> In the hour of trial, amidst smoking ruins, among the holocausts of dead which marked the prolonged, bloody and terrible battles on land and sea, the spirit of the nation quailed, and there was really no great leader to recall it to the ways of honour and duty.[29]

The reading public, damned by Le Queux himself as "the weak, excitable population of the towns," took avidly to the heady blend of pessimism and scaremongering, and *The Invasion of 1910* sold over a million copies in book form. It was also translated into twenty-seven languages, including German, although this version, as we shall see, differed significantly from the original.

Le Queux not only attacked the complacency of the Liberal government in the face of the accelerated German naval programme, but also introduced two motifs that were to flourish in 1914. The first was the legend of the German spy, of armies of German ex-soldiers employed in England as waiters, clerks, bakers, and servants, whose loyal collaboration was essential to the successful German invasion. This proposition led to questions in the House about the 66,000 German reservists who were supposed to be living in the Home Counties, and rumors of a German military establishment in Epping.[30] The second legend launched by Le Queux concerned the brutality that was to be expected of the invading Germans — a theme that further unsettled an already nervous public. The spy scares and the general ground swell of uncertainty fostered by Le Queux were developed in several books published in 1907. The worst, worthy of Le Queux himself, was *The Clash of Empires*, by Rowland Thirlmere, which suggested that every German soldier could pass an examination on the topography of Eastern England, a proposal that he backed up with vivid accounts of German officers making a tour of the East Anglian coastline on horseback in 1905, and of an actual landing undertaken in 1907 by Dr Kurt Wegener, a lieutenant in the Elisabeth-Garderegiment. Like Le Queux's novel, Thirlmere's yarn was also trans-

lated into German.[31] A better book from the 1907 crop was Austin
Harrison's *England and Germany*, a thoughtful account based on the
author's first-hand knowledge of Germany, where he had worked as a
journalist. Like Thirlmere, however, Harrison concluded that a war between the two nations was inevitable. This fatalistic conclusion, aggravated in 1908 both by German naval manoeuvres in the North Sea and
by the Bosnian crisis, prompted a new burst of invasion novels towards
the end of the decade.

Among the titles like *When England Slept, The Great Raid*, and *The
War Inevitable*, was one with a subtitle that suggested a certain levity in
the face of the Hunnish hordes. This was *The Swoop, or, How Clarence
Saved England*, published in 1909. Its author, P. G. Wodehouse, was
then 28 years old and had just given up his daily column on the London
Globe in order to visit America for the first time. The title was borrowed
from J. Blyth's 1909 novel, *The Swoop of the Vulture*, in which the inevitable German fleet invaded England. Tiring of this simple formula, Wodehouse contrived a more complex plot:

> Not only had the Germans effected a landing in Essex, but, in addi-
> tion, no fewer than eight other hostile armies had, by some remark-
> able coincidence, hit on that identical moment for launching their
> long-prepared blow. England was not merely beneath the heel of the
> invader. It was beneath the heels of nine invaders. There was barely
> standing-room.[32]

In addition to the Germans in Essex, the Russians had come ashore in
Yarmouth, and the Mad Mullah in Portsmouth. The problem was com-
pounded by the Swiss navy, which had bombarded Lyme Regis "and
landed troops immediately westward of the bathing machines" (21),
while China had captured Lllgxtplll in Wales. The final insults are
Monaco's seizure of Scarborough, the capture of Brighton by Moroccan
brigands, and of Margate by "dark-skinned warriors from the distant isle
of Bollygolla," who are mistaken by the bank-holiday excursionists as "a
troupe of nigger minstrels on an unusually magnificent scale" (23). The
multiple invasion is met initially with irritated disinterest, as a distraction
from the true concerns of life: the newspaper hoarding that first anounces
the German landing does so only in very small print, below the banner
headline "SURREY DOING BADLY," and the stop press only just manages to
squeeze in the news between the cricket scores ("Fry not out, 104. Surrey
147 for 8") and the results of the Loamshire Handicap ("Spring Chicken,
1; Salome, 2; Yip-i-addy, 3. Seven ran") (16). Indeed, the threat to the
sporting calendar is regarded as the most serious aspect of the whole
business. As Wodehouse notes:

Far-seeing men took a gloomy view of the situation. They laid stress on the fact that this counter-attraction was bound to hit first-class cricket hard. . . . The desire to see the invaders as they marched through the country must draw away thousands who otherwise would have paid their sixpences at the turnstiles. (31)

The British army had long since been disbanded, and organized resistance is left to the Boy Scouts. Fortunately for England, they are equal to the task, thanks to the wit of one Scout in particular, Clarence Chugwater. Clarence is a model Scout: "He could low like a bull. He could gurgle like a wood-pigeon. He could imitate the cry of a turnip to deceive rabbits" (10). As luck would have it, two senior German officers, Prince Otto von Saxe-Pfennig and Captain Graf von Poppenheim, decide to commandeer Nasturtium Villa, the home of Clarence's parents:

The visitors seated themselves, there was an awkward silence.
"Warm day "said Mr. Chugwater.
"Very!" said the Prince, a little constrainedly.
"Perhaps a cup of tea? Have you come far?"
"Well — er — pretty far. That is to say a certain distance. In fact, from Germany." (18)

In the end, Mr Chugwater rents his house to the Prince at a favorable rate, while his aide-de-camp is prevailed upon to buy both a life insurance policy and a motor bicycle. The two men are also sold tickets for an amateur theatrical, and stagger out of the house bemoaning the horrors of an invasion — for the invaders.

While the English are portrayed exactly according to the stereotype, as polite, money-grubbing, and sports-mad, the Germans fare no better:

Captain von Poppenheim approached and saluted.
"Please, sir, the men say, 'May they bombard London?',"
"Bombard London!"
"Yes, sir; it's always done."
Prince Otto pulled thoughtfully at his moustache. "Bombard London! It seems — and yet — ah well, they have few pleasures."
He stood awhile in meditation. So did Captain von Poppenheim. He kicked a pebble. So did Captain von Poppenheim — only a smaller pebble. Discipline is very strict in the German army. (36)

Fortunately no one is hurt by the bombardment as it is August and there is nobody in town (except Carruthers, perhaps), and the general feeling among the returning populace is in favor of the destruction. The Albert Hall had been struck by "a merciful shell," and "the burning of the Royal Academy proves a great comfort to all."[33] For relieving them of these shrines to *Kultur*, the philistine Londoners send Prince Otto a hearty vote of thanks.

The Kaiser is less pleased, however, and sends the following telegram: "At once mailed fist display. On get or out get — WILHELM" (42). But progress is slow, and as all the other combatants have abandoned the field, Germany and Russia are left facing each other across London, depressed by the lack of English resistance. There is no hate to be seen among the natives, only the supercilious stare, which thoroughly unnerves them. Wodehouse explains: "There is nothing so terrible to the highly-strung foreigner as the cold, contemptuous, patronizing stare of the Englishman . . . They felt like men who had been found travelling in a first-class carriage with a third-class ticket" (82).

Resistance *is* being organized, however, at a Scout camp in the Aldwych.

> On arriving at the camp, Clarence asks the sentry what the other Scouts are up to, and is told: "Some of them are acting a Scout's play, sir; some are doing Cone Exercises; one or two are practising deep breathing; and the rest are dancing an Old English Morris Dance."
>
> Clarence nodded. "They could not be better employed." (60)

By poking fun at the Scouts, Wodehouse also scored against the agitators for national service and against Lord Roberts, who, like Baden-Powell, was a hero of the Boer War.

The ultimate solution of the impasse, however, does not come from the Scout skills of woodcraft or toggle-tying, but rather from Clarence's own ingenuity. To break the monotony of a London summer, both Prince Otto and his Russian counterpart, Grand Duke Vodkakoff, have taken up careers as music-hall artists. Both command record fees, leading to protests from Harry Lauder and from the Water Rats, and Clarence, in his position of cub reporter, is able to stir up trouble between the two generals about the size of their respective incomes. Was one getting more than the other? This leads to a duel of the theatrical giants and to the *Daily Mail* headline: "Scene at the Lobelia: Prince Otto of Saxe-Pfenning given the bird by Russian soldiers. What will be the outcome?" (92). The outcome is a battle fought in thick fog, unobserved by the English war correspondents, who are unable to find it. So thick is the fog, in fact, that Edgar Wallace is found two days later in Steeple Bumpstead, in an almost starving condition. The Germans win, but lose most of their army in the process. After the battle Prince Otto lies sleeping in his tent in Tottenham:

> He was worn out. In addition to the strain of battle, there had been the heavy work of seeing the interviewers, signing autograph books, sitting to photographers, writing testimonials for patent medicines, and the thousand and one other tasks, burdensome but unavoidable,

of the man who is in the public eye. Also he had caught a cold during the battle. (113)

This is the moment to strike. The Boy Scouts, led by Clarence and armed with catapults and hockey sticks, surround the surviving Germans and take them prisoner. On capturing Prince Otto himself, Clarence launches into a patriotic oration:

> "England, my England!" cried Clarence, his face shining with holy patriotism. "England thou art free! Thou hast risen from the ashes of thy dead self. Let the nations learn from this that it is when apparently crushed that the Briton is to more than ever be feared."
> "That's bad grammar," said the Prince critically. (116)

In the final scene, Clarence appears on the music-hall stage as England's highest-paid artist, doing those things that Boy Scouts do best . . . deep breathing, twisting the right foot round the neck, hopping on one foot across the stage, and animal impersonations.

As Wodehouse noted in his preface, his story was written purely from a feeling of patriotism and duty: "Mr. Alston Rivers' sensitive soul will be jarred to its foundations if it is a financial success. So will mine."[34] Luckily for both author and publisher, the book was entirely out of step with the spirit of the moment, and sank without trace. His willingness to poke fun at his countrymen, when all around him the blimps and hacks were preparing for war, was a foretaste of things to come, and his levity was as little appreciated in 1909 as it was in 1941.

Far from being inclined to laugh at or dismiss the German threat, the public developed an insatiable appetite for Germanophobe literature in the immediate prewar years. As before, the novelists and playwrights were responding to a demand created by the popular press and by the increasing friction in Anglo-German relations. The apparently inexorable descent into armed confrontation, via the Daily Telegraph crisis of 1908, the success of the Conservatives' naval expansion platform in the 1910 election, the Agadir crisis of 1911, Lloyd George's Mansion House speech, and Tirpitz's supplementary naval bill of 1912, has been documented and discussed in minute detail and is not the direct concern of this study.[35] Symptomatic of the literary response, however, was Guy du Maurier's play *The Patriot*, which was put on by his brother Gerald at Wyndham's theatre in January 1909, and which told the sorry tale of the woefully unfit, ill-prepared, and physically deficient Brown family, and of their haplessness in the face of invading troops from a country named "Nearland." To a modern reader, the inability to fire a gun or dress gunshot wounds might seem to have some virtue, but in 1909 these were portrayed as singular deficiencies. The play had no presumptions to quality, and the invaders were apparently decked out in costumes more appropriate to light opera than to a serious tale of invasion. But, as *The Times* correspondent noted, it offered

> startling testimony to the hold which the great National Defence question has taken on the thoughts and imagination of the English public. The thing itself is crude enough, and indeed somewhat amateurishly done; what is significant is that the thing should have been done at all.[36]

Even more significant, perhaps, was the play's impact on the public: a special recruiting office was set up in the theatre foyer to enlist the newly converted recruits to the London Territorials.

The depressing catalogue of books forecasting the increasingly inevitable confrontation can be followed right up to the outbreak of hostilities. Most of them are deservedly forgotten, as are their authors, who were often pseudonymous. Examples are *A Derelict Empire*, published by Mark Time in 1912, *The Battle of the North Sea in 1914*, by Searchlight (who was actually Rear-Admiral Eardley-Wilmot) also dated 1912, and *Private Selby*, by Edgar Wallace — last heard of in Steeple Bumpstead. There were, however, exceptions to the general level of literary mediocrity. One was Conan Doyle's warning of the danger of a submarine blockade, first published in the *Strand Magazine* in July 1914 under the title "Danger," but actually written eighteen months earlier. It was accorded the accolade of two different German translations. H. G. Wells, abandoning alien beings from outer space, chose German invaders in *The War in the Air* (1908), another tale of British unpreparedness, and in *The World Set Free* (1914), he described, with exact topographical detail, the dropping of atomic bombs on Berlin. After flying in over Spandau, Charlottenburg, and the Tiergarten, Wells's aviator dropped his "Carolinum" bomb on the Berliner Schloß:

> In the open garden before the Imperial castle a shuddering star of evil splendour spurted and poured up smoke and flame towards them like an accusation. They were too high to distinguish people clearly, or mark the bomb's effect upon the building until suddenly the façade tottered and crumbled before the flare as sugar dissolves in water.[37]

More or less simultaneously, Kaiser Wilhelm marched into London in Saki's novel *When William Came*, published shortly before the outbreak of war. By a happy coincidence, the German domination of England was halted by no lesser body than the Boy Scouts, who refused to parade for the German Emperor in Hyde Park. In spite of this similarity, Saki's values were those of Le Queux and Lord Roberts rather than of Wodehouse, and, as Samuel Hynes has pointed out,

Saki celebrated them all in the peculiarly overripe prose that he reserved for the description of emotions about abstractions or about
scenes without human figures. These are the values that in their
more attractive forms we call patriotic; but as Saki represented them
they emerge more often as militaristic, arrogant and xenophobic —
the values that made the Empire and at the same time made England's enemies.[38]

It was exactly these qualities that were attacked in German popular fiction
between 1900 and 1914.

The German Response

The Transvaal Crisis in 1896 not only turned the British public against
Germany for the first time, but also had the obverse effect in Germany.
Twenty percent of the foreign capital invested in the Transvaal was German. Germans held the whisky and dynamite monopolies — a potent
combination; they ran the National Bank and were strongly represented
by large firms like Krupp, Siemens and Halske, and Lippert. The German
diplomatic reaction to the Jameson raid was catastrophically inept, and
the Kaiser had to be dissuaded from fantastic schemes like extending a
German protectorate, or sending in German troops to fight the British in
a localized war.[39] The Kruger telegram was a milder alternative, but still
one that outraged British opinion. As Gordon Craig has noted: "The
German attempts to apply to foreign policy Frederick William I's prescrip-
tion of using chastisement to compel love had been a miserable failure. In
1896 Anglo-German relations were at their lowest ebb."[40] The outbreak
of the Boer War in October 1899 and the brutality of the British response
served to strengthen German hostility. In A. J. P. Taylor's words, the
Boer War "brought first the culmination and then the end of an arrogant,
boastful epoch, in which British public opinion seemed to have abandoned principles for power."[41] These traits were also noted by opinion-
makers in Germany, and the Boer War novel was invented as a vehicle for
displaying the callousness of the British and the inherent nobility of the
"Teutonic" Boers. The most successful novel of this type was probably
Hans Grimm's *Volk ohne Raum*, first published in 1927. A good example
from the period, however, is Karl Bleibtreu's *Bur und Lord*, which appeared in 1900. Bleibtreu, to quote the *Deutsches Literatur-Lexikon*,
"produzierte zahllose Romane, besonders 'poetische Schlachtbilder,' und
nahm in vielbändigen popularisierenden Werken zu sämtlichen
Weltfragen Stellung. Vielschreiber-Typus der Gründerzeit. Dramatiker,
Erzähler, Kritiker und Übersetzer"[42] (Bleibtreu produced countless novels, particularly "poetical battlescapes," and expressed a view on all questions of international import in multi-volume works of popularization).

While his taste for warfare may well have derived from his father, Georg Bleibtreu, who was a celebrated painter of battlescapes, Karl Bleibtreu was neither a militarist nor an Anglophobe. In 1887 he founded the *Magazin für die Literatur des Auslandes,* and in the same year published his *Geschichte der Englischen Litteratur in der Renaissance und Klassicität* [*sic*]. The book begins with Bleibtreu describing his debt to English literature:

> Von Jugend an mit der britischen Litteratur genährt, dem Studium derselben besonderen Eifer widmend, haben wir uns von jeher der Überzeugung hingegeben, daß diese stammverwandte Litteratur die Spitze und Blüthe des europäischen Geisteslebens bedeute und daß, wie es seit der Mitte des vorigen Jahrhunderts auch thatsächlich der Fall gewesen, die deutsche Dichtung nur durch Befruchtung mit der britischen gesunde Früchte zeitigen könne.[43]

> [Nurtured from childhood on British literature and devoting particular effort to its study, we have always been convinced that this literature, related to ours, was the peak and acme of Europe's spiritual heritage, and that, as indeed proved to be the case from the middle of the last century onward, only through cross-fertilization with it could German literature produce healthy fruits].

By the time of writing, however, Bleibtreu was less convinced of the continuing English literary preeminence. Britain as a cultural driving force was on the decline, while German literature, formerly the poor relation, was in ascendancy:

> Auch glauben wir zu keiner oberflächlichen Phantasmagorie zu verleiten, wenn wir wähnen, das heutige neudeutsche Geistesleben unter der Hegemonie des deutschen Reiches dürfe sich wohl so ziemlich decken mit dem englischen unter der Weltherrschaft des "British Empire," unter Pitt, Wellington und Nelson.[44]

> [We believe too that we are not straying down paths of self-deception when we offer the view that present-day German creative life under the aegis of the German Empire is pretty well the equal of anything the English achieved under the worldwide domination of the "British Empire" under Pitt, Wellington, and Nelson.]

The reason for the British decline, felt Bleibtreu, was arrogance and immodesty: "diese insulare Selbstüberschätzung, dieses Hinaufschrauben aller britischen Verdienste zu schwindelnder Höhe"[45] (this excessive, insular self-esteem, this puffing up of all British achievements to vertiginous heights) — exactly the qualities displayed in the British handling of their South African interests.

In *Bur und Lord* Bleibtreu contrived to work in virtually all of the stereotyped deficiencies attributed, and not without some justification, to the British. The narrative is presented in the form of the diary of an English officer with the improbable name of Alfredus Magnus. Magnus had gone to fight in South Africa not, as one might think, to escape the career of pastry-cook for which his name had preordained him, but to give meaning to his idle and pampered life. On the very first page of the novel he asks:

> Wie soll man mit dem Leben anfangen! Ewig Football und Lawn-Tennis spielen, ersteres mit langweiligen Herrn, letzteres mit kurzweiligen Damen, scheint auf die Dauer doch kein ausreichender Lebenszweck. Die Garden-Parties, die Five o'Clocks und die Routs gleichen sich in unabänderlicher Folge und die Clubs sind nur gut genug, um eine verlorene Stunde der Verdauung hinzugähnen. Mit dem Sport wird man zuletzt noch stumpfsinning. Ich beneide die Kerle, die für eine Regatta von Oxford und Cambridge oder den altehrwürdigen Derbytag ihr Leben lassen.[46]

> [What's to be done with one's life? Endlessly playing games of football and tennis, the former with boring gentlemen, the latter with amusing ladies, doesn't really seem like a life-fulfilling goal. Those garden parties, those five o'clock drinks and tedious routs are all so boringly the same, and Clubs offer, at best, a tolerable hour's worth of digestion-settling. In the long run, sport clogs the brain. I envy those chaps who give their lives for an Oxford & Cambridge Regatta or good old Derby Day.]

By describing the action in Magnus's words, Bleibtreu is able to muster all the arrogance and narrow bigotry that he felt were typical of the British governing class. Magnus obliges by damning the liberals and socialists who are against the war, and by railing — in a condescending way — against the Germans for arming the Boers and for allowing German volunteers to fight in the so-called "Freicorps." "Dem deutschen Büffel die Hundepeitsche!" (25: A whip for the German buffalo!) as Magnus puts it. British cant, condemned by Germans from Fontane on, is examined closely, particularly after a patrol of German volunteers, including a "Graf von Zeppelin," is cut to ribbons by British dum-dum bullets. Magnus's first uncertainties about the validity of the British cause appear here, in a particularly grisly description of the effect of the forbidden bullets:

> Im zuckenden Fleisch öffnet sich das reizvolle Kügelchen wie eine Tulpe und seine gräßliche — pardon, bewunderungswerte Rotationskraft reißt Muskeln und Knochen, brüderlich zu Brei vermengt, mit sich fort. Ein hinreißender Vorgang, doch wir fechten ja für Fortschritt und Zivilisation. (29)

[The charming little bullet opens up like a tulip in the trembling flesh, and its grisly — apologies, its amazing rotation rips away muscle and bone, turning them into companionable pulp. A ripping process! But we of course are fighting for progress and civilization.]

As his uncle explains in a letter responding to Magnus's account of the war: "Nun, England ist die von Gott verordnete Obrigkeit über alle Heiden- und Barbarenländer, Christenliebe und Kultur zu verbreiten, dazu hat es die Gewalt" (40; Now, England is the authority ordained by God to spread Christian charity and civilization throughout barbarian and heathen lands, and it has the power to do so). As Magnus's nascent doubts about his cause develop in the course of long conversations with an educated German prisoner, the regular letters from his philistine uncle and aunt are used by Bleibtreu as a measure of the ever-widening gap between Magnus and the English jingoists. The aunt's views on literature are especially noteworthy:

> Und Byron, Shelley, ich bitte Sie, und andre Chosen — welche Gesinnung! Selbst Shakespeare und dergleichen — große Dichter, gewiß, aber nicht zu empfehlen, besonders nicht für Damen, und für die soll der Litterat doch schreiben, da der gereifte Mann sich nur mit Praktischem beschäftigt. (37)

> [And Byron and Shelley, I ask you, and other such types — their attitudes! Even Shakespeare and the like — great poets, of course, but not to be recommended, especially not for ladies, and it's for them that literary folk should be writing since mature men are only concerned with practical matters.]

Here, Bleibtreu offers a variation on the then prevalent theme, that the survival of Shakespeare's works and reputation had been a German achievement, achieved in the face of British indifference.

The author's prejudices are revealed strongly in a long passage in which Magnus confides to his diary his admiration of the Jews. Having praised the achievements of Jewish businessmen and entrepreneurs in creating the basis of the British financial domination of world markets, Bleibtreu then has Magnus write of the Jews:

> Seid fruchtbar und mehret euch, und besorgt die Buren-Expropriierung, um ein neues Kanaan im Goldland zu finden . . . Mit der heiligen Allianz des Judentums vereint, werden wir es durchsetzen, deß bin ich sicher, das "Größere Britannien!" (46)

> [Be fruitful and multiply, and carry out the expropriation of the Boers in order to discover a new Canaan in the Land of Gold . . . In sacred alliance with Jewry we shall achieve it, that I am sure of — "Greater Britain"!]

Anti-Semitism like this was a significant component of pre-1914 German Anglophobia, and is a theme that will be treated in the next section. Magnus's aunt's intimation that Rudyard Kipling was actually a Jew called Cohen is worth noting here, however, as it brings together two anti-British themes at one stroke. Kipling was particularly disliked at the time among German literati, and the contemporary Kipling mania in Britain was the subject of several articles in the German periodicals. Very typical was a review of *Stalky and Co.* (published in English by Tauchnitz of Leipzig in 1899), which concluded:

> Und nun die Moral dieser tiefsinnigen Erzählung? Das Schlußkapitel zeigt Stalky als einen Offizier, der an der Spitze seiner Sikhs eine märchenhafte Tapferkeit und List entfaltet. Und: "Indien ist voll von Stalkys — Jungen aus Cheltenham, Haileybury und Marlborough" (untergeordneten Public Schools), die nicht (wie die aus Eton oder Rugby), in erster Klasse-Wagen in die Front fahren. . . . Für die Enthüllung seiner geheimsten Gedanken in Betreff des Holzes, aus dem er sich die Verwirklicher seiner imperialistischen Träumereien geschnitzt denkt, hätte Kipling keine unglücklichere Zeit wählen können als die kurz vor Beginn des Burenkrieges.[47]

> [And now the moral of this weighty tale? — the final chapter shows Stalky as an officer displaying fairytale courage and cunning at the head of his Sikhs. And "India is full of Stalkys — lads from Cheltenham, Haileybury and Marlborough" (minor Public Schools) who (unlike those from Eton or Rugby) do not travel to the front in first-class carriages. . . . To reveal his innermost thoughts about the timber from which he was carving the characters he imagined achieving his imperialist dreams, Kipling could hardly have chosen a more inauspicious moment than just before the Boer War.]

By calling Kipling a Jew, Bleibtreu managed to link the gung-ho heroics of the public school with the more sinister machinations of the financier, thereby denying the heroics any moral dimension.

Magnus would definitely have traveled first-class to the front, but nevertheless differs from his fellow officers in that he is increasingly unsure of the morality of his crusade, and, at the same time, repulsed by the philistinism of his relations back in England. Long conversations with a German prisoner, an educated man who is also a committed socialist, transform Magnus from a hardened cynic who believed that God was always on the side with the biggest guns into a radical advocate of a people's democracy. The final revelation comes during a murderous battle with the Boers, which is described by Bleibtreu in proto-Sombartian terms, as a battle between *Händler und Helden*:

Dies Volk [the Boers] hat den Tanz ums goldene Kalb nicht
mitgemacht, den wir "Kultur" nennen; es ist geblieben, wie seine
Väter waren. Eine Auferstehung des Mittelalters ohne dessen dunkle
Schatten der Unwissenheit und Roheit, zum Trotz der perversen
Hyperkultur. . . . Gewiß, wir Lords und Börsenjobber — das ist heut
eins und dasselbe — werden nicht ablassen, unsre Söldnermassen
und freiwilligen Sportsmen als Mordpatrioten so lange auf die Freien
zu schleudern, bis unser Hurrahgebrüll sie betäubt und ihre Stimme
erstickt. Doch ich ahne, hinter den Buren steht eine höhere
unsichtbare unüberwindbare Macht: die Demokratie der Zukunft.
(138–39).

[This people (the Boers) has not joined in the dance around the
Golden Calf which we call "culture"; it has remained the way its fathers were. A resurrection of the Middle Ages without their darker
sides of ignorance and rudeness, in spite of a perverse hypercul-
ture. . . . No doubt about it, we Lords and Stock Exchange jobbers
— the same thing these days — will not cease to fling our masses of
mercenaries and volunteer sportsmen as ultimate patriots against the
freeborn until the din of our cheering deafens them and stifles their
voices. And yet I sense that a higher, invisible, undefeatable power
stands behind the Boers: the democracy of the future.]

The victory of true democracy, described as "die schlichte Gemeinde
ohne Herren" (Commons only, no Lords), could be the only outcome of
the war, and Magnus concludes "Ob Brite siegt ob Bur, der Lord ist ver-
loren" (149; Be it Briton or Boer who wins, there is no future for Lords).

Bleibtreu attacked the British from a socialist position for their imperialism and for their cynical worship of power and money. Although a
Berliner, Bleibtreu was no fan of Prussian militarism. This can be seen
very clearly in a pamphlet published in 1901 by the *Verlag Aufklärung*, a
revisionist-socialist outfit on the Bebel/Bernstein wing of the SPD. Towards the end of his text, after a long tirade against militarism, Bleibtreu
enlists the support of Wagner:

Richard Wagner sprach das große Wort gelassen aus: "Deutsch sein
heißt etwas der Sache wegen thun." Wer echten deutschen National-
stolz besitzt, der sich nicht an preußischen Junkermilitarismus,
sondern die Großthaten unserer Kultur knüpft, wird freudig
bekennen, daß in dieser Wagnerschen Übertreibung unseres Vorzugs
vor andern Völkern wohl etwas Wahres — war. Aber nicht im
Neudeutschland byzantischer Streberei und rohster Gewinnsucht.[48]

[Richard Wagner let fall a pearl of truth: "Being German means doing a thing for its own sake." Anyone possessed of true German national pride, not linked to Prussian Junker militarism but to the great

deeds of our people, will gladly admit that, in this exaggeration of Wagner's, there lay a certain truth about the preeminence of us Germans — once upon a time. But not in the byzantine striving and blatant profit-mongering of modern Germany.]

Bleibtreu's position prefigured that taken by many German intellectuals in 1914, most notably Thomas Mann, who saw the war as a struggle between German intellect and *Geist*, and British utilitarianism and materialism. There were, of course, other Germans — as Bleibtreu noted — who were convinced of the need to compete with the British Empire in material terms.

A year before his accession to the throne, the future Kaiser Wilhelm II said that one couldn't hate the British too much, and warned: "England kann sich vorsehen, wenn ich einmal etwas zu sagen habe."[49] (England can watch out when the day comes that I have something to say.) Once in power, the Kaiser began to implement his vision of a German future "auf dem Wasser," of an empire to rival the British Empire. In Alfred von Tirpitz he found a brilliant collaborator, who skillfully manipulated both political and public opinion in favor of naval expansion. As Volker Berghahn has explained:

> The Navy was to act as a focus for divergent social forces which the government hoped to bribe into a conservative "Sammlung" against the "Revolution." Promises of a great economic and political future were made with the aim of maintaining the big landowners, the military and the bureaucracy in their key positions within the power structure.[50]

The first result of Tirpitz's labors was the naval bill of 1898, which, as Gordon Craig has shown, was aimed directly at British naval power.[51] The mobilization of commercial, industrial, and agrarian interests in support of the new naval policy became a new literary industry. A typical piece, aimed at an educated readership, was *Zukunftskrieg und Zukunftsfriede* by Hans Delbrück. After expounding at length on the horrors of modern war and the power of modern military and naval technology, Delbrück nonetheless remained convinced that colonial expansion was essential: "Es ist eine Lebensfrage für uns, wenn wir eine große Nation bleiben wollen, hierbei neben den bereits etablierten Kolonial-Nationen einen gleichwerthigen Besitz zu erlangen" (For us it is imperative, if we wish to remain a great nation, to acquire possessions equal in value to those of already established colonial nations). Although he felt that expansion would ideally be achieved without armed conflict, Delbrück accepted that this was unlikely, and concluded that an empire "ist ein Gut, das auch um noch so viel Blut nicht zu theuer erkauft wäre"[52] (is a possession that cannot be achieved at too great a cost in blood). The great public success of this imperialist strategy can be measured in the membership of the Navy League in Germany, which had 86,675 members in November 1899, 275,272 in 1905, 315,420 in 1906, and 324,372 in 1907.[53]

Quite predictably, a new branch of popular fiction blossomed at this time, dripping with salt water and the tang of sea air. A pioneer of the genre was Graf Bernstorff, described on the title page of his first book as "Korvettenkapitän a. D." The book, *Unsere blauen Jungen*, was published in 1899, and promised "Ernstes und Heiteres aus dem Leben der Matrosen unserer Kriegsmarine" (serious and light-hearted moments from a sailor's life in our navy). On the niveau of the comparable English yarns published at the time in *Gem* and *Magnet*, Bernstorff tells the story of a great sea battle somewhere off the German coast, following the surprise attack on Danzig by an unnamed enemy. While the enemy is unnamed, England is clearly intended, and Bernstorff ascribes the success of the German fleet both to the courage of the German commanders and to the inferiority of the opposing ships, many of which are of an older construction. Even as early as 1899, the inevitability of war is unquestioningly accepted, and Bernstorff provides a popular version of Delbrück's argument. Bernstorff's style is less subtle, however, and the first paragraph gives a foretaste of what is to follow:

> Was erwartet, ist geschehen! Die Würfel sind gefallen! Der Krieg ist erklärt! Der Mund der Diplomaten schweigt. Statt ihrer werden die Geschütze ihren Feuermund öffnen und mit Donnerworten reden![54]
>
> [The expected has come to pass! The die is cast! War is declared! The diplomats have fallen silent. In their place the artillerymen will open fire and speak in words of thunder!]

After a preliminary skirmish, the enemy regroups to make a surprise attack on the main German fleet. The Germans, however, are much too clever to be caught out: "Der überraschende Angriff, welchen der Feind geplant hatte, ist dank der Aufmerksamkeit der Beobachter vereitelt"[55] (The surprise attack planned by the enemy has been thwarted by the alertness of our guards). After the necessary heroic sacrifices, a great victory is won, and the proud but battered fleet returns to Friedrichsort, the fortress guarding the approaches to Kiel harbor:

> Da braust es empor aus voller Brust, aus bewegtem, dankerfülltem Herzen, wie ein Jubelschrei bis an die Wolken dringend, das deutsche Hurra! Das deutsche Volk grüßt seine blauen Jungens, seine siegreichen Söhne, die hinausgezogen zum blutigen Streit, zum Schutze des Vaterlands und seiner Ehre! Mit Muth hinaus zum Kampf! Mit Gott hinaus zum Siege! . . . Hoch flattert die Flagge am Mast, wie Adlers Flüge rauschen! Flieg, deutscher Aar, weit über das blaue Meer! Dein ist's und wird es immer bleiben! Denn in den

Herzen deiner blauen Jungens steht es treu und unerschütterlich: "Allzeit mit Gott für Kaiser und Reich!"[56]

[Then, bursting forth from roaring lungs and thank-filled hearts, rising to the clouds with a cry of triumph, the German Huzza! The German people greets its boys in blue, its victorious sons who sallied forth to bloody strife in defense of fatherland and honor! Marching with courage to battle! Marching with God to victory! . . . The standard flutters from the mast, hissing like eagle's pinions! Fly, German eagle, fly across the ocean blue! Yours it is and ever more will be so! For firm in the hearts of your boys in blue lies the resolve: "Now and forever with God for Kaiser and Reich!"]

Not all the naval fantasies of the early fleet-building era were quite so inane, however, and Dr. Karl Eisenhart, in *Die Abrechnung mit England* (1900), describes how German sea power wrests Gibraltar from Britain, together with all her African possessions. Others were less optimistic, and wrote dire tales of German naval defeat in order to stimulate the further expansion of the fleet: Gustav Adolf Erdmann's *Wehrlos zur See: Eine Flottenphantasie an der Jahrhundertwende* (1900) is a good example.

With the reconciliation of Britain and France in 1904 and the beginning of the entente, Anglo-German animosity became more focused. Delbrück, in an article written in 1904, just after the Anglo-French agreement, and significantly entitled: "Deutschland in der Weltpolitik: Der Krieg," states quite baldly: "Als der große Zweck des neugebildeten Deutschen Reiches hat sich immer mehr herausgestellt, zu verhindern, daß die Welt englisch werde"[57] (The great objective of the newly formed German Reich has become increasingly clear: to prevent the world becoming English). The growing tension between the two leading European powers produced a bumper crop of novels prophesying war. In Germany, as in Britain, 1906 was an *annus mirabilis* of the genre. The fears of Lord Northcliffe, General Roberts, and William Le Queux that the British would be unable to resist a German invasion did not go unheard in Germany and were clearly welcomed as proof of the growing status of the nation's arms. As already noted, *The Invasion of 1910* appeared in German translation shortly after its publication in English. The translated version enjoyed considerable success, and 30,000 copies were sold within the first few months of publication. Part of this success may be attributable, however, to the happy ending that was added by the translator, Traugott Tamm. In the English original, the resistance of the English population finally drives out the German conquerors, and an unsatisfactory peace is concluded. In Tamm's version, in contrast:

Der Kaiser bot ritterlich die Hand zum ehrenvollen Frieden, und alle Bedingungen, auf denen er bestand, hatten nur den Zweck, die

Zahlung der zwar hohen, aber nicht unerschwinglichen Kriegs-entschädigung, sowie die ungefährdete Heimkehr des deutschen Landheeres zu verbürgen.[58]

[The Kaiser chivalrously offered his hand for peace with honor, and all the conditions he insisted on had only one objective: to guarantee payment of not inconsiderable but far from unaffordable reparations, and also the unhindered return home of the German Army.]

In exchange for a safe passage, with the undefeated British colonial fleets withdrawn to Malta, the Kaiser makes no territorial demands on the British. The purpose of this selfless gesture, and the moral of the whole tale, in its German reinterpretation, is spelt out on the last page:

Das britische Volk konnte sich der Einsicht nicht verschließen, daß die Invasion des Jahres 1910, wohl das blutigste Kapitel seiner ganzen Geschichte, keinen anderen Zweck gehabt hatte, als ihm zu zeigen, wo sein Panzer verwundbar wäre, und daß es am besten täte, dem Vetter jenseits der Nordsee fortan nicht mehr mit dem altgewohnten Hochmut und der erbitternden Eifersucht ent-gegenzutreten.[59]

[The British people could not fail to see that the invasion of 1910 — perhaps the bloodiest chapter in its whole history — had had only one goal, namely to show where its defences were vulnerable, and that they would do well henceforth not to confront their cousins across the North Sea with their old accustomed arrogance and em-bittering jealousy.]

1906 saw several other German contributions to the invasion scare, usually published under pseudonyms. The cover of Beowulf's novel *Der Deutsch-englische Krieg* showed an island in the vague shape of Britain, with four battleships steaming towards it. Moritorus proposed a longer route in his book *Mit Deutschen Waffen über Paris nach London*, while Hansa (actually Kapitän Hoepner a. D.) warned against German compla-cency in *Hamburg und Bremen in Gefahr!*, in which he reversed the usual plot and suggested that the British might invade Germany. The most suc-cessful book in the 1906 batch was undoubtedly *"1906"* — *Der Zusam-menbruch der alten Welt* by Seestern, the pseudonym of Ferdinand Grautoff. In a year the book sold 100,000 copies, and an English transla-tion was published in 1907. The plot diverged from the usual North Sea invasion fare and involved a conflict on a much wider scale. The global pretensions of the plot are immediately apparent in the first few pages, set in Samoa — a location with some significance for advocates of German colonial expansion. The plot is rather convoluted, as befits a world war, and starts with a skirmish between British and German ships in Samoa, an incident fomented by American duplicity. At the beginning of formal hostilities, Britain is joined by France, Spain, and Portugal; Germany by Austria and a hesitant Italy. Russia remains neutral, as does America, and both eventually emerge from the conflict as the only real winners. "Die amerikanische Gefahr" was to recur several times in other prewar forecasts of conflict, and Bleibtreu, as we shall see, was particularly insistent that any war between the British and the Germans could only favor the Americans.[60] In Seestern's narrative, the Americans sit back, having sparked off the explosion, and have first pick at the wreckage. The wreckage in the plot is fairly extensive, with set-piece naval battles off Cuxhaven (home win for Germany), in the Mediterranean (a victory for the British over the Italians), and off Heligoland (an away win for the British, in which all but one of the German ships are sunk). On land the Germans are more successful and push the French and British back to Bordeaux. After eight months of carnage, the war finally comes to an end when the news arrives in Europe of a series of uprisings in Africa and Asia against the colonial powers. Following an armistice generously offered by the Kaiser, the European powers are free to put down the black and yellow rebellions. This does not mean a return to the prewar order, however, since the decimation of the French, German, and British fleets meant that naval domination had passed over to America, and power on the land to Russia — St Petersburg and Washington had taken the places of London and Berlin. Under American pressure, the British were to withdraw from their Caribbean colonies, and the European governments forced to observe the terms of the Monroe Doctrine.

The breadth of Grautoff's vision, which in its final resolution anticipated the balance of world power after 1945, the technical expertise displayed in his descriptions of battle, and his narrative power, all point to the superiority of *"1906"* over comparable German or British rivals. Two extracts make this clear. The first describes the scene in Berlin Cathedral shortly after the outbreak of the war:

> Der gewaltige Prachtbau des Berliner Domes war bis auf den letzten Platz gefüllt. Fast nur Uniformen; hier war noch einmal die Führerschaft der Armee, soweit sie schon an der Grenze stand, um ihren Kaiser versammelt. Als die kaiserliche Familie ihre Loge betrat, ging ein Gemurmel durch die Versammlung. Ein metallisches Klirren und Knirschen des kriegerischen Schmuckes, aller Augen wandten sich einen Moment dem Herrscher zu und eine rauschende Bewegung ging durch die Menge.[61]

> [The magnificent edifice of the Berliner Dom was filled to the last seat. Almost exclusively uniforms; here the army leadership, insofar as they were back within the country, were assembled around their

Kaiser. As the imperial family entered their pew a murmur went up through the company. A metallic clinking and chinking of military regalia, the eyes of all turned for a moment to the ruler and a rustling movement stirred through the company.]

The second extract, a reflection on the anonymity of the combatants, indicates the superiority of Grautoff's text to the gung-ho patriotism of Bernstorff, or even Delbrück:

Wie der Krieg die wildesten Leidenschaften entfacht, wie er die tierischen Instinkte aufpeitscht, wenn der Soldat die Waffe auf einen Gegner richtet, der ihm persönlich nichts zuleide getan, der ihm unbekannt und gleichgültig, auch ein Mensch, um dessen Leben daheim Weib und Kinder zittern, um den sich die Eltern sorgen, um ihn, der nun zum Manne erwachsen die Stütze ihres Alters sein sollte. Mensch zu Mensch, nur verschieden nach dem Volksempfinden und nach den Farben der Uniform. Ja die Kugel ist eine Törin, dieses kleine Stückchen Metall, es weiß nicht, von wannen es kommt und wohin es fährt, und welche Tränensaat dem Boden entsprießt, auf dem sein Opfer verblutet.[62]

[How war sets alight the wildest of passions, how it whips up the animal instincts when a soldier aims his gun at an enemy who has done him no harm personally, who is neither known to him nor of interest, but who is also a man with wife and child at home trembling for his safety, whose parents are anxious about him, the man who, an adult now, they count on for support in their old age. Man to man, different only in their sense of belonging and the color of their uniform. The bullet is indeed blind, this little piece of metal, it knows not whence it comes nor whither it goes, nor the crop of tears that will blossom from the soil on which its victims bleed to death.]

The English translation was published in 1907 as *Armageddon 190–*, and the translator noted that "Seestern, as he calls himself, still retains his anonymity. Speculation has variously ascribed his work to the Emperor, to different distinguished naval officers, and — less frequently — to prominent journalists. The first-mentioned guess is of course not correct."[63]

With its exact details of naval tonnage, displacements, gun range, and so on, Grautoff's book contributed to the scientific debate on the likely form of the next war. This debate was generally conducted in non-fictional terms, although there were semi-fictional contributions. Symptomatic of the influence of fiction on this whole debate was a contribution to Landsberg's series *Moderne Zeitfragen* by Karl von Bruchhausen, entitled *Der kommende Krieg* (1906). Although dismissive of the invasion novels, Bruchhausen does single out the books by Seestern and Hansa as worthy of attention:

Solche Phantasiestücke — ich vermeide ausdrücklich den Ausdruck "Romane" — liegen aus älterer wie auch neuerer Zeit in Menge vor; aus neuster, also allein brauchbar für unsere Zwecke, "Seesterns" *1906* und Hansas *Hamburg und Bremen in Gefahr.*[64]

[Such works of imagination — I consciously avoid the term "novels" — are available in substantial numbers from both days gone by and more recent times; most recently, and therefore the only ones of use to us, are "Seestern's" *1906* and Hansa's *Hamburg and Bremen in Danger.*]

In particular, Bruchhausen agreed with Seestern's thesis that the Americans might promote a European war, "um dann hinterher — sich neutral haltend — das Fett abzuschöpfen und ohne Aufwendung eines einzigen Dollars die Weltherrschaft zur See zu gewinnen" (19; in order then afterwards, maintaining neutrality, to draw off the fat and, without spending a single dollar, to gain worldwide command of the seas.) He also supported Hansa's argument that the German coastal defenses could not provide adequate defense from a British invasion. The converse, however, was not the case, for as Bruchhausen insisted: "Träume von einer Landung an der englischen Küste sind also — Träume" (47; dreams of a landing on the English coast are just that — dreams). This was also the conclusion reached by Karl Bleibtreu in a book of staggering tedium, called *Die Offensiv-Invasion gegen England: Eine Phantasie.* In spite of its title, the text is entirely devoid of novelistic fantasy, and reads like a précis of *Jane's Fighting Ships.* It begins, in Bernstorffian manner: "Am Spätabend des 4. Mai 19. . . schlängelte sich plötzlich eine lange Kette grauer Schiffsleiber über die Nordsee" (Late on the evening of May 4, 19. . . a long chain of grey ships snaked out across the North Sea). The reason was given shortly after:

Englands Animosität gegen Deutschland in allen Weltteilen und bei jeder nur erdenklichen Reibungszone hatte nach allen Friedens- und Abrüstungsphasen so bedenkliche Schärfe angenommen, daß sich die Lenker deutscher Politik in keiner Täuschung darüber wiegten, weitgehendste Verträglichkeit könne den ernsten Konflikt nicht aufhalten.[65]

[England's antagonism towards Germany in every corner of the globe and in every conceivable area of conflict had reached a level of intensity after all peace and disarmament phases such that the shapers of German policy were in no way lulled into imagining that mutual tolerance, even at its most liberal, could survive the first conflict.]

The purpose of the attack was not to invade, however, but merely to blockade. At the time of the attack the British capital ships were all dispersed to the north of Scotland and in various places around the world, and the Kaiser and his advisers had taken this opportunity to attack, using the example of *perfides Albion*: "Nur mit schwerem Herzen entschloß man sich, das System Englands mit der feststehenden Doktrin plötzlichen Überfalls ohne Kriegserklärung nachzumachen"[66] (Only with heavy hearts was the decision taken to imitate England's system of sudden attack without prior declaration of war) — the gentlemanly Germans adopting opportunistic British tactics. After initial successes, the German fleet was totally destroyed by superior British numbers and firepower, and this was the moral of Bleibtreu's tale: "Selbst unter Beihülfe der französischen und italienischen Marine, worauf schwerlich zu rechnen wäre, hätte ein Seekrieg Deutschlands gegen England immer nur unglücklich enden müssen" (69). (Even with the assistance of the French and Italian navies, which could hardly be relied upon, a naval war against England could only ever end unhappily.) The only hope for Germany, he said, was not confrontation with England but rather collaboration between the two nations against the economic threat posed by America and the non-European nations: "Nur dauerndes Freundschaftsbündnis der beiden großen Germanenrassen kann Europa retten.... Seid einig, einig, einig!"[67] (Only a lasting treaty of friendship between the two great Germanic races can save Europe.... Be united, united, united!) Although informed opinion saw no prospect of a successful water-borne invasion of England, the fantasists had an exciting new weapon in their armory, the airship. Here too, informed opinion was skeptical. In his *Offensiv-Invasion*, Bleibtreu was dismissive about the role of the airships: "Das britische Militärluftschiff wirkte hier natürlich ebensowenig mit wie das deutsche Parsevalsche" (57; The British military airship operated in this field as little as did Germany's Parsival). Delbrück, writing in the same year, also questioned the strategic significance of the airship: "Zwar sind sich die Fachmänner darüber klar, daß diese Erfindung weder als Waffe noch als Transportmittel eine wesentliche Bedeutung erlangen könne" (The experts are admittedly clear that this invention will not achieve real significance either as a weapon or as a means of transport). He recognized, however, that:

> "In der Volksmeinung . . . sieht man schon Armeen durch die Lüfte fahren und die feindlichen Länder von oben her angreifen," adding: "Die Erfindung der lenkbaren Luftschiffe trägt dazu bei, die Nervosität im englischen Volke zu steigern."[68]

> [In the public's imagination . . . whole armies are already traveling through the air, attacking enemy countries from the skies. . . . The invention of air-borne dirigibles serves to increase nervousness amongst the English people.]

This nervousness led Excubitor, the author of an article in *The Fortnightly Review*, to urge the British government to invest heavily in a program of airship construction, claiming: "This is the only policy compatible with safety, and to that policy we must now bend all our splendid industrial and scientific resources if we are not to incur the risk of our naval supremacy passing from us."[69] As one would expect, the redundancy of British naval power in the face of the new aeronautical technology was a theme eagerly taken up in Germany by combative literati.

The leader in the genre was Rudolf Martin. In *Das Zeitalter der Motorluftschiffahrt*,[70] he included chapters on "Der Truppentransport durch die Luft" and "England keine Insel mehr," and he developed these themes in a second book published in the same year, *Kaiser Wilhelm II. und König Edward VII.* (1907). His arguments were based on the *Einkreisung* theory, which held that the entente powers were trying to encircle and ultimately crush Germany: "Die gegen Deutschland gerichtete Koalition zwingt die Deutschen zur Vorbereitung einer Landung durch die Luft in England"[71] (The coalition against Germany forces Germany to prepare for an air-borne invasion of England). This was technically possible, said Martin, in aluminum Zeppelins with a fourteen-meter diameter, each carrying seventy soldiers. Although he admitted that such a ship would cost half a million marks, Martin proposed that: "Auf 4000 Motorluftschiffen dieser Art kann man in einer Nacht 280 000 Mann durch die Luft von Norderney nach England werfen"[72] (In motorized dirigibles of this kind 280,000 men could be launched in a night by air from Nordeney to England) — the *Riddle of the Sands* given wings! Flying at a height of 1,500 meters, the German airships could float over the English maritime defenses, merely pausing to destroy the home fleet in a hail of aerial bombs and torpedoes.

Such visions of the power of the airship naturally lent themselves to even more extravagant fantasies. Maurus, the pseudonymous author of *Ave Caesar! Deutsche Luftschiffe im Kampfe um Marokko*, avenged the diplomatic defeat suffered by Germany in the 1905 Moroccan crisis by sending in the airships. As the hero explained to the airship captain:

> Und heute soll Deutschland, das Reich der siebzig Millionen Menschen, von der Suche nach nährender Erde ausgeschlossen sein, indes der unfruchtbare gallische Hahn in törichter Ländergier seine Krallen in das saftige Fleisch Marokkos schlägt und England über Ägypten den Landweg nach Indien sucht?[73]

> [And are we to accept that Germany today, a Reich of 70 million people, is to be excluded from the search for nourishing lands at a time when the barren Gallic cockerel, driven by a crazy lust for land,

buries its claws in the juicy flesh of Morocco while England strikes overland through Egypt into India?]

After performing miracles with the airships "Kastor" and "Pollux" and driving the French out of Morocco, the Germans turned their attention to England:

> Am letzten Maientag umwogte abermals eine riesige Volksmenge die Hangars von Friedrichshafen. Erschauernd fühlte sie den geheimnisvoll wehenden Atem des großen Augenblicks, der das ewig glimmende Feuer in der Esse des Völkerwerdens zur Flamme anfacht, zum Segen oder zum Unheil. . . . Wie geblendet vom Lichtmeer schob sich der Riesenleib des "Wilhelm" langsam aus dem Hangar. "Deutschland, Deutschland über alles . . ." Männer, Frauen, Kinder sangen das erhabene Lied. (221)

> [On the last day of May another massive crowd poured around the hangars in Friedrichshafen. With a shiver they sensed the secret whispering of that great moment when the eternal glow in the forge of nation-growth bursts into flame — for bane or blessing. . . . As if blinded by the sea of lights, the massive torso of the "Wilhelm" edged slowly out of the hangar. "Deutschland, Deutschland über alles . . ." Men, women and children sang the sublime hymn.]

Arriving over Windsor Castle the German airship dropped a bomb that devoured a group of beech trees in front of the castle:

> Aus den Lüften dröhnte ein Sprachrohr: "Der Meister vom Bodensee bittet seine Majestät um eine Audienz" . . . Der König der Meere empfing den Herrn der Luft. (227)

> [A megaphone called down from the sky: "The Lord of the Bodensee requests an audience with his majesty" . . . The King of the Oceans received the Lord of the Skies.]

Unless Britain gave up its plans for war, conceived "nur um sich seiner wirtschaftlichen Konkurrenz zu entledigen" (only to rid itself of economic competitors), the Germans threatened to attack Windsor Castle, London, and the Home Fleet lying off the Dogger Bank. The King procrastinated . . . a further explosion rocked the castle: "Sir, ehret den Frieden der Völker. Seht hinauf, die Kriegsaare rüsten zum Kampfe" (Sir, honor the peace amongst nations. Look above: the war-eagles are preparing for battle). The King paused again . . . another explosion. The King was beaten: "Hier meine Hand. Ich verbürge mich mit meinem Königsworte für den Frieden . . . Der König lächelte trübe. 'Ihr habt mich dazu gezwungen'" (230; My hand on it. I stand guarantee for peace with my royal word. . . . The king smiled dully. "You forced me to it.")

The same theme was aired at even greater length in a novel published a year later, in 1910: *Englands Feind: Der Herr der Luft* by Ewald Gerhard Seeliger. Seeliger was a very productive writer, who favored tales of the sea, and novels set in and around Hamburg. His airship novel, in contrast, is set principally in Funchal, and the early plot evolves around the efforts of Waldemar Quint, a German inventor, to build an effective airship motor. This he achieves, using a machine driven by a *Wasserstoffkristall.* Armed with this new machine, and an assortment of highly potent new weapons, he sets off to pursue his idealistic goal:

> das Meer zu befreien und die Mächte der Menschheitsentwicklung, die sich in den mörderischen Rüstungen der Völkerkriege erschöpften, für das höhere Ziel der Völkereintracht zu entfesseln.[74]

> [to set free the ocean and the powers of human development, exhausted by the murderous arms race of international war, releasing them in the interests of the higher goal of peace between nations.]

The fear of Quint's airborne power was to be used to bring peace to the world, and to this end, Quint sinks the British cruiser *Hermes*, together with 419 of its crew, off the island of Thule. The British send a battleship and two more cruisers to the same spot, to find out the identity of the mysterious aggressor. Once again, Quint strikes, the two cruisers are sunk, and the battleship is allowed to limp back to England. At this point Quint makes radio contact with the British War Minister, who asks:

> "Was bezwecken Sie?"
> "Die Aufrichtung des Weltfriedens."
> "Das ist auch unser Ziel. Weshalb bekämpfen Sie uns?"
> "Um die Menschheit zu befreien. Sie rüsten Ihre Flotte ab. Sammeln alle Schiffe auf der Reede von Portland, wo ich sie in einer Nacht vernichten werde. . . . Meine Kampfmittel sind in ihrer Wirkung unbegrenzt. Ich könnte aus London einen Schutthaufen machen."
> . . .
> "Warum sollen gerade wir den Anfang machen?"
> "Weil England die Wurzel alles Unfriedens ist. Weil England die erste Macht war, die schwimmende Mordmaschinen auf das freie Meer hinausgeschickt hat. Weil England die Hälfte der Erdkugel gestohlen hat." (219)

> ["What is your purpose?" — "To establish peace on earth." — "That is our goal too. Why are you fighting against us?" — "To set mankind free. Disarm your fleet. Assemble all your ships in the roads off Portland where I shall destroy them in one night. . . . My weaponry is unlimited in its effects. I could reduce London to a heap of

rubble." ... — "Why is it we who have to make the start? — "Because England is the greatest threat to peace. Because England was the first power to send floating vessels of destruction out into the free ocean. Because England has stolen half the globe."]

The British refuse to accept these conditions, and Quint gives them a six-month remission before the planned beginning of his destruction of the British fleet. After endless further complications, some involving the American newspaper proprietor, William Randolph Hearst, and his star reporter, Horace Toddy, the day of reckoning approaches. Quint's secret base on Madeira has been betrayed to the British who close in. John Splendy, the leader of the British hunters, tells Quint's English wife that her husband has already sunk fourteen British ships and asks her to lead the British to him, Delilah-style: "Du bist eine Engländerin. Wir erwarten deine Hilfe!" (343; You are an Englishwoman. We expect your assistance). At the last moment, however, her resolve weakens, and her love for Quint proves stronger than her patriotism. She urges him to flee, but in vain, for the British shoot him out of the sky as he tries to escape in his last remaining airship. The British fleet survives, continuing to rule the waves, but the message is clear: Even capital ships are defenseless against the new technology of the air.

Although the Zeppelin threat existed more in the minds of the literary fantasists than of the military strategists, it had a potent effect on the British imagination, and the theme flourished after the outbreak of war. In *Zeppelin Nights* (1916) — a book described by J. M. Barrie as one of the worst potboilers ever published in London — Viola Hunt and Ford Maddox Hueffer said of the new threat: "It was this pre-eminently German spectre which rode us all those summer months terrifying some of us beyond mental endurance; making us all, strong and weak, profoundly wretched and uneasy, filled with a restlessness that was worse than pain."[75] An earlier book by Viola Hunt, *The Desirable Alien*, describes her honeymoon journey down the Rhine as a German bride after her marriage to Ford Maddox Hueffer. Returning across the Belgian border, she sees piles of railway track stacked up on the German side, ready to be laid during a future war — "a frightful omen," as Firchow calls it, "even for a desirable alien."[76] While she and Hueffer were able to abandon any lingering fondness for Germany at the outbreak of war, the choice was not always so easy. Indeed, the conflict between national and personal loyalty, a question also thrown in by Seeliger towards the end of *Englands Feind*, points to another favored vehicle for fictional discourse on Anglo-German animosity in the years leading up to the First World War.

"Only Connect"

In a book entitled *Deutschland und England*, Karl Bleibtreu offers ironical thumbnail sketches of the characteristics of the two nations, each seen through the eyes of the other. In the sight of the English:

> Deutschland ist bekanntlich eine einzige Militärkaserne und bildet überhaupt einen Übergang zu Halbasien, Rußland, an dessen politisches System es sich anlehnt. Mag man sonst viel sogenannte Bildung dort pflegen, politisch bleibt es ein ganz rückständiges Land, das jeden freien Briten mit tiefster Abneigung erfüllen muß. Die Institutionen sind teilweise mittelalterlich feudal. Gesellschaftlich haben die Deutschen bekanntlich die schlechtesten Manieren, wie man an allen internationalen Kurorten beobachtet. Sie kleiden sich schlecht, schwatzen laut, sind unreinlich, essen unappetitlich, meist noch mit dem Messer. Ihre Küche ist abscheulich, Biersaufen ist ihre Nationalnahrung. Im Charakter sind sie arrogant, zänkisch, brutal, von besonderer stupider Wut gegen alles Englische verzehrt, natürlich aus Neid. Die Frauen sind häßlich und ungebildet, die Männer bekommen nur durch den Militärdienst eine gewisse wohlfeile Strammheit, treiben aber keinen Sport und sind daher, mit Ausnahme der Offiziere, physisch unbeholfen. Letztere sind aber meistens Gecken und führen mit einer für englische Augen empörenden Aufdringlichkeit ihren bunten Rock spazieren. Die studentischen Faxen berühren auch mittelalterlich, ebenso das gottlose Duellieren. . . . Der Dummstolz ihrer sogenannten Junker, eines pauvren Geschlechts mit antediluvianischen Anschauungen, ist sprichwörtlich. Der Bürger gilt überhaupt nichts, hat nur das Recht, hohe Steuern zu zahlen. Die Polizei mengt sich so frech in alles, ganz russisch, daß dem Ausländer das Leben bald unerträglich wird.[77]

[Germany is, notoriously, one great barracks and, in general, serves as a staging post en route for half of Asia and Russia, whose political system it is aligned with. Irrespective of how much education is pursued there, the country remains politically backward, bound to fill every free-born Briton with profound distaste. Its institutions are, in part, medieval and feudal. Socially, the Germans are the clumsiest of all, as can be witnessed at any international spa. They dress badly, talk loudly, lack cleanliness, eat noisily, still using their knives by and large. Their cuisine is ghastly. Beer is their national dish. In character they are arrogant, quarrelsome, brutal, consumed by a particularly stupid rage at all things English — out of envy, of course. Their women are ugly and uneducated, their men achieve a certain basic deportment thanks to service in the army but they don't play sport, so, apart from their officers, they are physically clumsy. The latter, on

the other hand, are mostly fops and, to English eyes, look outrageously pushy swaggering out in uniform. Student pranks come
across as medieval, so does their godless dueling. . . . The crass
stupidity of the so-called Junkers, a miserable class of people with
antediluvian attitudes, is proverbial. Ordinary citizens count for
nothing, their only right: to pay high taxes. The police meddle in
everything with such impertinence — entirely à la Russe — that for-
eigners soon find life there intolerable.]

Conversely, in the eyes of Germany:

> Nichts Komischeres als den langstieligen, storchbeinigen Briten mit
> karrierten Hosen und Bartkotelettes und die eckige, knochige Miss
> mit Schmachtlocke und Kneifer. Die Leute sind meist groß und
> stark, treten mit keckem Selbstbewußtsein auf, als wollten sie fragen:
> was kostet die Welt! Sie pochen auf ihren Geldbeutel, denn sie haben
> ja meistens viel Geld, und Geld allein gilt bei ihnen, nur der
> Kaufmann regiert. Darum heißen sie mit Recht "a nation of
> shopkeepers." (145)

> [There's nothing funnier than a lanky, stork-legged Briton with his
> checkered breeches and sideburns, and an angular, boney Miss with
> her kiss curl and pince-nez. Mostly the people are tall and strong,
> they step out with bold self-confidence as if asking: what price the
> world? They point to their wallets, for they mostly have lots of
> money, and money is the only thing that counts: the merchant is
> king. That's why they are rightly called "a nation of shop-keepers."]

In these negative characterizations, Bleibtreu anticipates the propaganda
literature of the First World War, and the simple dialectic of good and
bad, *Händler und Helden*. Regardless of all appeals to racial affinity, to
cousins across the water and related monarchs, two nations with such different characters would appear to be entirely irreconcilable. For those
happy to stay at home, comfortably cocooned in their national prejudices,
these differences were of little personal import. As soon as the borders
were crossed, however, and emotional links established, the differences
took on an existential significance. The difficulties involved in trying to
resolve or accommodate these national conflicts within a marriage became
a popular fictional theme in the prewar years, a favored vehicle for airing
wider prejudices.

A German example first, with an obviously propagandistic intent:
Rudolph Straß, *Seine englische Frau*.[78] The story tells of the impoverished
Lieutenant Merker, who marries his rich English cousin, Edith. On moving to England, his wife's wealth enables him to live the life of an English
gentleman. This pleasant state loses its charm for him, however, as he
grows more and more deadened by a life of cultivated indolence, shared

with a vain, obstinate wife. Abandoning both Edith and her country, Merker returns to Germany and atones for his sins of omission by serving in a remote garrison on the Eastern borders. The bankruptcy of his father-in-law obliges him to renounce his commission, however, and return to England. Reunited with his wife, now reformed by her new-found poverty, Merker succeeds as a businessman in England thanks to his application and *Zielstrebigkeit*. He is saved from this profitable but unworthy existence, however, by an inheritance from a rich uncle in Frankfurt, and with these new means he is able to return to the service of the Kaiser as an officer in the German navy. Implied, but not stated in this resolution of the plot, is the probability that his checkered life will be given an ultimate purpose when, at some time in the future, he gets the chance to blow his English relatives out of the water.

Almost more interesting than the book itself is a review of it published in the increasingly warlike *Preußische Jahrbücher*, which proclaimed:

> Es blicken so viele mit Neid und einer gewissen Bewunderung über den Kanal und preisen uns englisches Wesen und englische Kultur zur Nacheiferung an. Haben sie recht? Straß beantwortet diese Frage mit einem sehr entschiedenen Nein.[79]

> [So many people look with envy and a certain admiration across the Channel and recommend us to imitate English customs and culture. Are they right? Straß answers this question with a very clear No.]

Describing Merker's beckoning career in the navy as "ein Leben in freiem Gehorsam gegen die Vorgesetzten und in ernster Pflichterfüllung und gemeinnütziger Tätigkeit" (a life of freely accepted obedience to one's superiors, of conscious devotion to duty and action in the interests of all), the review ends by recommending the book as a "Gegenmittel gegen das Übel der Engländerie" (an antidote to the evil of Englishry).

What Edith thought of all this is unclear, and Straß's book, which revels in the crass stereotypes caricatured by Bleibtreu, anticipates the one-dimensional propaganda of the war years. There were, however, a number of novels written at this time in English on the theme of Anglo-German marriages, which shun the black and white of the propagandist in favor of more subtle differentiations. These novels allowed for criticism of both nations, and any praise for one side carried with it an explicit or implicit criticism of the other. Most were the result of first-hand experience in Germany by the English-speaking writers. In a descending sequence of quality, one could draw up a list of novels that would include: E. M. Forster, *Howards End* (1910); Elizabeth von Arnim, *The Pastor's Wife* (1914); I. A. R. Wylie, *Dividing Waters* (1911); and three books of lesser pretension by Sybil Spottiswoode: *Marcia in Germany* (1908), *Hedwig in England* (1911), and *Her Husband's Country* (1911). This list could also be enlarged by Wylie's two non-fiction books on Germany: *My Year in Germany* (1909), and *Eight Years in Germany* (1914), and also Lawrence's *Mr Noon*, written 1920–22, but based on a prewar journey through Germany with Frieda von Richthofen. Further examples of fiction, which do not directly involve mixed marriages, but nevertheless throw light on British attitudes to German society, include Jerome K. Jerome: *Three Men on the Bummel* (1900), the collection of short stories by Katherine Mansfield: *In a German Pension* (1911), and Lawrence's short story: *The Prussian Officer* (1914). Close links exist between the Anglo-German books of Forster, von Arnim, Lawrence, and Mansfield, and between their authors. Von Arnim and Mansfield were cousins, Forster worked as a tutor to the von Arnim family in Nassenheide in 1905–6,[80] and Mansfield provided the model for Gudrun in Lawrence's *Women in Love* (1920). These books have also, to varying degrees, been the subject of scholarly enquiry and are all still available in paperback. The novels of Wylie and Spottiswoode, by contrast, have vanished from view, and deserve some attention. Rather than describe each of these novels individually, it would perhaps be more profitable to look for shared motifs — motifs that helped form the fictional stereotypes of the two countries.

I. A. R. Wylie's first impression on arriving in Germany was one of order. In *My German Year*, she dismisses the large cities and points to the medium-sized towns like Karlsruhe as typically German. To walk through such a town

> is to gain an impression of light, fresh air and cleanliness. A whole army of neatly uniformed individuals are busy morning, noon and night sweeping, watering and sand-strewing according to orders . . . And over everything the policeman watches with a paternal, wakeful eye. If you wish to prove his wakefulness you need only leave your particular piece of pavement in an untidy state, and in a few minutes a polite but firm arm of the law will spring apparently from nowhere to recall you to a sense of duty.[81]

Thanks to the policeman, says Wylie, there are no beggars, street musicians, or rowdies to upset the prevailing sense of calm and order. While Wylie found this entirely positive, an earlier visitor, Jerome K. Jerome was less sure, and he ventured that the German government tells the individual: "You get yourself born, we do the rest. Indoors and out of doors, in sickness and in health, in pleasure and in work, we will tell you what to do, and we will see to it that you do it."[82] Jerome was by no means anti-German, and described the race as "the best people in the world; an amiable, unselfish, kindly people" (199), but nevertheless marveled at what he called "blind obedience to anything in buttons" (201). This points forward not only to Wilhelm Voigt — who in 1906 took over the *Stadtkasse* in Köpenick dressed as a *Hauptmann* — but also to a short article by the sociologist Ferdinand Tönnies, published in *Die neue Rundschau* in 1908. It was entitled "Glückliches England," and suggested that in spite of its other shortcomings, England was fortunate in having a liberal, if ineffiient, State apparatus:

> Der Brite nennt sich den Untertan seiner Krone; aber er fühlt sich als Staatsbürger. Wir, so scheint es, müssen uns als Untertanen fühlen, selbst wenn wir uns Staatsbürger nennen dürfen. Der Engländer weiß, daß jeder Beamte, daß die Armee und die Flotte ihm zu dienen und zu helfen bestimmt sind, nicht ihn zu bevormunden und zu demütigen. Glücklicher Engländer! du hast als Bürger nie den Korporalstock, nie den Säbel des Polizeimannes dauernd über deinem Haupt gesehen.[83]

> [Britons call themselves servants of their monarch but feel themselves to be citizens of the state. We Germans are permitted to call ourselves citizens, but it seems we are obliged to feel ourselves subservient. An Englishman knows that every civil servant, the army, and the navy exist to serve and to assist him, not to treat him like a child or humiliate him. Fortunate Englishman! As a citizen, you have never seen a truncheon or a policeman's sabre constantly hovering over your head.]

Tönnies's negative view of the ubiquitous *Beamte* was shared by Lawrence, who recounted Gilbert Noon's encounter with a German ticket inspector as follows:

> He glared at Gilbert's ticket and glared at Gilbert — and broke into a torrent of abuse in a vile Rhenish accent. . . . Snarling and flourishing in the pretty [*sic*] Prussian official manner in front of the offender's nose, while all the others in the carriage looked either virtuous or rebuked! Snarl snarl snarl went the beastly person — and Gilbert's brain turned to cork.[84]

Although invested with endless power to obstruct, the *Beamte*, when viewed as an individual rather than as a representative of the state, is portrayed by the British novelists as a poor specimen. "Herr Amtschreiber Felde" in a later novel by Wylie, *Towards Morning*, felt "red with shame right to his very soul" when the birth of his child made him late for work. "He knew that *Groß-herzogliche Staatsbeamte* never ran. Nor were they ever late. They were always at their post, weaving their little pattern into the vast national design with absolute efficiency and dignity, without haste or disorder."[85] *Frau Hofpostamtdirektor Kohlschlegel* did no better in *Marcia in Germany*, where she was pictured at a charity bazaar "perspiring copiously into her new, tight clothes."[86]

The authority of the *Beamte* derived less from his individual ability than from his exactly defined place in a rigid social hierarchy, and this formalization of German society naturally attracted the attention of the British authors. At the bottom of the pile, in contrast to British practice, are the businessmen, and the stereotype of the fat, greedy German tends to be limited to this class. Nora, the heroine of Wylie's novel *Dividing Waters*, on hearing that she is about to go and live in Germany, exclaims:

> "You mean," she began slowly, "that I should go and live in a German family?"
> "Yes."
> "With a lot of fat, greasy, gobbling Germans?"[87]

This picture of the gobbling German was specifically linked to the commercial classes by Katherine Mansfield, who has a "Traveller from North Germany" explain over the meal table: "I eat sauerkraut with great pleasure, but now I have eaten so much of it that I cannot retain it. I am immediately forced to —."[88] Similarly, it is Herr Schlund, the businessman at the pension chosen for the honeymoon of Spottiswoode's heroine in *Her Husband's Country*, who talks with his mouth full. This is particularly galling to Patience, the heroine, as the subject of his speech is the decline of England.[89] A very damning dismissal of the German business class is the portrait of Frau von Sasswitz in the same book, the loud and vulgar daughter of a Berlin fancy-goods manufacturer, who intersperses her conversation with French and English expressions, "bragging of the glories of their huge Berlin villa, outstripping all the others on the Kurfürstendamm by its elaborate architecture and its palatial equipment" (366).

The disparaging treatment accorded to the commercial classes is explained in terms of anti-Semitism. In her non-fictional account *Eight Years in Germany*, Wylie writes:

> For a long time German trade was almost exclusively in the hands of Jews, thus becoming doubly distasteful to a people whose antipathy to the Jewish population, as unfortunate as it is fundamental, was inevitably increased by an unreasonable if natural bitterness.[90]

The exclusion of the Jews from polite society in Germany, and their total rejection by the military caste, is a recurring theme in the novels of Wylie and Spottiswoode. It also carries an implicit critique of the British, for their more liberal treatment of the Jews. In Spottiswoode's *Marcia in Germany* the Jewish subplot is particularly developed, when one of the sons of the *Gräfin* who is Marcia's hostess develops a passion for the daughter of a Jewish businessman. While the *Gräfin* herself is also inclined to British liberality, another son defends the correct German standards. This provokes the following dialogue:

"My dear mamma," Ernst interrupted impatiently. "She may have great taste and she may be American, but you can't blink the fact that old Rosenbaum is a dirty little Jew, who made his money in old clo', or God knows what disreputable business . . ."

"Why are we so horribly narrow-minded in Waldberg?" the *Gräfin* sighed. "Frau Rosenberg was telling me that in England they have a Prime Minister married to a Jewess, and the Rothschilds are the most important persons in the country. She says Jews rule society, and everyone runs after them there."[91]

Ernst's views on the matter were also aired in *Hedwig in England* — the successor to *Marcia in Germany*. Here Spottiswoode merely reverses the plot, and allows her visiting German girl to be amazed and shocked that her English hostess should not only dine with Jews, but speak of them in flattering terms. Hedwig concluded: "Evidently it was true that the English would sell their souls for luxury and riches."[92] This link between English capitalism and Jewishness was a recurring feature in anti-English propaganda in Germany. It was a central argument in a book published in the same year as the Hedwig novel by Alexander von Peetz, and entitled *England und der Kontinent*. Peetz, an Austrian industrialist, claimed that King Edward and the leading Jewish financiers in the City of London belonged to various secret organizations, adding: "Aus dem Umstande, das durch die City eine fremde Nationalität oft ein gewichtiges Wort spricht, erklärt sich manche Unstimmigkeit in der Haltung Englands"[93] (From the circumstance that, thanks to the City, foreign nationals often carry great weight, we can understand many a faux pas in England's behavior). This obsession, satirized by Spottiswoode, lay behind the notion of an Anglo-Jewish conspiracy against the Boers, already noted in Bleibtreu's *Bur und Lord*. It should also be remembered, however, that the English could indulge in anti-Semitism in the other direction. As Rupert Brooke sat in the Café des Westens in Berlin in May 1912, pining for Grantchester, he was particularly oppressed by "Temperamentvoll German Jews."[94]

High above the *Beamten*, the businessmen, and the Jews was the military caste, the very pinnacle of German society, and the immediate context of the two major novels by Wylie and Spottiswoode, *Dividing Waters* and *Her Husband's Country* respectively. The plots of both books are strikingly similar. An English girl, from narrow, provincial circumstances, goes to Germany and is courted by an officer in the German army. Wylie's heroine, Nora Ingestre, is the daughter of a self-obsessed art collector; her counterpart in Spottiswoode's book, Patience Thaile, is the daughter of a country vicar who has lost all his money in a risky speculation in Mexico. Escaping from these suffocating home surroundings, the two heroines are easily impressed by the martial splendor of life in a German garrison town. Nora falls for her future husband, Wolff von Arnim (a happy coincidence of name!) while out riding:

> His gaze was set resolutely ahead; his lips beneath the short, fair moustache were compressed in stern, thoughtful lines which changed the whole character of his face, making him older, graver. . . . She saw Arnim in a new light, as the worker, the soldier, the man of action and iron purpose. Every line of the broad-shouldered figure suggested power and energy, and the features, thrown into shadow by his officer's cap were stamped with the same virile characteristics translated into intellect and will.[95]

Spottiswoode's heroine is equally struck by the military machine, telling her future husband, Helmuth Rabenstedt: "Each day I am here I am more impressed with the observed militarism of everything. I now realize what is meant by a 'nation in arms.'"[96] Even Lawrence, who hated German militarism, was struck by the external trappings: "They were handsome, on the whole, the cavalry: so strong, so healthy looking, powerful, with that strange military beauty which one never saw in England."[97] For Wylie and Spottiswoode, however, the infatuation is not simply for blood and iron, and both authors provide a musical backdrop for their romances, showing that the German officer was not merely a soldier, but also had qualities of intellect. In Rabenstedt's case, these are fairly slight, and he pursues his courtship to the strains of *Carmen*. Wolff von Arnim, however, is altogether a more thoughtful person, and his developing love for Nora is accompanied by *Tristan*, played by the two lovers as a piano duet. On completing the first act:

> He turned and looked at her.
> "Did you understand it?"
> "Not at all. I feel that there are many more wonders to fathom which are yet too deep for me. But I understand enough to know that they are there — and to be glad."
> "It is the noblest — most perfect expression of love and of the human heart that was ever written or composed," he said.[98]

In addition to all the qualities expected of a military hero, Wylie invested von Arnim with a depth of intellect and spirit that went far beyond that of his English counterpart, and rival for Nora's hand, Captain Arnold, who is depicted as decent but unthinking. All this accords perfectly with Sombart's dialectic, and in both books the initial infatuation with things German is contrasted against images of English weakness and decadence.

Compared to the muscular German supermen, with Wagner ringing in their ears, the English menfolk are given a very bad press. The fathers in both *Dividing Waters* and *Her Husband's Country* are weak and self-centered, and Mr Thaile has the added disadvantage of liking Turner watercolors and William Morris wallpapers. Both men are only able to function thanks to their strong, competent wives, and the novels share a distinctly feminist reading of the unfair lot of these oppressed wives, nobly suffering under the folly of doltish husbands. Of the other menfolk, the two English suitors are shown to be weak and unexciting, and Nora's brother Miles is a caricature of all the worst qualities of the English in the Bleibtreu/Mommsen version:

> — a shiftless, idle, gambling fool, who responds to the news of her sister's engagement by exclaiming: "Just think of it people! 'Wolff' for my brother-in-law! A German bounder in the family! Many thanks!"[99]

A confrontation between the enfeebled English bourgeois and the German officer caste is reached late in the book, after Miles insults an officer at a ball in Berlin. Explaining to his German challenger that the English don't fight duels, Miles is told: "No; you go to law and take money for your injured honour. . . . That is the revenge of shopkeepers — not of gentlemen" (120). This challenge is issued simultaneously with a German ultimatum to England, and the duel echoes on the private level the crisis that looms on the international stage.

Dueling and the concept of honor clearly had considerable attraction to both authors. In her two non-fiction books on Germany, Wylie goes to some length to explain that it is a German officer's *duty* to defend forcibly his honor against civilian insult. Citing the celebrated Zabern affair, which had been widely reported in the British press, she insisted that the uniformed lieutenant had no option but to draw his sword and kill the cobbler who had threatened him: "If the army is the nation then the uniform is obviously symbolical of the national honour. . . . An insult to the nation involves either war or dishonour. An insult to an individual bearer of the symbol involves, logically, death or dishonour."[100] This was a theme picked up again by Spottiswoode, who has Hedwig explain to her English hostess the principles of honor behind German dueling, adding that the English tendency to turn the other cheek or accept some financial compensation "seems terribly degrading," for "'if duelling is abolished, you abolish also the rigid notions of keeping your honour untarnished at the price of your own life-blood' . . . Mrs. Ilford yawned."[101] Her reaction was later shared by the wartime propagandists in Britain, who invariably pointed to the Zabern affair and to the sight of women being pushed into the gutter by officers on Unter den Linden as proof of the absurdity of the German notion of honor.

What was behind this concept of military and family honor? Very little, as the two English heroines were to find out, only a "brilliant misery" — the phrase used by both authors. The problems begin directly after the marriages, when the cavalier officers suddenly appear more Teutonic, less dashing. This impression strikes home most forcibly when the respective husbands appear for the first time in civilian clothing. In Nora's case this happens when Wolff von Arnim appears in England for the wedding: "She would hardly have recognized him in the plain tweed suit and bowler hat . . . it was all too evident that the suit was 'ready-made.'"[102] The same shock is awaiting Patience on her honeymoon, when "she realized this was her husband, denuded of the uniform in which she had heretofore seen him, and clothed in the ill-cut and grotesque garments which constitute the usual attire of the ruck of Germans who have not come under the influence of English tailordom."[103] Clothes play an important part in delineating the national conflicts. While the poor cut of the husbands' suits reveals to the English wives the superficiality of the military splendor, the fine clothes favored by the English women attracts the criticism of the German regimental wives, as being incompatible with the Prussian military ideal of austerity. The appalling dress sense of German womanhood is a theme that crops up frequently in both books. The negative impact of "good" English taste on the German military mind is spelled out by Spottiswoode in her account of Patience's first meeting with her husband's commanding officer:

> The Colonel eyed her suspiciously . . . "I insist upon simplicity in my officers and their families — any tendency to ostentation and extravagance I put an instant stop to." He fixed an accusing stare upon the broad sweep of Patience's plumed hat and continued meaningly [sic] "I usually find that the people of the best family and position are those who adhere most rigidly to simplicity. It is the *parvenu* and the business classes who love a fashionable show and display."[104]

This is the confrontation of *Händler und Helden*, of English luxury versus Prussian austerity, being fought out on the vestimentary front.

There were other fronts too. Bathing was an important source of conflict, adding a further dimension to Wylie's title, and the English preference for regular baths was criticized by the officer husbands as decadent and extravagant. Furnishings, too, prove a point of bitter contention. Having fled from the precious artsiness of her father, Nora slowly realizes that the products of the English Arts and Crafts movement were, indeed, preferable to the cheerless, lumpy furniture of the German *Gründerzeit*. Both in the small garrison town and later in Berlin, Nora finds her surroundings ugly and uncomfortable, only made bearable by her love for her husband. Patience, in contrast, is made of less resilient stuff, and her dismay at the furnishings in her marital home provokes her husband, Helmut, into a nationalistic outburst:

"The furnishings may be considered correct here," she said icily, "but if so, complete absence of taste must be the correct thing in Germany." "Patience," he said, using her Christian name for the first time, and pronouncing it in an unrecognizable manner. "I cannot allow you to speak like that. I cannot, as a German officer, stand by and hear my beloved country disparaged."[105]

When Patience refurbishes part of the flat according to current English taste, she is thoroughly rebuked by the wives of her husband's fellow officers. Behind these external sources of conflict, however, lies a deeper malaise — the refusal of the English-born wives to accept the humbling role of a German officer's wife, who is brought up to regard plainness and austerity as virtues, and expected to shop, cook, and serve her master, untrammeled by any higher ambitions. Wylie concluded her account *Eight Years in Germany* with the hope that the German woman would free herself from male tyranny, since "in her are the fires that are destined to bring light into the dark places of German medievalism."[106] In *Her Husband's Country*, Patience resolves to break the mold, and offer an alternative to "these unappreciated and downtrodden wives" (130). She refuses, accordingly, to learn to shop economically, to sew, mend, or cook in the skillful manner expected of an officer's wife, and is ostracized for her efforts — or lack of them. The difference between the Spartan Prussian ethic and the luxuriousness and comfort enjoyed by the English bourgeoisie is summed up in Patience's marvelous complaint: "I hate cooking! It spoils one's temper, one's hands and one's health! It's far less tiring to play three rounds of golf than to make a couple of fritters" (279).

Patience's failure to break out of the constraints of German domesticity, aggravated by her husband's gambling and infidelities, all increase her yearning for England and English society. Although resolved to change her ways and support her husband in all his Germanness, and against her native inclinations, she is able to return to her roots because of the death of her husband in a riding accident. Back in rural England she sees new prospects in Captain Cunningham Roper, V.C., D.S.O., a paragon of all the supposedly English virtues, who had made a fleeting appearance earlier in the book, when he was admired for his "bright and capable look" and the excellent fit of his shooting suit (45). The fact that Roper was standing as Conservative candidate, against the pacifist Liberals in her father's set, suggests that Roper might succeed by violent means where Patience had failed in love, to put the German saber-rattlers in their place.

Wylie's denouement is much more sophisticated. Her brother's disgrace in Berlin over the duel and the threat of war prompt her to leave her husband and return to England. The British government backs down, however, since the army is totally unprepared for a war with Germany. As Captain Arnold explains to her:

Nothing was ready. . . . If there had been a war it would have been a repetition of 1870, with London for Sedan, and they knew it. No horses, reduced regiments, a crowd of half-trained men pitted against a nation which has been ready for war any day in the last years! . . . It's all wrong, Nora, all wrong! We have grown too easy-going, too fond of smooth comfort. . . . We can't see that the world has changed, that we have to face a race that has all our virtues in their youth and strength — all our tenacity, all our bulldog purpose, all our old stoicism.[107]

Nora's torn loyalties are resolved by her mother, in a passage closely similar to E. M. Forster's celebrated "Rainbow Bridge" section in *Howards End*:

"You will go back," says her mother, "and bravely take up the work which lies before you — the work of reconciliation. You will fight the unhappy influence of the narrow-hearted fools and braggarts who have helped to bring catastrophe into your life and upon whole nations . . . you will help build the bridge between the country of your birth and the country of your adoption."[108]

Forster's "Rainbow Bridge" "that should connect the prose in us with the passion," the English and the Germans, the Wilcoxes and the Schlegels, suggests that reconciliation was possible. "Only connect! That was the whole of her [Margaret Schlegel's] sermon. Only connect the prose and the passion, and both will be exalted, and human love will be seen at its highest."[109]

This Wagnerian link between German idealism and English materialism symbolizes in *Rheingold* the temporary victory of love over gold. Yet as Firchow has shown, it also corresponds to Bifrost in the Norse Myths, the scene of apocalyptic destruction on the judgment day.[110] In *Howards End* the destruction of the present race of gods at Bifrost is symbolized by the destruction of the Wilcox dynasty, and the reader is left with a slight hope for a new race in the child of Helen Schlegel and Leonard Bast. In *Dividing Waters* war is averted, and Nora returns to Berlin as an Isolde figure, in whose arms her husband dies: "Love had pronounced the last, triumphant word, and the sea between them had rolled away for ever."[111]

Conclusion

Although both are concerned with perceptions of the supposed enemy, the two types of popular novel considered in these pages, the invasion novel and the mixed-marriage novel, offer two different resolutions to the Anglo-German conflict. The invasion novel, strictly a male preserve on both sides, proposes that only strength of arms and national preparedness could repel the imminent attack from the other side. In this battle of words, both sides measure strength against strength, ship against ship, in a conflict of two avowedly incompatible systems. In the mixed-marriage novel, by contrast, neither side is granted an absolute monopoly of virtue, and the possibility of reconciliation is held open to the very end. Significantly, the principal influences for good in these novels are female: Ruth Wilcox and Margaret Schlegel in *Howards End*, the two mothers in *Dividing Waters* and *Her Husband's Country*. In all the mixed-marriage novels female frailty in some way threatens male superiority and the empty concepts of honor and of national pride.

While it is certain that the invasion novels actually encouraged the war psychosis on both sides of the Channel, there is little evidence that the novels of reconciliation had any effect as an antidote. The "Rainbow Bridge" proved a chimera, and Bifrost revealed itself as the scene of terrible destruction.

Notes

[1] Hermann Kellermann, *Der Krieg der Geister* (Weimar: A. Duncker, 1915), 64–68. For accounts of the propaganda war, see: Cate Haste, *Keep the Home Fires Burning: Propaganda in the First World War* (London: Allen Lane, 1977); Kellermann, above; and Klaus Bohme, ed., *Aufrufe und Reden deutscher Professoren im Ersten Weltkrieg* (Stuttgart: Reclam, 1975).

[2] H. G. Wells, "The Sword of Peace," *Daily Chronicle*, August 7, 1914.

[3] H. G. Wells, "The War of the Mind," *The Nation*, August 29, 1914.

[4] Ford Madox Hueffer, "High Germany — 1: How it Feels to be Members of Subject Races," *The Saturday Review* 112 (September 30, 1911): 421–22; "High Germany — 2: Utopia," ibid. (October 7, 1911): 454–56.

[5] Peter Edgerly Firchow, *The Death of the German Cousin: Variations on a Literary Stereotype, 1890–1920* (London and Toronto: Associated University Presses, 1968), 94. Firchow's work was an important model and stimulus for this text.

[6] Ford Madox Hueffer, *Between St Dennis and St George* (London: Hodder & Stoughton, 1915), 32–33.

[7] Cecil Chesterton, *The Prussian Hath Said in His Heart* (London: Chapman & Hall, 1914), 129–30.

[8] John Cowper Powys, *The War and Culture* (New York: Arnold Shaw, 1914; repr., London: Village Press, 1975), 46.

[9] Arnold Bennett, *Liberty: A Statement of the British Case* (London: Hodder & Stoughton, 1914), 44.

[10] Stefan Zweig, *Die Welt von Gestern* (Stockholm: Bermann-Fischer Verlag, 1944), 268. Zweig also offers an amusing account of Lissauer's attempt to volunteer in 1914: "Als dann der Krieg ausbrach, war es sein erstes, hinzueilen in die

Kaserne und sich als Freiwilliger zu melden. Und ich kann mir das Lachen der Feldwebel und Gefreiten denken, als diese dicke Masse die Treppe heraufkeuchte. Sie schickten ihn sofort weg. Lissauer war verzweifelt" (ibid., 267 Then when war did break out, the first thing he did was rush to the barracks to volunteer. And I can just imagine the sergeants and corporals laughing as this podgy figure panted up the stairs. They immediately sent him away. Lissauer in despair).

[11] Ernst Lissauer, "Haßgesang gegen England" (1914), quoted in Kellermann, *Krieg der Geister*, 461–62. For a contemporary appreciation of Lissauer's verse, see Benno Diederich, "Ernst Lissauer, ein Lyriker unserer Zeit," *Preußische Jahrbücher* 175 (July–September 1914): 193–224.

[12] See Waldeyer and Erdberg, eds, *Deutsche Reden in schwerer Zeit*, 3 vols. (Berlin: Carl Heymanns Verlag, 1915). Particularly interesting are the sections on Hans Delbrück, "Über den kriegerischen Charakter des deutschen Volkes," 1:47–74; on Alois Riehl, "1813 — Fichte — 1914," 1:191–210; on Franz von Liszt, "Von der Nibelungentreue," 1:325–50; on Alois Brandl, "Byron im Kampf mit der englischen Politik und die englische Kriegslyrik von Heute," 2:209–40; Friedrich Meinecke, "Deutsche Kultur und Machtpolitik im englischen Urteil," 3:67–94; and Ernst Troeltsch, "Der Kulturkrieg," 3:207–50.

[13] Richard Dehmel, "An meine Kinder," *Berliner Tageblatt*, October 9, 1914.

[14] Werner Sombart, *Händler und Helden: Patriotische Besinnungen* (Leipzig: Duncker & Humblot, 1915), 4.

[15] Sombart, *Händler und Helden*, 65.

[16] See, for example, Powys, *War and Culture*, 57: "There was indeed something that Nietzsche hated more even than Christian morality, and that was this very 'Philistine Culture' which modern German arms are seeking to force upon the world." See also: J. A. Cramb, *Germany and England* (London: John Murray, 1914), 75, on the animosity between Treitschke and Nietzsche.

[17] Sombart, *Händler und Helden*, 56. Subsequent references to this work are cited in the text using the page number alone.

[18] Anon., "Ein englisches Tagebuch von Theodore Fontane," *Die Neue Rundschau* 25 (1914), 1385. On the question of stereotypes, see also: Günther Blaicher, "Zur Entstehung und Verbreitung nationaler Stereotypen in und über England," *Deutsche Vierteljahrsschrift für Literaturwissenschaft und Geistesgeschichte* 51, no. 4 (1977): 549–74.

[19] Chesterton, *The Prussian Hath Said in His Heart*, 75–76.

[20] Wilhelm Dibelius (1914), quoted by Wolfgang J. Mommsen, "Zur Entwicklung des Englandbildes der Deutschen seit dem Ende des 18. Jahrhunderts," in *Studien zur Geschichte Englands und der deutsch-britischen Beziehungen*, ed. Lothar Kettenacker, Manfred Schlenke, and Helmut Seier (Munich: Wilhelm Fink Verlag, 1981), 385.

[21] I. F. Clarke, *Voices Prophesying War: 1763–1984* (London: Oxford UP, 1966), 138.

[22] George Chesney, "The Battle of Dorking," *Blackwood's Magazine*, May 1871, quoted in Clarke, *Voices Prophesying War*, 34. Chesney's text was also published as

a book in the same year: George Chesney, *The Battle of Dorking: Reminiscences of a Volunteer* (Edinburgh: Blackwood, 1871).

[23] Chesney, "Battle of Dorking," in Clarke, *Voices Prophesying War*, 34.

[24] Quoted in Gordon A. Craig, *Germany, 1866–1945* (Oxford: Clarendon, 1978), 247.

[25] Quoted in Haste, *Home Fires Burning*, 8.

[26] Erskine Childers, *The Riddle of the Sands* (23rd ed., London: Sidgwick & Jackson, 1946), viii. Subsequent references to this work will be given in the text using the page number alone.

[27] Childers, *Riddle*, 289: "Is it not becoming patent that the time has come for training all Englishmen systematically either for the sea or for the rifle?"

[28] Quoted in Haste, *Home Fires Burning*, 11.

[29] See Clarke, *Voices Prophesying War*, 149, 152–53.

[30] William Le Queux, *The Invasion of 1910* (London: Eveleigh Nash, 1906), 542.

[31] Rowland Thirlmere, *The Clash of Empires*, trans. as *Der Zusammenprall der Weltmächte* (Berlin: Verlag von Karl Curtius, 1907).

[32] P. G. Wodehouse, *The Swoop! or How Clarence saved England* (London: Alston Rivers, 1909), 21.

[33] Wodehouse, *The Swoop!*, 42. One is reminded of John Betjeman's poem "Slough," beginning "Come friendly bombs and fall on Slough." See John Betjeman, *Collected Poems* (London: John Murray, 1958), 21.

[34] Wodehouse, *The Swoop!* preface, signed: "P. G. Wodehouse, The Bomb-Proof Shelter, London W."

[35] See, for example, Fritz Fischer, *Germany's Aims in the First World War* (London: Chatto & Windus, 1967); James Joll, *1914: The Unspoken Assumptions* (London: Weidenfeld & Nicolson, 1968); Fritz Fischer, *War of Illusions: German Policies from 1911 to 1914* (London: Chatto & Windus, 1971); Volker Berghahn, *Germany and the Approach of War in 1914* (London: Macmillan, 1973); Paul Kluke, *Außenpolitik und Zeitgeschichte* (Wiesbaden: Steiner Verlag, 1974); James Joll, "War Guilt 1914: A Continuing Controversy," in *Aspekte der deutsch-britischen Beziehungen im Laufe der Jahrhunderte*, ed. Paul Kluke and Peter Alter (Stuttgart: Klett-Cotta, 1978), 60–80; Bernd Faulenbach, *Ideologie des deutschen Weges* (Munich: C. H. Beck, 1980); and Geoff Eley, *Reshaping the German Right: Radical Nationalism and Political Change after Bismarck* (New Haven and London: Yale UP, 1980).

[36] Quoted in Samuel Hynes, *The Edwardian Turn of Mind* (Princeton, NJ and London: Princeton UP, Oxford UP, 1968), 46.

[37] H. G. Wells, *The World Set Free* (1914; repr. London & Glasgow: Collins, 1956), 101.

[38] Hynes, *Edwardian Turn of Mind*, 51.

[39] See Craig, *Germany, 1866–1945*, 246.

[40] See Craig, *Germany, 1866–1945*, 247.

[41] A. J. P. Taylor, "The Boer War," in *Essays in English History* (Harmondsworth, UK: Penguin, 1976), 182–83.

[42] Bruno Berger and Heinz Rupp, eds., *Deutsches Literatur-Lexikon* (Bern and Munich: Francke Verlag, 1968), 1, 563.

[43] Karl Bleibtreu, *Geschichte der englischen Litteratur in der Renaissance und Klassicität* (Leipzig: Wilhelm Friedrich, 1887), iii.

[44] Bleibtreu, *Englische Litteratur*, vi.

[45] Bleibtreu, *Englische Litteratur*, 577. Interestingly, Bleibtreu cited in this context the Waterloo Lectures by Colonel Charles Chesney, a relative, perhaps, of Sir George Chesney of Dorking fame.

[46] Karl Bleibtreu, *Bur und Lord* (Heilbronn: Eugen Salzer, 1900), 1.

[47] Anon., "Englische Literatur," *Preußische Jahrbücher* 107 (January-March 1902): 329. For other negative responses to Kipling, see also "Englischer Literaturbericht," ibid. 102 (October–December 1900): 548–49; and "Englische Literatur," ibid. 104 (April–June 1901): 538–39.

[48] Karl Bleibtreu, *Der Militarismus im 19. Jahrhundert* (Berlin: Verlag Aufklärung, 1901), 56.

[49] Wilhelm II, in J. C. G. Röhl, *Kaiser, Hof und Staat* (Munich: Beck, 1987), quoted in *Die Zeit*, September 4, 1987.

[50] Berghahn, *Approach of War*, 29.

[51] Craig, *Germany, 1866–1945*, 309.

[52] Hans Delbrück, "Zukunftskrieg und Zukunftsfriede," *Preußische Jahrbücher* 96, no. 11 (May 1899): 228–29.

[53] Figures from Geoff Eley, *Reshaping the German Right*, 102.

[54] Graf Bernstorff, *Unsere blauen Jungen* (Berlin: W. Paulis Nachf., 1899), 149.

[55] Ibid., 164.

[56] Ibid, 175. Bernstorff continued to write similar nautical nonsense right up to the outbreak of war. In *Ran an den Feind* (Leipzig: C. S. Amelings Verlag, 1913), he is still described as a "Korvettenkapitän a.D.," a lack of promotion that suggests that he was as bad at sailoring as he was at writing.

[57] Hans Delbrück, "Deutschland in der Weltpolitik: Der Krieg," *Preußische Jahrbücher* 116 (April–June 1904): 375–83.

[58] William Le Queux, *Die Invasion von 1910*, trans. Traugott Tamm (Berlin: Concordia Deutsche Verlags-Anstalt, 1906), 271.

[59] Le Queux, *Die Invasion von 1910*, 272.

[60] On relations between Germany and America at this time, see Reiner Pomerin, *Der Kaiser und Amerika: Die USA in der Politik der Reichsleitung, 1890–1917* (Cologne: Bohlau, 1986).

[61] Seestern (Ferdinand Grautoff), *"1906" — Der Zusammenbruch der alten Welt*, 17th ed. (Leipzig: Dieterich'sche Verlagsbuchhandlung, 1907), 41.

[62] Seestern, *"1906,"* 163.

[63] Seestern (Ferdinand Grautoff), *Armageddon 190—* (translation of Seestern, *"1906" — Der Zusammenbruch der alten Welt*; London: Kegan Paul, Trench, Trubner & Co., 1907), vi.

[64] Karl von Bruchhausen, *Der kommende Krieg: Eine Studie über die Militarische Lage Deutschlands* (Berlin: Pan-Verlag, 1906).

[65] Karl Bleibtreu, *Die Offensiv-Invasion gegen England: Eine Phantasie* (Berlin: Verlag von Schall und Rentel, 1908), 3.

[66] Bleibtreu, *Die Offensiv-Invasion*, 8.

[67] Bleibtreu, *Die Offensiv-Invasion*, 70. Bleibtreu developed this conviction at length in a subsequent novel: *Weltbrand* (Berlin, Schwetschke & Sohn, 1912).

[68] Hans Delbrück, "Politische Korrespondenz," *Preußische Jahrbucher* 133 (July–September 1908): 376.

[69] Excubitor, "Sea and Air Command: Germany's New Policy," *The Fortnightly Review*, new series 1007 (1 May 1913): 889.

[70] Rudolf Martin, *Das Zeitalter der Motorluftschiffahrt* (Leipzig: Theod. Thomas, 1907).

[71] Rudolf Martin, *Kaiser Wilhelm II. und König Eduard VII.* (Berlin: Verlag Dr. Wedekind, 1907), 62. Other books by Martin on similar themes are *Berlin-Bagdad: Das deutsche Weltreich im Zeitalter der Luftschiffahrt, 1910–1931* (Stuttgart and Leipzig: Deutsche Verlags-Anstalt, 1907); and *Deutschland und England: Ein offenes Wort an den Kaiser* (Hanover: A. Sponholtz, 1908).

[72] Martin, *Kaiser Wilhelm II. und König Eduard VII.*, 63.

[73] Maurus, *Ave Caesar! Deutsche Luftschiffe im Kampfe um Marokko* (Leipzig: Dieterich'sche Verlagsbuchhandlung, 1909), 14.

[74] Ewald Gerhard Seeliger, *Englands Feind: Der Herr der Luft* (Wiesbaden: Westdeutsche Verlagsgesellschaft, 1910), 193.

[75] Violet Hunt and Ford Maddox Hueffer, *Zeppelin Nights* (London: John Lane, 1916), 2. Quoted in Firchow, *The Death of the German Cousin*, 98.

[76] Firchow, *Death of the German Cousin*, 98.

[77] Karl Bleibtreu, *Deutschland und England*, 2nd ed. (Berlin: Karl Curtius, 1909), 43.

[78] Rudolf Straß, *Seine englische Frau* (Stuttgart and Berlin: J. Cotta'sche Buchhandlung, 1913).

[79] Martin Havenstein, "Notizen und Besprechungen," *Preußische Jahrbücher* 155 (January–March 1914): 162–63.

[80] See: E. M. Forster, "Recollections of Nassenheide," *The Listener* (January 1, 1959), 12–14.

[81] I. A. R. Wylie, *My German Year* (London: Mills & Boon, 1910), 15.

[82] Jerome K. Jerome, *Three Men on the Bummel* (Harmondsworth, UK: Penguin, 1983), 198.

[83] Ferdinand Tönnies, "Glückliches England," *Die Neue Rundschau* 19, no. 3 (March 1908): 458.

[84] D. H. Lawrence, *Mr. Noon* (London: Grafton, 1986), 231.

[85] I. A. R. Wylie, *Towards Morning* (London: Cassell, 1918), 9.

[86] Sybil Spottiswoode, *Marcia in Germany: An Indiscreet Chronicle* (London: Heinemann, 1908), 21.

[87] I. A. R. Wylie, *Dividing Waters* (London: Mills & Boon, 1911), 17.

[88] Katherine Mansfield, *In a German Pension* (Harmondsworth, UK: Penguin, 1985), 10.

[89] Sybil Spottiswoode, *Her Husband's Country* (London: Heinemann, 1911), 221–23.

[90] I. A. R. Wylie, *Eight Years in Germany* (London: Mills & Boon, 1914), 102.

[91] Spottiswoode, *Marcia in Germany*, 23.

[92] Sybil Spottiswoode, *Hedwig in England* (London: Heinemann, 1909), 25.

[93] Alexander von Peetz, *England und der Kontinent* (Vienna and Leipzig: Carl Fromme, 1909), quoted in *Preußische Jahrbücher* 160, no. 2 (May 1915): 326.

[94] Rupert Brooke, "The Old Vicarage, Grantchester," in *The Poetical Works of Rupert Brooke* (London: Faber & Faber, 1950), 67 and 141.

[95] Wylie, *Dividing Waters*, 94.

[96] Spottiswoode, *Her Husband's Country*, 119.

[97] Lawrence, *Mr. Noon*, 223.

[98] Wylie, *Dividing Waters*, 82.

[99] Wylie, *Dividing Waters*, 132.

[100] Wylie, *Eight Years in Germany*, 183.

[101] Spottiswoode, *Hedwig in England*, 139–40. For a surprisingly thoughtful discussion of the German duel and of the student "Mensur," see Jerome K. Jerome, *Three Men on the Bummel*, 182–88.

[102] Wylie, *Dividing Waters*, 138.

[103] Spottiswoode, *Her Husband's Country*, 215–16.

[104] Spottiswoode, *Her Husband's Country*, 260–61. Exactly the same message was delivered to Ingeborg, the un-English sounding Englishwoman who became a German pastor's wife in Elizabeth von Arnim's novel. At their first meeting her mother-in-law was dressed absolutely plainly, with no decoration, and her hair drawn tightly back: "Ingeborg suddenly felt that she herself was a thing of fal-lals, — a showy thing, bedizened with a white collar and hat she had till then considered neat, but that she now knew for a monstrous piece of frippery crushed on to insufficiently pinned-up hair" (Elizabeth von Arnim, *The Pastor's Wife* (London: Virago, 1987), 135).

[105] Spottiswoode, *Her Husband's Country*, 255. In fact the "Kulturpolitiker" in Germany had long recognized the superiority of English domestic architecture and design over its German counterpart, and the architect Hermann Muthesius was posted to London for seven years between 1896 and 1903 as "Attaché für Architektur" at the German Embassy. The fruits of his studies were published in three volumes as *Das englische Haus* (Berlin: Wasmuth, 1904).

[106] Wylie, *Eight Years in Germany*, 242.

[107] Wylie, *Dividing Waters*, 380–81.

[108] Wylie, *Dividing Waters*, 365.

[109] E. M. Forster, *Howards End* (Harmondsworth, UK: Penguin, 1985), 189.

[110] See Firchow, *Death of the German Cousin*, 72.

[111] Wylie, *Dividing Waters*, 411.

2: Perversion and Pestilence:
D. H. Lawrence and the Germans

Helena Ragg-Kirkby

I AM MAD WITH RAGE . . . I would like to kill a million Germans — two million."[1] D. H. Lawrence's somewhat negative view of our European neighbors is probably quite typical of the average Englishman during the years leading up to the First World War. However, what is perhaps not quite so typical is that he based his view on firsthand experience of German militarism rather than on mere stereotypes. This experience he gained from his 1912 visit to Metz with Frieda Weekley, with whom he was having a clandestine affair, and whose family still lived there. Their "just good friends" cover was (unsurprisingly) blown when Lawrence wrote to Weekley's husband, Professor Ernest Weekley, revealing all — and when he was almost arrested as an English spy:[2]

> Mrs Weekley and I were lying on the grass near some water — talk-
> ing — and I was moving round an old emerald ring on her finger,
> when we heard a faint murmur in the rear — a German policeman.
> There was such a to-do. It needed all the fiery Baron von Richt-
> hofen's influence — and he is rather influential in Metz — to rescue
> me. They vow I am an English officer. (*TI*, xxvi)

Lawrence soon turned this experience (on May 7, the day before he had to leave Metz "quick"[3]) into the subject of a newspaper article, "How a Spy is Arrested" (like all sensible writers, he also recycled it in *Mr Noon*). He then sent the essay, along with three others ("The English and the Germans,"[4] "French Sons of Germany," and "Hail in the Rhine-Land") to Walter de la Mare,[5] in the hope that he would be able to place them for him. Lawrence explained in the covering letter: "I wonder if any of this stuff . . . would be any good to the *Westminster*, or if anybody else would have it. I don't know the papers a bit . . . would you mind offering the ar-ticles to somebody you think probable. I am reduced to my last shilling again . . . so I must work" (*TI*, xxvi). De la Mare did in fact manage to place three of the articles with the *Westminster Gazette*, but the fourth ("How a Spy is Arrested") was rejected by the paper's editor, John Alfred Spender, "as being too violently anti-German."[6] "French Sons of Germany" and "Hail in the Rhineland" appeared in the *Westminster* in August 1912, although, in true newspaper-editor style, Spender ultimately failed to use "The English and the Germans" despite having put it through the typesetting process.[7]

So are the essays really so warmongeringly anti-German — or was the *Westminster Gazette* getting in a stew over nothing? Perhaps Lawrence didn't study his market carefully enough. The paper was, after all, not likely to look favorably on his piece: it was "more or less the accredited organ" of parliamentary Liberalism,[8] and was "campaigning for understanding of the German point of view,"[9] criticizing other newspapers for stoking up the flames of Anglo-German discord, and quoting at length from Stein's entente campaign as well as including long reviews of German books (one of which appeared in the column next to "French Sons of Germany").[10] The *Gazette*'s arguable over-sensitivity aside, it is easy to imagine how Lawrence's essays could be seen as provocative to say the least. Remarks in "The English and the Germans" about a possible German attack could no doubt be regarded as scaremongering if not warmongering, and the portrayal of German officiousness in "How a Spy is Arrested" could, as Paul Eggert suggests, be read as "the irresponsible endorsement of a stereotype" (*TI*, xxx).

Let us look in more detail at the two offending essays. "The English and the Germans" gets off to a hostile start: watching the soldiers, Lawrence notices — or chooses to focus on — their sloppiness, thickness, and lack of height; in other words, the way in which they are different from *our* proud and upstanding men of honor:

> I am tired of German soldiers.
>
> They are not like English soldiers . . . As we watch our soldiers go flaunting down the street, we feel the pride of the human creature. With the German soldiers it is not so. There marched past me this morning a squad of men with stumpy helmets and trousers bagging over their boots, short, thick men, and they looked for all the world like a division of bears shuffling by. (*TI*, 7)

"In the German soldier," he carries on, "the worst national characteristics seem most pronounced — lack of intuition, clumsy sentimentality, affectation; a certain clumsiness of soul, a certain arrogance of stupidity, a certain stupid cleverness" (*TI*, 10). What's more, his hostility is not confined to the military. No, Lawrence's scathing comments apply to the Germans in general: they are "fat and untroubled" (*TI*, 8); they may be better-looking than Nottingham's miners, but "I can't find anywhere among them the fine faces of men that are to be seen in the streets at home" (*TI*, 8); and his own countrymen are, he says, "superior in soul" (*TI*, 10). It is, he continues, "the lack of wonder that spoils the German" (*TI*, 8), while the English, for their part, need to reinforce their souls rather than their fleet to make them safe from "any German attack" (*TI*, 9). For Lawrence, the difference between England and Germany is that between civilization and brutality — Germany "is *not* a civilised nation" (*TI*, 10); and "why should the more brutal nation in the end always conquer the highly civilised nation?" (*TI*, 9).

If "The English and the Germans" would hardly have been contributing to the *Westminster Gazette*'s international peacekeeping mission, "How a Spy is Arrested" doesn't exactly help the European cause either. Here we find Lawrence and Frieda (disguised in this instance as "I" and "Anita") lying in the grass — when along comes a uniformed German who attempts to arrest them for two heinous crimes: being on forbidden land, and being English spies.[11] Lawrence's anger manifests itself in a vicious attack on the whole German spirit of *Pflicht* and *Verbot*: "'Verboten!' One is not in Germany five minutes, without seeing or hearing this word: only it is usually, 'Strengstens verboten'" (*TI*, 12; strictly forbidden), he rages, as he looks at the "young, officious fool" (*TI*, 13) playing his "babyish game of authority" (*TI*, 14). Moreover, his anger is directed not only at this particular interfering busybody but at the whole of the Germany he represents: "one felt the vast, stupid mechanism of German officialdom behind him" (*TI*, 14). Anita herself admits that she ought to have known her dreadful countrymen better: "I ought to know these German officials — every tiny scrap of a fellow thinks himself as important as the Kaiser" (*TI*, 15). Even Anita's father is characterized as the archetypal humorless German: he doesn't laugh when the incident is recounted to him and, as Lawrence remarks, is typical of the whole nation: "these fussy little things seem important to them, instead of comic" (*TI*, 15).

"French Sons of Germany" and "Hail in the Rhineland," for their part, *were* published — though that by no means implies that Lawrence relaxed his anti-German stance. From the outset of "French Sons" he declares himself to be firmly on the side of all things French in Metz, before we find the inevitable German officer looking at him "coldly and inquisitively" (*TI*, 17). Lawrence's response seems to leave us in no doubt as to his feelings:

> I look at him with a "Go to the devil" sort of look, and pass along. I wonder to myself if my dislike of these German officers is racial, or owing to present national feeling, or if it is a temperamental aversion. I decide on the last. (*TI*, 17)

As in "The English and the Germans," the soldiers also come in for criticism: "Everywhere these short, baggy German soldiers, with their fair skins and rather stupid blue eyes!" (*TI*, 17), he complains. "I do not like German soldiers" (*TI*, 20).

Likewise, "Hail in the Rhineland" clearly conveys his dislike of all things German — though in a more ironic than aggressive manner. Walking to Nümbrecht, he and "Johanna" encounter an old man whose oxen are being plagued by flies. Johanna asks him if he can't help them, and Lawrence's suggestion is playful yet at the same time another attack on the culture in which everything is "streng verboten": "You could write a card and stick it between their horns, "Settling of flies strictly forbidden here" (*TI*, 22).

So, far from coming to understand Germany better during his stay there during 1912 and 1913, it seems that Lawrence discovered a new dislike of the country. Indeed, his travels around south Germany seem to have sparked off a narrative poem, set in Wolfratshausen, which he sent to Edward Garnett in 1912, "The soldier with bloody spurs," full of a sense of the cruelty of the German military, echoed a year later in *The Prussian Officer*.[12] As Ronald Gray puts it, Lawrence "instinctively recoiled both from the German nation and from the very atmosphere of Germany."[13] Even as late as 1924, he would still be writing about Germany in unambiguously negative terms — perhaps even anticipating the rise of Nazism. "Immediately you are over the Rhine, the spirit of place has changed," he remarks in "A Letter from Germany." "There is no more attempt at the bluff of geniality. . . . The moment you are in Germany, you know. It feels empty, and, somehow, menacing."[14] The sense of German menace persists throughout the entire "Letter": he writes of the "latent sense of danger, of silence, of suspension" which marks the return of "the ancient spirit of prehistoric Germany"; he is scared by the "silence . . . secrecy . . . stealth" of the "swarms of people," seeing the atmosphere as heralding a return "to the days of the silent forest and the dangerous, lurking barbarians."[15] "Something about the Germanic races is unalterable," he concludes. "White-skinned, elemental, and dangerous . . . the northern Germanic impulse is recoiling towards Tartary, the destructive vortex of Tartary."[16]

Let us return to the First World War period, though. It is all very well to see this warmongering attitude in Lawrence's own travel writings — but what of his fiction? After all, he was the one who warned us: "Never trust the artist. Trust the tale."[17] Would it have been just as likely to stir up anti-German sentiment in Britain? On the face of it, yes. Take *The Prussian Officer*. Published in 1914, it is the story of a sadistic Prussian officer who beats and humiliates his orderly to the point that the said orderly kills him before destroying himself too.[18] The officer, a Prussian aristocrat, is admittedly "handsome," with "amazing riding-muscles" (*PO*, 2) — but the emphasis is firmly on his unpleasantness: on his "full brutal mouth," the "cold fire" of his look, his "hostile and irritable" air (*PO*, 2), his eyes "sneering with restless contempt" (*PO*, 5). His relationship with his orderly, who is — rather like Kleist's puppet[19] — so full of "natural completeness in himself," so "free and self-contained" (*PO*, 3), serves to highlight his own Germanic "suppression" that is "always on the point of breaking out" (*PO*, 4) in his "tense, rigid body" (*PO*, 3). Furthermore, his German military bearing is expressed by his "rage" (*PO*, 4) and by the way he becomes "harsh and cruelly bullying, using contempt and satire" (*PO*, 5) — to such an extent that the orderly (whose perspective, incidentally, we are encouraged to share) fears his master is going "irritably insane" (*PO*, 5).

Similarly, *Mr Noon* does little to bridge the Anglo-German gap. True, it wasn't written until 1920, but it warrants consideration here, as many of the incidents fictionalized in it were taken from Lawrence's 1912 Metz visit.

The first ambassador of Germany we find in the text is Alfred, the Herr Professor. And what a typical German he is: "fretful," "restless and fidgetty," "petulant and fussy," "fussy, rather woe-begone," he "felt himself at some sort of disadvantage before the world, and so was often irritable and tiresome" (*MN*, 100).[20] What's more, he is a classically anally retentive German: his meanness is most terribly tested by Gilbert's unforgivable habit of taking too much coffee and honey: "He begrudged the Englishman his bigger share of coffee, and he almost wanted to snatch the honey dish off the table" (*MN*, 101). Gilbert Noon, for his part, represents typical, reliable, we-can-pull-it-all-together England: as the narrator remarks, Alfred "was one of those Germans who find the presence of an Englishman soothing and reassuring, seem to derive a certain stability from it" (*MN*, 100).

Alfred, at least, is humorous for all his "pettyfogging" (*MN*, 101). The military in Detsch (that is, Metz), on the other hand, are treated just as viciously in the novel as they are in the travel essays: Gilbert, for instance, watches the military parade asserting German superiority and ownership of the area, detesting the "peculiar assertive German callousness" (*MN*, 145). The whole of the "Detsch" chapter clearly brings out the problems Lawrence observed in Metz — in particular the French loathing of everything German, as well as his own sympathy with the French. Gilbert encounters a peasant-farmer and innkeeper, who is educating his children in France in order to avoid their being contaminated by the vile Germans, and he shares the man's feelings in a tirade of anti-German feeling:

> Gilbert sympathised sincerely. This rampant Germanism of Detsch was beginning to gall him: a hateful, insulting militarism that made a

man's blood turn to poison. It was so forcé, unnatural too. . . . It was an insulting display of militaristic insolence and parvenu imperialism. The whole thing was a presumption, a deliberate, insolent, Germanistic insult to everybody, even to the simpler Germans themselves. The spirit was detestably ill-bred, such a mechanical heel-clicking assumption of haughtiness without any deep, real human pride. When men of a great nation go a bit beyond themselves, and foster a cock-a-doodling haughtiness and a supercilious insolence in their own breasts, well, then they are asking for it, whoever they may be. (*MN*, 159–60)

The anti-German — warmongering? — mood persists in his fictionalization of his near-arrest in the same chapter. Here, the man ("soldier or police individual, whatever he was"; "a cunning, solid lump of a fellow," [*MN*, 167]) creeps towards them "with the loathsome exultant officiousness of all police or soldier individuals on duty, and of German specimens in particular," addressing the couple with "the foul sound of German officious insolence" (*MN*, 166) and "impertinent officiousness" (*MN*, 167), as he carries out his orders and does his duty. Even when he has let them go, the effect on Gilbert remains, and he develops an overpowering — one might even say Germanic — sense of guilt for existing: "the grating sound of officious, aggressive militarism was getting on his nerves and making him feel almost guilty of something — perhaps of being a mere civilian" (*MN*, 168). Unsurprisingly, he is glad to leave Detsch, "which place he hated with so deep a hatred, with all its uniforms and its *verbotens*" (*MN*, 172).

In order to escape, though, Gilbert is doomed to have a final encounter with German rules and regulations: he fails to pay his *Zuschlag* (supplementary fare), and an altercation ensues with a ticket-collector. Again, Gilbert's hostility towards the individual is couched as hostility towards his German-ness: his accent is "like the tearing of badly made calico," as he stands there "snarling and flourishing in the pretty Prussian official manner in front of the offender's nose" (*MN*, 183); and he represents the "system — wonderful system" (*MN*, 183) that Germany is so obsessed with. Indeed, Gilbert rages, the whole of Germany bows down before the gods of order, system, and officialdom:

Dear Gilbert mused on the god-almighty ferocity of Prussian officials. Nay, the shabbiest porter was an olympic — or at least a Wotan God — once he had put his holy cap on. And all the mere civilians grovelled before a peak-official-cap as before some nimbus. What a funny world! They saw in it the symbol of Germanic Over-Allness. (*MN*, 184)

For good measure, he ends with an attack on Goethe, saying that what he needed was "a good kick in [the] toga-seat" (*MN*, 184).

Goethe takes me neatly onto the next victim of Lawrence's warmongering stance: German literature. True: "Über allen Gipfeln" was one of the poems that, so he said, meant most to him;[21] and he viewed Goethe as "pure male"[22] — a huge compliment in the Lawrentian scheme of things. But in a letter to Aldous Huxley, he called the great man of German literature a "grand pervert" (along with other luminaries such as Kant, Rousseau, and Louis XIV) for his falsification of the "phallic consciousness":

> I think *Wilhelm Meister* is amazing as a book of peculiar immorality, the perversity of intellectualised sex, and the utter incapacity for any *development* of contact with any other human being, which is particularly bourgeois and Goethean. Goethe *began* millions of intimacies, and never got beyond the how-do-you-do stage, then fell off into his own boundless ego. He perverted himself into perfection and God-likeness. But do do a book of the grand orthodox perverts. Back of them all lies ineffable conceit.[23]

But if Goethe fares badly in his perverted perfection and boundless ego, Thomas Mann fares even worse. In July 1913, as anti-German feeling in England was increasing ever more, Lawrence did little for Anglo-German literary relations when he wrote a piece for the *Blue Review* on his German contemporary, lambasting him for indulging in the "craving for form" currently sweeping Germany. Artists such as Mann, who don't "give themselves to life as well as to art," who are "afraid, or despise life" (and let's not forget that Life is one of Lawrence's pet topics) would, he claims, "ferment and become rotten" — and this is what has happened to poor Mann: "He is physically ailing, no doubt. But his complaint is deeper: it is of the soul."[24] Lawrence then starts digging around in *Der Tod in Venedig* to prove that this sickness is a part of Mann's entire *Weltanschauung* (in the process failing, unfortunately, to distinguish between Mann and Aschenbach), concluding:

> It [*Der Tod in Venedig*] is absolutely, almost intentionally, unwholesome. The man [Aschenbach? Or Mann himself? It is not clear] is sick, body and soul. He portrays himself as he is, with wonderful skill and art, portrays his sickness. And since any genuine portrait is valuable, this book has its place. It portrays one man, one atmosphere, one sick vision. . . . Thomas Mann seems to me the last sick sufferer from the complaint of Flaubert. The latter stood away from life as from a leprosy. Physical life is a disordered corruption, against which he can fight with only one weapon, his fine aesthetic sense, his feeling for beauty, for perfection, for a certain fitness which soothes him

and gives him an inner pleasure, however corrupt the stuff of life may be. There he is, after all these years, full of disgusts and loathing of himself, as Flaubert was, and Germany is being voiced, or partly so, by him.[25]

So the position seems pretty clear: Lawrence was a patent warmonger who did his utmost to reinforce all the stereotypes of Germany: *Ordnung*, *Pflicht*, brutality, petty-minded bureaucracy — not to mention its lack of Life. On occasion, he even treated his wife as "The Enemy": in a letter to E. M. Forster, he wrote that the kind of fate she was cut out for was to be killed by a bomb dropped by her own countrymen.[26]

But is it really that simple? No. For a start, Lawrence's attitude to the First World War *per se* was anything other than enthusiastic: he even embarked on an antiwar lecture tour with Bertrand Russell (though they then fell out due to "philosophical differences"). That doesn't mean he was a "pacifist" as such; indeed, he was no stranger to violence.[27] However, as Jeffrey Meyers argues, he was strongly opposed to the First World War, partly as a result of his "non-conformist heritage that taught him to think independently and to reject prevailing modes of thought."[28] His "pacifism" "was not religious or moral, but a commonsensical opposition to meaningless death."[29] And, while he rejected conscientious objection as "a kind of Christian turning-of-the-cheek, an outmoded asceticism,"[30] he saw himself as one of the architects of a new social order that had to emerge after the war.[31]

Lawrence's views are particularly clearly expressed in the essay "With the Guns," which was a direct response to the outbreak of the First World War on August 4, 1914. Only five days before, Lawrence had set out on a walking tour in the Lake District with three companions — and his initial reaction to the news was quite positive: "Then we came down to Barrow-in-Furness, and saw that war was declared. And we all went mad."[32] However, he was soon "very miserable about the war"[33] — and the result was the disturbing "With the Guns," in which he recalled the moment when he "followed the Bavarian army down the Isar valley" (*TI*, 81) in the autumn of 1913. It was published (with the byline "H. D. Lawrence") on the back page of the *Manchester Guardian* on August 18, 1914.[34]

In this essay, Lawrence's "misery about the war" expresses itself in a prophecy. Again, the Germans don't get off scot-free — he mentions the "hard, tearing, hideous voice of the German command" (*TI*, 81) — but his main emphasis is on the process of mechanized war rather than on the German enemy: "I could see what war would be like — an affair entirely of machines, with men attached to the machines as a subordinate part thereof, as the butt is the part of a rifle" (*TI*, 81). Watching the firing practice, Lawrence is particularly struck by the fact that the man who shoots has no way of knowing whether he "hit or missed, killed or did not touch" (*TI*, 82) — and this in turn leads him to contemplate the horror of man serving machine:

> What was there to feel? — only the unnatural suspense and suppression of serving a machine which, for ought we knew, was killing our fellow-men, whilst we stood there, blind, without knowledge or participation, subordinate to the cold machine. This was the glamour and glory of the war: blue sky overhead and living green country all around, but we, amid it all, a part in some insensate will, our flesh and blood, our soul and intelligence shed away, and all that remained of us a cold metal adherence to an iron machine. (*TI*, 82)

The essay ends on a grim note:

> But what is it all about? I cannot understand; I am not to understand. My God, why I am a man at all, when this is all, this machinery piercing and tearing?
> It is a war of artillery, a war of machines, and the men no more than the subjective material of the machine. It is so unnatural as to be unthinkable. Yet we must think of it. (*TI*, 83–84)

So it seems that Lawrence's objection was to the war itself rather than to "the Hun." But let's look more closely at his wartime attitude towards the Germans and at the specific remarks he made about the enemy. As Maddox remarks, England was generally characterized by "a prevailing hatred of all things German," and the war was "widely viewed as a consequence of German national characteristics such as subservience and aggressiveness which led its population docilely to follow the dictates of Prussian militarism"[35] — but this was a view that Lawrence explicitly rejected, declaring that he found the hatred of all things German positively distressing: "My chief grief and misery is for Germany — so far . . . I can't help feeling it a young and adorable country — adolescent — with the faults of adolescence," he wrote in the early days of the war.[36] He had no doubt that Germany should not and could not win it, "but they are a young, only adolescent, nation, and they don't know what to do with themselves."[37] Indeed, such was his dislike of the war as a whole that, as he wrote to Lady Cynthia Asquith in October 1915, it really made no difference to him who won it: "give the Germans England and the whole Empire, if they want it, so we may save the hope of a resurrection from the dead, we English, all Europe."[38]

What, though, of his fiction? After all, we've seen the overtly anti-German sentiments in *The Prussian Officer* and *Mr Noon*. But if we look at another story, written during the war and one of the four that directly deal with it, we see another perspective at work — one that throws into doubt that of "Lawrence-as-warmonger." "England, my England"[39] shows Lawrence being both antiwar and decidedly *not* anti-German — to such an extent that when he sent it to his London agent, J. B. Pinker,[40] he enclosed a letter saying "I send you a story, which England will not publish, I am afraid, but which America may" (*EME*, xxxii) (in fact, he was mistaken: the *English Review* published it in October 1915). In the 1915 version, Winifred (whose sexual interest in her husband Evelyn seems to have increased since he became a soldier) tries to tell him that he is now, in this new soldierly role, "one of the saviours of mankind" — but it falls on deaf ears:

> He listened to these things; they were very gratifying to his self-esteem. But he knew it was all cant. He was out to kill and destroy; he did not even want to be an angel of salvation. Some chaps might feel that way. He couldn't; that was all. All he could feel was that at best it was a case of kill or be killed. As for the saviour of mankind: well, a German was as much mankind as an Englishman. What are the odds? We're all out to kill, so don't let us call it anything else. (*EME*, 226)

How many other writers would have declared a German to be "as much mankind as an Englishman" in 1915? True, the 1915 version by no means excludes the brutality of the German soldiers, but this is matched by Evelyn's own actions: neither side is "right" — and both are victims of a mechanical process.

This is made even clearer in the 1920 revision of the story. Here, Evelyn, now called Egbert, sins on two counts: he rejects the war, and — even worse — contradicts all the prevailing anti-German sentiments. For him, Germany isn't worse than England — it's simply different:

> So when the war broke out his whole instinct was against it: against war. He had not the faintest desire to overcome any foreigners or to help in their death. He had no conception of Imperial England, and Rule Britannia was just a joke to him. He was a pure-blooded Englishman, perfect in his race, and when he was truly himself he could no more have been aggressive on the score of his Englishness than a rose can be aggressive on the score of its rosiness.
>
> No, he had no desire to defy Germany and to exalt England. The distinction between German and English was not for him the distinction between good and bad. It was the distinction between blue water-flowers and red or white bush-blossoms: just difference.[41] The difference between the wild boar and the wild bear. And a man was good or bad according to his nature, not according to his nationality.

Hardly the talk of a warmonger! What's more, even the stories that *do* quite explicitly criticize the Germans — and in particular the German military — aren't unambiguously anti-German. In fact, England also comes in for some fierce criticism. In "The English and the Germans," we read about the "coldness and indifference" of an Englishman's glance (*TI*, 7); the English are "stiff and brittle and unworkable" (*TI*, 8), "sad almost to despair" (*TI*, 8); the average Englishman "cares vitally for nothing whatsoever, except his own security in daily life" (*TI*, 8); it is our "own souls" that we need to deal with if we are to resist German attack (*TI*, 9); we are remarkable for our "mania for self-starvation" (*TI*, 9); and we may be civilized, but "what is the good of being noble and of doing nothing?" (*TI*, 9). Unlike those of the "healthy and lusty" Germans, our souls — and in particular those of our women — have "atrophied" (*TI*, 9). As for the German threat — what threat? It's all part of "this strange, perverted will to destroy ourselves, which is common everywhere in England" (*TI*, 10). The pro-German sentiments reach a peak towards the end of the essay: "the German nation has a warmth and generosity of living, like a full fire roaring, that makes us look very pale. They have none of our wavering, uncertain look about them" (*TI*, 10).[42] You could perhaps even suspect him of anti-English warmongering!

What of that other anti-German tract, *Mr Noon?* Again, the evidence isn't quite so clear-cut. Yes, we English may inhabit the "Islands of the blest" (*MN*, 97), but the narrator refuses (in a pre-echo of postmodernism, perhaps?) to capitulate to the "gentle reader's" desire to "browbeat" him into describing Gilbert's German accommodation as a scruffy brothel full of insalubrious characters: on the contrary, it's a comfortable, sunny room furnished in the Biedermeier style — it is even centrally heated! (*MN*, 98). What's more, this positive vision extends beyond the domestic interior to the whole of European geography. As he and Alfred stand on the mountain "surveying the world," Gilbert the proto-Europhile is struck by the beauty and glamour of the German landscape, by its vastness and sense of liberation (especially compared to the provincial English Midlands) — and by the way, it is part of a greater European whole:

> Many magical lands, many magical peoples, all magnetic and strange, uniting to form the vast patchwork of Europe. The glamorous vast multiplicity, all made up of differences, mediaeval, romantic differences, this seemed to break his soul like a chrysalis into a new life. (*MN*, 107)

This vista in turn leads him to reevaluate his feelings about England — to such an extent that he feels himself to have become "un-Englished":

For the first time he saw England from the outside: tiny, she seemed, and tight, and so partial. Such a little bit among all the vast rest. Whereas till now she had seemed all-in-all in herself. Now he knew it was not so. Her all-in-allness was a delusion of her natives. Her marvellous truths and standards and ideals were just local, not universal. They were just a piece of local pattern, in what was really a vast, complicated, far-reaching design. . . . His tight and exclusive nationality seemed to break down in his heart. He loved the world in its multiplicity, not in its horrible oneness, uniformity, homogeneity. He loved the rich and free variegation of Europe, the manyness. His old obtuseness, which saw everything alike, in one term, fell from his eyes and from his soul, and he felt rich. There were so many, many lands and peoples besides himself and his own land. And all were magically different, and it was so nice to be among many, to feel the horrible imprisoning oneness and insularity collapsed, a real delusion broken, and to know that the universal ideals and morals were after all only local and temporal. (*MN*, 107–8)

So let's look at the evidence again. Around the period of the First World War, Lawrence declared himself on the one hand to be implacably hostile to German bureaucracy, brutality, and even books — but at the same time, his writing and indeed his whole being was colored by German-ness. As Ronald Gray remarks: "Lawrence's relationship to Germany was more intimate *and* critical than that of any other English writer."[43] Let's not forget that he married a German at what was probably the most incendiary time to do so — and not any old German, but a cousin of the star of the German air force, the "Red Baron" (Baron Manfred von Richthofen) — a man so notorious that Frieda's family name led to her and Lawrence's expulsion from the Cornish resort of Zennor on the grounds that they were German spies. In addition to this, his novels are suffused with German words and concepts: *Women in Love*, for instance, focuses on the central concepts of "Blutbrüderschaft" (blood-brotherhood, which was of central importance *generally* to Lawrence) and "Wille zur Macht" (the will to power) — not to mention the "Glücksritter" desired by Gudrun;[44] and *The Rainbow*'s whole inspiration was arguably Germanic, its nudity, al fresco sex scenes and lesbianism being received rather badly in what Maddox calls the new atmosphere of "war-inspired English prudery."[45]

Moreover, we can't even take Lawrence's anti-Goethe and anti-Mann remarks as a sign of seriously, warmongeringly anti-German feeling. For the fact is that he was not exactly complimentary about his fellow writers in general, regardless of their nationality. Blake, for instance, was one of those "ghastly, obscene knowers"; H. G. Wells apparently thought he (Wells) was "the centre of the universe"; Proust was "too much water-jelly; Dostoyevsky was "a lily-mouthed missionary rumbling with ventral howls of derision and dementia"; and Chekhov was "a second-rate writer and a willy wet-leg."[46]

So: warmonger or peacemaker? English spy in Germany, or German spy in England? Traitor to the cause, or raiser of the British Standard abroad? Reactionary provincial miner's son, or forward-thinking proto-European? D. H. Lawrence is all of them at once. Perhaps what matters is something beyond what he and his novels explicitly say. And that is: in the era of the First World War, when German songs were banned, when having a German wife was as frowned upon as owning a dachshund, Germany's influence over Britain, for better or for worse, could not be eradicated, however much the spin-doctors of the day might have wanted to convince us.

Notes

[1] Letter of May 1915 to Lady Ottoline Morrell, cited in Brenda Maddox, *The Married Man: A Life of D. H. Lawrence* (London: Minerva, 1994), 207.

[2] For full details of Lawrence's visit to Metz and the events leading up to it, see *Twilight in Italy and Other Essays*, ed. Paul Eggert, 1994), in *The Cambridge Edition of the Letters and Works of D. H. Lawrence*, ed. James T. Boulton et al. (Cambridge UP, various dates), xxiii–xxvi. Henceforth referred to in the text of this essay as *TI*.

[3] *Twilight in Italy*, xxvi.

[4] Title editorially supplied by the *Cambridge Edition*.

[5] Heinemann's reader. He had also been arranging a proposed volume of Lawrence's poems.

[6] *Twilight in Italy*, xxvi. Lawrence expected at least one of the articles — probably "How a spy is arrested" — to cause trouble: in a letter of 9 May, he proclaimed: "I have written a newspaper article that nobody on earth will print, because it's too plain and straight. However, I don't care" (*Twilight in Italy*, xxvii).

[7] For details of the essays' fates, see *Twilight in Italy*, xxvi–xxix.

[8] Stephen Ross, *The Rise and Fall of the Political Press in Britain* (1984), ii 10. Quoted in *Twilight in Italy*, xxx.

[9] See Mark Kinkead-Weekes, *D. H. Lawrence: Triumph to Exile, 1912–1922* (Cambridge: Cambridge UP, 1996), 764–65 n. 30. See also *Twilight in Italy*, xxx.

[10] See *Twilight in Italy*, xxx.

[11] This incident apparently gave Lawrence "an instant and fierce antagonism to German militarism" (Maddox, *The Married Man*, 125).

[12] See Harry T. Moore, *The Priest of Love: A Life of D. H. Lawrence* (Harmondsworth, UK: Penguin, 1980), 231.

[13] Ronald Gray, *The German Tradition in Literature, 1871–1945* (Cambridge UP, 1965), 340.

[14] D. H. Lawrence, "A Letter from Germany," in *Selected Essays* (Harmondsworth, UK: Penguin, 1981), 175–76.

[15] "Letter from Germany," 178.

[16] "Letter from Germany," 178–79.

[17] Anthony Beal, ed., *D. H. Lawrence: Selected Literary Criticism* (London: Mercury, 1961), 297.

[18] Lawrence in fact took issue with the implications of the title given to the story by Edward Garnett (Lawrence had wanted to call it "Honour and Arms"): "DHL's angry exclamation "what Prussian Officer?" (*Letters*, 2:241) may refer to the fact that, although the captain is a Prussian and an officer, he is not serving in the Prussian army, which until the First World War was quite distinct from the Bavarian army: cross-postings between the two armies were very rare" (*The Prussian Officer and Other Stories*, ed. John Worthen, 1983, in *The Cambridge Edition of the Letters and Works of D. H. Lawrence*, 249); henceforth referred to in the text of this essay as *PO*.

[19] See *Über das Marionettentheater*.

[20] The abbreviation *MN* refers to *Mr Noon* (ed. Lindeth Vasey), in *The Cambridge Edition of the Letters and Works of D. H. Lawrence* (1984).

[21] Beal, *Selected Literary Criticism*, 6.

[22] Beal, *Selected Literary Criticism*, 71.

[23] Letter to Aldous Huxley, 27 March 1928, in *Selected Literary Criticism*, 148.

[24] Beal, *Selected Literary Criticism*, 261.

[25] Beal, *Selected Literary Criticism*, 264–65. Funnily enough, Lawrence had a taste of his own medicine when T. S. Eliot said he was "spiritually sick" — see *D. H. Lawrence: A Collection of Critical Essays* (New Jersey, Prentice-Hall, 1963), ed. Mark Spilka, 2.

[26] Quoted in Maddox, *The Married Man*, 207.

[27] Maddox, *The Married Man*, 235.

[28] Jeffrey Meyers, *D. H. Lawrence: A Biography* (London: Macmillan, 1990), 156.

[29] Meyers, *Lawrence: A Biography*, 158.

[30] Maddox, *The Married Man*, 215.

[31] Maddox, *The Married Man*, 216.

[32] Letter of January 31, 1915, cited in *Twilight in Italy*, xl.

[33] Letter of August 5, 1914, ii, 205; cited in *Twilight in Italy*, xl.

[34] See *Twilight in Italy*, xl–xli.

[35] Maddox, *The Married Man*, 191.

[36] Harry T. Moore, *The Priest of Love*, 266.

[37] Maddox, *The Married Man*, 191.

[38] Quoted in the introduction to *D. H. Lawrence: The Mortal Coil and Other Stories* (Harmondsworth, UK: Penguin, 1988).

[39] D. H. Lawrence, *England, My England and Other Stories*, ed. Bruce Steele, 1990, in *The Cambridge Edition of the Letters and Works of D. H. Lawrence.* Henceforth abbreviated in the text of this essay to *EME*.

[40] James Brand Pinker was D. H. Lawrence's agent from July 1914 to December 1919 — see *England, My England*, xxi.

[41] Elsewhere, the English and the Germans are not even necessarily different: "masses of English folk are identically the same as the Germans" (*Twilight in Italy*, 10).

[42] The other "too anti-German" essay, "How a Spy is Arrested," likewise shows Lawrence to be not entirely immune to the charms of the Germans, for all his carping. "The Germans have not yet lost the faculty for enjoying themselves simply and happily together," he observes at the outset (*Twilight in Italy*, 11).

[43] Gray, *German Tradition*, 340.

[44] Ronald Gray sees *Women in Love* as showing clear parallels to *Die Wahlverwandtschaften*, Nietzsche, Rilke, and even Hölderlin. See Gray, *German Tradition*, 341.

[45] See Maddox, *The Married Man*, 220. According to her, a Home Office memo suggests that the novel's suppression had as much to do with Lawrence marrying the enemy as anything else (ibid., 222).

[46] Richard Foster, "Criticism as Rage: D. H. Lawrence," in Spilka, *Critical Essays*, 152.

3: *"Und muß ich von Dante schweigen, zieht Italien gegen uns?"*: Carl Sternheim's Opposition to the First World War

Rhys W. Williams

THE QUOTATION IN MY TITLE — "And must I cease to speak of Dante if Italy marches against us?" — is taken from Carl Sternheim's adaptation of Friedrich Maximilian Klinger's drama *Das leidende Weib*. Its sentiment was to acquire a curious poignancy, in that when the play was written (October 3–18, 1914) Italy was not one of the belligerent powers. Nor indeed was Italy at war when the first private performance, in a Max Reinhardt production for the Kammerspiele des deutschen Theaters in Berlin, was permitted by the censor on March 31, 1916. But by the time the play was first performed for a public audience on October 30, 1916 the issue had only historical significance: on August 29, 1916 Italy had declared war on Germany.

The outbreak of war in August 1914 was a personal and professional disaster for Carl Sternheim. From 1911 onwards he had established a major literary reputation with his comedies *Die Hose, Bürger Schippel,* and *Der Snob,* in effective collaboration with Max Reinhardt. But his difficulties with the censor, initially on moral grounds, began to give him the reputation of a liability on the German stage, and this fact, combined with his decision to move to Brussels in 1912, made his position in 1914 highly precarious. His personal experiences in Belgium on the outbreak of hostilities were harrowing. Having set out for Germany from the family home, La Hulpe, south of Brussels, Sternheim was briefly arrested as a potential German spy and then kept in protective custody. He managed to persuade his captors of his credentials and then, after a series of frantic journeys, he and the family reached Germany via Holland. His encounter with the chauvinistic passions unleashed by the war precipitated a nervous collapse that contributed to his being rejected as unfit for military service in Düsseldorf on August 23, 1914, a procedure that was to be repeated frequently in the following years, thanks to repeated medical certification and brief stays in sanatoria. The family moved to Bad Homburg, not returning to Belgium until April 1916. It was not until December 1916 that the family was finally able to take up residence in the family home, and the German evacuation of Belgium less than two years later, again under appalling circumstances, marked a provisional end to Sternheim's residence in Belgium.[1] He was not to return there until 1928, after the breakdown of his marriage to Thea Sternheim, and it was in Brussels that he died in 1942.

The war radically disrupted Sternheim's professional career. His prewar difficulties with the censor made him suspect, and the polarization of intellectual life in Germany in 1914 found him consigned to the opponents of Germany's war aims. His problems with German nationalism began early in 1914. Four years previously he had published an essay in the periodical *Hyperion* on Vincent van Gogh that contained the phrase "mit dem aufrichtigen Ekel vor allem Deutschtum, das es längst nicht mehr ist"[2] (with honest disgust at all things German which have long ceased being so). This statement, unmistakably critical of German cultural values, had caused offense in 1910, and Hans von Weber, publisher of the offending article, had chosen to distance himself in a disclaimer inserted in the next issue of the journal. Sternheim, it seems, had mobilized his friends to go round the bookshops of Munich removing the disclaimer from all copies of the journal (6:465). The debate on Sternheim's un-German values resurfaced in 1914 in the Berlin press. Sternheim defended himself in the *Berliner Börsen-Courier,* glossing his statement with the words: "Ich beklage und verabscheue die Rohheit des ästhetischen Urteils in Deutschland, soweit es fremden Einflüssen erliegend, versnobt und nicht mehr deutsch sei" (6:18; I lament and reject the coarseness of aesthetic judgments in Germany to the extent that they are subject to foreign influences, snobbish, and no longer German). The formulation, with its emphasis on "versnobt," was not wholly unconnected with the fact that Sternheim, never one to miss the chance of some publicity, wanted to draw attention to the fact that his play *Der Snob* was at the start of a successful run in Berlin. The *Deutsche Tageszeitung* was not mollified and pursued him with increasing vigor. In a letter to Thea on December 7, 1914 he reported his immense relief that the newspaper had finally retracted its claims, contenting itself with the assertion that Sternheim was himself to blame because his German was so difficult to understand. Sternheim's relief was not unconnected with the fact that he was in Berlin to oversee the production of *Das leidende Weib,* a crucial theatrical venture for him, as his prewar comedies were unlikely to be performed. Thea's diary records in September 1914: "Die Leute des Deutschen Theaters sollen ihm schlankweg gesagt haben, seine Stücke seien nun auf mehrere Jahre für das Theater erledigt" (10/2: 1184[3]; the Deutsches Theater people have apparently said to him straight, that they will now not put on his plays for years to come).

Das leidende Weib is Sternheim's first major statement about the war. It illuminates the wide polarization of German intellectuals in response to the war, and offers a fascinating insight into a major political controversy surrounding the German Ambassador in London. That Sternheim was drawn towards adaptations is hardly surprising. Sheltering behind the claim that he was merely re-creating the work of others, he was better able to defend himself against censorship. Between 1914 and 1921 he adapted for the stage six literary works, five of which are from French literature, which he clearly elected to champion at a time when such commitment was tantamount to pacifism, if not outright disloyalty to Germany. Why Sternheim should have been inspired to adapt *Das leidende Weib* is unclear. He obviously felt that the play displayed thematic similarities to the current situation and he would have been aware of the recently published three-volume edition *Friedrich Maximilian Klingers dramatische Jugendwerke,* edited by Hans Berendt and Kurt Wolff, published by Ernst Rowohlt in 1912, his own publishers. But what is most striking about the adaptation is its dissimilarity to the original. Direct verbal borrowings are few: in all, only just over a hundred lines are directly borrowed in a play which has well over a thousand lines. In only five of the thirty-six scenes (act 2, scenes 1, 2, and 5, act 3, scene 10, and act 4, scene 6) are there substantial borrowings. It seems clear, therefore, that Sternheim's strategy was, in part, to mislead the reader (or at least the censor) into thinking that his play was more similar to Klinger's than it was and thus allay fears about its topicality. The plot, too, bears only a superficial resemblance to Klinger's. The main action of the Klinger play concerns the dilemma faced by the Ambassadress, who had previously been in love with Brand, an officer, but who had married the Ambassador in deference to her father's wishes. When she meets Brand again, she is still tormented by passion and its accompanying guilt. After Brand has killed Graf Louis, who was trying to blackmail her, the Ambassadress dies, a victim of stricken conscience. Brand stabs himself on her grave. Sternheim's version of *Das leidende Weib* is radically different in plot, structure, and frame of reference.

Its most significant feature is the transposition of the action to 1914: Dietrich von Brandt is given four brothers (all invented by Sternheim). Their clipped military jargon and the pervasive atmosphere of the officers' mess suggest parallels with Fritz von Unruh's *Offiziere* (1911) or Otto Erich Hartleben's *Rosenmontag* (1900), both of which explore the Prussian military ethos. Sternheim depicts Brandt as a conventional officer, burning to see action at the front, yet initially condemned to remain behind to train raw recruits and later convinced that it is his duty, as an officer and gentleman, to uphold a code of chivalry by remaining in the town to protect the Ambassadress from the unwelcome advances of Graf Louis.

It is the military ethos that supplies Brandt's inner conflict. Brandt's affair with the Ambassadress is sudden, brief, and passionate, motivated on her part by the knowledge that he is about to depart for certain death on the battlefield without having experienced the love of a woman. Their affair is witnessed by Louis, with whom Brandt first fights a duel, and whom he then murders. Between the third and fourth acts the Ambassadress confesses her infidelity to her husband, but privately affirms her continued love for Brandt. While her husband interprets her sudden illness as a token of her guilt, the audience is left in little doubt that she is brokenhearted at Brandt's departure. Brandt himself accepts a suicidal mission at the front and dies of his wounds. As far as the broader framework of the plot is concerned, Sternheim manages to suggest that he is having the best of both worlds. The willing self-sacrifice of Brandt's four brothers appears to uphold the Prussian values of 1914, and while Dietrich von Brandt himself has purely personal reasons for wishing to sacrifice himself, he does so in an act of patriotic service. The ultimate expression of individual self-fulfilment, the hallmark of Sternheim's plays after 1914, coincides with an act of nationalistic fervor. He was clearly hoping that the censor would be sympathetic enough about the nationalist sentiment and be persuaded to overlook any other subtleties.

A number of alterations to the original bear the stamp of topicality. Sternheim adapts a subplot involving two minor characters, Franz and Julie, to permit him to make some general observations on literature and nationalism. Julie is transformed into an actress of French nationality who is so carried away by the prevailing atmosphere of chauvinism that she is prepared to spurn the love of a German. Franz, who suffers this rebuff, becomes the mouthpiece of Sternheim's own opposition to the war. As "der zähe Verteidiger des Friedens" (act 2, 105; robust defender of the peace) he refuses to subordinate literary and intellectual values to current nationalistic prejudices: "Ich habe auf der Hofbühne Molière ebenso gespielt wie Schiller" (2:110; I have performed Molière on stage as much as Schiller). After Holbein and Dürer he extols the virtues of "die französischen Maler bis in unsere Tage" (2:110; French artists down to the present day) and he reads Stendhal with the same delight as Goethe's *Wahlverwandtschaften*. Not inappropriately, in view of the atmosphere of seduction and adultery, he has been discussing Tolstoy's *Anna Karenina* with the Princess and he wonders: "Und muß ich von Dante schweigen, zieht Italien gegen uns?" (2:113). Franz's literary and artistic tastes reflect Sternheim's commitment to a common European literary tradition. Both here and in his essays he kept faith with more broadly European cultural values. His continued allegiance, above all, to French literature was to be reflected throughout the war years; indeed, his championing of French literature became more strident as his opposition to the war grew. Thea

Sternheim, too, later published an article in *Die Aktion* on Tolstoy, an article which the editor Franz Pfemfert had refused to publish in February 1915, as Sternheim reports in a letter to his wife: "Weil man ihm einen Wink gegeben, die Zeitung würde dann verboten" (*Briefe*, 2:160; because he had been dropped a hint that the paper would then be banned).

A further topical reference is included in act 3 of *Das leidende Weib*. The Ambassador inquires of Blum whether he would be willing to add his name to an "Aufruf" (appeal): "Alle bedeutenden Männer des Landes versichern darin der Welt auf ihre Ehre, trotz gegenteiliger Behauptung ist der Deutsche kein Barbar" (In it, all the leading men of the country assure the world upon their honor that, despite assertions to the contrary, Germans are not barbarians). Blum's response, "Steht das ohne die Versicherung nicht einigermaßen fest?" prompts the Ambassador's retort: "Durch Goethe, Kant und den großen König nicht genug" (2:138–39; Is that not more or less the case without our needing this assurance? . . . Despite Goethe, Kant, and our great king, it is not enough). This refers to the infamous "An die Kulturwelt! Ein Aufruf," a manifesto defending Germany's war aims that appeared in the *Frankfurter Zeitung* on October 4, 1914, as well as in a number of major newspapers. *Die Aktion* reprinted it without commentary, but clearly with subversive intent, on 29 May 1915. The document, signed by ninety-three intellectuals, denied German responsibility for the war, denied that Germany had violated Belgian neutrality, denied that Belgian citizens had been intentionally killed, denied that Louvain had been destroyed, denied that the High Command had violated the laws of international justice, and asserted that any attack on German militarism was an attack on German culture. The declaration concluded with the statement: "Glaubt, daß wir diesen Kampf zu Ende kämpfen werden als ein Kulturvolk, dem das Vermächtnis eines Goethe, eines Beethoven, eines Kant ebenso heilig ist wie sein Herd und seine Scholle"[4] (Believe this! We shall pursue this struggle to its conclusion as a *Kulturvolk*, for whom Goethe, Beethoven, Kant are no less sacred than our hearths and homes). Among the signatories were Richard Dehmel, Herbert Eulenberg, Gerhart and Carl Hauptmann, Max Reinhardt, and Karl Vollmöller; the presence of the last two names highlights the desperate efforts made by the Deutsches Theater in Berlin to demonstrate commitment to the German cause and hence escape the worst repercussions of censorship.

The outbreak of war unleashed both an outburst of patriotic fervor and powerful anti-war sentiments. While many writers and intellectuals rushed to the defence of German war aims, others strove to assert their beliefs in the internationalism of culture and counter the bellicose nationalism of much of cultural life. The Declaration of Ninety-Three Intellectuals was only one manifestation of the polarization of cultural and political life. "Wir kannten sie ja, diese Welt des Friedens. . . . Gor und stank sie nicht von den Zersetzungsstoffen der Zivilisation. . . . Krieg! Es war Reinigung, Befreiung, was wir empfanden, und eine ungeheure Hoffnung."[5] (We knew it, of course, this world of peace. . . . Did it not brew and stink from the decaying acids of civilization? . . . War! What we sensed was purification, release, and an enormous surge of hope). Thomas Mann's words in his essay *Gedanken im Krieg,* written in August and September 1914, would have fallen largely on sympathetic ears. Heinrich Mann, by contrast, belonged to a group of writers who, by their silence, or by outspoken criticism of nationalist propaganda, laid themselves open to the charge of disloyalty to the nation in its hour of peril. In particular, the periodicals *Die Weißen Blätter* and *Die Aktion* provided a focus for anti-war sentiments.[6] It was in *Die Weißen Blätter* that Heinrich Mann's "Zola" essay appeared in November 1915, and here that Sternheim had published his short story *Busekow* in 1913. When René Schickele took over the editorship of *Die Weißen Blätter* in 1915, Sternheim became a regular contributor. Schickele published a counterblast to Thomas Mann's *Gedanken im Krieg* in *Die Weißen Blätter* in 1915; he elected in 1916 to move with his journal to Zurich in order to retain an editorial freedom that censorship threatened to limit severely in Germany. Franz Pfemfert, the editor of *Die Aktion,* adopted a rather different policy to circumvent censorship: he published, without editorial comment, extreme nationalistic utterances from the German press under the rubric "Ich schneide die Zeit aus" (Excerpting the times — they speak for themselves). Readers were left to draw their own conclusions. His editorial policy was to emphasize the internationalism of culture, as illustrated by the special numbers on culture in Russia, France, Britain, Belgium, Italy, Czechoslovakia, and Poland. He refused to accept contributions from anyone who was, in his opinion, a supporter of the war, even from those who had come to see the futility of war after a period of initial enthusiasm. Any contributor whose work appeared in *Die Aktion* after August 1914 may therefore be deemed to have been an opponent of the war. That Sternheim was acceptable to Pfemfert as a contributor gives a clear indication of his anti-war position.

Das leidende Weib was also a defense of a much-maligned public figure in 1914. As contemporary reviewers hinted, after the play's belated release from censorship in 1916, the Ambassador is modeled on a contemporary figure, Karl Max, Prince Lichnowsky, who was German Ambassador in London from 1912 to 1914 and had made strenuous efforts to prevent the outbreak of war. When he returned to Germany in 1914 he had to contend with the widespread assumption that he was to blame for Germany's involvement in a war of encirclement. It was generally assumed that Lichnowsky had misled the German Foreign Office by implying that British attitudes to Germany were more positive than they were. The German Foreign Office had wrongly assumed that a violation of Belgian neutrality would not cause Britain to declare war. When Sir Edward Grey promptly, if with profound reluctance, did so, Lichnowsky was made the scapegoat. Lichnowsky's embittered reaction to the charges would have been perfectly well known to Sternheim, who was in close contact with the Lichnowskys and frequented circles in Berlin in which they moved. By the time *Das leidende Weib* was released for wider public consumption in October 1916, the issue of German war guilt and Lichnowsky's role had begun to have significant reverberations.

In the summer of 1916 Lichnowsky wrote *Meine Londoner Mission, 1912–1914*, defending his own integrity and pointing up the disastrous trends in German foreign policy of the previous decade.[7] The manuscript was complete by August 1, 1916. His mission in London, he insisted, had been to eliminate the tension between Britain and Germany that had arisen because of naval rivalries, and to bring about a wider understanding between the two nations. This goal he believed was within reach when war intervened. Germany's decision to tie itself to Austro-Hungary would, he predicted, have disastrous effects, for a war of encirclement could not be won and the colonies would be lost. Eight copies of the pamphlet were prepared and circulated by Lichnowsky to his friends, including Maximilian Harden, Albert Ballin, and Richard Witting, a member of the anti-war *Bund Neues Vaterland*. Recognizing the importance of the document, Witting made further copies, which he distributed widely to politicians and army officers. Lichnowsky was immediately instructed by the German Government to recall all his copies, an order with which he swiftly complied. In January 1918 the pamphlet suddenly became widely available in printed form: the *Bund Neues Vaterland* appears to have been responsible, though the publisher's name was fictitious. On March 6, 1918 the Swedish newspaper *Politiken* began to serialize the document. The Allies welcomed the propaganda advantages that accrued to them; the *Times* acquired a copy and published an English version. The whole pamphlet, *My Mission to London, 1912–1914*, with a preface by Gilbert Murray, appeared in English early in 1918. By May 1918 four million copies had been distributed in Britain, mainly among industrial workers in the North of England; many of the copies were free. During 1918 six different editions appeared in Switzerland, five in France, four in the United States, and three in Italy; copies were even dropped by airplane on German trenches on the Western Front.

That British sources should have a vested interest in publicizing Lichnowsky's views is unsurprising. What is striking, however, is the vehemence of Lichnowsky's attack on his political masters in the German

Foreign Office and his damning indictment of aspects of the German political and military tradition:

> Have they not proved to be right who declared that the spirit of
> Treitschke and Bernhardi governed the German people, that spirit
> which glorified war as such, and did not loathe it as an evil, that with
> us the feudal knight and junker, the warrior caste, still rule and form
> ideals and values, not the civilian Gentleman; that the love of the
> duel which animates our academic youth still persists in those who
> control the destinies of the people? Did not the Zabern incident and
> the parliamentary discussions about it clearly demonstrate to foreign
> countries the value we place on the rights and liberties of the citizen
> if these collide with questions of military power?[8]

The reader of this passage will note the parallels with Heinrich Mann's
analysis of the authoritarian structures of Wilhelminian Germany in *Der
Untertan*. Certainly, when Mann's novel was first published in 1919, ten
copies were privately printed in a luxury edition: one was dedicated to
Mechtilde von Lichnowsky, the Ambassador's wife.

Sternheim's motives in supporting Lichnowsky were not disinterest-
edly political. He had met Mechtilde von Lichnowsky, née Gräfin von
Arco-Zinneberg, in Berlin early in 1911, a relationship which later developed briefly into a love affair, by no means an unusual experience for
Sternheim. He was invited to the Lichnowsky residence in February 1911
after the premiere of *Die Hose*, and in April of the same year Mechtilde
was a guest at Sternheim's house in Höllriegelskreuth near Munich. In
1913 the relationship developed further: she visited Sternheim in Munich
in January, when he read the first version of the short story *Busekow* to
her. In May of that year, he visited her in London, staying at the German
Embassy in Carlton House Terrace. After this visit the intimate relationship continued only for a short time, although Sternheim remained in
touch with her for many years, taking a lively interest in her literary efforts. Looking back on his own early literary career in *Vorkriegseuropa im
Gleichnis meines Lebens* (1936), he includes in his reminiscences three letters from Mechtilde Lichnowsky, all written from London in 1913.[9]
When he read Klinger's *Das leidende Weib*, Sternheim must have been
struck by certain analogies between the plot and both his personal relationship and the wider political situation. This autobiographical element
accounts for his decision to alter the ages of Klinger's characters to bring
them into line with his real-life models: in Sternheim's version the Ambassadress is in her thirties (Mechtilde was thirty-five in 1914), while the Ge-
heimer Rath's twenty years service is increased to thirty and his function
conflated with that of the Ambassador. (Lichnowsky had been in the diplomatic service for thirty-one years in 1914.) The Ambassadress's infidel-

ity was a distracting element in Sternheim's play, but it suggests that the autobiographical element was a significant stimulus to him, however indiscreet his confession might have appeared.

Immediately after completing *Das leidende Weib* on October 18, 1914, Sternheim went to Berlin to read the manuscript to Max Reinhardt. November saw rehearsals at the Deutsches Theater. Sternheim was full of enthusiasm for the production: "Ich glaube doch, aus dem Stück wird etwas Schönes, da ich Reinhardt immer mehr davon ergriffen sehe" *(Briefe* 2:149), but on 20 November 1914, the first doubts about the censor's reactions are given:

> Wir telefonieren sofort zum Polizeipräsidium und richtig, Glasenapp, ohne sich definitiv zu erklären, murmelt etwas, von schweren Einwendungen.
>
> Nun ging sofort ein neues Teater [sic] los: Holländer muß sich mit dem ordentlichen Professor für Litteratur an der Berliner Universität Geheimrat Roethe in Verbindung setzen, der ein Gutachten abgeben soll. (*Briefe* 2:150)

> [We immediately telephone the police HQ and, sure enough, Glasenapp, without going into details, mutters something about serious objections.
>
> That immediately set off a fresh hullabaloo. Holländer has to get in touch with the Ordinarius for Literature at Berlin University, Geheimrat Roethe, who is to provide a reference.]

On December 2, 1914 the censor banned the performance, and even though Sternheim was able to force the *Deutsche Tageszeitung* to withdraw its accusations against him the ban was not lifted. The Berlin Chief of Police Jagow insisted in his response "daß diese Bedenken nicht in allgemein polizeilichen Gesichtspunkten, sondern im wesentlichen in der Rücksicht auf die gegenwärtige große Zeit und die kämpfenden Offiziere wurzeln"[10] (that these doubts are not prompted by general policing considerations, but basically by a concern for the officers in the field and the great times we are presently passing through). It was Regierungsrat Klotz who was responsible for the detailed criticism of the play that was appended to Jagow's statement:

> Das vorliegende Stück ist meines Wissens das erste, in dem ein dramatischer Schriftsteller von Ruf den gegenwärtigen Krieg zum Gegenstand oder Anlaß eines dramatischen Werks gemacht hat. Daß gerade Sternheim, dessen undeutsche Gesinnung hinlänglich erwiesen ist, und dessen Darstellungsweisen auch sonst schon Gegenstand heftiger Kritiken gewesen ist, diesen Schritt unternommen hat, verspricht von vornherein nichts Gutes.[11]

[To the best of my knowledge, this play is the first in which a play-
wright of renown has taken the present war as its subject or as a reason for writing a play. The fact that it should be Sternheim who took
this step — whose un-German attitudes have been sufficiently
proven and whose manner of presentation has also been the subject
of sharp criticism — hardly bodes well.]

Regierungsrat Klotz referred disparagingly to Sternheim's *Van Gogh* essay
and went on to single out for criticism a number of incidents in the play.
Accordingly, Jagow banned performances of the play as calculated to af-
front public sentiments and not conducive to public order. Certainly, the
experience with *Das leidende Weib* was to be repeated with other plays,
and by October 1915 seven of Sternheim's plays were banned from performance. In March 1916 Reinhardt agreed to make a further attempt to
stage the play. The Deutsches Theater applied to the censor for permission on 31 March 1916; this was granted on condition that the performance should be a "closed" one, a private afternoon performance before an
invited audience. No sale of tickets or any reviews in the press were permitted. Regierungsrat Klotz took pains not only to prevent any review in
the Berlin papers but also to ensure that newspapers outside his jurisdic-
tion were unable to report the performance. Moreover, he insisted that
certain scenes be cut and that the whole action be transposed to the Napoleonic wars. As a result of the closed performance, which the censor attended, the emasculated version was granted a license for public
performance, which however did not take place until 30 October 1916.
Despite Sternheim's high hopes, the play ran for only four performances.

One of the reasons for the failure of the play was the press reaction,
which was uniformly negative. The effect of the censor's interference was
to reverse Sternheim's literary strategy, with confusing consequences. It
seemed to contemporary reviewers that Sternheim was concerned, above
all, to project back into history ideas of 1914, while his original concern
had been to employ a historical model to explore a topical theme in such
a way as to obviate difficulties with censorship. Thanks to the censor's insistence that the play be transposed to the Napoleonic wars, the topical
references to 1914, far from being diminished in impact, stood out the
more for jarring with the Napoleonic setting. Small wonder that it was to
these topical references that the reviewers took exception. The reviewer of
the *Berliner Lokal-Anzeiger* noted: "Manchmal greift diese Absicht aufs
Zeitgemäße so nahe ungeniert an das Gefühl des Zuhörers heran, daß er
abwehrend zurückzucken muß"[12] (Sometimes this targeting of present
circumstances challenges the listener's sensitivities so much that he must
react defensively). The *Vossische Zeitung* was more outspoken. Stefan
Großmann argues that the play was depressing "weil es gegen den
menschlichen Takt verstößt"[13] (because it offends against human tact).

In more recent times the play has been subject to widely differing interpretations. It has been argued both that it panders to the audience's enthusiasm for the war and that it is directed against that enthusiasm.[14] There seems little reason to doubt that Sternheim was an opponent of the war, so why should he have presented it in *Das leidende Weib* in such an ambiguous light as to suggest that he was glorifying war? The reasons will, I hope, have emerged from my paper. First and foremost, he was facing extreme difficulties with censorship and had to pretend, at the very least, that he had put his "undeutsche Gesinnung" behind him. Second, he wished to present in the play the notion that radical individualism and personal self-fulfilment transcend all social and moral constraints; if the "Liebestod" coincides with a "Heldentod," the reader (and the censor) might be unaware of the difference. Third, he was alluding to both a highly personal and private relationship with Mechtilde Lichnowsky on the one hand and a wider issue involving Prince Lichnowsky on the other. On both counts he may justly be regarded as violating "den menschlichen Takt." The play was a failure, but because it helps to lay bare the pressures operating on writers of the time, it is a particularly fascinating and instructive failure.

Notes

[1] For an account of Sternheim's links with the German community in Brussels, see Ulrich Weisstein, "Der letzte Zivilist? Carl Sternheim at La Hulpe," in *The Ideological Crisis of Expressionism: The Literary and Artistic German War Colony in Belgium, 1914–1918,* ed. Rainer Rumold and O. K. Werckmeister (Columbia, SC: Camden House, 1990), 115–31.

[2] *Carl Sternheim: Gesammelte Werke,* ed. Wilhelm Emrich and Manfred Linke, 10 vols. (Neuwied and Darmstadt: Luchterhand, 1963–76), 6:7. All subsequent references to Sternheim's work are to this edition and are cited with volume and page reference after quotations in the text. References to Sternheim's letters are to *Carl Sternheim: Briefe,* ed. Wolfgang Wendler, 2 vols. (Darmstadt: Luchterhand, 1988); these, too, are given after quotations in the text.

[3] Excerpts from Thea Sternheim's diary were first published in the notes to the *Gesammelte Werke,* to which this reference refers; her diaries have since appeared as *Tagebücher 1903–1971 und Kommentar,* 5 vols., edited by Thomas Ehrsham and Regula Wyss (Göttingen: Wallstein, 2002).

[4] Quoted in *Expressionismus: Manifeste und Dokumente zur deutschen Literatur, 1910–1920,* ed. Thomas Anz and Michael Stark (Stuttgart: Metzler, 1982), 314–15.

[5] Thomas Mann, *Gedanken im Krieg,* in *Gesammelte Werke in dreizehn Bänden* (Frankfurt am Main: Fischer, 1974, vol. 13: *Nachträge,* 527–45, here 532–33).

[6] For a detailed discussion of the policy of literary journals, see Eva Kolinsky, *Engagierter Expressionismus: Politik und Literatur zwischen Weltkrieg und Weimarer Republik* (Stuttgart: Metzler, 1970), 8–48, and Anz and Stark, *Expressionismus,* 293–301.

[7] I am indebted here to Harry F. Young, *Prinz Lichnowsky and the Great War* (Athens: U of Georgia P, 1977), 146–87.

[8] Karl Max, Prince Lichnowsky, *My Mission to London, 1912–1914* (London: Heinemann, 1918), 40–41.

[9] These letters are misdated as having been written in 1912.

[10] Quoted by Karl Deiritz, *Geschichtsbewußtsein, Satire, Zensur: Eine Studie zu Carl Sternheim* (Königstein im Taunus: Forum Academicum in der Verlagsgruppe Athenäum, Hain, Scriptor, Hanstein, 1979), 174.

[11] Deiritz, *Geschichtsbewußtsein, Satire, Zensur,* 174.

[12] Deiritz, *Geschichtsbewußtsein, Satire, Zensur,* 150.

[13] Deiritz, *Geschichtsbewußtsein, Satire, Zensur,* 151.

[14] For the former view, see Rudolf Billetta, "Carl Sternheim" (unpublished Ph.D. thesis, University of Vienna, 1950), 283; for the latter, see Wilhelm Emrich's editorial comments in *Carl Sternheim: Gesammelte Werke* 2:552.

4: The Martians Are Coming!
War, Peace, Love, and Reflection in H. G. Wells's *The War of the Worlds* and Kurd Laßwitz's *Auf zwei Planeten*

Ingo Cornils

Introduction

A T THE END OF THE NINETEENTH CENTURY, "news from Mars" ex-
cited scientists, writers, journalists, and the general public. The dis-
covery of the lines on the Martian surface and the suggestion that these
were "canals" cut by intelligent Martians prompted *The War of the Worlds*
in a newspaper serial in 1897, describing the invasion of peaceful Victorian England by technologically superior, "unsympathetic" Martians.
Wells's monsters wreak havoc in Surrey and London with their heat rays
and black poison gas, before Earth's bacteria destroy them.

What is little known is that in the same year that *The War of the
Worlds* was first read in England, a German writer, Kurd Laßwitz, quite
independently published a book about Martians coming to Earth, entitled
Auf zwei Planeten.[1] Laßwitz, a scholar, physicist, and humanist, came up
with a vision at least as exciting and thought-provoking as Wells's. His
Martians come to Earth as benevolent culture-bearers. They have reached
a highly advanced stage of technical and scientific development, but, more
important, they have reached a moral maturity that makes them appear
almost godlike in the eyes of men. Their home world is presented as a
technological and social utopia, and it is this advanced state that they
want to share with us, albeit on their terms.

In this paper, I aim to show how Wells and Laßwitz started from the
same premise and yet came up with completely different visions of the future. We will see how Victorian England and Wilhelmine Germany
shaped their imagination, in particular their critique of the main threat to
peace posed by their respective regimes: colonialism and imperialism.
Both authors offer unique responses to the challenge of the scientific
revolution, and both pose fundamental questions about mankind's moral
evolution in the face of scientific and technological progress.

War

I. F. Clarke ranks Wells's *The War of the Worlds* as "the perfect nineteenth-century myth of the imaginary war."[2] By this he means that Wells had combined a number of elements already in the public psyche at the time and given it expression and meaning in a symbolic representation that was immediately understood. These elements or ideas were all based on scientific or technological discoveries: Darwin's theory of evolution, the experience of changing methods of warfare, and the theory that man might not be alone in the universe. Wells drew his own conclusions from the violence with which colonial wars were fought, which seemed to support the social Darwinian idea of the "survival of the fittest." He was also quick to realize that military technology had advanced to such an extent that any future war would involve not just the combatants but the civilian population as well; that these wars would be mechanical; and that the side with the most advanced technology would prevail.

Much of this was standard fare for the contemporary readers of sensationalist novels and pamphlets. The future had become the canvas for war games: the arms race on land and sea inspired authors in England, France, and Germany to ever-bloodier depictions of imaginary battles. In direct response to the Franco-Prussian War, where the efficient Prussian army with its superior technology had won an unexpectedly swift and decisive victory against the supposedly greatest military power in the world, English writers such as George Chesney in his *Battle of Dorking* focused on the potential threat coming from the new German empire.

It is a moot point whether the Martians in *The War of the Worlds* are Germans dressed up as bogeymen. There are passages in the novel that seem to signify that Wells was thinking about the threat coming from Germany, but I believe that in this case the novel is really depicting a more general threat. That doesn't mean that Wells was not taking the threat of a war with Germany seriously; indeed, he does his very best to prepare his readers for what they might encounter.[3]

The Martian style of war that Wells depicts is all-engulfing: it enters every home, it does not discriminate between classes, it does not spare women, children, or the clergy, and it offers no quarter. The narrator in *The War of the Worlds*, who is himself initially swept up by the "war fever," is deeply disturbed by such a ruthless and "efficient" enemy: after a near mental breakdown, he realizes that he has to come to terms with this new reality. Mankind has been pushed from its throne: "the fear and empire of man had passed away."[4]

Wells was convinced that the ability to build and control machines would be the decisive factor in a future conflict. His Martians employ excavating and building machines, which in turn assemble the Martian tripods. These tripods themselves are highly mobile, impervious fighting machines that can destroy the English guns and warships at will and cover ground quickly.

The ability to maneuver freely also occurred to Laßwitz as a major advantage in any armed conflict. But while Wells drops the idea of flight once the Martian projectiles had made their way from Mars to Earth, Laßwitz imagines a whole civilization built on a technology that is able to control gravity, with armed and armored Martian airships that can reach any point on the planet in a matter of hours.

Auf zwei Planeten takes a global viewpoint: following the moment of first contact, when three German scientists in a balloon expedition to reach the North Pole are rescued by Martians who have built a base there, it soon becomes clear to the explorers that the Martians are planning to conquer Earth. The Martians, an old civilization, have a keen sense of their own superiority. This attitude is partly based on their observation of the Eskimos, the only humans they have encountered so far. The Martians believe that if the rest of mankind is on the same cultural level, they are justified in taking control and using the planet's resources for their own benefit. Any objections by the protesting German explorers are brushed aside with the comment: "We come to you to bring you the benefits of our culture."[5] When it becomes clear to the Martians that the humans don't want to be conquered, they are faced with an ethical dilemma and have to reconsider their plans. They conclude they must get a clearer picture of mankind first, and set out on an expedition to learn more about us.

Unfortunately their next encounter with "civilized" human beings is with an English warship. A misunderstanding leads to an exchange of gunfire, Martians are taken hostage, and the Martians in the airship try to force the English to release the hostages. Captain Keswick and his hot-headed Lieutenant Prim, self-important lords of the sea, cannot bear the humiliation. For them, it is a question of honor to defeat the new enemy and to bring the Martians to London in triumph. They continue the unequal fight and, even though the Martians try not to inflict any damage, the English warship is lucky to escape the awesome power of the Martian weapons. This restraint is taken as a sign of weakness, whereupon the English mobilize their fleet.

The Martians conclude that mankind is simply too immature to master its own affairs. They demand compensation from the English government and set an ultimatum for the English to comply, threatening quarantine if they do not. The English government refuses to acknowledge these conditions, which in turn forces the Martians to place an embargo on all English harbors. In an ironic reversal of sides, the greatest colonial power becomes the helpless victim of Martian "gunboat diplomacy."[6] At

Portsmouth, the English try to break the embargo and in the ensuing battle they lose most of their ships. In spite of all efforts by the Martians to prevent any loss of life, the English only surrender when their flagship is sunk.

With the fleet destroyed, England's power is broken. The colonies declare their independence, and other countries rush in to secure the trade regions for themselves. This brings the English to their senses. To save what is left of their empire, they sue for peace. Rather predictably, the squabble over English colonies starts further wars, and the Martian representative has no alternative but to declare the whole Earth a Martian protectorate, and to enforce the disarmament of all nations.

It is no accident that the English are singled out by Laßwitz as the main adversaries of the Martians. After all, they were the greatest sea power of the time, and it is with a sense of pride that he can set the explorer spirit of the Germans against the nation that rules the sea. Laßwitz is not above national sentiments,[7] but is seldom jingoistic.[8] The English may be arrogant and unable to deal with the new realities, but their valor is undeniable. Whilst Wells's sea battle between the English and the Martians in *The War of the Worlds* is a struggle between good and evil, Laßwitz's sympathies are more equally divided. The English defense in the "battle of Portsmouth" is a matter of misplaced pride, and the ships sent against the Martians defend not just the English upper classes but also the freedom of mankind. On the other hand, the inability on the part of the English to negotiate and reason with the superior Martians simply because that would be an acknowledgement of their own inferiority shows a dangerous lack of common sense. Interestingly, Laßwitz does not portray the Germans to be any better than the English, and the German Imperial Guard is destroyed in an equally spectacular manner: in a chapter on the "unfortunate events in the fatherland," he presents a masterpiece of ironic political criticism, skillfully disguised to avoid prosecution by the Imperial censors. Like Wells, he employs a narrative device to distance himself from the message he delivers: his narrator quotes from a newspaper report about the "shameful events" that leave Prussia without an army and the Emperor without his clothes.

When the Germans do not follow the order for global demobilization, Martian airships turn up over Berlin to force the Emperor to comply. The "report" gives a detailed description of how the imperial guard was disarmed: the Emperor, mustering a parade designed to show off his military power, openly displays his defiance to the Martians. But the Martians use powerful magnets and pull everything metallic into the air; the "invincible" Prussian war machine is tossed about like straw in the wind. In a brilliant parody that foreshadows Heinrich Mann's *Der Untertan* (1919), the belligerent Emperor shouts: "Meine Herren! Hier gibt es nur einen Weg — hindurch!"(*ZP*, 607; Gentlemen! There's only one way here — straight through!). The Martians are ready for the stubborn advance — they inform the Emperor that they have his son on board their ship and invite the Emperor to join him for peace talks, on their terms, of course. The mighty German army has been beaten without a shot fired.

Following a conservative backlash on Mars, where outraged Martian citizens demand that the "savage" humans be taught respect (*ZP*, 458), the Martians on Earth embark on a program of re-education. Germany is governed by a Martian "Kultor" in Berlin. Physically weakened by the effects of the Earth's heavier gravity and moister atmosphere, however, the Martians are unable to resist the corrupting effect of power; and in time their rule becomes despotic. While the humans are benefiting materially from the way the Martians clean up production and end hunger, they lose their spirit because they have no say in their own affairs any more. Naturally, after several years of suppression, a resistance movement springs up: the "league of humans."

What unites Wells and Laßwitz when writing about war is their satirical and enlightened approach to the colonial politics of the imperialist powers. Both present a mirror to the greedy nations that have carved up the planet amongst them, a satirical mirror that turns all the colonial powers into well-organized Martian colonies. Wells allows his native England to suffer the fate that it was forcing upon its colonies at the very time the book was published, and Laßwitz criticizes the imperialistic stance of all powers involved by ridiculing them. Rudi Schweikert, the editor of the recent reissue of *Auf zwei Planeten*, suggests that what he is after is "die Läuterung der menschlichen Moral"[9] (the purification of human morality), and this is achieved by suffering under and then emulating the lofty Martian spirit, while resisting the oppression when the Martians are "contaminated" by human egotism.

There is a certain grim satisfaction in seeing one's own side beaten. Wells's mixed feelings towards the ruling classes in late Victorian England are well known, and one could argue that Laßwitz also took delight in humiliating his blinkered, arrogant, and unscientific superiors. However, mankind does not deserve to be beaten in *The War of the Worlds*: it is simply overpowered by an adversary that literally fell out of the sky. It is a different story in *Auf zwei Planeten*: the English deserve to be beaten in the sea battle because they don't use their brains, and the Germans deserve to be made an example of with their stubborn pomp and misplaced pride. The decisiveness of the defeat is a clear signal that change is going to come, that the old order and the old certainties are no more. Yet while Wells, like Chesney, looks back to what used to be, bemoaning the loss of that "safe" feeling pervading their society, Laßwitz looks forward, embracing the change and the opportunities that exposure to the Martian culture can bring.

Peace

Wells argues in *The War of the Worlds* that peace can only be found after a war has been fought. Laßwitz on the other hand expends considerable energy in *Auf zwei Planeten* to show how peace could be achieved even when faced with a superior adversary. At a time when the German Empire set out to claim its "Platz an der Sonne" (place in the sun) by acquiring and extending its own colonies, Laßwitz added his voice to those who warned of the fatal consequences of such militaristic adventures. This did not go down well with the critics of the time. His noble Martians were described as "Typen der internationalen Friedensapostel" (typical international peace apostles), and he was accused of undermining the German spirit by spreading the "the cold breath of (socialist) tendencies."[10] His views were compared to those of the controversial pacifist Bertha von Suttner,[11] who was one of the few who had favorably reviewed *Auf zwei Planeten* in 1898. Indeed, von Suttner was perceptive enough to recognize that what Laßwitz was offering not only went completely against the dominant Zeitgeist but also mapped out an alternative to the pursuit of "Machtpolitik." To her it was obvious that the function of the Martian "takeover" was to create "international solidarity" amongst human beings, and that the book contained "socialist thinking."[12]

Perhaps this interpretation overstates the intentions of the book, but Laßwitz, a descendant of classical Weimar and fully committed to its ideal of humanism and its sense of cultural mission, firmly believed in the amelioration of mankind. By portraying a morally and ethically advanced civilization, he aimed to show by what steps humanity itself could reach this higher level of maturity. These steps are: an advancement in science and technology; moral education; and a general appreciation of the miracle of life, which teaches us to respect other cultures instead of forcing them to adhere to our own values.

We get a clear sense of what science and technology might deliver to counter the main reason for war, namely the economics of scarcity, the lack of basic resources that forces mankind to engage in endless battles for survival, control, and domination. The scientific dream that we could somehow create our basic resources and end the vicious circle of hunger and greed is splendidly described in *Auf zwei Planeten* in the way the Martians have used their technological mastery to eradicate want and hunger:

> Steine in Brot! Eiweißstoffe und Kohlehydrate aus Fels und Boden, aus Luft und Wasser ohne Vermittlung der Pflanzenzelle! — Das war

die Kunst und Wissenschaft gewesen, wodurch die Martier sich von dem niedrigen Kulturstandpunkt des Ackerbaues emanzipiert und sich zu unmittelbaren Söhnen der Sonne gemacht hatten. (*ZP*, 393)

[Stones to bread! Protein and carbohydrates from rocks and soil, from air and water without the photosynthesis of the plant cell! This was the progress by which the Martians had emancipated themselves from the early cultural stage of farming and how they had become direct sons of the sun. (*Two Planets*, 181)]

Perceiving that war is a constant threat for all humanity, the Martians set about the task of reeducating man: to show him how he can escape from Kantian "self-inflicted immaturity."[13] They know that humans are capable of this because they have seen the integrity and selfless behavior of the German explorers. What unites the two races, they argue, is the dream of peace,[14] and the peaceful pursuit of knowledge. One instance of this common disposition is the scientific exploration of the planet, as exemplified by the three German balloonists who encounter the Martian explorers at the North Pole. A second, more powerful, moment occurs when the Martians take the Germans up to their space station high above the Pole. Looking down on Earth, they realize that they share the capacity for awe in the face of creation:

In tiefem Schweigen standen die Deutschen, völlig versunken in den Anblick, der noch keinem Menschenauge bisher vergönnt gewesen war. Noch niemals war es ihnen so klar zum Bewußtsein gekommen, was es heißt, im Weltraum auf dem Körnchen hingewirbelt zu werden, das man Erde nennt; noch niemals hatten sie den Himmel unter sich erblickt. Die Martier ehrten ihre Stimmung. Auch sie, denen die Wunder des Weltraums vertraut waren, verstummten vor der Gegenwart des Unendlichen. (*ZP*, 212)

[In deep silence the humans stood completely fascinated by the sight which no Earthly eye had ever beheld. More clearly and more overwhelmingly than ever before, they realized what it meant to be whirled about in space on a small particle named Earth. Never had they seen the sky underneath them. . . . The Martians respected their thoughtfulness. They, too, to whom the wonders of space were familiar, became silent in the presence of the infinite." (*Two Planets*, 92)]

At this moment we see the link between Martians and humans, a link that is stronger than the differences. We are accepted as potential equals, a spiritual band linking the two planets, whereas there is only the vastness of empty space in *The War of the Worlds*.

Significantly, the final step on the way to peace between the two planets is the unselfish act of Ell, son of a stranded Martian explorer and a human mother, who had instigated the German polar expedition in the hope that it would encounter Martians there. When human resistance-fighters[15] have taken Martians hostage and Martian public opinion demands the extermination of the "barbarians," it is he who sacrifices himself in order to avoid a catastrophic confrontation.[16] Interestingly, this ultimate sacrifice is not only dictated by Martian logic, but also by human love.

Love

Wells's Martians are all brain and no heart. The narrator believes that they communicate telepathically, though the content of their communications is beyond his comprehension. He witnesses how the Martians produce buds on their bodies, small copies of themselves, and from this he deduces that they have no genders. For Charles Gannon, the symbolism of this method of reproduction has complex and crucial implications, in that "Wells eliminates a basic reason for, and force in, communal relations, love, compassion, selflessness, and sensuality."[17]

The consequence of their advanced mental evolution "may entail horrific social, even physiological, alterations."[18] Their dedication to self-interest and efficiency is shown to lead to egoism, narcissism, intolerance of difference, and indifference to other species. This is in marked contrast to the very human form of love represented by the close relationship between the narrator and his wife, who are separated at the beginning of the conflict. Only at the end, against all hope, are they reunited, and the narrator can reflect on the ultimate value of their relationship.

Laßwitz, too, shows human suffering in separation, and presents love as the greatest bond between humans, a bond that defines our humanity. The twist in *Auf zwei Planeten* lies in the fact that one of the explorers, Saltner, actually falls in love with a Martian woman, La. Laßwitz's portrayal of "loving the alien" may have been his greatest risk, but it is also one of his greatest achievements. The developing relationship between Saltner and La shows up vital differences between the races. In addition, Laßwitz confronts us with a beautiful female Martian who is vastly superior to humans in intelligence and spirit.

La falls for Saltner in rather conventional, sentimental circumstances: he saves her life when she falls into a crevasse, and she realizes that he has qualities such as courage, selflessness. and generosity of spirit that a more logical-thinking Martian would lack. La and her girlfriend Se initially play with the humans, making them fall in love to test their reactions. But for Saltner, who interprets these signals within a human framework, her affection is an unexpected gift from the gods. Overcome by the overwhelming sense of awe on board the space station, looking down on his home planet, Saltner gives La a timid kiss. She allows it, but immediately warns him that Numean love never comes at the cost of freedom: "Vergiß nicht, daß ich eine Nume bin. . . . Die Liebe der Nume macht niemals unfrei" (*ZP*, 214; Don't forget that I'm a Martian. . . . The love of a Martian never takes away her freedom). They journey to Mars together, but she increasingly withdraws from him, and, when he is required to return to Earth, she stays on Mars.

After a separation of two years, La returns to Earth in her own luxury cruiser. She has realized that she cannot live without Saltner, but wishes to explore human life before committing herself to the indignities and the burden of terrestrial gravity for good. When she and her friend Se are surprised by a summer thunderstorm, La realizes that Earth offers sensations that the Martians have forgotten. She begins to understand that physical sensations are a necessary part of the human experience, and decides for herself that the Martian way of life is poorer with its rarified tastes. She rescues Saltner from the bureaucratic Martians he has offended and offers him asylum in the private room on board her airship, which gives Saltner the status of a Martian. The investigating Martian officer respects the inviolability of her bedroom. From her "impregnable" dress to the sanctuary in her private room, Laßwitz uses sexual imagery rather as a thought-experiment than a simple male fantasy. If the highly developed culture of Martians is due to "their exclusion of the body,"[19] then the terrestrial sensations of gravity, food, rain, even smells and light, are the counterbalance required to lead a complete life.

La decides to help Saltner to flee Europe, and, by sharing her Martian technology with the resistance, to give mankind a chance to fight against their suppressors. This is more than simply a message that love conquers all. In contrast to Wells's artilleryman, who fantasizes about an underground life where the men reproduce the human race by having sex with plenty of women, Laßwitz shows us that an evolved humanity must necessarily also lead to a more mature relationship between the sexes.

Laßwitz explores human love in very modern terms of dependence versus freedom: love becomes a utopian theme, a bond between Martians and humans that gives substance to the possibility of emancipation and equality, as training ground for the mature individual. La explains it to her friend Se in a moving monologue that may be full of pathos but is nevertheless a programmatic statement that underlines Laßwitz's ability to go beyond the framework of Kantian philosophy:

> Die Bestimmung ist nur eine, es ist die der Vernunft im zeitlosen Willen, daß ich sein soll und daß wir das eine, dasselbe Ich sein sollen — das ist die Liebe. Dieser Bestimmung folgen ist Freiheit. Dieser Bestimmung genügen ist Würde. (*ZP*, 712)

[Destiny — this is reason within timeless will, that I am to be and that we are to be this one being consisting of two creatures: namely, love. To follow destiny is freedom; to satisfy it is dignity. (*Two Planets*, 336)]

Reflection

The War of the Worlds sends us on a circular journey: the narrator returns to his house, and rereads the paper he was working on when the first cylinder landed:

> It was a paper on the probable developments of Moral Ideas with the development of the civilising process; and the last sentence was the opening of a prophecy, "In about two hundred years," I had written, "we may expect —" (*WW*, 187)

At the end of the novel, we know what to expect. We may be wiped out by a ruthless enemy, just like the "primitive" races that were wiped out by colonial powers. However, this message, carried by a narrative that so obviously sets out to entertain and terrify its reader, encourages us to escape into fatalism: what good is all "development of moral ideas" if survival is a matter of chance?

And yet the message seems so full of idealism. Even at the turn of the century, it was clear to Wells that advanced technology wasn't the same as superior intellectual capacity, a notion that dominated the imperialist ideologies of the Victorian Age.[20] Somehow, mankind had to adapt to the world it had created. How this could be achieved was a question that would exercise him for the rest of his life. Reading *The War of the Worlds* closely, we can make out the direction his thoughts would take: man would have to abandon his supreme confidence in the future, accept that the evolutionary process would continue, improve through universal education, and unite in a league of nations to avoid destruction by the very means he created to establish his power. However, the odds that Wells gave us, even before the First World War, were not good.

Laßwitz was, generally speaking, more optimistic. He held high hopes that there was a way to overcome our "Unfähigkeit, das Ziel zu sehen, dieser Eigensinn, daß die Dinge nicht auch anders gingen" (*ZP*, 286; inability to see the ultimate goal, this refusal to accept that things might be done differently). Writing against the Zeitgeist, he created a vision of a golden age of happiness and peace, which would be possible if only we would give up our outdated way of thinking. By supplying us with a vantage point from which to view our "folly," he magnified man's flawed activities and criticized the shortsightedness of his greed. To give an example: when the Martians see the smog over our cities, they ask:

"Woher kommen diese Nebel über Ihren Städten?" "Hauptsächlich von der Verbrennung der Kohle." "Aber warum nehmen Sie die Energie nicht direkt von der Sonnenstrahlung? Sie leben ja vom Kapital statt von den Zinsen." (ZP, 223)

[What causes these fogs over your large cities?" one of the Martians asked. "Mainly the burning of coal," Grunthe replied. "But why don't you take energy directly from the sun-rays? You should not be living on the capital but on the interest instead. (*Two Planets*, 98)]

What is apparent here is Laßwitz's belief that if only we had the proper insight into things, we would act rationally and do what's best. The Martians recognize that our inability (or unwillingness) to follow the ethical course of action is a general human trait, on which they comment with the remark: "Ko Bate!" ("Poor Earthlings!").

Laßwitz expounded this view on several levels. In *Auf zwei Planeten*, Ell explains to La that the humans simply lack the ability to act rationally, that they need help to grow up. The problem, as he sees it, is that humans tend to attach emotional value to simple rational decisions. Religion, Fatherland, and self-preservation are all causes of destructive egoism. Only enlightenment can lead mankind onto a higher level.

Laßwitz combines his social criticism with a constructive vision of the remedy that is required. In a brilliant passage written in a style reminiscent of Jonathan Swift's *Gulliver's Travels* or Johann Gottfried Schnabel's *Die Insel Felsenburg*, he provides us with a mirror in which we can see what exactly is wrong with our society. In a Martian newspaper, conditions on Earth are described as hair-raising: humans have no concept of justice, honesty, and freedom; they are divided and fight constantly. The economic consequences of war lead to squalor, and the population then has to be kept in check by brutal force. Corruption is rife, classes are divided, and the more powerful states do not hesitate to make a massacre of so-called "uncivilized" peoples. The article concludes: "Es sind wilde Tiere, die wir zu bändigen haben" (ZP, 457; they are like wild animals, and it is our task to tame them).

From this extreme point of view, there is not a big difference between "wilde Tiere" and the image of microbes under a Martian magnifying glass used by Wells. And yet Laßwitz's and Wells's reflections are worlds apart. For Laßwitz, the only chance to make headway in the "civilizing process" was to anticipate the future and then strive to be worthy of it. Thus he evokes the idea of an enlightened humanity in combination with the dream of a different way of life made possible by scientific and technological progress. In his essay "Über Zukunftsträume" (1899; On Dreams of the Future), he laid the foundation for a different aesthetics. This "aesthetics of the future" was to refute traditional assumptions, to embrace science and technology, and to speak of them in poetic terms. By acknowledging that man's scientific and technological activity was in fact a paradigm for his ability to progress, his poetic efforts would encourage the reader to make similar efforts on the side of ideas, ethics, and morals. The "scientific fairy tale" would thus convey to the reader the new discoveries on a subjective, emotional level: "Es gilt, das neue Naturgefühl persönlich zu gestalten."[21] (Our task is to give personal shape to this new sense of Nature).

It follows that Laßwitz never intended to paint the grand utopian state — it is the perfectibility of the individual that he is interested in, to such an extent that his creaking plot, wooden dialogue, and lack of characterization — all points of derision for the traditional literary critic — seem all but irrelevant. What he focused on was the noble idea, the fascination with the wonders of science, the opening of the mind in the context of ever-new discoveries of the universe around us, which could not fail but have a "civilizing" effect on us.[22]

Conclusion

One last nagging question remains: Why is *The War of the Worlds* still so popular while *Auf zwei Planeten* is relatively unknown? Franz Rottensteiner suggests that it has a lot to do with the culture and language in which these works were published. If *Auf zwei Planeten* had been published in English, it would be widely recognized today as an early science fiction classic. But language isn't the only problem. As a pacifist, antiauthoritarian, democratic and liberal-minded outsider, Laßwitz was ostracized in Wilhelmine Germany. Following a period when he was relatively popular during the Weimar Republic, the Nazis seized on this critical writer and suppressed any further printing of his work. After the war, the "normative" mode of Anglo-American science fiction dominated the market, and by the time that efforts were made to remember his contribution, his labored conventional style and apparent inconsistency precluded a wider audience.[23]

The problem with *Auf zwei Planeten* is perhaps that Laßwitz tried too hard. On the one hand, his Martians have developed a tolerant society based on the ideals of reason and humanity. On the other hand, they represent a satirical counterfoil for human behavior. For the modern reader, Wells's depiction of Martians as monsters is simply easier to grasp. This does not mean, though, that his novel fails to make its mark. Whilst in the Anglo-American realm it was (just) possible to write science fiction and remain within the cultural mainstream, in Germany utopian and fantastic thought was cut off. It went against the grain of a society that refused to come to terms with the cultural consequences and possibilities of its (belated) industrial revolution until this progress was turned into nationalistic saber-rattling by the ruling elites. German idealism had solidified to create an authoritarian mentality characterized by unquestioning obedience to the Emperor and his power-hungry generals. Laßwitz's dogged insistence on the potential of the human spirit to rise up against repression, his unwavering faith in the ultimate freedom of the individual, provides a powerful antidote to the dominant Zeitgeist. It is for this reason that *Auf zwei Planeten* deserves to be regarded not only as a premier work of science fiction, but also as a courageous statement of utopian ideals.

Notes

An earlier version of this essay appeared in *Comparative Literature* 55, no. 1, winter 2003: 24–41.

[1] In spite of several striking parallels between *Auf zwei Planeten* and *The War of the Worlds* — the invasion of superior Martians and the disastrous effect of terrestrial conditions of life on the invaders being the most obvious — the two writers were unaware of each other: "there was no influence, direct or otherwise, of one story upon the other. Indeed, it is impossible to see how there could have been as the two stories appeared almost simultaneously" (Mark R. Hillegas, "Martians and Mythmakers: 1877–1938," in *Challenges in American Culture*, ed. Ray B. Browne, Larry N. Landrum, and William K. Bottorff (Bowling Green, OH: Bowling Green U Popular P, 1970), 160.

[2] I. F. Clarke, *Voices Prophesying War: Future Wars, 1763–3749*, 2nd ed. (Oxford and New York: Oxford UP, 1992), 84.

[3] Wells only mentions the Germans once in *The War of the Worlds*. At the beginning of chapter 8, the narrator writes that the arrival of the Martians has caused less "sensation" than an ultimatum to the Germans would have done. The implication is twofold: Wells and his readers are aware that there is a potential of conflict with Germany, but also that the Germans, for once, are not the object of fear and aggression.

[4] H. G. Wells, *The War of the Worlds* (Harmondsworth. UK: Penguin, 1974), 154. Subsequent references to this work will be given in the text using the abbreviation *WW* and the page number.

[5] "Wir kommen zu ihnen, um ihnen die Segnungen unserer Kultur zu bringen." Kurd Laßwitz, *Auf zwei Planeten* (Munich: Heyne, 1998), 264 (translation IC). Subsequent references to this work are given in the text using the abbreviation *ZP* and the page number. An abridged English version was published in 1971 under the title *Two Planets*.

[6] "die Kolonialmacht England wird sehr schnell zum hilflosen Opfer einer Kanonenbootpolitik der Martier." See Götz Müller, *Gegenwelten: Die Utopie in der deutschen Literatur* (Stuttgart: Metzler, 1989), 160.

[7] Like Wells, Laßwitz was not oblivious to his country's nationalistic fervor. Twelve years after *Auf zwei Planeten*, he wrote a surprisingly naive article following his first glimpse of the new Zeppelin (shaped very much like his imagined Martian airships), expressing his pride in this "representation of an idea." See Angela and Karlheinz Steinmüller, *Visionen 1900 2000 2100: Eine Chronik der Zukunft* (Hamburg: Rogner & Bernhard, 1999), 28.

[8] The humiliation of Britain did not go down well with Edwin Kretzmann, an American Germanist who wrote one of the first reviews of *Auf zwei Planeten* for an English-speaking audience in 1938: "Several little incidents cast interesting sidelights on contemporary conditions. . . . It becomes quite evident that the Martians are really a glorified German race and have the same imperialistic tendencies as that nation" (E. M. J. Kretzmann, "German Technological Utopias of the Pre-War Period," *Annals of Science* 3, 4 [1938]: 417–301; here, 427). I believe that we must put this interpretation down to war fever before the Second World War, for there is nothing in *Auf zwei Planeten* that would support this interpretation.

[9] See Rudi Schweikert, "Von Martiern und Menschen, oder: Die Welt, durch Vernunft dividiert, geht nicht auf," in *Auf zwei Planeten*, 849–50.

[10] "kühle Atem der Tendenz" — see Bölsche, *Vom Bazillus zum Affenmenschen* (Leipzig: Diederichs, 1900), 337.

[11] Von Suttner was a famous advocate for peace at the time. Her novel *Die Waffen nieder!* first appeared in Dresden in 1889, and was widely read. Though ultimately derided and ineffective against the military elites in her native Austria and in Germany, she was successful in organizing peace societies and in convincing Alfred Nobel to institute the Nobel Peace Prize, which she won in 1905. For an accessible biography see Brigitte Hamann, *Bertha von Suttner: Ein Leben für den Frieden* (Munich: Piper, 1986).

[12] See Bertha von Suttner, "Die Numenheit" (1898), in Dietmar Wenzel, *Kurd Laßwitz: Lehrer, Philosoph, Zukunftsträumer: Die ethische Kraft des Technischen* (Meitingen: Corian, 1987), 109–16; here, 116. See also Rudi Schweikert, "Von Martiern und Menschen," 878–80.

[13] Kant's famous definition of Enlightenment is "der Ausgang des Menschen aus seiner selbstverschuldeten Unmündigkeit" (*Was ist Aufklärung?* 1784; mankind's emancipation from its self-inflicted immaturity) — this, according to Rudi Schweikert, is the philosophical "center" of the novel. (Schweikert, *Von Martiern*, 881).

[14] The cover of the 1917 Volksausgabe, which depicts two outstretched hands across the vastness of space, illustrates this well.

[15] With their slogan "Numenheit ohne Nume" (Numedom without Nume).

[16] See William Fischer, *The Empire Strikes Out: Kurd Laßwitz, Hans Dominik, and the Development of German Science Fiction* (Bowling Green, OH: Bowling Green U Popular P, 1984), 140: "By far the most important alien figure, and perhaps the central character in the entire novel, is Ell. It is he who mediates between the two worlds and to whom the title alludes."

[17] Charles E. Gannon., "'One swift, conclusive smashing and an End': Wells, War and the Collapse of Civilisation," *Foundation* 28, no. 77 (1999): 35–46; here, 42.

[18] Gannon, "Wells, War and the Collapse of Civilisation," 42.

[19] Götz Müller makes the point that the highly evolved culture of the Martians cannot bear any reference to physical needs or animal instincts: see his *Gegenwelten*, 161.

[20] For an elaboration of this point, see Patrick Parrinder, "How Far Can We Trust the Narrator of *The War of the Worlds?*" *Foundation* 28, no. 77 (1999): 15–24; here, 20.

[21] Franz Rottensteiner, "Kurd Laßwitz — Erkenntnis und Ethik dazu," in Kurd Laßwitz, *Homchen und andere Erzählungen*, Heyne Science Fiction Classics 4309 (Munich: Heyne, 1986), 11–12.

[22] See Kurd Laßwitz, "Über Zukunftsträume," in *Homchen*, 468.

[23] See Rottensteiner's foreword in Kurd Laßwitz, *Homchen*, 18–19.

Thinkers

5: Nietzsche as Hate-Figure in Britain's Great War: "The Execrable Neech"

Nicholas Martin

> Meine Brüder im Kriege!
> Ich liebe euch von Grund aus,
> ich bin und war Euresgleichen.
> Und ich bin auch euer bester Feind.[1]

[Brother warriors, / I love you intensely, / I was, and am, one of you, / And I am also your best enemy.]

IT IS COMMONLY ASSUMED that the first wholesale abuse of Nietzsche's thought for the purposes of political propaganda took place in Nazi Germany and was aggravated by the response of Allied propagandists during the Second World War. In fact, as early as 1914 Nietzsche had provided a convenient lens through which warmongers, whether British or German, Austrian or Australian, were able to focus their hatreds and self-justifications.[2] Given Nietzsche's contempt for virulent nationalism, particularly its German strain, and his comparative obscurity in Britain before 1914, this development requires some explanation.

The three principal aims here are to examine how his thought was presented by British commentators and propagandists at the beginning of the First World War; to explain how the singular view of Nietzsche that emerged was due not only to the demands of wartime propaganda but also to the malleability of Nietzsche's texts; and to counter the view that his impact on public opinion was negligible.[3] It must be stressed that this discussion is not another attempt to absolve Nietzsche or to domesticate his thought. As will become clear, his ideas were exploited in a cavalier and highly selective fashion in 1914, but Nietzsche was not entirely blameless. His ambivalent pronouncements on war and barbarism lent themselves to exploitation by British propagandists.

Gavrilo Princip, the young Serb who assassinated Archduke Franz Ferdinand and his wife in Sarajevo on 28 June 1914, thereby triggering the sequence of events that led Europe into war in early August, was an ardent Nietzschean. It is said that at meetings of the "Black Hand," an underground movement resisting Austria's annexation of Bosnia, he and his fellow terrorists liked to recite Nietzsche's verses, in particular the poem "Ecce Homo":

> Ja! Ich weiss, woher ich stamme!
> Ungesättigt gleich der Flamme
> Glühe und verzehr' ich mich.
> Licht wird Alles, was ich fasse,
> Kohle Alles, was ich lasse:
> Flamme bin ich sicherlich. (V 2:39)[4]

[Yes! I know where I come from! Insatiable as flame I burn and am consumed. What I grasp turns to light, what I leave is ash. Indeed — I am a flame.]

Princip, it seems, was possessed by Nietzsche, *ergo* Nietzsche was the immediate cause of the First World War. While this claim is patently absurd, no less absurd claims were made in Britain and throughout the Empire in the first weeks and months of the conflict, suggesting that Nietzsche was directly or indirectly responsible both for the war and for the allegedly brutal conduct of German troops advancing through Belgium and northern France. In this period a rash of articles, books, and pamphlets appeared in Britain, claiming that Nietzsche had fueled, if not created, the Germans' supposed love of killing and conquest.

In works with improbable titles such as *Fighting a Philosophy*, or *Nietzsche and Treitschke: The Worship of Power in Modern Germany*, or *Nietzsche and the Ideals of Modern Germany*, British propagandists accused Nietzsche, who had died in 1900, of leading a posthumous conspiracy with his "followers," the historian Heinrich von Treitschke — dead since 1896 — and the ageing military strategist General Friedrich von Bernhardi (1849–1930), to foster a mood of aggressive imperialism in Germany.[5] Bernhardi, a career cavalry officer, was the outstanding military writer of his day and had published *Deutschland und der nächste Krieg* in 1912. From 1898 to 1901 he was chief of the war historical section of the General Staff, and in 1909, shortly before retirement, he became the general in command of the Seventh Army Corps. *Deutschland und der nächste Krieg* was written in the shadow of the second Morocco crisis, and Bernhardi scarcely disguises his impatience with the German government's lack of resolve. Criticism of Germany's current leadership is implicit throughout. Invoking a higher morality and the logic of history, Bernhardi advocates aggressive war, for which the nation had to be prepared materially and psychologically. Negotiating with rival Great Powers was not a serious option; it was instead a sign of weakness. The work preaches the necessity of war with an urgency bordering on panic and was believed by some in Britain to be the official blueprint for a war of aggression. In truth, Bernhardi did not have the ear of the German General Staff and was regarded by its members as, at best, a maverick. Yet his views were in keeping with those of extreme nationalists in the Pan-German League, who believed that war was both a right and a duty, a biological imperative sanctioned by the findings of Darwin. The choice was expansionism or certain death, "Weltmacht oder Untergang."[6]

Deutschland und der nächste Krieg was a publishing sensation. It was into its fourth German impression a few months after publication and had been translated into English. It was reissued in an inexpensive popular edition by Edward Arnold in August 1914 and hailed by the Times Book Club as "The Book of the Hour. . . . This book expresses in the highest degree the spirit of Pan-Germanism."[7] Its connection with Nietzsche is not obvious. Treitschke is mentioned on nearly every page, but Frederick the Great emerges as Bernhardi's great hero. A Nietzsche quotation, from the *Zarathustra* chapter, "Vom Krieg und Kriegsvolke," forms the epigraph to Bernhardi's work: "Der Krieg und der Muth haben mehr grosse Dinge gethan, als die Nächstenliebe" (Za I; VI 1:55: "War and Courage have achieved more great things than brotherly love"). Otherwise, Nietzsche is not mentioned in Bernhardi's tome, and the epigraph was not reproduced in the English edition. While it is clear that Bernhardi's views were not a phenomenon of the lunatic fringe, it is equally clear that, contrary to what many British commentators apparently believed, Bernhardi was not part of, and did not influence, the mainstream of German military and political thinking. He was, it seems, a Prussian officer of the old school, worried that Bethmann Hollweg's government was going soft.

Yet at the outbreak of the Great War, British commentators alleged that the bellicose ideas of the Nietzsche — Bernhardi — Treitschke "triumvirate" had permeated German society and shaped the bloodthirsty and expansionist ambitions of its ruling class. Extravagant conspiracy theories of this kind were rife at the beginning of the war. Oscar Levy, who had edited the first complete English translation of Nietzsche's works, later recalled how, in 1914, "der Refrain Nietzsche, Treitschke und Bernhardi grollte uns [Nietzschejüngern in England] aus den Spalten aller Blätter und Revuen, von der altehrwürdigen Tory-Wochenschrift *Spectator* bis zur 'aufgeklärten' liberalen *Daily News* entgegen."[8] (The chorus 'Nietzsche, Treitschke, and Bernhardi' shook its fist at us English Nietzsche-disciples from the columns of every newspaper and review, from the venerable Tory weekly *Spectator* to the 'enlightened' Liberal *Daily News*.) On hearing that Allied commentators were mentioning Treitschke, Bernhardi, and Nietzsche in the same breath, a horrified Thomas Mann wrote:

Man hat dort [im Ausland] ja wahrhaftig neuestens angefangen, Kritik und Erkenntnis des Deutschtums zu treiben, wenn auch unter dem Titel "Nietzsche, Treitschke und Bernhardi." Daß gerade Den, der gegen Unds so empfindlich war, diese Zusammenstellung treffen muß. Schon "Goethe und Schiller," "Schopenhauer und Hartmann" konnte er nicht ertragen: und nun dies.[9]

[Abroad they have indeed started to acknowledge and to criticize Germanness, even if under the heading "Nietzsche, Treitschke, and Bernhardi." How ironic that the very person who was so opposed to such Ands should find himself thus connected. He so much disliked even "Goethe and Schiller," "Schopenhauer and Hartmann," and now this happens.]

Mann reiterated this note of bemused contempt after the war in one of a series of brief "letters" he wrote for a Chicago journal:

The usual thing was to link together Nietzsche, Treitschke, and Bernhardi — a grotesque cacophony to the ear of all intellectual Germans, and not of the Germans alone. One might conceivably name Treitschke and General von Bernhardi in one breath, although there was a great injustice to Treitschke in this. But it was ridiculous that Nietzsche should be brought in to complete the symbol of German wickedness; and it remains ridiculous, even after one comes to understand how it was possible. The things responsible for this were his philosophy of power, his anti-Christianity (which he shared with Goethe, whose antipathy was less thoroughly grounded, however), and his enthusiastic glorification of aesthetic greatness, of the strong and the beautiful life. But to take this lyricism as a prophecy of militaristic industrialism means simply neither to understand the lyricism nor the industrialism.[10]

In view of his own contribution to the propaganda war, Mann protests too much. In November 1914 he had published a notorious essay, "Gedanken im Kriege," which celebrated the outbreak of war, though the war's significance seemed to him more aesthetic and cultural than political.[11] Within his overarching antithetical concepts of "Geist" and "Leben," Mann assigns "Krieg" to "Leben" in this essay, along with other expressions of creative vitality, namely "Kultur," "Kunst," and "Deutschland." Ranged against these, on the side of "Geist," are the over-refined and decadent notions of "Zivilisation," "Literatur," and "Frankreich." The war, to Mann, meant above all a liberation of vital, creative forces from sterile decadence, and while he may not appeal directly to Nietzsche here (though he does in the extended tome of 1918, *Betrachtungen eines Unpolitischen*), the essay is clearly indebted to Nietzsche's antithesis of "Leben" and "Dekadenz."[12]

The British press frequently mentioned Nietzsche during the first months of the war, but in connection with stories of alleged German atrocities in Belgium. Those who had not read him, and they were the overwhelming majority, would have concluded from these references that his writings were incitements to wanton cruelty, barbarism, and megalomania, and that without them there would have been no Pan-German boorishness and no Schlieffen Plan.[13] In the understandably feverish and often hysterical atmosphere that gripped the belligerent nations in 1914, the British attacks on Nietzsche served two main purposes. The first was to provide intellectual artillery support for the assault on the moral and cultural high ground. The second and no less important aim was to press home the charge that not only was Germany responsible for the present conflict but that it was also in her nature to provoke and prosecute war. The enemy had to be demonized.[14] Certain real or imagined elements of Nietzsche's philosophy were harnessed to this project. These included his vehement opposition to Christianity and conventional moral codes, his glorification of strength, his alleged German nationalism, and his exhortation to "live dangerously":

> Denn, glaubt es mir! — das Geheimniss, um die grösste Fruchtbarkeit und den grössten Genuss vom Dasein einzuernten, heisst: *gefährlich leben*! Baut eure Städte an den Vesuv! Schickt eure Schiffe in unerforschte Meere! Lebt im Kriege mit Euresgleichen und mit euch selber! Seid Räuber und Eroberer, so lange ihr nicht Herrscher und Besitzer sein könnt, ihr Erkennenden! (*FW* 283; V 2:206)

> [Yes, believe me! — the secret to gaining the greatest harvest and pleasure from existence is to *live dangerously*! Construct your cities on Vesuvius! Send your ships out into unexplored oceans! Live at war with your fellows and with each other! Be robbers and plunderers so long as you cannot be rulers and possessors, you who understand!]

A favored tactic was to assert that Nietzsche's philosophy had influenced the German temperament and then to tar them both with the same brush. In the words of one observer in November 1914, "like many another German, Nietzsche was in his work, as in his life, the victim of megalomania."[15] Oscar Levy, the editor and translator of Nietzsche's works in Britain, had an unpleasant encounter with this sort of jingoism at the beginning of the war, which indicated to him how rapidly, in some quarters at least, Nietzsche was becoming an outlet for hysterical anti-German feeling:

Es war in England — ganz am Anfange des Krieges, am 18. August
1914, wenn ich nicht irre — als ich des Morgens im Briefkasten
meines Londoner Hauses eine Nummer der Edinburger Zeitung *The
Scotsman* entdeckte, in der mit blauem Stifte ein Artikel angestrichen
war. Er handelte über "Nietzsche und der Krieg" und hatte einen
schottischen Geistlichen zum Verfasser, der zu beweisen versuchte,
daß die heidnische, anti-christliche Gesinnung Nietzsches, seine
Verachtung aller landläufigen Moral, seine Predigt des Willens zur
Macht und seine Verherrlichung des Übermenschen den Deutschen
den Kopf verdreht und sie zum Überfall des kleinen Belgien und zur
Aussendung von vier Kriegserklärungen in einer Woche veranlaßt
habe. Am Rande der Zeitung stand geschrieben: "*You* have brought
this poison to England."[16]

[In England — right at the start of the War, 18th August, if I remember correctly — I discovered in my letter-box in London that
morning a copy of the Edinburgh newspaper *The Scotsman* with an
article ringed in blue. It was about "Nietzsche and the War," written
by a Scottish clergyman who was attempting to prove that
Nietzsche's pagan, anti-Christian attitudes, his contempt for all ordinary morality, his preaching of the Will to Power and his veneration
for Superman had turned the Germans' heads and induced them to
invade innocent Belgium and to issue four declarations of war in a
week. In the margin were the words: "*You* have brought this poison
to England."]

Throughout the British Isles and Empire, scribblers of every description joined a headlong rush to blame Nietzsche for the war. The drama
critic William Archer, for example, writing in the long series of Oxford
Pamphlets, all of which were devoted to Germany and the war, claimed
there was "exact agreement between the precepts of Nietzsche and the
policy and practice of Germany," adding that there was "not a move of
modern Prussian statecraft, not an action of the German army since the
outbreak of the war, that could not be justified by scores of texts from the
Nietzschean scriptures." The ideas of Nietzsche, he continued, that "get
home to the mind of nine readers out of ten . . . are precisely those which
might be watermarked on the protocol paper of German diplomacy and
embroidered on the banners of German militarism."[17] Using an interpre-
tative technique to which Nietzsche's writings are notoriously susceptible,
Archer picks and mixes quotations from *Die fröhliche Wissenschaft, Ecce
homo, Jenseits von Gut und Böse,* and *Zur Genealogie der Moral* in order to
show "how strong is Nietzsche's claim to a posthumous Iron Cross of the
first class" (6). "In a very real sense," Archer concluded, "it is the philosophy of Nietzsche that we are fighting" (26). The *English Review* ran
an article in October 1914 concerning Nietzsche's responsibility for the

war, by an author calling himself A. "Blond Beast,"[18] and an enterprising bookseller in London's Piccadilly caught the mood with a prominent notice next to his window display of the English edition of Nietzsche's works: "The Euro-Nietzschean War. Read the Devil, in order to fight him the better."[19]

Even *The Times* soon abandoned its hitherto judicious position and began lending its voice to this increasingly shrill chorus. During the first two weeks of the war it had taken the view that Britain's involvement was a straightforward matter of defending her interests and honoring the 1839 treaty obligations to safeguard Belgian neutrality.[20] Unconfirmed reports of German atrocities in Belgium began to arrive on 18 August, claiming that some units on the right flank of the German advance were ill-treating wounded prisoners, raping nuns, bayoneting babies, and using civilians to shield infantry advances. There was some truth in these allegations, as recent research has confirmed, yet at the time *The Times* chose to report them without comment.[21]

The turning point in the attitude of *The Thunderer* to the war came a week later. On 25 August 1914 the Belgian city of Louvain (Leuven) was set ablaze by rampaging German troops who had panicked on hearing false reports of civilian insurrection and military counterattack. The collegiate church of St Pierre, many university buildings, and the incomparable library with its unique collection of early books and medieval manuscripts were all destroyed.[22] *The Times* editorial condemning this act bore the headline "The March of the Huns." The defense of British interests was now strengthened by a crusading note of moral outrage. Until this point, arguments concerning Germany's alleged motives and character had been conducted in the letters columns, but now the editor felt obliged to characterize the German armies advancing through Belgium as Huns and Vandals, atavistic reincarnations of their marauding ancestors. Their actions, *The Times* indicated, were the physical counterpart to the intellectual atrocities committed by Treitschke, Bernhardi, and Nietzsche.[23]

The destruction of Louvain prompted one correspondent to enquire whether the Germans were not "reverting under the joint inspiration of their sanctimonious 'War Lord' [the Kaiser] and of the impious Nietzsche to the barbarities of their ancestors."[24] Sir Arthur Evans, professor of archaeology at Oxford, was moved to describe the sack of Louvain as the "Prussian holocaust."[25] As late as 1962, in a passionate evocation of the "flames of Louvain," Barbara Tuchman echoed the grandiloquent generalizations of 1914 by asserting, without irony, that a "hundred years of German philosophy went into the making of this decision [to violate Belgian neutrality]." The voice was Schlieffen's but the guiding hands, Tuchman claims, were those of Fichte, Hegel, Treitschke, and, of course,

Nietzsche, "who told them [the German people] that Supermen were above ordinary controls."[26]

Although the torching of Louvain constituted a serious breach of the rules of war, it is not necessary to look for a presiding demon in order to understand how it came about. *The Times*, however, was not slow to provide one. A leading article on 2 September 1914, entitled "The Great Illusion," exclaimed:

> War to TREITSCHKE and GENERAL BERNHARDI and all the conscious or unconscious followers of NIETZSCHE is noble and splendid in itself . . . the peculiarity of Germany is that this notion of war as an end in itself has taken hold of the intelligence of the country, that her idealists now are not peace-loving but war-loving, that her national conscience has undergone the change of moral values which NIETZSCHE desired.[27]

As if to underline this new stance, Rudyard Kipling's "For All We Have and Are" appeared at the foot of the same page:

> Once more we hear the word
> That sickened earth of old:–
> "No law except the sword
> Unsheathed and uncontrolled."
> Once more it knits mankind,
> Once more the nations go
> To meet and break and bind
> A crazed and driven foe.[28]

A few days later *The Times* asserted that, in Germany, "Christianity is beginning to be regarded as a worn-out creed, a new creed of which Nietzsche was the prophet — 'the religion of valour,' the religion of 'might is right' — is beginning to take its place." On the same page, the second stanza of a poem by Edmond Holmes served to emphasize and exaggerate this new Anglo-German antithesis and its symbolic antagonists:

> Christ or Nietzsche? Right or might?
> Truth of Heaven or lies from Hell?
> Healing balm or bursting shell?
> Freedom's day or serfdom's night?[29]

As early as August 13, 1914, the publisher Humphrey Milford reissued the *Oxford Knapsack Bible*, bound in khaki, "for the use of those on active service."[30] Thousands of copies had been sold during the South African War some fifteen years earlier, and many thousands more would change hands in the First World War. Expedient appropriation of cultural heritage was not confined to Britain, of course. In Germany, a number of war anthologies and almanacs, with titles such as *Nietzsche-Worte: Weggenossen in großer Zeit*, as well as tens of thousands of copies of the durable "Feldausgabe" of *Also sprach Zarathustra*, were sold to the troops.[31] In the nearhysterical words of the philosopher and Nietzsche scholar Karl Joël:

> Lacht [, ihr Engländer und Franzosen,] auch über jene Auskünfte der Buchhändler in München und Metz, daß von den ausziehenden Kriegern am meisten und in Massen der *Faust*, die Bibel und der *Zarathustra* verlangt wurden. Lacht nur über all solche Zeichen, daß mit den Waffen die Seele dieses Volkes in den Kampf zog, das man als barbarisch verschrie![32]

> [Laugh, you English and French, laugh at the news from the booksellers of Munich and Metz that the books most frequently, and massively, demanded by the departing soldiers were *Faust*, the Bible and *Zarathustra*. So, laugh at the signs that, along with their weapons, this people went to war with their souls — a people who had been declared barbarian!]

For a time, *Also sprach Zarathustra* sold better than those other knapsack durables, *Faust* and the New Testament. Even non-Germans marched to the front with a copy of *Zarathustra* in their kitbags. Robert Graves (who was, admittedly, half-German),[33] Gabriele d'Annunzio, Herbert Read,[34] and Pierre Drieu La Rochelle are perhaps the best known. In the words of Steven E. Aschheim: "They could all take Nietzsche into battle because Nietzsche transcended national distinctions and conventional political categorization. Like the anticipated war experience itself, Zarathustra symbolized the longing for transcendence, for the exceptional, and for the heroic."[35] After the initial euphoria, however, Zarathustra's sentiments proved less hard-wearing in the trenches than in the armchairs and libraries of the home front. After all, it must have been hard for a front-line soldier, of whatever nationality and however avid a Nietzschean, to equate the wasteland of trench warfare with the Alpine peaks and the fantasies of danger that had inspired Nietzsche-Zarathustra.

Although it is conceivable that he would not have been entirely displeased by it, this unprecedented publicity campaign did Nietzsche an enormous disservice. As a rule, writers do not create climates of opinion; they flourish in climates ready to receive them, yet British opinionformers were crediting Nietzsche with the remarkable achievement of shaping the principles, policies, and prejudices of an entire nation. Never before, at least in modern times, had a philosopher been held responsible for a war. Many of Nietzsche's British critics in 1914 knew that they were overplaying their hand, but these desk-bound warriors were in the business of propaganda. Because the complex economic, military, and diplomatic realities of the war and its causes made for comparatively poor propaganda material, it was simpler to justify the war by pinning the blame for it on identifiable individuals.

The effects of this loosely orchestrated anti-Nietzsche campaign were twofold. The first was to reduce him to the level of a melodramatic villain. In Wyndham Lewis's ironic words, he was now the "execrable Neech."[36] He was cast in the role of intellectual war criminal, as the *éminence grise* of the German General Staff, a Mephistophelean figure directing German strategy from the underworld. This is a view endorsed by Robert Graves. He recounts how, as he lay wounded on the Somme in July 1916, he repeated to himself "a line of Nietsche's [*sic*], whose poems, in French, I had with me: 'Non, tu ne peux pas me tuer,' [no, you cannot kill me]" adding that "Nietzsche was execrated in the papers as the philosopher of German militarism; he was more properly interpreted as a William le Queux mystery-man — the sinister figure behind the Kaiser."[37] The second effect of the propaganda was to propel Nietzsche from relative obscurity to become almost a household name. The *New Age*, which had become the house journal for British Nietzscheans, was appalled by the treatment he was receiving at the hands of vulgarizers and propagandists and recounted an illuminating anecdote in its issue of 10 September 1914:

> Two regular Tommies went into a bookshop in Charing Cross Road last week for a work by "this Nich or Nych." The bookseller divined their want as something by Nietzsche, and showed them a book of extracts. They examined it together in blank astonishment for a while and then handed it back saying they couldn't find anything by the Kayser [*sic*] in it.[38]

The first complete English edition of Nietzsche's works, which had been selling slowly since its completion in 1913, was snapped up.[39] In Britain by the end of 1914 Nietzsche had metamorphosed into the many-headed hydra "Nichee—Neitschee—Neetschee," which he was to remain, in the Anglo-Saxon world at least, until the 1950s.[40] He was, of course, demonized once again during the Second World War, not least because, with the eager assistance of his sister, he had become the philosophical mascot and quasi-legitimizer of National Socialism. Nevertheless, the debate concerning his supposed guilt for underpinning Nazism in particular and the war in general lacked the fire and vehemence of the controversy twenty-five years earlier, perhaps because that earlier experience had already created the indelible impression in Anglosaxony that Nietzsche, aggression, and German nationalism, in whatever form or combination, were identical.[41] In 1914, as in 1941, much of the mudslinging was either groundless or based on crude twistings of Nietzsche's words and their context; yet it was so relentless that, inevitably, some of the mud stuck. In the words of Nietzsche's most devoted apologist, Walter Kaufmann:

During [the First World War], the "superman" began to be associated with the German nation; and militarism and imperialism were read into Nietzsche's conception of power, although nothing could have been further from his mind. Again, these misinterpretations were supported, and perhaps partly inspired, by the works of Nietzsche's sister. The French, incidentally, on whom Nietzsche had so frequently lavished his praise, on the whole have retained a far more favourable picture of his thought than have people in the Anglo-Saxon countries where the war-begotten misconceptions have never been eradicated from the popular mind. The advent of Hitler and the Nazis' brazen adaptation of Nietzsche have strengthened these misapprehensions.[42]

The British Nietzsche of 1914 bore only a passing resemblance to the ironic and incisive, elliptical and elusive Nietzsche who emerges from his texts. His saving subtleties, his anti-German tirades, and the spiritual dimension of his thought were explained away or more often ignored. What emerged instead was a swaggering Prussian brute. The "Übermensch" and the "blonde Bestie," carefully separated by Nietzsche, became inseparable in the popular mind and were forced into the same ill-fitting, field-gray uniform of a faceless nation on the march. Nowhere does Nietzsche discuss the "Übermensch" systematically, but it is evident from Zarathustra's first address, "Von den drei Verwandlungen," that the "Übermensch" is a vision of an authentic, self-justifying, and self-determining subject, who is at once the polar opposite of the modern condition and, Nietzsche thinks, the means of overcoming it (*Za* I; VI 1:25–27) The "blonde Bestie," by contrast, is a lion (an unfortunate metaphor, perhaps) and represents man as predator, a savage slave to his instincts (*GM* I:11; VI 2:289) The "Übermensch," and this is the crucial distinction, will not be the reincarnation of this savage slave to instinct or of the cowed modern slave to "Life-impairing" intellectual and moral codes. He will instead rein in and redirect these destructive forces to the task of reshaping himself as a self-creating being. Instinct and intellect will be conjoined in an autonomous individual who has freed himself from the Life-denying servitude of his savage and his civilized forebears. Yet Nietzsche's picture of the "blonde Bestie" is undoubtedly crisper and betrays traces of the refined intellectual's yearning for barbaric simplicity and raw power.[43]

This distinction between "Übermensch" and "blonde Bestie," and other nuances in Nietzsche's thought, became blurred or were deliberately overlooked in British propaganda. A leading figure in this campaign of simplification and vilification was the 74-year-old Thomas Hardy. On hearing the news that German gunners had bombarded Rheims cathedral, Hardy wrote indignantly to the *Manchester Guardian* in early October:

> Should [the shelling of Rheims cathedral] turn out to be a pre-determined destruction . . . it will strongly suggest what a disastrous blight upon the glory and nobility of that nation has been brought by the writings of Nietzsche, with his followers Treitschke, Bernhardi, etc. I should think there is no instance since history began of a country being so demoralised by a single writer, the irony being that he was a megalomaniac and not truly a philosopher at all.[44]

Thomas Beecham condemned Hardy for this "light-minded and ill-considered attack on a writer with whose works he is very slightly acquainted."[45] It seems likely, though, that Hardy's real target was not Nietzsche, but rather his literary admirers in the English-speaking world, who included Wyndham Lewis, James Joyce, and Ezra Pound. Conservatives like Hardy were suspicious of these writers' admiration for Nietzsche before the war and were quick to seize the opportunity in 1914 to vilify him and, by extension, his admirers.

Nietzsche had enjoyed a limited following in Britain since the turn of the century, and there were at least two journals devoted to propagating and discussing his ideas. *The Eagle and the Serpent,* an eccentric and entertaining potpourri of socialism, Nietzscheanism and anarchism, appeared as early as 1898 but suffered an early demise in 1902. The more scholarly *Notes for Good Europeans* was founded in 1903 and written almost entirely by its editor, the improbably named Thomas Common.[46] As was the case in Germany before the First World War, Nietzsche's principal devotees were to be found among the literary and artistic avant-garde. Before 1914 he was barely appreciated outside salons, garrets, and ateliers.[47] Elsewhere the attitude towards his thought was uncomprehending and generally dismissive, as Nietzsche's obituary in *The Times* in August 1900 reveals:

> Nietzsche's philosophy, being revolutionary and altogether unpractical, obtained a certain number of followers in this country, as any violent view of life, violently expressed, always will. . . . His glorification of personal force as the only power that ought to rule the universe was little to the taste of the time in which he lived, and his works were certainly not taken very seriously in England.[48]

That *The Times* produced an obituary so rapidly (Nietzsche had died only two days earlier) would indicate that, as early as 1900, he was already a familiar, if despised figure in conservative circles. This was also true in Germany at the time, as one of Elisabeth Förster-Nietzsche's early collaborators recalled much later, after he had resigned in protest over her links with the Nazis:

Man möchte weinen, wohin Nietzsche und das Nietzsche-Archiv gekommen sind. Noch eins: daß dieser alten sechsundachtzig-jährigen Frau der mächtigste Mann Deutschlands [Adolf Hitler] und die Frau des früheren Kaisers heute den Hof machen. Letzteres fast grotesk nach der Einstellung S[einer] M[ajestät] zu Nietzsche vor dem Kriege! . . . Damals war Nietzsche Revolutionär und fast ebensosehr vaterlandsloser Geselle wie die Sozis.[49]

[One could weep at what has become of Nietzsche and the Nietzsche-Archive. And also at the fact that this 86-year-old lady is being paid court to by the most powerful man in Germany [Hitler] and by the wife of the former Kaiser. The latter is almost grotesque in view of His Majesty's attitude to Nietzsche before the War! In those days Nietzsche was a revolutionary and almost as much disowned by the country as were the Socialists.]

His followers in Britain before the Great War were equally marginalized. As Oscar Levy put it in the postscript to his Nietzsche edition in 1913:

We were an insignificant minority in a state of war with a vast major-ity. . . . We were a hopelessly small garrison in the midst of alarm-ingly hostile surroundings. Everybody was against us: not openly, to be sure, but, what is worse, silently, sullenly, instinctively. In front of us stood a most powerful phalanx composed of everything that di-rects the intellect of this country — a phalanx of priests and profes-sors, politicians and petticoats.[50]

In view of his acerbic and outspoken criticisms of the Wilhelmine Reich, it seems astonishing that Nietzsche should have been chosen as a scapegoat by British propagandists in 1914. "Ich halte das jetzige Preußen für eine der Cultur höchst gefährliche Macht (I regard present-day Prussia as a very great threat to culture," Nietzsche wrote in Novem-ber 1870, two months before the Prussian-led unification of Germany.[51] His works and letters seethe with hostility towards this new Germany and the arrogant philistinism, material greed, and saber-rattling stupidity he detected at its core.[52] In the context of one of his many paeans to Goethe ("der letzte Deutsche, vor dem ich Ehrfurcht habe" [the last German for whom I feel veneration]), Nietzsche observes: "Man fragt mich öfter, wozu ich eigentlich *deutsch* schriebe: nirgendswo würde ich schlechter ge-lesen, als im Vaterlande" (*GD* 51; VI 3:147; People often ask why I actu-ally write in *German*, since I am nowhere so badly understood as in Germany); and in *Ecce homo*, his review of his outlook and preview of his impact, he notes:

"Deutsch" ist ein Argument, "Deutschland, Deutschland über Alles" ein Prinzip, die Germanen sind die "sittliche Weltordnung" in der

Geschichte. . . . Es giebt eine reichsdeutsche Geschichtsschreibung, es giebt, fürchte ich, selbst eine antisemitische, — es giebt eine *Hof-*Geschichtsschreibung und Herr von Treitschke schämt sich nicht . . . ich spüre Lust, ich fühle es selbst als Pflicht, den Deutschen einmal zu sagen, was sie Alles schon auf dem Gewissen haben. *Alle grossen Cultur-Verbrechen von Vier-Jahrhunderten haben sie auf dem Gewissen!* . . . (*EH,* "WA," 2; VI 3:356–57)

["Germany" is an argument, "Deutschland, Deutschland über Alles" is a principle; in history the *Germani* provide "the world's moral order." . . . There is an Imperial German historiography, there is also, I'm sorry to say, an anti-semitic one, there is a *court* historiography, and Herr von Treitschke is not ashamed . . . I feel the desire, I feel it even a duty to tell the Germans what they have on their consciences. *All the great crimes against culture over four centuries are on their consciences!*]

Nietzsche is here reasserting his belief that the sterile, "Life-denying" ethos of the German Reformation was a resentful uprising against the "Life-affirming" spirit of the Italian Renaissance. As he explains elsewhere:

Die Deutschen haben Europa um die letzte grosse Cultur-Ernte gebracht . . . — um die der *Renaissance.* . . . Die Renaissance — ein Ereigniss ohne Sinn, ein grosses Umsonst! — Ah diese Deutschen, was sie uns schon gekostet haben! Umsonst — das war immer das *Werk* der Deutschen. — Die Reformation; Leibniz; Kant und die sogenannte deutsche Philosophie; die Freiheits-Kriege; das Reich . . . Es sind *meine* Feinde, ich bekenne es, die Deutschen: ich verachte in ihnen jede Art von Begriffs- und Werth-Unsauberkeit, von *Feigheit* vor jedem rechtschaffnen Ja und Nein. (*AC* 61; VI 3:248–50)

[The Germans have robbed Europe of its last great cultural harvest . . . — that of the *Renaissance.* The Renaissance — an event without meaning, a great "in vain"! — Ah, these Germans, what they have cost us! "In vain" — that has always been the Germans' achievement. The Reformation, Leibniz, Kant and so-called German philosophy, the Wars of Freedom, the Reich . . . They are my enemies, I admit it, the Germans: I despise in them every inadequacy of concept and value, their cowardice in the face of every honest yes and no.]

It was the notion of individual self-overcoming not national self-aggrandizement that appealed to Nietzsche. Those in Britain who had bothered to read him at all, let alone at all carefully, recognized that patriotism was utterly alien to him, though his fierce opposition to nationalism by no means entails a humane, cosmopolitan outlook:

Nein, wir [Heimatlosen] lieben die Menschheit nicht; andererseits sind wir aber auch lange nicht "deutsch" genug, wie heute das Wort "deutsch" gang und gäbe ist, um dem Nationalismus und dem Rassenhass das Wort zu reden, um an der nationalen Herzenskrätze und Blutvergiftung Freude haben zu können, derenthalben sich jetzt in Europa Volk gegen Volk wie mit Quarantänen abgrenzt, absperrt. (*FW* 377; V 2:312)

[No, we stateless individuals do not love mankind; nor, on the other hand, are we anywhere near "German" enough, as "German" is commonly understood these days, to give the lie to nationalism and race hatred, to take any pleasure in the national heart-searching and poisoning of the blood, on whose account the peoples of Europe are now separating and cutting themselves off from each other as if in quarantine.]

For understandable reasons, few in Britain stood up to be counted as defenders of Nietzsche during those first few months of the war. Important exceptions were John Cowper Powys, who published the ironically entitled *The Menace of German Culture,* and Oscar Levy, who mounted a spirited rearguard action in the *New Age,* but British Nietzscheans were a beleaguered minority.[53] It is no doubt true, as Levy claims, that "zu Ehren der Nietzschefreunde in England sei es gesagt, that they stuck to their gun [*sic*]," but their gun lacked both range and penetration.[54] The *Times Literary Supplement* did, however, print an eloquent and informed counterattack on October 1, 1914:

When the outcome of a doctrine he denounced so fiercely is called a "Nietzschean war," Nietzsche, who knew so little quiet in his tormented life, can know no more in the grave. . . . Nietzsche, in short, has been misunderstood because, while caring nothing for the popular mind and taking no trouble to make himself intelligible to it, he nevertheless deeply struck it by the incisive vigour of his characteristic phrases. Like every preacher who is also a poet, he taught in paradoxes and hard sayings, deliberately intending to be understood only by those who would be at the pains to understand. . . . If instead of putting our own interpretations on Nietzsche's intentionally provocative aphorisms, we seek familiarity with the noble and passionate mind which produced them, . . . this sinister philosophy begins to change its colour. It begins to look more like discipline than violence, disinterestedness than egotism, culture than anarchy.[55]

Nietzsche's greatest fear was this: "Ich habe eine erschreckliche Angst davor, dass man mich eines Tags *heilig* spricht" (*EH;* VI 3:363; It scares me stiff that, some day, I may be pronounced a saint). While he may not have been canonized in 1914, something equally shameful happened to Nietzsche. He was pronounced German.

Notes

A version of this article, entitled "'Fighting A Philosophy': The Figure of Nietzsche in British First World War Propaganda," appeared in *The Modern Language Review* 98 (2003). It is reprinted here by kind permission of The Modern Humanities Research Association.

[1] Friedrich Nietzsche, *Also sprach Zarathustra* I, "Vom Krieg und Kriegsvolke," in Nietzsche, *Werke: Kritische Gesamtausgabe* [*KGW*], ed. Giorgio Colli, Mazzino Montinari, et al. (Berlin and New York: de Gruyter, 1967–), VI 1:54. Subsequent references to Nietzsche's works will be to this edition and will give the abbreviated name of the work, followed by the section number, or chapter title and section number, and the *KGW* division, volume, and page numbers (e.g., *FW* 350: V 2:268). Abbreviations used: *AC* — *Der Antichrist*; *EH* — *Ecce homo*; *FW* — *Die fröhliche Wissenschaft*; *GD* — *Götzen-Dämmerung*; *GM* — *Zur Genealogie der Moral*; *MA* — *Menschliches, Allzumenschliches*; *WA* — *Der Fall Wagner*; *Za* — *Also sprach Zarathustra*.

[2] The first, and very successful, attempt to manipulate Nietzsche's texts in a conscious and systematic fashion was undertaken by his sister, Elisabeth Förster-Nietzsche, and her philological henchmen at the Nietzsche Archive in Weimar from the mid-1890s onwards. It was largely thanks to her tireless campaigning and publishing in 1914 that Nietzsche was enlisted in the service of German war propaganda and thus came to the attention of a wider audience in Britain. For further comment and discussion, see Richard Frank Krummel, *Nietzsche und der deutsche Geist*, 3 vols. (Berlin and New York: de Gruyter, 1974–98), vol. 2 (1983), 571–84; Ben Macintyre, *Forgotten Fatherland: The Search for Elisabeth Förster-Nietzsche* (London: Macmillan, 1992), 149–75; and Klaus Goch, "Elisabeth Förster-Nietzsche: Ein biographisches Portrait," in *Schwestern berühmter Männer*, ed. Luise F. Pusch (Frankfurt am Main: Suhrkamp, 1995), 363–413; here, 387–401.

[3] Michael Howard, for example, dismisses "the much-touted influence of Nietzsche and of Bergson among intellectuals [before and during the war] — the creed of liberation from old social norms, of heroic egotism, of action as a value transcending all others. How widespread was their influence? Did it make the idea of war more generally acceptable than it otherwise would have been? Intellectuals, I am afraid, tend to overrate the importance of other intellectuals, or at least attribute to them an influence which becomes important only among later generations" (Michael Howard, "Europe on the Eve of the First World War," in *The Coming of the First World War*, ed. R. J. W. Evans and Hartmut Pogge von Strandmann [Oxford: Oxford UP, 1988], 1–17; here, 16).

[4] See Vladimir Dedijer, *The Road to Sarajevo* (London: MacGibbon & Kee, 1967), 288, and James Joll, *1914: The Unspoken Assumptions: An Inaugural Lecture Delivered 25 April 1968* (London: Weidenfeld & Nicolson, 1968), 17–18. The poem itself is the penultimate in a series of sixty-three short, self-contained stanzas, which Nietzsche included as a prelude to the first four books of *Die fröh-*

liche Wissenschaft (1882), with the title "'Scherz, List und Rache': Vorspiel in deutschen Reimen" (V 2:39).

[5] William Archer, *Fighting a Philosophy*, Oxford Pamphlets 1914–1915, 65 (Oxford: Oxford UP; London: Humphrey Milford, 1915), Ernest Barker, *Nietzsche and Treitschke: The Worship of Power in Modern Germany*, Oxford Pamphlets 1914, 20 (Oxford: Oxford UP; London: Humphrey Milford, 1914), Herbert Leslie Stewart, *Nietzsche and the Ideals of Modern Germany* (London: Edward Arnold, 1915). See also J. H. Muirhead, *German Philosophy and the War*, Oxford Pamphlets 1914–1915, 62 (Oxford: Oxford UP; London: Humphrey Milford, 1915), 19–26.

[6] Friedrich Adam Julius von Bernhardi, *Deutschland und der nächste Krieg* (Stuttgart and Berlin: Cotta, 1912). For further discussion of Bernhardi's impact in Britain, see James Joll, "The English, Friedrich Nietzsche and the First World War," in *Deutschland in der Weltpolitik des 19. und 20. Jahrhunderts*, ed. Imanuel Geiss and Bernd Jürgen Wendt (Düsseldorf: Bertelsmann, 1974), 287–305; here, 302–3, and also Bridgham, chap. 7 in this volume.

[7] *The Times*, 20 August 1914, 9. The edition referred to is Friedrich von Bernhardi, *Germany and the Next War*, popular edition, trans. Allen H. Powles (London: Edward Arnold, 1914).

[8] Oscar Levy, "Nietzsche im Krieg: Eine Erinnerung und eine Warnung," *Die weißen Blätter* 6 (1919): 277–84; here, 278. Levy had edited *The Complete Works of Friedrich Nietzsche*, 18 vols. (Edinburgh and London: T. N. Foulis, 1909–13). Examples of this scapegoating of Nietzsche in the early months of the war include Barker, *Nietzsche and Treitschke*; Canon E. MacClure, *Germany's War-Inspirers, Nietzsche and Treitschke* (London: Society for Promoting Christian Knowledge, 1914); Members of the Oxford Faculty of Modern History, *Why We Are At War: Great Britain's Case* (Oxford: Clarendon, 1914); Paul More, "Lust of Empire — The Responsibility for the Present War — Nietzsche and Bernhardi," *Nation* [New York] 99 (1914): 493–95; Dora M. Jones, "Nietzsche, Germany, and the War," *London Quarterly Review* 245 (January 1915): 80–94; and John Vance, "Nietzsche: A Study in Paganism," *British Review* 9 (January 1915): 13–28.

[9] Letter to Ernst Bertram, 4 May 1915, in *Thomas Mann an Ernst Bertram: Briefe aus den Jahren 1910–1955*, ed. Inge Jens (Pfullingen: Neske, 1960), 25.

[10] Thomas Mann, "German Letter," *The Dial* 74 (January–June 1923): 609–14; here, 610–11.

[11] Thomas Mann, "Gedanken im Kriege," *Die neue Rundschau* 25 (1914): 1471–84; repr. in Thomas Mann, *Gesammelte Werke*, 13 vols. (Frankfurt am Main: S. Fischer, 1974), 13:527–45.

[12] For further discussion of "Gedanken im Kriege," see Hermann Kurzke, "Die politische Essayistik," in *Thomas-Mann-Handbuch*, ed. Helmut Koopmann (Stuttgart: Kröner, 1990), 697–98; wider questions surrounding Mann's "unpolitical" stance during the First World War are analyzed in T. J. Reed, *Thomas Mann: The Uses of Tradition*, 2nd ed. (Oxford: Oxford UP, 1996), 179–225.

[13] The Schlieffen Plan, named after its originator, Count Alfred von Schlieffen, was drawn up in 1905 as a response to the fear of encirclement. Any war for Germany

would be a war on two fronts. The Schlieffen Plan envisaged knocking France out of the war in forty-two days, before Russia could complete her mobilization. German forces would then be able to turn eastwards and defeat the Russian armies.

[14] For fuller accounts of this process, see Harold D. Lasswell, *Propaganda Technique in the World War* (London: Kegan Paul; New York: Knopf, 1927), 77–101; Cate Haste, *Keep the Home Fires Burning: Propaganda in the First World War* (London: Allen Lane, 1977), 79–108; and M. L. Sanders and Philip M. Taylor, *British Propaganda during the First World War, 1914–18* (London: Macmillan, 1982), 137–63.

[15] Anon., "Musings without method," *Blackwood's Magazine* 196 (July–December 1914): 694–705; here, 700.

[16] Levy, "Nietzsche im Krieg," 277.

[17] Archer, *Fighting a Philosophy*, 3–4.

[18] A "Blond Beast," "Nietzsche," *English Review* 18 (August–November 1914): 392–96.

[19] See Levy, "Nietzsche im Krieg," 278

[20] For further discussion of the debate in Britain surrounding her obligations and interests during July and early August 1914, see Michael Brock, "Britain Enters the War," in *The Coming of the First World War*, ed. Evans and Strandmann, 145–78.

[21] See John Horne and Alan Kramer, *German Atrocities, 1914: A History of Denial* (New Haven and London: Yale UP, 2001), 9–42 and 435–43.

[22] See "Louvain in Ashes: Terrible Act of German Vandalism," *The Times*, August 29, 1914, 8. For a more balanced account of events at Louvain, see Horne and Kramer, *German Atrocities*, 38–42.

[23] *The Times*, August 29, 1914, 9.

[24] Letter to the editor, *The Times*, September 10, 1914, 7.

[25] Letter to the editor, *The Times*, September 1, 1914, 12.

[26] Barbara W. Tuchman, *August 1914* (London: Constable, 1962), 33.

[27] *The Times*, September 2, 1914, 9.

[28] Ibid. Kipling donated his (then) enormous fee of £50 to the Belgian Relief Fund.

[29] *The Times*, September 13, 1914, 3.

[30] See *Times Literary Supplement* 13 (1914): 381 [August 13, 1914].

[31] Nietzsche, *Nietzsche-Worte: Weggenossen in großer Zeit*, ed. Hermann Itschner (Leipzig: Kröner, 1915). See also "Friedrich Nietzsche: Vom Kriege (Aus den Werken)," in *Kriegs-Almanach: Insel-Almanach auf das Jahr 1915* (Leipzig: Insel, 1914), 147–52. This cut-and-stick compilation comprises "Der Krieg unentbehrlich" (*MA* 477), "Vom Krieg und Kriegsvolke" (*Za* I:10), "Unser Glaube an eine Vermännlichung Europas" (*FW*, 362), and aphorisms 729 and 982 of the so-called *Der Wille zur Macht* (VIII 2:429–30 and VII 2:4). Other Yuletide morale-boosters in this almanac include Klopstock's "Wir und sie" (77–79), Hölderlin's "Der Tod fürs Vaterland" (85), Hebbel's "Requiem" (221–22),

and Hofmannsthal's "Die Bejahung Österreichs' (208–12). See also Ernst Rolffs, "Treitschke, Nietzsche, Bernhardi," *Die christliche Welt* 30 (1916): 857–65, 882–88; here, 859. As late as 1917, over 140,000 copies of the Kröner "Taschenausgabe" of *Also sprach Zarathustra* were sold. For further discussion, see Joll, *1914: The Unspoken Assumptions*, 20.

[32] Karl Joël, *Neue Weltkultur* (Leipzig: Wolff, 1915), 88; see also Richard Groeper, "Nietzsche und der Krieg," *Die Tat*, 8/1 (April 1916): 25–38.

[33] Graves's mother, Amalie von Ranke Graves, was a great-niece of the German historian Leopold von Ranke (1795–1866).

[34] See Herbert Read, *The Contrary Experience: Autobiographies* (London: Faber, 1963), 61–70.

[35] Steven E. Aschheim, *The Nietzsche Legacy in Germany, 1890–1990* (Berkeley, Los Angeles, and London: U of California P, 1992), 134.

[36] Wyndham Lewis, *Blast*, no. 2 (July 1915):10.

[37] Robert Graves, *Good-bye to All That: An Autobiography* (London: Jonathan Cape, 1929), 272–73. William le Queux (1864–1927) was a popular author of some 220 books, mostly spy novels. His publisher, Hodder & Stoughton, styled him "The Master of Mystery."

[38] *New Age* 15 (1914): 455.

[39] *The Complete Works of Friedrich Nietzsche*, ed. Oscar Levy, 18 vols. (Edinburgh and London: T. N. Foulis, 1909–13).

[40] Between 1900 and 1950 only two doctoral theses on Nietzsche were completed at British universities; see Gernot U. Gabel, *Friedrich Nietzsche: Ein Verzeichnis westeuropäischer und nordamerikanischer Hochschulschriften, 1900–1980* (Cologne: Gemini, 1985), 23.

[41] Crane Brinton, for example, claimed that Nietzsche had provided the essential points of Nazi ideology ("The National Socialists' Use of Nietzsche," *Journal of the History of Ideas* 1 (1940): 131–50); see also the same author's full-length but no less abrasive study, *Nietzsche* (Cambridge, MA: Harvard UP, 1941). For further discussion of Nietzsche in Second World War propaganda, see Eric Bentley, *The Cult of the Superman: A Study of the Idea of Heroism in Carlyle and Nietzsche, with Notes on Other Hero-Worshippers of Modern Times* (London: Robert Hale, 1947), 248–55.

[42] Walter Kaufmann, *Nietzsche: Philosopher, Psychologist, Antichrist*, 4th ed. (Princeton: Princeton UP, 1974), 8–9.

[43] For further discussion and clarification of Nietzsche's easily misunderstood "blonde Bestie" metaphor, see Detlef Brennecke, "Die blonde Bestie," *Germanisch-Romanische Monatsschrift* 20 (1970): 467–69, and T. J. Reed, "Nietzsche's Animals: Idea, Image, and Influence," in *Nietzsche: Imagery and Thought; A Collection of Essays*, ed. Malcolm Pasley (London: Methuen, 1978), 159–219; here, 163–64.

[44] Letter to the editor, *Manchester Guardian*, October 7, 1914, quoted in Patrick Bridgwater, *Nietzsche in Anglosaxony: A Study of Nietzsche's Impact on English and American Literature* (Leicester: Leicester UP, 1972), 144.

[45] Letter to the editor, *Manchester Guardian*, October 9, 1914. Hardy's letter provoked a number of other critical responses (e.g. C. M. S. McClellan, letter to the editor, *Daily Chronicle*, October 8, 1914, and Beatrice Marshall, letter to the editor, *Daily News*, October 12, 1914), to which Hardy replied in a letter to the *Manchester Guardian* on October 13. See also Anon., "Not up on Nietzsche," *Literary Digest* [New York] 49 (1914): 889–90, and Oscar Levy, "Thomas Hardy and Friedrich Nietzsche," *New Outlook* 61 (1928), 217–18.

[46] Common was a wealthy Scot, a lapsed Presbyterian, who devoted his considerable energy and resources to promoting Nietzsche's works in Britain. He is perhaps best remembered as the translator of two volumes of the abortive first English edition of Nietzsche's works: *The Works of Friedrich Nietzsche*, ed. Alexander Tille, 4 vols. (London: T. Fisher Unwin, 1899–1903). See also Manz's essay, chap. 8 in this volume.

[47] Valuable introductions to the nature and extent of Nietzsche's impact on British (and Irish) life and letters before 1914 are Oscar Levy, "The Nietzsche Movement in England (A Retrospect — A Confession — A Prospect)," in Levy, *The Complete Works of Friedrich Nietzsche*, xviii, ix–xxxvi, and M. E. Humble, "Early British Interest in Nietzsche," *German Life and Letters* 24 (1970/71): 327–35. For more detailed surveys of this terrain, see David S. Thatcher, *Nietzsche in England, 1890–1914: The Growth of a Reputation* (Toronto: U of Toronto P, 1970), and Bridgwater, *Nietzsche in Anglosaxony*, 7–148. Nietzsche's importance to the British literary scene in the years 1896–1914 is discussed in Patrick Bridgwater, "English Writers and Nietzsche," in Pasley, *Nietzsche: Imagery and Thought*, 220–58. See also the illuminating introductory essay in Nancy Snider, *An Annotated Bibliography of English Works on Friedrich Nietzsche*, Ph.D. dissertation, University of Michigan, 1962, iv–xix.

[48] *The Times*, August 27, 1900, 4.

[49] Harry Graf Kessler, *Tagebücher, 1918–1937*, ed. Wolfgang Pfeiffer-Belli (Frankfurt am Main: Insel, 1961), 682 [August 7, 1932].

[50] Levy, "The Nietzsche Movement in England," xx.

[51] Nietzsche. *Briefwechsel: Kritische Gesamtausgabe*, ed. Giorgio Colli, Mazzino Montinari, et al. (Berlin and New York: de Gruyter, 1975–), II 1:155.

[52] Nietzsche's most sustained criticism of (German) nationalism occurs in the chapter "Völker und Vaterländer" in *Jenseits von Gut und Böse* (240–56). Other key passages in this context are the chapter "Was den Deutschen abgeht" in *Götzen-Dämmerung* (VI 3:97–104), and "Die Unzeitgemässen," in *Ecce homo* (VI 3:314–19).

[53] John Cowper Powys, *The Menace of German Culture* (London: William Rider and Son, 1915); for an account of Levy's publishing activities, see Diane Milburn, *The "Deutschlandbild" of A. R. Orage and the "New Age" Circle* (Frankfurt am Main: Peter Lang, 1996), 139–42.

[54] Levy, "Nietzsche im Krieg," 279. For further discussion, see Humble, "Early British Interest in Nietzsche," 333–35.

[55] M. A., "The Nietzschean War," *Times Literary Supplement* 13 (1914): 442.

6: Darwinism and National Identity, 1870–1918

Gregory Moore

WHEN WAR BROKE OUT in August 1914, intellectuals on both sides exchanged fire in a barrage of manifestos and pamphlets, seeking to discover the underlying causes of the catastrophe, not in mundane political events, but in the dominant ideologies and native intellectual traditions of the Great Powers. For many observers, the Great War was more than anything a "war of ideas." In Germany, an impressive array of thinkers sought to elucidate the deeper meaning of the war by arguing that the crisis of 1914 was a truly world-historical conflict rooted in the mutual antagonism that existed between two fundamentally different forms of life, a confrontation that the sociologist Werner Sombart famously summed up as the battle between the rapacious "Händler" of materialistic Britain and the idealistic German "Helden," between a shallow, degenerate "civilization" and a spiritually profound *Kultur*.

Allied intellectuals conceived the war in similarly apocalyptic terms, a struggle pitting "humanity" against "un-humanity." The Oxford historian Ernest Barker thought Germany was pervaded by a "spirit of mastery" that asserted the right of the strong to rule the weak in the struggle for existence. Many other commentators observed that brutality permeated all levels of German life, "from the Cancellarial [*sic*] spluttering about 'hacking through' a practically defenceless neutral State, to the unembarrassed air with which a sixteen-stone Berliner will crowd a woman out of the corner seat in a tram."[1] British propaganda argued that there was a radical fissure in the German tradition; a deep split lay between the dreamy cosmopolitanism of the *Goethezeit* on the one hand and the rise of Prussian hegemony on the other, assisted by the material success of unification and the dominance of materialist philosophy at the expense of idealism. As is well known, British commentators invariably linked this development in German thought with Friedrich Nietzsche, the nationalist historian Heinrich von Treitschke, and General Friedrich von Bernhardi.[2]

What these three very different figures had in common, in the opinion of many British writers, was a sanguinary imagination, a lust for conquest, and a tendency to celebrate war as a natural, elemental force and the ineluctable destiny of all nations — it was, in Bernhardi's infamous phrase, a "biological necessity." All this seemed to be nothing more than crude and abhorrent social Darwinism. Yet some German commentators were no less certain that the deeper meaning of the war lay in a fundamental misunderstanding, an egregious misuse, of evolutionary theory. It is this dispute over perhaps the dominant philosophical and scientific principle of the age — the theory of evolution — that I want to focus on here, a small skirmish that is nevertheless emblematic of the wider ideological battles being fought. What interests me is the ways in which Darwinism was appropriated both before and during the war by intellectuals in both Germany and Britain and made a constitutive element of national identity: Darwinism as an example of the way in which both countries came to attribute to their supposed enemies those characteristics that they wished to surmount in themselves: materialism, modernity, and the dehumanizing consequences of advanced technology.

The View from Britain

To British eyes, Nietzsche's concept of the *Übermensch* and his critique of traditional morals seemed, inevitably, particularly suspicious in this regard.[3] Thomas Escott, a journalist and former lecturer in logic, was certain that Nietzsche's ideas involved "some plagiarism from Darwin." And Bishop Charles Down, in a letter to *The Times*, argued that what he called the "German spirit" is simply "Darwinism turned into an ethical principle . . . That is the principle which is animating modern Germany, and it is neither Kant, nor Hegel. It is Nietzsche; and Nietzsche is Darwinism turned into a rule of life for men and nations."[4]

Down's words provoked an immediate response from Darwin's son, Major Leonard Darwin, president of the Eugenics Association. In a letter published the next day, he sought to dissociate his illustrious family name from any direct involvement in the development of militarism. With perfect justification, he pointed out that his father had been unwilling to apply his theory of evolution by natural selection to human affairs; nor had he believed that it was possible to derive a moral or political philosophy — and certainly not an ethic of military efficiency — from the principle of the struggle for existence in nature. What is more, Darwin argued that modern warfare is positively harmful to the race, for it involves the indiscriminate slaughter of its best specimens — those very men who enlist in the army. The German ideology, the son concluded, had its origins in a misappropriation of Darwin's theory: "It is the worship of brute force and not the doctrine of evolution which must stand condemned."[5] These arguments were repeated time and time again by many other eminent commentators. The biologist Sir Peter Chalmers Mitchell wrote a book entitled *Evolution and the War*, in which he took issue with the tendency of social Darwinism to extrapolate from a biological "law" such as "the struggle for existence" to human rules of conduct. Similar views were expressed by James Crichton-Browne in his book *Bernhardi and Creation: A New Theory of Evolution*, and by Harry Campbell in *The Biological Aspects of Warfare*, and by Havelock Ellis, to name just a few. These figures are representatives of what the historian Paul Crook has termed "peace biology," a tradition of biological thought that predates the war — indeed can, as these men were so keen to point out, be traced right back to Darwin himself — and which viewed war as a genetic disaster for humankind. The task of evolutionary biology was to promote peace. Of course, there were German warmongers who really did deploy the rhetoric of social Darwinism — Max von Gruber, for example, in his 1915 speech *Krieg, Frieden und Biologie*. But there were British social Darwinists too, just as there were biologist peacemeakers in Germany — like the dissident professor of physiology at Berlin, G. F. Nicolai, who, sickened by the war and especially by the conduct of his fellow German intellectuals, published *Die Biologie des Krieges* in 1917. In British propaganda, however, the "biological justification of war" exemplified by Bernhardi came to be seen as something typically "German." For Chalmers Mitchell, though this way of thinking was not *uniquely* German, it had nevertheless "seized the imagination of the German nation consciously rejoicing in the splendour of material progress, and it appears to have contributed in no small measure to the catastrophe which is devastating civilization." Others were less even-handed and referred to something called "Darwinism 'made in Germany.'"[6]

Another kind of British commentator took a more theistic view of evolution. The Liberal MP William Chapple maintained that evolution should not be considered in purely materialistic terms; human beings, he argued, are at the present stage "evolving to the moral and spiritual." Germany, however, recognized only the evolution of physical strength, of physical power, a throwback to when "force was the only factor in the struggle." In contrast, truly civilized nations embraced a different conception of power: the "power of spirit, the power of freedom and liberty" that was unknown in so-called German culture. In his book *German Philosophy in Relation to the War*, Prof. John Henry Muirhead of the University of Birmingham concurred. Darwinism, correctly interpreted, he thought, ultimately "joins hands with the Idealism it is thought to have superseded." The theory of evolution, British writers agreed, presupposed a profoundly spiritual conception of the universe and of humanity's place within it.[7]

The German interpretation of Darwinism was held to have had a corrosive effect on morals, whereas evolutionism as Darwin himself conceived it certainly did not lead to a transvaluation of values. The latter is true, to an extent: the social order did not collapse with the dissemination of Darwinism in the late nineteenth century. Victorian culture was pliant and confident enough to tolerate and adapt evolution, provided it was not couched in terms that violated accepted civilized and ethical values — which was precisely what the Germans were supposed to have done. The majority of Victorians could not accept that the ubiquitous conflict entailed by the notion of a struggle for existence was entirely without purpose. Their faith in progress was an essential means of reassuring themselves that whatever the short-term suffering, there was a meaningful goal to be achieved, that evolution was a process leading inexorably towards moral and intellectual improvement. Biologists looked to evolution as a source of spiritual values, and sought to discover indications and proof of an underlying order and meaning in Nature.[8]

That the fundamental idea that lay behind all nineteenth-century theories of evolutionary progress was a moral and religious one is perhaps indicated most clearly by Darwin's own account of the development of morality in *The Descent of Man*, which is obviously motivated by a strong desire to leave inviolate the moral "truths" of Christian teaching instilled in him during his childhood. Although Darwin believes that a moral sense originated through the natural selection of those tribes in whom the social instinct was strongest, he recognizes that this primitive ethic gradually developed into a "higher morality" through the effects of habit, rational reflection, and religious instruction. Not "the survival of the fittest" but "as ye would that men should do to you, do ye to them likewise" has come to be regarded as the true maxim of human conduct. Nor is moral progress at an end: virtuous habits will grow stronger, becoming fixed by inheritance: "In this case the struggle between our higher and lower impulses will be less severe, and virtue will be triumphant." This theistic notion of evolution as an ever-upward progression away from earlier forms of animal life and towards spiritual and social perfection came to be inseparable from the way Darwinism was received and interpreted. As J. H. Muirhead admitted, Darwin's view "has, on the whole, been in growing degree the view taken in England."[9] It is the very foundation of Herbert Spencer's elaborate system of thought and is present in L. T. Hobhouse's 1906 book *Morals in Evolution*, to name just two examples.

But in Germany, according to Muirhead, Darwinism was inevitably perverted by a quarter of a century of materialistic thought. One of the thinkers he singled out as having contributed to the development of a distinctively German brand of Darwinism was the eminent biologist Ernst Haeckel, the man who had done much to popularize evolutionary theory in Germany in the late nineteenth century and who had raised it to the level of an all-encompassing worldview, encapsulated in his so-called "monistic" philosophy. He was not alone. Other British commentators weighed in against Haeckel, their arguments often recapitulating the polemics that, ten years before, had greeted Haeckel's best-selling books *Das Welträtsel* and *Die Lebenswunder*, both in Britain and Germany, particularly from Christian writers horrified by Haeckel's attempt to replace Christianity with a secular religion with evolutionism at its center. According to the theologian Robert Newton Flew, it was *Das Welträtsel*, "more than any other work," that had "poisoned the intellectual atmosphere of Germany." Baron Friedrich von Hügel, an anglophile former German consul, pointed to the supposedly materialistic worldview exemplified in *Das Welträtsel* as the source of a growing "pedantic barbarism" in Germany, a coarsening of human feeling, thinking, and theory. Another pair of writers concurred with this estimation of the baneful influence of what they called the "upside-down philosophy of Haeckel's variant of Darwin's rule of efficiency." Haeckel's radical materialism was supposedly taken up by Nietzsche, who represents the climax of the "German gloss on Darwinism." Haeckel may have held Christian ethics in "materialistic contempt," but at least he "recognised it, and tried, if he failed, to reconcile it with his own doctrine." Nietzsche, on the other hand, showed no compunction in brutally sweeping away the old morality and replacing it with his own notion of "super-humanity." This creed had subsequently become a "living influence" in Germany, where it had been "ridden to death" by Bernhardi and his ilk.[10]

This distinctive "Germano-Darwinism" was often held to underpin that peculiar form of civilization that the Germans proudly called their *Kultur*. That evolutionary theory was the "*prima facie* element which gave origin and cohesion to German *Weltpolitik*" is the central claim of the Scottish anthropologist Robert Munro's aptly titled book *From Darwinism to Kaiserism*. Munro maintained that the notion of the survival of the fittest had for many years been the guiding principle of German scientists and politicians. They reasoned that if dominance was ultimately attained in plant and animal life by the degree of adaptedness or biological efficiency that individual organisms are able to achieve within a given milieu, the same effect could be reproduced in the human sphere by imitating nature's methods. The Imperial government therefore promoted efficiency in all areas of national life, particularly in industry and the military, giving rise to the sophisticated technocratic society that German chauvinists hailed as their superior *Kultur*. Most British writers shared Munro's suspicion of the enemy's claims to cultured refinement. *Kultur* was not to be confused with "culture" in Matthew Arnold's sense, understood as the pursuit of "sweetness and light." Rather, as Sir Peter Chalmers Mitchell explained, the concept of "Kultur" corresponded to a much older, scientific use of the English word "culture," surviving "in such a phrase as the bacteriological term 'culture-media.'" *Kultur* included "the operation of the whole set of forces, partly selective, partly directive, political, educational, social, environmental, that go to the moulding of the national character." In other words, *Kultur* was nothing more than the sum of environmental pressures acting upon the German "species." And its goal? To bring forth a "race of Supermen." For this, the German people as a whole "accept the fate of the mediocre." The German people as a whole willingly made sacrifices for the sake of this higher goal, receiving in return "the reward of the mediocre: good government, a perfect mechanical organisation."[11] In sum: British commentators portrayed Germany as a repressive society based on a nightmarishly modern combination of the law of the jungle and the technology of the machine. In Britain, meanwhile, Darwinism had been interpreted as promising an ultimate release from the exigencies of struggle and conflict.

The View from Germany

But the Germans of course did not see themselves as slaves to a brutal military-industrial complex rooted in the Darwinian struggle for existence and merely masquerading as "culture." On the contrary: this was precisely how they viewed the British. For German writers, the real threat to European civilization was the materialism and mercantilism of British society, and this was most clearly manifested in Darwinism.

One of the ironies of British commentators' seeing in Nietzsche's thought a misinterpretation of Darwin was that Nietzsche himself had devoted considerable energies trying to refute Darwin. To Nietzsche's way of thinking, Darwin's theory of natural selection — the idea that advantageous adaptations to specific environmental conditions are preserved by a struggle for the means of subsistence — misconstrues the very essence of life. Vital processes are not primarily characterized by a passive adaptation to the prevailing circumstances, whether biological or social, but rather by an active, form-giving force inherent in nature itself — the will to power. Nor is Nature frugal, as Darwin supposed; organisms do not fight amongst themselves for scraps of food like poverty-stricken urchins of the urban proletariat — here Nietzsche claims to catch the whiff of "englische Uebervölkerungs-Stickluft" (stifling atmosphere of English over-population) wafting around Darwin's theory. Anyway, in such an unseemly struggle, it is not the fittest, the strongest, the remarkable individuals who prevail, but the rabble, the herd, the weak — through sheer weight of numbers: just look, Nietzsche says, at the average modern European.[12]

But Nietzsche's scorn was not reserved for Darwin alone. Darwinism was for him just one manifestation of the egalitarian and democratic ideology of industrial Britain. The British way of life, with its good-natured bad taste, its comfortable *laissez-faire*, and its resolutely unheroic aspirations and indigestible food was anathema to Nietzsche and seemed to him to be the modern breeding ground of the herd instinct. Just as symptomatic of British intellectual mediocrity was John Stuart Mill, the author of utilitarianism, the moral theory for which the highest ethical good is the "greatest happiness of the greatest number" — a notion that Nietzsche dismissed as base, ignoble, fundamentally perverse. But the figure whom Nietzsche saw as perhaps the most characteristic British thinker was the philosopher and sociologist Herbert Spencer, who combined Mill's utilitarianism and Darwin's evolutionism to create a doctrine according to which the "greatest happiness of the greatest number" was the inevitable end of evolution, a wholly necessary development brought about by increasing social adaptation and natural selection of the morally fit. Spencer's dream of future contentment was a nightmare for Nietzsche; a society founded on Spencerian principles, he declared, "schiene uns der Verachtung, der Vernichtung wert!" (would seem to us worthy of contempt, of annihilation).

Now, Nietzsche may not have influenced the development of German militarism or foreign policy, as British observers suspected, but his Anglophobic attacks on Darwin and Spencer certainly helped to shape the prewar and wartime opinions of a later generation of German intellectuals. For if Nietzsche or Bernhardi were the social Darwinist bogeymen of British propagandists, then their German counterparts cast Herbert Spencer in a similar role.

Spencer was a particularly apt choice of villain for the Germans, for he divided society into two forms that seemed to describe perfectly the two warring camps in 1914: the militant and industrial types. The militant society was exemplified by Russia and Prussia, where the state appropriates industry, and political control slides back towards the military. In the more highly evolved industrial society, such as Britain, the historical trajectory is towards free trade, liberalism, and a gradual decline in the role of the state. Spencer's position that warlike societies are superseded by industrial ones, that peaceful international commerce replaces conflict between nation states, is the exact opposite of that of Werner Sombart, who saw the Great War as a battle between noble military *Helden* and vulgar British *Händler*. Unsurprising, then, that Sombart viewed Spencer as the British thinker par excellence because he combined "die spezifisch-englische, also flache Ethik mit der spezifisch-englischen, also flachen Entwicklungstheorie" (specifically English, that is, gutless, ethics, with a specifically English, that is, gutless, theory of development). He excoriated Spencer not only for daring to present industrialization as a perfectly necessary development, but also for believing that the dangerous superficiality and commercialism of British civilization that has debased the human spirit was somehow a morally superior form of life *precisely because* it was supposedly the product of a natural evolution. For Sombart, then, there was a heroic and a mercantile, a right and a wrong, a German and an English conception of nature.[13]

These views were echoed by Sombart's friend, the philosopher Max Scheler, who would go on to become the most prominent German thinker of the 1920s. In his pamphlet *Der Genius des Krieges und der Deutsche Krieg*, Scheler agreed with Nietzsche and Sombart: that the "englische Biologie" of Darwin and Spencer merely consisted in the projection and universalization of the liberal and utilitarian principles of the "englischen Kaufmannsphilosophie" onto the whole realm of organic life: its individualism, the coarse mechanism of its metaphysics, the subordination of the noble to the useful, the prioritization of adaptation, and the conception of the organism as machine. War was not an extension of the struggle for existence, as Spencer claimed, something that humanity would in time outgrow because evolution is a process of progressive civilization, of humanity's increased adaptation to its surroundings and fellow beings — Scheler explicitly rejects *both* pacifism *and* militant social Darwinism. Following Nietzsche, Scheler proposed that the true root of all war lay not in a conflict for finite resources among nations, or as a consequence of imperfect adaptation (the human organism is not an inert object modified by environmental pressure), but rather in the fact that in all life there is an innate tendency to expand and grow, to unfurl its rich potentialities. Scheler adopts another Nietzschean argument, but gives it a suitably nationalistic twist. If war were really simply an amplification of the struggle for existence, in which the best adapted and adaptable won out — then the sheer numbers of what he terms the "die niedrigeren Lebensformen" would destroy the superior and aristocratic peoples, who are always in a minority. Those who possessed the virtues and vices of the adaptable — slyness, flexibility, industry, but also cowardice, mistrustfulness, deceitfulness, servility, egoism — that is, the English — would outlive that endangered minority with noble and heroic qualities — and here he is referring to what he terms the "Germanic-Celtic-Slavic peoples of western Europe" — whose nobility consists not in increased adaptability to all possible natural and social circumstances but in their readiness to perish rather than to live under any old conditions. Such self-sacrifice is inevitable and praiseworthy; Darwin was wrong to assume that war is both morally wicked and harmful to the race because it ensures that its best specimens are eliminated. On the contrary, says Scheler, the desire to save the manliest individuals from a warrior's death in the service of the Fatherland is a sure sign of the "biologischen Niedergangstendenz" (biological decline) of a people. The willingness of the best specimens of a race to sacrifice themselves for such a goal was a sign of higher life: "Alles hochgeartete Leben ist verschwenderisch mit seinen Kräften" (every noble form of life is profligate with its powers).[14]

What is interesting is that before the war, Scheler had already, in his 1912 book *Ressentiment im Aufbau der Moralen*, portrayed the prevailing mechanistic paradigm exemplified by Darwin and Spencer as itself a symptom of cultural malaise. But here his ideas are couched in less explicitly Anglophobic terms, and figure as part of a more general *Kulturkritik*. Scheler uses the Nietzschean concept of *Ressentiment* to explain how the erroneous mechanistic understanding of life has come to dominate the biological sciences. But unlike Nietzsche, Scheler believes that not Christian ethics but rather that specifically modern form of asceticism, bourgeois morality, is the product of the poisonous "*Ressentiment* der Lebensuntüchtigeren gegen die Tüchtigeren" (*resentment* of those less fit for life towards those who are more fit). The steady rise of the biologically inferior bourgeoisie, the victory of industrialism and commercialism over the military and theological-metaphysical spirit, and the rise of the *Gesellschaft* at the expense of the *Gemeinschaft*, have brought with it the "tiefste Verkehrung der Wertrangordnung" (the most profound perversion of the hierarchy of values): the subordination of *Lebenswerte* to *Nutzwerte*, the elevation of instrumental reason and utilitarianism over everything that is noble, powerful, and healthy. Modern Darwinian biology views life as merely a complex of mechanical processes; the organism is reduced to a mere machine, its organs tools whose function is primarily to promote the survival of the structure as a whole. Life is thereby stripped of any independent worth apart from its utility value. This impoverished understanding of life represents nothing more than the projection of the values and concerns of the rabble onto nature; the entire mechanistic worldview is only the "ungeheure intellektuelle *Symbol* des Sklavenaufstandes in der Moral," a "Dekadenzerscheinung" (monstrous intellectual symbol of the slave revolt in morality . . . a symptom of decadence):

> So stellt der Geist der modernen Zivilisation nicht, wie Spencer meinte, einen "Fortschritt," *sondern* einen *Niedergang* der Entwicklung der Menschheit dar. Er stellt die Herrschaft der Schwachen über die Starken, der Klugen über die Edlen, der bloßen Quantitäten über die Qualitäten.

> [Thus the spirit of modern civilization does not represent progression, as Spencer thought, but a decline in humanity's development. It represents the dominion of the weak over the strong, the clever over the noble, mere quantity over quality.]

In 1914, Scheler now portrays the British as the sole bearers of degenerate bourgeois morality, the source of the contagion that has spread all over Europe. The war is the means to regeneration, to restoring *Lebens-werte* to their rightful place in the hierarchy of values, to effect a trans-valuation of values in the Nietzschean sense. By defeating England, Germany will destroy the vulgar materialism and the shallow utilitarianism and mercantilism afflicting modern European life.[15]

Scheler's understanding of evolution was profoundly influenced by Jakob von Uexküll, a Baltic German biologist and friend of Houston Stewart Chamberlain. Uexküll combined an anti-Darwinian evolutionism (expressed most clearly in his objection to the idea that living things are the passive products of the environment) with Kantian epistemology in order to investigate the ways in which organisms actively create their own external realities. Each organism, Uexküll concluded, subjectively con-structs its own world around itself (which he termed the "Umwelt"), with different kinds of sensory organs giving rise to different realities. In his wartime essay "Darwin und die englische Moral," though, Uexküll blended biology and Kantianism in a rather different way.

As we have seen, British commentators often railed against the sup-posed amorality of the Germans, who had systematically replaced civilized ethics with a vulgar social Darwinism. Yet it was the development of mo-rality that raised humanity above the remorseless struggle for life. Com-munal existence, governed by what the Germans, with Nietzsche, derided as the "law of the herd," presupposed forms of mutual obligation and al-truistic behavior that were far more advanced than the "soulless egoism of the primitive brute." Uexküll turned the tables on such critics. Like Nietzsche before him, he accused English morality itself of being an expression of herd mentality and attacked Darwin's account of moral evo-lution, as outlined in *The Descent of Man*, as a typical example of the su-perficial English mind: "Darwins Standpunkt kann man kurz dahin zusammenfassen: *Je größer die Herde, um so höher die Moral*" (Darwin's view can be summarized thus: *the greater the herd, the higher the morality*). The fundamental, irreconcilable differences separating the English and German moral universes were clearly visible in the contrast between Kant's categorical imperative, which appealed to eternal ideals woven into the very fabric of the world, and Darwin's moral imperative, which might be phrased as: "Handle so, daß deine Handlungen durch die Billigung und Mißbilligung deiner Mitmenschen dauernd bestimmt bleiben" (Act in such a way that your actions are always determined by the approval or disapproval of your fellow-men). The English, then, have not so much a morality as a "Moralersatz"; like Darwin, whose evolutionary ethics amounts to nothing more than a biologization of national prejudice, they recognize no higher authority than public opinion, the praise and censure of one's fellow beings. Darwin, in his moral as well as in his biological thought, has failed to recognize the divinity, profundity, and beneficence of nature. German moral philosophy, however, presupposes the sovereign individual and requires him to despise the "allgemeine Meinung" and "völlig frei von Lob und Tadel der anderen seine eigenen Handlungen moralisch zu werten" (to judge the moral value of his own actions quite independently of the praise or reproaches of others). He is guided not by the whims of the masses, but by transcendental values, for the German moral tradition is predicated on a mystical union with "einer planmäßigen Naturgewalt, die nichts mit Physik oder Chemie zu tun hat" (a predetermining force of Nature which has nothing to do with physics or chemistry). Adopting another Kantian argument, Uexküll declares that immediate, intuitive access to the secrets of nature are not granted to us by scientific observation, but by the individual moral conscience:

> Wohl können wir den biologischen Beweis für die Existenz einer solchen planmäßigen Naturgewalt bringen, denn ein jeder Gestaltungsvorgang in der Körperwelt der Lebewesen verläuft nach planmäßigen Gesetzen. Aber die planmäßige Naturgewalt selbst wird uns durch unsre Sinne immer nur mittelbar zur Kenntnis gebracht. Bloß im Gewissen kann sie sich uns unmittelbar offenbaren, weil diesem die Gestaltung unserer Gefühle und Empfindungen zu einem harmonischen Ganzen übertragen ist.[16]

> [No doubt we can provide biological proof for the existence of such a predetermining force of Nature, since every formative process in the physical structure of living things develops along predetermined lines. But the predetermining force of Nature can itself be known to us only partially through our senses. Only in our consciences can it reveal itself to us directly, because it is the conscience that bears responsibility for shaping our feelings and emotions to a harmonious whole.]

Another philosopher who fulminated against the decadent materialism of British thought — as manifested in the evolutionary theories of Darwin and Spencer — was Karl Joël. Joël was a German-Jewish thinker who before the war had written a book called *Nietzsche und die Romantik,* and whose own neo-Romanticism was expressed in such works as *Seele und Welt* and *Antibarbarus,* the latter favorably reviewed by Max Scheler just after the beginning of hostilities. Joël viewed the war as a struggle for mastery between what he termed the mechanical principle and the organic principle. The overthrow of the former, both in politics and the sciences, would usher in a brave new "Weltkultur." He dismissed British propaganda claims that German *Kultur* was absolutist and totalitarian; on the contrary, absolutism really resided in the systematizing and atomizing tendencies of mechanist and materialist thought. The organic principle, on the other hand, represented a holistic view of nature and society. It expressed a philosophy of freedom liberating one from the constraints of external causes and laws, a philosophy celebrating living nature over and against the dead and merely mechanical, a philosophy of *Entwicklung* that recognizes that organic change is the product, not of the brutal *Manchestertum* of Darwin's struggle for life, but of the unfolding of life's inherent creative energies. This Romantic vitalism was a profoundly, uniquely German way of thinking. The same inexhaustible vital impulse that propels nature had inspired Germany's philosophers and poets — from Goethe to Nietzsche — and now guided the German people to even greater deeds on the battlefield. If the organic principle was humanity's salvation, its redemption from soulless abstraction, then the Germans — as the "Volk der Selbsterneuerung, des inneren Werdensdranges, des ewigen 'Stirb und Werde'" (the people of self-renewal, of the inner compulsion to develop, of the eternal "die and become"), as the only truly evolving, vital nation, the most in tune with nature — were the agents of this salvation.[17]

In a sense, British writers were right to say that Germans had developed a novel brand of Darwinism or *Darwinismus*. It has often been said that Darwinism, though born in England, "found its spiritual home in Germany"; it was here more than any other country that evolutionary theory achieved the status of "a kind of popular philosophy."[18] But this had little to do with social Darwinism — which was equally at home in Britain as in Germany. Even though some German biologists openly proclaimed themselves to be "Darwinians," their thought often turns out to be little more than a blend of Darwinian rhetoric — usually the evocation of the struggle for existence — with attitudes that are in reality a legacy of a pre-Darwinian view of nature. This may have been due to the fact that, even before the publication of the *Origin of Species*, many German naturalists were already evolutionists in the sense that they accepted the gradual unfolding or *Entwicklung* of a purposeful trend in the history of life, ideas that had their roots in the dynamic view of nature fostered by Romantic and pre-Romantic *Naturphilosophie*. While there were some German scientists who followed Darwin in holding that natural selection — or at least some combination of external, environmental factors — was the mechanism of species mutation, a significant number of prominent biologists either wholly rejected Darwin's theory of natural selection or attached less importance to it. In its place, many articulated a *pre-Darwinian basic commitment to non-adaptive models of evolutionary change*. Loyal to the vitalistic traditions of their science, nineteenth-century German biologists resurrected the concept of the *Bildungstrieb*, and held an internal directive or transformative force to be the main engine of evolution. This is at the heart of the "organische Entwickelungstheorie" proposed as a replacement for Darwinism by Eduard von

Hartmann, perhaps *the* most widely read philosopher in late nineteenth-century Germany, and certainly one of the first to incorporate evolutionary theory into his thinking. The theory of descent and the doctrine of the unity of nature belonged, he argued, not to natural science but to *Naturphilosophie.* He claimed that the "Anhänger der Descendenztheorie in Deutschland" (disciples of the theory of descent in Germany), and Ernst Haeckel in particular, were shaking off the spell of Darwinism and working towards "einer solchen dem Volke der Denker mehr entsprechenden Auffassung" (a conception more appropriate to the people of thinkers). Evolution had become for Hartmann an expression of national identity, and it seems significant that he was making these demands in the early 1870s, when nation-building was high on the political agenda in Germany. Haeckel himself had already gone down this road, regarding evolutionary biology as an objective foundation for nationalism and an ideology of social integration. Where Hartmann saw Kant as a forerunner of the evolutionary worldview, Haeckel, in his best-selling 1866 work *Generelle Morphologie der Organismen,* declared Goethe to be the "*selbständig[e] Begründer der Deszendenz-Theorie in Deutschland*" (the independent originator of the theory of descent in Germany). Haeckel was not alone; there were many in Germany who downplayed Darwin's achievements in favor of Goethe: Julius Langbehn, Houston Stewart Chamberlain, Jakob von Uexküll, Karl Joël. And Nietzsche himself claimed: "Darwin neben Goethe setzen / heisst: *die Majestät verletzen*" (placing Darwin alongside Goethe is *lèse-majesté*).[19]

This appeal to Goethe was not just a sop to national pride; Goethe came to represent the antidote to Darwinian materialism and the positivism of modern natural sciences. Just as Goethe himself had rebelled against the rigid mechanism of Newtonian physics, so his successors sought to revive his aesthetic-teleological vision of living nature in their fight against the mechanism of the man hailed as the new Newton: Darwin. But Goethe's rich and colorful world promised an alternative, not just to the apparently aimless destructiveness of the Darwinian universe and the reductive materialism and mechanism of modern science, but also to the materialism and mechanism of the rapidly industrializing, modernizing Bismarckian Reich, which had left so many so disappointed. What was going on in Germany in the late nineteenth century was not just an abstract debate over the legitimacy of competing biological theories; it was an integral part of the experience of modernity, which was characterized, in the words of Friedrich Meinecke, by the fact that:

> eine neue tiefere Sehnsucht nach dem Echten und Wahren, aber auch ein neuer Sinn für die zerissene Problematik des modernen

Lebens erwachte und von seiner zivilisierten Oberfläche wieder in die bald unheimliche, bald lockende Tiefe zu tauchen versuchte.[20]

[there arose a new, deeper longing for what is true and genuine, but also a new sense of the fissured, problematic nature of modern life — and attempted to dive back into the depths, now eerie, now beckoning, away from the civilized surface.]

The *Reichsgründung* or establishment of the Empire could not by itself overcome the fragmentation and individualism of modern life, its "Entzauberung" (disenchantment), in Max Weber's famous words. Julius Langbehn put it most clearly in *Rembrandt als Erzieher*, when he suggested that, just as Bismarck had provided external unity for Germany, so now there was an acute need for a leader with the aesthetic vision to give Germany back her internal, cultural unity.

The war of course intensified these long-held hopes for renewal, for the resurgence of those moral sources of social cohesion that had been threatened by the materialism of Wilhelmine culture. Scheler's and Joël's Nietzsche-inspired calls for a radical renewal of German-European culture — symbolized by the rejection of a British-Darwinian conception of nature — are part of this discourse. This anti-Darwinism is a form of the, at times, virulent Anglophobia in German society, which, like the increasingly intellectually respectable anti-Semitism, was itself merely a mask for a wider antimodern attitude. Darwinism, as one of the very symbols of modernity, had to be reinterpreted, reconciled with an older tradition to purge science and philosophy of its instrumentalism and utilitarianism, to replace it with a more holistic character. And that organic worldview would serve as the model for a new organicist, collectivist society. As Fichte had urged over 100 years before in his *Reden an die deutsche Nation*, Germany must throw off the yoke of foreign influence and return to its own vital beliefs and practices.

The "war of ideas," the "conflict between two different and irreconcilable conceptions of government, society, and progress," which many saw as the true meaning of the Great War, was not just a struggle over rival philosophical and political traditions, over the relative merits of *Kultur* against civilization; it was also a struggle over the true meaning of the theory of evolution, with both sides claiming for themselves the ability to appreciate its true spiritual significance. This was a war not just between competing conceptions of culture, but also of competing conceptions of nature. As such, Darwinism — or rather, one's relationship to it, one's own particular interpretation of it — became a key component of national identity, an expression of indigenous intellectual traditions.

Notes

[1] A. S. Ellwell-Sutton, *Humanity vs. Un-Humanity* (London, Unwin, 1916); Ernest Barker, "Nietzsche and Treitschke: The Worship of Power in Modern Germany" (Oxford: Oxford UP, 1914); E. C. Bentley, "The German State of Mind," *Fortnightly Review* 97 (1915), 42–53; here, 50.

[2] On this, see Gregory Moore "The Super-Hun and the Super-State: Allied Propaganda and German Philosophy during the First World War," *German Life and Letters* 65 (2001): 310–30.

[3] See particularly James Joll, "The English, Friedrich Nietzsche and the First World War," in *Deutschland in der Weltpolitik des 19. und 20. Jahrhunderts*, ed. Imanuel Geiss and Bernd Jürgen Wendt (Düsseldorf: Bertelsmann Universitäts-verlag, 1973), 287–305.

[4] T. H. S. Escott, "German Culture in the Crucible," in *British Review* 9 (1915), 321–43; here, 335; *The Times*, September 25, 1914, 9.

[5] *The Times*, September 26, 1914, 9.

[6] Paul Crook, *Darwinism, War and History: The Debate over the Biology of War from "The Origin of Species" to the First World War* (Cambridge: Cambridge UP, 1994); Peter Chalmers Mitchell, *Evolution and the War* (London: Murray, 1915); Max von Gruber, *Krieg, Frieden und Biologie* (Berlin: Heymanns 1915); G. F. Nicolai, *Die Biologie des Krieges* (Zurich: Fuessli, 1917); James Crichton-Browne, *Bernhardi and Creation: A New Theory of Evolution* (Glasgow: James Maclehose & Sons, 1916); Harry Campbell, *The Biological Aspects of Warfare* (London: Baillière & Co., 1918); Havelock Ellis, *Essays in War-Time: Further Studies in the Task of Social Hygiene* (London: Constable, 1917); W. Morris Colles and A. D. McLaren, "The War of Ideas," *Nineteenth Century* 86 (1919), 1114–24; here, 1118.

[7] W. A. Chapple, "German Culture," *Contemporary Review* 107 (1915), 355–60; here, 358; J. H. Muirhead, *German Philosophy in Relation to the War* (London: Murray, 1915), 95.

[8] For a discussion of these themes, see: Robert J. Richards, *Darwin and the Emergence of Evolutionary Theories of Mind and Behavior* (Chicago: U of Chicago P, 1987); and Peter Bowler, *The Non-Darwinian Revolution: Reinterpreting a Historical Myth* (Baltimore: John Hopkins UP, 1992).

[9] Charles Darwin, *The Descent of Man, and Selection in Relation to Sex*, 2nd ed., 2 vols. (London: Murray, 1877), 1:124–25.

[10] R. Newton Flew, "Kant and Modern Prussianism," *London Quarterly Review* 13 (1917), 264–68; here, 267; Friedrich von Hügel, *The German Soul* (London: Dent, 1916), 185; W. Morris Colles and A. D. McLaren, "The War of Ideas," 1118.

[11] Robert Munro, *From Darwinism to Kaiserism* (Glasgow: James Maclehose & Sons, 1919), 129; P. Chalmers Mitchell, *Evolution and the War*, 67; A. S. Ellwell-Sutton, *Humanity vs. Un-Humanity*, 206.

[12] Friedrich Nietzsche, *Die fröhliche Wissenschaft*, §349, in *Sämtliche Werke, Kritische Studienausgabe* (Munich: Deutscher Taschenbuch Verlag; Berlin: Mouton de Gruyter, 1988), 3:585. I have discussed Nietzsche's relation to Darwinism in more detail in Gregory Moore, *Nietzsche, Biology and Metaphor* (Cambridge: Cambridge UP, 2002).

[13] Werner Sombart, *Händler und Helden: Patriotische Besinnungen* (Munich: Duncker & Humblot, 1915), 21.

[14] Max Scheler, *Der Genius des Krieges und der Deutsche Krieg*, in *Gesammelte Werke* (Bern: Franke, 1954–97), 4: 31, 36, 38, 41.

[15] Max Scheler, *Ressentiment im Aufbau der Moralen*, in *Gesammelte Werke* 3: 137, 131, 145, 147.

[16] Colles and McLaren, "The War of Ideas," 1117; Jakob von Uexküll, "Darwin und die englische Moral," *Deutsche Rundschau* 173 (1917): 215–42; here, 223, 225, 228. The glorification of public opinion eventually led to parliamentary democracy, which Uexküll, with the disdain of a nobleman, denigrated as mob rule. Uexküll developed his biological arguments against democracy in "Biologie und Wahlrecht," *Deutsche Rundschau* 174 (1918): 183–203.

[17] Karl Joël, *Neue Weltkultur* (Leipzig: Wolff, 1915), 70.

[18] Emanuel Rádl, *The History of Biological Theories* (London: Humphrey Milford, 1930), 42.

[19] Eduard von Hartmann, *Wahrheit und Irrthum im Darwinismus: Eine kritische Darstellung der organischen Entwickelungstheorie* (Berlin/Leipzig: Duncker, 1875), 148–49; Ernst Haeckel, *Generelle Morphologie des Organismen* (Berlin: Reimer, 1866), 2:160; Friedrich Nietzsche, "An die deutschen Esel," in *Sämtliche Werke*, 9:317.

[20] Friedrich Meinecke, *Erlebtes, 1862–1919* (Stuttgart: Verlag, 1964), 111. On the reaction against materialism and mechanism in Germany, see Anne Harrington, *Reenchanted Science: Holism and German Culture from Wilhelm II to Hitler* (Princeton: Princeton UP, 1996).

7: Bernhardi and "The Ideas of 1914"

Fred Bridgham

The Book that Caused the War?

DEUTSCHLAND UND DER NÄCHSTE KRIEG (1912), by the retired cavalry general Friedrich von Bernhardi (1849–1930), has been aptly called "a best seller and a political disaster."[1] It ran through five impressions in 1912 alone, and nine by 1914, by which time an English "popular edition," *Germany and the Next War*, had reached a sixth reprint.[2] *Deutschland* was itself extracted from an even larger treatise, *Vom heutigen Kriege*, part of which had already appeared in English as *Cavalry in Future Wars* (1906);[3] a second volume of *Vom heutigen Kriege* (1912) duly became, rather more pointedly, *How Germany Makes War* (1914).[4] Much of *Germany and the Next War* likewise focuses on military technicalities, to the extent that one wonders who but specialists will have read through to the end. But the early chapters, notably those vividly evoking not only Germany's "right to wage war" but her "obligation to wage war" to achieve her "historic mission," namely "world-power or downfall,"[5] are, in the words of a contemporary critic, "very curious . . . messroom metaphysics, and worth explaining. . . . It is a blessing to the world that the men who wanted war, and got a war much bigger than they wanted, had a spokesman so simple and frank in proclaiming all their plans as General von Bernhardi."[6]

Yet a third version of Bernhardi's ideas reached English readers shortly after the outbreak of war as a two-shilling paperback, *Britain as Germany's Vassal*, its cover declaring it to be "The Book That Caused the War." A literal and less sensational rendering of *Unsere Zukunft: Ein Mahnwort an das deutsche Volk* (1913) would be "Our Future: A Word of Warning to the German Nation," but its translator defends the choice of title as an attempt "to summarize more correctly its chief contents as it affects this country."[7] In spite of the title, it too is a sensitive and sympathetic translation.[8] *Unsere Zukunft: Ein Mahnwort an das deutsche Volk* was published in Germany a year after *Deutschland und der nächste Krieg* at less than half the length and a fifth of the price. The foreword to the

English version tells us it is "more popular in tone, more outspoken, more striking and more up to date," "contains after-thoughts," and is, in sum, "perhaps the more important of the two," with "far greater circulation in Germany and far greater influence upon German public opinion."

Its impact on British public opinion was certainly enhanced by two appendices, both included in *Britain as Germany's Vassal* though not in *Germany and the Next War*. The first of these — *Kriegsbrauch: The Customs of War*, published by the German General Staff (Berlin, 1902)[9] — must have helped promote the belief that Bernhardi was writing with official approval, even if there is "some debate over whether it [the *Kriegsbrauch*] did reflect the views of the General Staff or merely of 'Young Turks' in the officer corps."[10] But a year later, in 1915, another translation of the *Kriegsbrauch*, by J. H. Morgan, dubbed it the "Handbook of the Hun."[11] Professor Morgan had been currently investigating reports of German executions of franc-tireurs and reprisals against Belgian citizens, collecting depositions for the Home Office that were fed into the official Bryce Report (1915). He then depicted the behavior of the army during the invasion of Belgium in even more lurid terms in his own *German Atrocities: An Official Investigation* (1916).[12] Inevitably, guilt by association would have further blackened Bernhardi's name.

Soon, though, memory appears to have fused or confused *Unsere Zukunft / Britain as Germany's Vassal* with *Germany and the Next War*. Thus Emil Ludwig during the Second World War quotes the title of the one but extracts from the other: "Except for the style, which retains a certain fluidity, Bernhardi's book, *Germany's Future*, published in 1912, resembles for whole pages at a time the book Hitler wrote later."[13] *Britain as Germany's Vassal* repeats many of the ideas and some of the formulations of *Germany and the Next War*, but it is otherwise a different book, which omits the "metaphysics" almost entirely. It does, however, share that ease of expression (of "the cavalry general from his high horse," as Ludwig puts it) that had persuaded the enterprising Cotta, Goethe's erstwhile publishing house, to take up Bernhardi. This connection "endowed him with a literary aura" that others, too, have recognized and indeed thought his due.[14]

Finally, Bernhardi's extensive memoir, *Eine Weltreise, 1911/1912*, deserves consideration too, although it did not appear until 1920, avowedly unaltered in the light of hindsight though with a long appendix detailing "Germany's collapse," by which time there was clearly no call for an English translation. His world tour provided Bernhardi with firsthand experience of British colonialism and of the United States, which nicely complements the arguments presented in *Germany and the Next War* and probably contributed to the slight shifts of emphasis in *Britain as Germany's Vassal*.[15]

Unofficial Conduit or Lunatic Fringe?

Germany and the Next War argues for a preemptive or preventive war to secure the very survival of idealistic German culture against encroaching Western materialism, and the universal benefits of a subsequently dominant *Kultur* commensurate with Germany's entitlement to world-power status. Its target readership, according to Wolfgang Mommsen, was thus appropriately the *Bildungsbürgertum*, notably *Studienräte*, the élite of the teaching profession;[16] others, however, heard, and still hear, primarily the voice of aggressive militarism, "the Prussian masterplan for world domination."[17] There can be little doubt, though, that Bernhardi's book(s) added momentum to "the rise of the Anglo-German antagonism"[18] by giving lucid expression to the issues alleged to be at stake. Sir Arthur Conan Doyle responded promptly in 1912 with "Great Britain and the Next War,"[19] an article soon followed by a stream of pamphlets in which Bernhardi became "the favourite whipping boy of British propaganda,"[20] such as "The New (German) Testament" by Anthony Hope Hawkins, D. S. Cairns's "An Answer to Bernhardi," D. A. Wilson's "Bernhardi and the Germans," and A. Clutton-Brock's "Bernhardism in England."[21]

Fritz Fischer tells us that German historians at the time also dismissed the book, viewing it however as the scribblings of a maverick Pan-German, its thinking remote from that of the General Staff and political leadership.[22] Gerhard Ritter took the same line in the 1950s and 1960s in his exhaustive four-volume account of German "Militarismus" (his scare-quotes), maintaining that "the fact that *Deutschland und der nächste Krieg* was written in a purely private capacity by an outsider not in the General Staff's good graces was completely ignored. It was cited on countless occasions as proof that the German General Staff was systematically fostering war, with the aim of making Germany the principal power in the world."[23] And Hew Strachan, in the first volume of "what promises to be the definitive history of the war" (John Keegan), still makes the same distinction: "Despite his place in entente demonology, Bernhardi perhaps matters least as an indicator of military thought, since he was at odds with much of the prevailing ethos of the general staff."[24]

Bernhardi certainly distances himself from then current government diplomacy in the foreword to *Deutschland*, written in October 1911 in the wake of the second Morocco crisis, but, as Fischer shows, his vision of Germany as a *Weltmacht* (world power) was a very precise reflection of official German intentions: first, the elimination of France (as proclaimed almost verbatim in Bethmann Hollweg's September 1914 program); second, the foundation under German leadership of a Central European confederation with which weaker states would seek protective *Anschluß* — a departure from the principle of balance of power in Europe as favored by

Great Britain; and third, German expansion — through the acquisition and cultural proselytization of new colonies, and consequent growth of political and economic influence over them — to world power status within a system of world states (von Bülow's *Weltpolitik* having become a widely held German aspiration).[25] These aims were not necessarily contradicted by the fact that "the traditionalist General Staff . . . had little enthusiasm at all for *Weltpolitik*."[26] Fischer reminds us, further, that colleagues initially reacted to his own provocative reassessment of German war guilt by denying continuity between the prewar period and the war, stressing that Germany was merely reacting to the entente, and restricting responsibility for imperialistic expansionism to the "evil" Pan-Germans.[27]

The issue — of whether Bernhardi was a conduit for widely held views or simply part of "the lunatic fringe"[28] — is a complex one. After all, he was one of Schlieffen's own candidates to succeed him as Chief of the General Staff in 1906,[29] and a far cry from the Kaiser's unfortunate choice of the great Moltke's nephew. According to Arden Bucholz, Moltke the Younger "lacked both a detailed understanding of the war plan and the confidence that it would work." He "began reading Rudolf Steiner [his wife's close adviser] in 1904, apparently to clarify his understanding of Nietzsche and Haeckel," remarking later "that before reading Steiner he had understood neither one, but now everything was clear." His "deep inner quest for life after death, nourished by fears, anxieties, and expectations of the imminent second coming of Christ amid an apocalyptic battle between German and Slav" led to two severe nervous breakdowns during mobilization, and finally dismissal in November 1914.[30] On the face of it, Moltke was scarcely one to call Bernhardi "a perfect dreamer,"[31] for Moltke, too, held a "belief in the inevitability of a coming war, ordained within the cosmic scheme of world history."[32]

This belief certainly sits oddly with the fact that "the years from 1906 to 1912 were ones of almost complete cessation of army growth."[33] Niall Ferguson addresses this seeming contradiction and suggests that, though often "cited as a classic text of Prussian militarism, [Bernhardi's] book really needs to be read as Army League propaganda." (The *Wehrverein*, a propaganda organization that quickly surpassed the Navy League in effectiveness, was founded in 1912 by Bernhardi's friend August Keim, another retired general.)[34] Ferguson points out that the book attacks "not only the pacifism and anti-militarism of the Left, but also the German government's pusillanimity in the second Morocco crisis and — most importantly — the arguments advanced by conservatives within the Prussian military for the maintenance of a relatively small army"[35] (chief among them reluctance to mobilize the urban proletariat with its socialist sympathies).

Whatever Bernhardi's real or perceived status vis-à-vis "official" Germany, many must have assumed that, as erstwhile Chief of the General Staff's Department of Military History (1898–1901) and commander of the VII Army Corps in 1909,[36] "on account of his rank, he could be regarded as speaking officially."[37] It also seems probable that he was acting "as ghost-writer to top military men."[38] In this, as Stuart Wallace points out, he resembles Lord Roberts's speechwriter Professor J. A. Cramb, the cover of whose posthumously published lectures — *Germany and England* (1914) — proclaimed "Treitschke Expounded," "Bernhardi Explained";[39] or indeed, and more closely, Lord Roberts himself, President of the National Service League, who had resigned his post as commander-in-chief of the British army to promote — in Roberts's case, unsuccessfully — a scheme for universal conscription.[40] (Universal conscription, according to Bernhardi, contributes to the love of peace, for it involves everyone in suffering; but barely half of those capable of bearing arms in Germany currently did so, whereas France had effective universal conscription.)[41]

Nietzsche, Treitschke, Bernhardi

Mention of Nietzsche and Treitschke (names that lent themselves to mocking abbreviation and mispronunciation when war came, notably as Nitch and Tritch — though spelling varied, as it regularly did among "serious" commentators, too) completes the trio of writers to whom "the ideas of 1914" were, and still are, generally ascribed. But interpreting Nietzsche, particularly at such a time, is fraught with difficulty.[42] William Archer famously asserted in *Fighting a Philosophy* (1915) that "in a very real sense, it is the philosophy of Nietzsche that we are fighting," and other commentators, too, saw Treitschke and Bernhardi as "merely symptoms; the underlying cause was Nietzsche."[43] But Nietzsche, notably through publication of the *Complete Works in English* (18 volumes under Oscar Levy's general editorship, 1909–13), had many admirers,[44] so that "to lump Nietzsche in an undifferentiated way along with Treitschke and Bernhardi as a sort of '*spiritus rector*' of German expansionism, as many Britons did during the war years, is to compound that sin of misinterpretation."[45] Wallace provides a different perspective again: by 1914 "the dead historian Treitschke, Hegel, and General von Bernhardi constituted the unholy trinity, with Nietzsche in reserve for those who wished to leave nothing to chance," for "Hegel's state rather than Nietzsche's 'blond beast' was at the centre of attention." This realignment, though it failed to take hold then or since, at least gives due weight to the "life or death" struggle between the Hegelian and anti-Hegelian camps in both British (largely Oxford versus Cambridge) and German philosophy.[46]

Strachan, however, plays down Hegel's significance: "The 'ideas of 1914,' however much they tapped into the thought of Kant, Hegel, or Fichte, were essentially a new departure."[47] Nevertheless, as we shall see, the legacy of this further trio, representing the main strands of German idealism, echoes throughout *Deutschland und der nächste Krieg*.

If we accept perhaps the least contentious combination: "pundits explained how the spirit of Treitschke and Bernhardi had conquered the German mind,"[48] for these were the "two names which were soon to appear in every pamphlet and article on the war."[49] What, then, of Heinrich von Treitschke? Gordon Craig has provided a telling sketch of how this Berlin professor "fed the stream of rabid nationalism that engulfed his country in 1914": "For a quarter of a century students heard this deaf, hoarse-voiced, but compelling *praeceptor Germaniae* fulminate against Germany's neighbors, calling for the destruction of British sea power and glorifying war as a German destiny, provided by a beneficent Deity as a means of purging the nation of the sins of materialism and of allowing it to manifest and fulfill its cultural superiority. That his teachings left their mark upon the prewar generation of German leaders is undeniable, and his influence is most painfully evident in the thought and actions of such of his auditors as Alfred von Tirpitz, Friedrich von Bernhardi, Carl Peters, the explorer, and Heinrich Class, the founder of the Pan-German League. His lectures were the embodiment of injustice and lack of objectivity, filled with emotional judgments and wildness of language."[50] Class himself, of course, put it rather differently — "Treitschke was my master, who determined my life" — and Paul Kennedy cites further influential figures, including von Bülow, who absorbed what they took to be Treitschke's "noble message."[51] But Wallace points out that "in Germany Treitschke had suffered neglect since his death in 1896," being eclipsed among younger historians by Ranke, so that, in the words of a recent biographer, "Germans were surprised to find the almost forgotten Treitschke singled out as one of the intellectual instigators of the war."[52] True, his standard history of nineteenth-century Germany began to appear for the first time in English in 1915, but at the outbreak of war, as one contemporary British historian put it, "To the great majority of Germans, as to the great majority of Englishmen, Treitschke can be little more than a name."[53]

The Schlieffen Plan and Belgian Neutrality

If so, it was indeed Bernhardi's book(s) that probably did most, in both German and English, to propagate "the ideas of 1914." This term was popularized by Rudolf Kjellen, a Swedish economist, in *Die Ideen von 1914* (1915), and further by Johann Plenge in *1789 und 1914* (1916), the subtitle of which, "Die symbolischen Jahre in der Geschichte des politischen

Geistes," drew attention to an alleged progression of "the political spirit" between the beginning and the end of the long nineteenth century. Both authors, Strachan summarizes, "associated the French Revolution with freedom and the ongoing German revolution with its replacement by order and responsibility."[54] More obviously, of course, Germany's revolutions — of the Left and the Right — lay in the postwar decades. Nor was a conservative revolution necessary to implement "order and responsibility" in prewar Berlin. But "the ideas of 1914" do give a coherent voice to the contemporary conservative imagination, a "transvaluation of values" *made in Germany* though in a very un-Nietzschean sense. Their later convergence with a better known, native-born French version produces the very antithesis of the good Europeanism Nietzsche had hoped for. Thus, Philip Thody writes that Marshal Pétain's "instruction to the French to exchange what he saw as the decadent urban values of liberty, equality and fraternity for the peasant virtues of acquiescence implied in the Vichy motto *Travail, Famille, Patrie* merged rather easily, it will be remembered, into the recommendation that they should also collaborate with the Germans."[55] At all events, the new *Weltanschauung* was quite alien to those like Gilbert Murray, who in his own words in 1915 were "always aiming at culture in Arnold's sense not Bernhardi's."[56]

Bernhardi had already caused a stir in Germany with an anonymous pamphlet in 1890, *Videant consules, ne quid res publica detrimenti capiat* (Let the Consuls take care that the Republic comes to no harm),[57] which gives a fair summary — perhaps even anticipation — of the Schlieffen Plan (1895; the strategy for winning a war): "first settle the score with France, then reach a settlement allowing us next to turn the full vigor of the *Volk* against Russia" — a "vast cultural undertaking" rather different from that facing the Goethe Institut today. Its aim: "to force Slav barbarism back towards the East and South-east, its natural sphere, and safeguard West European culture against pan-Slav violation."[58] This objective gained additional force after Russia's defeat by Japan in 1905, when her sights turned again to Europe, but Bernhardi's "singularly influential and sensational publication" (Fischer)[59] of 1890 already spelt out the inevitability of a "preventive" war against Russia.

Of Estonian extraction, Bernhardi was one of a group of Baltic Germans who wielded influence close to the center of power. Although he is not mentioned directly in the Kaiser's memoirs, his Baltic compatriot and another of Treitschke's protégés, the historian Theodor Schiemann, appears there as an esteemed adviser and "champion of Germanness against Slav presumption,"[60] who had advised the Kaiser that "ein frischer, fröhlicher Krieg" ("a jolly good war") was the best possible way of warding off democracy and socialism.[61] In 1909, Bernhardi tells of being assured by Schiemann, "who should know," that Russia was presently incapable of waging war.[62] Paul Rohrbach, author of *Der deutsche Gedanke in der Welt* (1912 — a book still widely read in the Weimar years), believed, like Schiemann, that Russia was a colossus with feet of clay, its imminent economic collapse about to clear the way for Germany's *Kulturimperialismus*.[63] Johannes Haller is yet another historian from the Baltic provinces preaching their liberation from Russia to a receptive Kaiser and public.[64] Bernhardi, too, finds it not unlikely that the struggle for power between Germans and Slavs[65] will be decided once more by arms. By contrast, those who still respected Bismarck's key policy of avoiding war on two fronts found a spokesman in the former Chancellor's confidant, Maximilian Harden, a central figure in German journalism during the Wilhelmine era, who used his periodical *Die Zukunft* to attack these Baltic Germans as "dangerous warmongers active in the interest only of some Baltic barons."[66] Yet *Die Zukunft* published an article by Bernhardi in praise of Kant in 1912.[67] In fact, Bernhardi was not at all close to the aggressively anti-British Pan-German League until *after* publication of his book in 1912, let alone when he was still in active service (until 1909).[68] On the other hand, it is true that in *Britain as Germany's Vassal* he focused even more pointedly on the inevitable conflict of interests between England and Germany, though still in the context of advocating a Central European federation under German leadership (a *Kontinentalpolitik* at variance with the traditional British policy of maintaining a European balance of power) as the necessary basis for colonial expansionism and *Weltpolitik*.[69] This is essentially the thinking behind the concept of *Mitteleuropa* as popularized in the book of that name in 1915 by the Liberal economist and parliamentarian, Friedrich Naumann.

And against whom exactly would Germany be fighting in the next war? Russia apart — and many, following Bismarck, still regretted the deterioration of the long-standing Hohenzollern-Romanov friendship, exacerbated as it had been by Czarist Russification policy in the 1870s and 1880s[70] — Bernhardi lists several possible permutations. Thus, Schiemann had already suggested that Germany, England (*passim* in most German writing of the time), and America might find themselves in alliance.[71] But though a reconciliation of England and Germany would also be Bernhardi's preferred solution,[72] he rejects it as a fata morgana, unworthy of pursuit, especially if the Unionists return to power, as it would require a total English rethink of her opposition to German colonial and trade expansion. Nevertheless, the rising power of America as she emerged from her Monroe Doctrine isolation points towards her inevitable clash with England (especially after England's alliance with the main US rival in the Pacific, Japan), at which point German and English interests might coincide.[73] Alternatively, political links and sympathies between German-Americans and Irish-Americans could bring Germany and America together against England, while England would need to destroy the German fleet before embarking on war with America for global hegemony.[74] All of the anti-Slav Balts were agreed, however, that good relations with England were desirable until such times as England aggressively opposed Germany's cultural and "power-political" claims.[75] England might yet seek an accommodation with Germany that paid at least lip service to the widespread assumption of English neutrality in the event of a European war. Here lay the crucial German misreading of Britain's likely response to the unavoidable violation of Belgium's guaranteed neutrality built into the Schlieffen Plan — even more unavoidable after Moltke's emendation of the Plan to respect Dutch neutrality.[76]

Bernhardi contributed to this still much-debated issue in two ways. First, in the light of Belgium's extensive gains in the scramble for Africa, scarcely envisaged by her collective guarantors in 1831 and 1839, he professed only contempt for her simultaneous claim on neutrality — a neutrality that extended to Leopold II's personal fiefdom in the Congo (recognized, albeit not guaranteed, by the Berlin Africa Congress, 1885), the notorious exploitation of which had become an international scandal by 1908. "Permanent neutrality," Bernhardi declared, "contradicts the essence of statehood inasmuch as a state can only achieve its highest moral goals in competition with other states."[77] Bethmann-Hollweg's dismissal of the Belgian guarantee as "a scrap of paper" (prompting Ambassador Lichnowsky's frantic warnings from London to the contrary) helped Asquith's government to ignore Belgium's colonial record and turn the issue into one of principle, playing the "rights of small nations" card against Bernhardi's "ethical" gloss on "power politics."[78]

Second, though he does not mention the (officially secret) Schlieffen Plan in *Deutschland*, Bernhardi's focus there is on justifying the action of a sovereign state based solely on its power, that is, Germany's "necessary" violation of Belgian neutrality in defiance of international "conventions" and "law" based on the French Liberal doctrine of non-interference in the affairs of another state.[79] In this, he was very much in step with "official" Germany.[80] Interestingly, though, on a different issue Bernhardi was perceived to have become the most influential of Schlieffen's critics, according to Strachan, by arguing in *Vom heutigen Kriege* (1912) that "breakthrough and flank attacks should often be combined."[81] And Moltke, indeed even Schlieffen himself by 1912, allegedly also recognized the force of this "more pragmatic and less mechanistic" strategy, though the vacillating Moltke did not, or in the event could not, adequately implement it. If so, Bernhardi was no doubt mindful of the "totally neglected" traditional role of the cavalry (as highlighted in *Deutschland*),[82] which would be more effective spread out along the line. The core of the Schlieffen Plan — a massive attack through Belgium to envelop the French forces — was indeed weakened. The shift in balance between the right and left wings of the German front — from 7:1 in Schlieffen's final memorandum to 3:1 in 1914 — seems to speak for itself and to support postwar critics of the Plan's dilution, notably Groener and Liddell Hart. Strachan plays down these astonishing statistics, however, concluding merely that the right wing "was not quite as strong as envisaged in the 1905 memorandum," and listing reasons for the change — Holland no longer a target; the inability to pour more troops through the narrow Belgian front; the increased likelihood of French counterattack elsewhere and opportunities for a German breakthrough.[83] It seems unlikely that British or French readers during the war years knew of their debt to Bernhardi.

The Will to Power

A brief synopsis of the opening chapters of *Deutschland* should take us beyond the commentaries cited earlier, which go little beyond invective. The book's motto is taken from Nietzsche's *Also sprach Zarathustra*: "War and courage have brought about more great things than loving thy neighbor. It has always been your courage, not your compassion, that saved life's hapless wretches. What is good? you ask. Courage is good."[84] And the foreword continues by contrasting the "pusillanimity" of German diplomacy (in the second Morocco crisis) with the professedly indubitable "will to power" ("Wille zur Macht," *D*, iv) of the German people, now aroused, whose manifest enthusiasm to answer the call to arms in defense of its honor and its future is offset only by doubts about its (or rather, the Reichstag's) readiness to shoulder the financial burden (*D*, v). The argument, as we shall see, is so often couched in terms of "will" and "power" that further explicit acknowledgement of Nietzsche and "the phrase which launched a thousand ships"[85] was scarcely necessary — or indeed wise, given Nietzsche's known skepticism towards a German "Herrenvolk" (which Bernhardi promptly invokes, albeit in the past, *D*, 2),[86] let alone a contemporary German "Kulturstaat." Nietzsche, for instance, maintains that "Culture and the state — let no one be deceived on this point — are antagonists: a 'culture-state' is merely a modern idea."[87]

Bernhardi's introduction nevertheless begins with the present "Kulturwelt" — with Germany as one "Kulturstaat" among many, albeit with a distinctive conception of *Kultur* — in which the self-sacrificing, idealistic, martial spirit, notably prominent in Germany's past and crucial for its self-defense, has been undermined by rapidly increasing prosperity and the instant gratification it affords. Since Germany's astonishing rise from fragmentation and political impotence[88] to European preeminence, Germany appears to lack the will for further political and cultural expansion of power. All too peace-loving and easygoing (the stereotypical nineteenth-century "deutscher Michel"), Germany seeks "justice," foolishly believing other nations to do so, too, and naively refusing to acknowledge that the political world is ruled only by self-interest and the pursuit of power, not philanthropy. Germany has become accustomed to see war as a curse, not as the prime factor in promoting culture and power. Germany lives in hope that the power of the state will steadily increase without needing to fight for it, but if it should come to that, Germany is quietly confident and determined never passively to accept a diminution of power. This need for power is felt by the southern German states, long deprived of power, as keenly as it is by Prussia.[89]

Further examples of "will" and "power" abound, which prompts the question of how close Bernhardi comes to Nietzsche's own premises, or whether Thomas Mann's "bemused contempt" for the linking of their names,[90] and the social Darwinist "survival of the fittest" to which "Bernhardism" was most commonly reduced by hostile critics, are indeed more apposite. We might bear in mind Nietzsche's own critique of social Darwinism: "even life itself has been defined as an ever-more expedient inner adaptation to external circumstances (Herbert Spencer). But this represents a failure to recognize the essence of life, its *will to power*; this overlooks the priority of the spontaneous, attacking, overcoming, reinterpreting, restructuring, and shaping forces, whose action precedes 'adaptation.'"[91] Or again, Nietzsche's insistence that "Ausbeutung" between peoples — the inevitable antagonism between predator and prey — which democratic or humanitarian socialism currently seeks to abolish, is "a consequence of the will to power, which is precisely the will to life," not merely an atavistic anachronism.[92] Such perspectives, which tend to relegate cautious *Realpolitik* and concern over shifting political alliances to what Nietzsche would call a "second-order activity, a mere reactivity,"[93] find at the very least linguistic echoes in Bernhardi and provide him with a schematic framework on which to erect his single-minded argument.

Thus only a state that aspires to increase the sphere in which it exercises power[94] creates conditions in which man can flourish: the state that renounces expansion of power and is content with *being*, not *becoming* — with the "bed of ease" Faust wagers he will never put before "sublime striving" (*D*, 20)[95] — that state becomes pitiful and soon degenerate. (Kurt Riezler makes the identical point in *his* celebrated prewar book *Grundzüge der Weltpolitik in der Gegenwart*: "To the aspirations of a people, just as to the striving of an individual, there is no limit and no end.")[96] One hesitates before citing any of Nietzsche's sundry expostulations on *Faust* as "the greatest German poem!" but his own ironically robust "philosophizing with a hammer" appears to lie somewhere between what Goethe calls the choice between "hammer or anvil" and von Bülow's adoption of the same metaphor — in the *reactive* sense of "do before it is done to you" — as Germany embarked on *Weltpolitik.*[97] Nietzsche as the advocate of constant self-overcoming — "Selbstüberwindung" as "will to power" over oneself — had fewer scruples about putting ironic distance between himself and Hegel: "The German himself does not *exist*; he is *becoming*, he is 'developing himself.'"[98] "We Germans are Hegelians, even if Hegel had never existed, inasmuch as we instinctively bestow on becoming and development a deeper meaning and more profound value than on that which 'is.'"[99] Such mockery of course subverts the view, advanced by its official philosopher at the beginning of the nineteenth century, of the Prussian state as already the apotheosis of the political life of man.

By 1871 the Barbarossa legend has come true (*D*, 4, 111–12), united Germany needs a new goal, and that, Bernhardi argues — in meta-Hegelian vein, so to speak — must be progression from European power to world power.[100] The balance of power that it is in England's interest to foster in Europe — currently by strengthening France and constraining Germany (*D*, 104), thereby allowing England a free hand elsewhere (*D*, 118–19) — must be replaced by a system of global powers (*D*, 46) based on real power factors, "for the rights of states can only be exercised by living power" [Bernhardi here quotes Treitschke]. The advancement of power is the prime task of the state — and there can be nothing above the state (*D*, 45–46). It is a good in itself, as Machiavelli first declared (*D*, 44), but to us, since the German Reformation, the state embodies "power in the service of protecting and promoting higher interests" [Treitschke again] (*D*, 45). It is war, not peace, that serves to expand power, providing the vital spark; only in war, too, do we fully experience "the transitoriness of the goods of this world" (*D*, 21; this is Bernhardi's only explicit reference to Hegel, and it is an indirect one — via Kuno Fischer's *Hegel*). The international arbitration system currently pursued by President Taft — US treaties with GB, Japan, France, and Germany (*D*, 10) — would favor the status quo and culturally declining states at the expense of a people striving to expand its power in order to carry out its cultural-cum-civilizing mission.[101] Diplomatic attempts to maintain the status quo are futile, for all is flux, we either progress or regress.[102] We are surrounded by states constantly seeking to expand their power. For example, the USA in reality wants not peace, but a free hand in Central America and Panama, while "perfidious Albion," whose empire is based on the power of money, wants to cover its back in the eventuality of war with Germany (*D*, 10).

And where would the power come from to implement international law? (*D*, 28) Scarcely from the "high court of international justice" established by the second Hague Conference (*D*, 28), still less from some — inconceivable — future universal state like the Roman Empire (*D*, 29).

Only war, not court decisions, can cement power, as illustrated by Frederick the Great's acquisition of Silesia against the coalition of European powers (*D*, 29). This is an example of Prussia's triumph over "encirclement" ("unser deutsches Vaterland von allen Seiten bedroht" *D*, 6; our German fatherland, threatened on all sides), which Thomas Mann also thought appropriate to celebrate in 1915.[103] (Curiously, Bernhardi later describes "die Einkreisungspolitik gegen Deutschland" as having been engineered with much adroit statesmanship by Edward VII [!], only to collapse on his death [*D*, 36–37].) Similarly, Japan's immensely daring decision to wage war against the growing power of the Russian colossus in the East was heroic, politic, and morally justified, for her rapid flowering as the dominant civilized power[104] in Eastern Asia required a commensurably expanded sphere in which to deploy that power.[105] Yet Bernhardi firmly rejects the possibility of any such German expansion within Europe (at most, in his *Weltreise, 1911/1912*, he proposes an exchange of territory and population along the Eastern border of Prussia),[106] even while half-evoking the *membra disiecta* (scattered body parts) theory of the annexationist Pan-Germans[107] and recalling that the source and mouth of the Rhine, "most German of all rivers," still lay outside German control (*D*, 79). Instead, German power must find expression in hegemony over *Mitteleuropa* and colonial expansion — including a "carve-up" of Portuguese colonies — perhaps already secretly agreed with England (*D*, 115). World power status, however, is ultimately predicated on awakening in our people a unanimous will to power.

And so Bernhardi returns at the end of these expository chapters to the question posed at the beginning. The will to become a civilized and cultured people[108] healthily reflects the will to political power.[109] Only through conscious willing[110] can Germany seize the propitious moment, if her will to victory[111] has not been weakened[112] by that now ubiquitous dream of eternal peace, the anemia afflicting most "Kulturvölker" (*D*, 11), which the "der alternde Kant" — that is, Kant in his dotage (*D*, 9) — first promulgated in 1795, attributing to the process of civilization the power to end all war.[113] But providence, using human willpower to achieve its ends (*D*, 36), has allotted Germany — the "Kulturvolk" *par excellence* (*D*, 7) — momentous tasks, for which it must be optimally prepared in the decisive struggle to come, even in the face of a more powerful enemy (*D*, 135).

As suggested by these examples, the crucial need for "will" that Bernhardi reiterates throughout *Deutschland und der nächste Krieg* is seldom more nuanced than the anatomy of "power" outlined earlier, so that any specific indebtedness to Nietzsche remains as elusive as the philosopher's own unsystematic portrayal of "will to power," something simply posited as a first principle. Let us instead examine how Bernhardi fleshes out the bones of his argument.

War as a Biological Necessity

War was recognized "long before Darwin" (*D*, 12) to be "the father of all things" (Heraclitus), a biological necessity, the great regulator (*D*, 11). War is always "biologically just" in deciding the outcome (*D*, 16); consequently — as Hegel, and at times Nietzsche, are taken to have said — "might is right."[114] Whichever people has "the greatest physical, spiritual, moral, material, and state power" (*D*, 13) will come out on top. Of these, spiritual[115] and moral power are most crucial for superiority in war, and to serve progress. Though German history is a classic case of weaker states in coalition overwhelming the intrinsically — that is, spiritually and morally — stronger one (*D*, 14), such defeats serve to revitalize the will for ultimate victory against numerical odds while erstwhile conquerors fall apart (*D*, 14). The later sections of *Deutschland und der nächste Krieg* often seem uncertain whether the next war will already provide this "dialectical" turning point, famously described by Hegel,[116] at which the underdog vanquishes his oppressor. But Bernhardi has no doubt that this will happen in British India, where the cultural gap is fast disappearing as the native population develops "higher ways of life and attitudes to life" (*D*, 15). While a people's right to colonize is determined by its higher culture (in the case of India it was, Bernhardi concedes, that of England; *D*, 151), the healthy demographic growth of Germany makes geographic expansion even more urgent (*D*, 15), if necessary by war (*D*, 15–16), simply to feed its excess population.[117] The third criterion for colonization is trade, which produces its own bitter wars, especially when the main export-dependent trading nations (America, England, Germany) compete with the erstwhile import-dependent, now tariff-seeking, but soon all too competitive developing world (*D*, 16–17).

Thus Germany would surely have fought France if trade with Morocco had been a more vital issue, just as, if threatened, England would fight to maintain its Indian market, presently the source of its power, as resolutely as it fought to protect its gold and diamond interests in South Africa (*D*, 17–18). "Free trade" is ultimately controlled by colonial power — that of England in Egypt, Japan in Manchuria, France in Morocco, Belgium in the Congo (*D*, 117). The impression Bernhardi gives of frustrated or thwarted German belligerence during the Morocco crisis is not incompatible with his admission that war unleashes man's original brutishness (*D*, 11); or that will to power exposes man's less admirable traits, among which he counts the pursuit of pleasure for its own sake and even of honor, as well as greed, envy, and the desire for revenge (*D*, 12). He acknowledges that the Hague Peace Conferences have helped humanize the conduct of war (*D*, 11), and even insists that the Germans are an essentially peace-loving people (*D*, 2) in part because they are also a born trading nation, once indeed, before the Thirty Years' War, the greatest trading nation of all — presumably a reference to the Hansa (*D*, 3). But although German business may presently believe peace essential for commerce, it forgets that political power was founded on recent military victories that facilitated forty years of upswing, the growth of the second-biggest merchant marine in the world, and the ubiquity of German trading houses, not least in England (*D*, 3) — a reminder of the wealth-creating talent lost through post-1848 emigration.

The fundamental philosophical distinction could scarcely be spelled out more clearly. On the one side, the maximization of happiness and avoidance of pain, a this-worldly philosophy that envisages a "minimal state" analogous to an insurance company guaranteeing the unimpeded pursuit of commercial and personal gain, and which consequently abhors war as the greatest evil imaginable (*D*, 18). Here we might well expect Nietzsche's famously contemptuous critique of the "English utilitarians"[118] to be cited in support. Instead, it is one of Prussia's great men whom Bernhardi has in his sights: Wilhelm v. Humboldt's treatise advocating limits on the activity of the state,[119] primarily to the protection of property and life (*D*, 18). Beyond its eighteenth-century, Physiocratic roots, Humboldt's eulogy to radical individualism and the ideal of *Bildung* denies any final purpose to the state at all. It seems equally distant from the youthful Humboldt, who advocated an all-powerful welfare state, and the later champion of the principle of necessity, who helped frame the Prussian Constitution.[120] Published only in extracts and overshadowed a year after its composition by his friend (and critic) Gentz's translation of Burke's *Reflections on the Revolution in France* (1793), Humboldt's book received perhaps more than its due on posthumous publication in 1851, the zenith of Liberalism, especially from his admirer John Stuart Mill. This in turn — and this is surely Bernhardi's cue — prompted Treitschke's counterblast in the essay "Die Freiheit" (1864), which proposed that "the purpose of the State, like that of all living things, is sufficient unto itself."[121]

The alternative to the minimal state is the philosophy that sees the final purpose of the life of individuals and peoples as "the development of spiritual and moral strength" (*D*, 18), the role of the state being "to secure for that strength the global influence by which humanity can progress." The moral task of the state, as Fichte taught, is to "fashion humanity for freedom,"[122] while for Schleiermacher the state "endows the individual with the highest form of life." But any attempt "to expand the concept of the state to that of humanity as a whole, presenting the indi-

vidual with ostensibly even higher duties in the process, is misguided, for
to conceive of humanity as a single entity is to eliminate life's most indispensable characteristic, namely struggle / conflict / strife ("der Kampf,"
D, 19). The desire for peace is "a false glimmer of higher humanity" (*D*,
32), and Germans have to learn that maintaining peace must never be the
goal of politics (*D*, 34, 38). Such universalism is an aberration, the sort of
utopian thinking that defies implementation (*D*, 19). Where the battle for
survival is eliminated — and this elimination is the goal of all efforts for
peace — the result is decadence; this is a law of nature (*D*, 31).

War, however, with its shared dangers, is a unifying force for a whole
people as our individual pursuits shrink into insignificance.[123] Rilke was far
from being an isolated voice when he evoked precisely this communal sac-
rificial spirit in his *Fünf Gesänge, August 1914*, just as the ecstatically ac-
claimed "God of War" was beginning his "human harvest": "for it was
always cause for celebration to live, not prey to individual anxieties, but in
a shared spirit of adventure, of exhilarating danger common and sacred to
all."[124] Here the Nietzschean challenge to live dangerously that only the
Hero could meet in Rilke's *Sixth Duino Elegy* (1913)[125] is supposedly es-
poused by a whole people. Or in Treitschke's words, cited by Bernhardi,
"The sacred power of love, which a just war awakes in a noble people, is
made manifold" (*D*, 21–22). Luther is cited as a key witness: "It is true
what people now say and write, that war is a great plague. But consider
how much greater the plague that is avoided through wars" (*D*, 55).[126]
The Christian precept that one must love one's neighbor as oneself in-
spires altruism towards one's community (*D*, 30), but not towards political enemies, where the Church Militant must promote "moral progress"
in accordance with Jesus' own words: "I bring you not peace but the
sword" — Matthew 10:34 (*D*, 24) — a reading still remembered and indignantly rejected by Egon Friedell in his celebrated *Kulturgeschichte der
Neuzeit* (1929).[127]

This leads Bernhardi to set Bismarck's publicly often repeated principle, "never initiate wars," against his practice of seizing the initiative under favorable conditions (*D*, 35–37) — a practice shared by the Great
Elector and Frederick the Great, though not (disastrously not) by Frederick William III in 1805[128] — to argue for a "free act" of "preemptive" war
in 1911 (when British neutrality was still thought likely) as the German
statesman's moral and political duty (*D*, 39). His criticism of Bethmann
Hollweg during the Morocco crisis for taking Bismarck's words at face
value (*D*, 38) was to be taken up by David Wilson in one of the British
propaganda pamphlets, which juxtaposes "Bismarck v. Bernhardi on Wanton War," depicting the former Chancellor as "a completely genuine man,
. . . truthful and good, one of the heroes of humanity," who "was most
explicit, as even Bernhardi admits (*D*, 38), in laying down the principle

that no nation should ever go to war unless and until it is forced," and who later "laid the chief blame for these wars on the newspapers."[129] Compared with Bismarck, the "simple and frank"[130] Bernhardi's defense of *Realpolitik* is inevitably strained — deliberate political deception is unworthy, but cunning stratagems permissible (*D*, 48) — and his belligerence more overt. To revert to Bernhardi's own formulations: a state that can no longer compete in an arms race with enemies who must soon win the upper hand has an obligation to seize the initiative (*D*, 53); it is even sometimes proper to go to war with no prospect of victory, solely as a matter of national honor; indeed — the quotation is from President Roosevelt in 1906[131] — "it can be far better to be defeated in war than never to have fought at all" (italicized, *D*, 52; the Boers' "heroic" struggle against England being a case in point [*D*, 42]).

A Note of Resignation

It is this note of resignation that prevails in the latter half of *Deutschland und der nächste Krieg*. War with England is indeed inevitable since Germany is compelled to acquire *Lebensraum* and overseas markets (*D*, 110), which England will indubitably resist. Indeed, England has already begun her onslaught on German banks (*D*, 327). Ideally, we should try to make France attack us (for the Franco-Russian defensive alliance would not then operate), or even England, though it is not in their interest to do so (*D*, 322). However disadvantageous Germany's strategic position (pending the crucial widening of the Kaiser-Wilhelm-Kanal),[132] the coming war must be fought, whatever the cost (*D*, 111), for Germany is also morally compelled to establish "the Empire of the Spirit" (*D*, 65) and "Germanness" worldwide (*D*, 112).[133] England has already performed "cultural work" of great magnitude, if all too exploitatively materialistic (*D*, 83), and continues to pursue Lord Rosebery's proud boast in 1893 of imposing her stamp globally (*D*, 82), not least through the ubiquity of the English language.[134] Now it is Germany's turn to take up what Bernhardi could only have agreed with Kipling is "the white man's burden."

But set against the excess of energy, enterprise, and idealism of the *Volk* is its "petty theoretical vindictiveness," the gift of the bad fairy (*D*, 295), manifest, for instance, in its unwillingness to accept higher taxation to fund essential military expenditure (*D*, 303). Like Fichte a century earlier, Bernhardi thinks education all-important in compensating for quantitative and material disadvantage. The army must be able to draw on all those capable of bearing arms (*D*, 191–94) and "the spiritual and moral level of the troops raised" (*D*, 236) by the cultivation of individual personality (*D*, 285) — an unlikely military sentiment, one might think, though Bernhardi bases it partly on the development of new weapons that make the individual soldier more specialized and responsibly independent, and authority more devolved (*D*, 205). But such individualization, imbued with patriotic historical awareness, has clearly some way to go when not one out of 63 recruits questioned know who Bismarck was (*D*, 289).

The indictment extends to the political immaturity of the German people as a whole, attributed in part to its long history of particularism, and its dependence on strong leadership. The German character is suited to the richest development of individual talents — intellectual, scientific, artistic — everything, in fact, except politics (*D*, 123). "No people is less fitted to rule itself" in a purely parliamentary, republican, "liberal" sense.[135] "It can be induced to undertake some great communal action only under the leadership of powerful personalities."[136] Such personalities must be allowed to act "freely, out of a sense of power, to achieve greatness through and for our people."[137] For all Bernhardi's insistence that Germany's unique cultural heritage underwrites her obligatory world-historical mission, latter-day readers cannot but be reminded instead of E. M. Forster's verdict that Germany's better self was lost when "Potsdam" replaced "Weimar."[138] Ultimately, Bernhardi's call for power-driven personalities to lead that mission to "Weltmacht oder Untergang" is horribly prophetic of an even more disastrous call to "world domination or annihilation" in the following generation.

Notes

[1] See Gerhard Ritter, *The Sword and the Sceptre: The Problem of Militarism in Germany* (= *Staatskunst und Kriegshandwerk: Das Problem des "Militarismus" im Deutschland,* 4 vols. [Munich: Oldenbourg, 1954, 1960, 1964, 1968), trans. Heinz Norden (Coral Gables, FL: U of Miami P, 1972), 113; also cited in Peter Buitenhuis, *The Great War of Words: Literature as Propaganda, 1914–18 and After* (London: Batsford, 1987), 31.

[2] Friedrich von Bernhardi, *Deutschland und der nächste Krieg* (Stuttgart and Berlin: J. G. Cotta'sche Buchhandlung Nachfolger, 1912), 333 pages, one map of Britain and northern Europe, focused on the North Sea (referred to hereafter as *Deutschland*). In English, *Germany and the Next War*, popular edition, trans. Allen H. Powles (London: Edward Arnold, 1914), 288 pages, no maps.

[3] Friedrich Adam Julius Bernhardi, *Cavalry in Future Wars*, trans. C. S. Goldman (London: John Murray, 1906).

[4] Ritter, *Sword & Sceptre*, 113. Buitenhuis, *Great War of Words*, 31.

[5] Chapters 1, 2, 4, and 5: "Das Recht zum Kriege," "Die Pflicht zum Kriege," "Deutschlands historische Mission," "Weltmacht oder Niedergang."

[6] David Alec Wilson, *Bernhardi and the Germans* (Manchester: National Labour Press, 1915), 4, 3.

[7] Friedrich von Bernhardi, *Unsere Zukunft: Ein Mahnwort an das deutsche Volk* (Stuttgart and Berlin, 1913), translated by J. Ellis Barker as *Britain as Germany's Vassal* (Bream Buildings, [London] E. C.: Wm. Dawson & Sons, 1914), 5. The British Museum acquisition stamp is dated November 11, 1914. In small format and large print, the book runs to 234 pages, including two short appendices (see note 11 below and accompanying text).

[8] Like *Germany and the Next War*, which for example renders "Herrenvolk" (*Deutschland*, 9) as "ruling people" rather than "Master Race," *Britain as Germany's Vassal* avoids the imminent linguistic distortions of the propaganda war.

[9] *Kriegsbrauch im Landkriege* — its full German title — is a handbook for German officers on land warfare. The other appendix is "Extracts from Regulations Adopted by the Hague Conference 1907 and Subscribed to by Germany."

[10] Thus Stuart Wallace in his excellent account, *War and the Image of Germany: British Academics, 1914–1918* (Edinburgh: John Donald, 1988), 183.

[11] J. H. Morgan, *The German War Book: being "The Usages of War on Land."* (London: John Murray, 1915), 1–11.

[12] Wallace mentions *Britain as Germany's Vassal* (*Image of Germany*, 257, n. 45), though he gives the date of the German edition (1913). He also omits mention of the appendices, giving the impression that Morgan's 1915 translation of the *Kriegsbrauch* is the first. Though Lord Bryce rejected Morgan's advocacy of reprisals against Germany, Wallace concludes that nevertheless the "roots of 'Vansittartism' were well and truly established during the First World War" (*Image of Germany*, 182–84; the reference is to Lord Vansittart's 1941 polemic, *Black Record: Germans Past and Present*).

[13] Illustrated by a half-page quotation from *Germany and the Next War* — Emil Ludwig, *The Germans*, trans. Heinz & Ruth Norden (London: Hamish Hamilton, 1942), 307. The unfairness of any comparison with *Mein Kampf* would need to be argued at length.

[14] Quotes from Ludwig, *The Germans*, 307. The liberal Hanseatic *Deutsche Wirtschaftszeitung*, in its review of 1 July 1912, thought the political and economic arguments of *Deutschland und der nächste Krieg*, while not original, had been formulated "mit Wärme und literarischem Geschick" — see Fritz Fischer, *Krieg der Illusionen: Die deutsche Politik von 1911 bis 1914* (Düsseldorf: Droste, 1969, repr, 1970), 345–46. For Thomas Mann's dissenting voice, see Nicholas Martin's essay above.

[15] Friedrich von Bernhardi, *Eine Weltreise, 1911/1912 und der Zusammenbruch Deutschlands*, 3 vols. (Leipzig: S. Hirzel, 1920).

[16] "die deutschen Bildungsschichten und namentlich die deutschen Studienräte" (Wolfgang J. Mommsen, *Bürgerliche Kultur und politische Ordnung* [Frankfurt am Main: Fischer, 2000]), 198. See Paul Kennedy's note on "the *Mittelstand*, especially (one suspects) the Pan-German schoolteachers" as likely readers of the anti-Semitic and anti-modernist tracts of the 1880s and 1890s (*The Rise of the Anglo-German Antagonism 1860–1914* [London: G. Allen & Unwin, 1980], 539).

[17] Peter Edgerly Firchow, *The Death of the German Cousin: Variations on a Literary Stereotype, 1890–1920* (London and Toronto: Associated University Presses, 1986), 160.

[18] Kennedy notes that in 1912 "the two political 'bestsellers' in Germany were General Bernhardi's *Deutschland und der nächste Krieg* and the Pan-German leader, [Heinrich] Class's *Wenn ich der Kaiser wär*" (in *Anglo-German Antagonism*, 448).

[19] Included in Conan Doyle, *The German War* (London: Hodder & Stoughton, 1914) — see Buitenhuis, *Great War of Words*, 3, 183.

[20] In Buitenhuis's apt phrase (*Great War of Words*, 31).

[21] Hawkins's *The (New) German Testament: Some Texts and a Commentary*. London: Methuen, 1914, contained four such pamphlets, the first ironically entitled "The Blessings of — War" (Buitenhuis, *Great War of Words*, 31). From 1914 Hawkins was chief literary adviser to the British propaganda effort based at Wellington House. Writing as Anthony Hope, he is probably better known as the author of *The Prisoner of Zenda*. D. S. Cairns, *An Answer to Bernhardi*, Papers for War Time, 12 (London: Humphrey Milford, Oxford UP, 1914); David Alec Wilson, *Bernhardi and the Germans*; A. Clutton-Brock, *Bernhardism in England*, Papers for War Time, no. 26 (London: Humphrey Milford, Oxford UP, 1915).

[22] "als Ausstreuung eines disziplinlosen Alldeutschen abgetan und in weiter Distanz zu den Plänen sowohl des Generalstabes als auch der Reichsleitung gesehen" (dismissed as the vain imaginings of an undisciplined Pan-German, and regarded as being far removed from the plans both of the General Staff and also the *Reich* leadership), Fritz Fischer, *Griff nach der Weltmacht* (Düsseldorf: Droste, 1961, repr. 1967), 35.

[23] Ritter, *Sword & Sceptre*, 113. Though he had himself grown up in the Treitschke-Bernhardi spirit and continued to write in this vein throughout his career, Ritter distorts Bernhardi's "outsider" status in polemical apology of Wilhelmine Germany against Fischer — see Imanuel Geiss, "Alt-Neues Licht auf Gerhard Ritter," in *Gerhard Ritter: Geschichtswissenschaft und Politik im 20. Jahrhundert*, ed. Christoph Cornelison (Düsseldorf: Droste Verlag, 2001). Buitenhuis also cites Ritter approvingly: "one would be led to believe that Bernhardi was a major influence on German policy before the war. He was instead a heaven-sent opportunity for Allied propagandists" (Buitenhuis, *Great War of Words*, 31).

[24] Keegan, review of Hew Strachan, *The First World War*, vol. 1, *Times Literary Supplement* (April 12, 2002), 25; Hew Strachan, *The First World War*, vol. 1 (Oxford: Oxford UP, 2001), 1127.

[25] Fischer, *Griff nach der Weltmacht*, 35.

[26] Kennedy, *Anglo-German Antagonism*, 430. Further: "many historians have correctly pointed to the reorientation of German interest from *Weltpolitik* to *Kontinentalpolitik* in the post-1911 period" (448). Niall Ferguson, in *The Pity of War* (Harmondsworth, UK: Allen Lane, Penguin, 1998), the first chapter of which is entitled "The Myths of Militarism," proposes an even more radical shift: "The evidence is unequivocal: Europeans were not marching to war, but turning their

backs on militarism" (30). Of relevance here is the question, pursued below, of whether Bernhardi's views corresponded to "official" policy.

[27] Fischer, *Krieg der Illusionen*, 11.

[28] See William Carr's polemically oversimplified gloss on the author and readership of "Bernhardi's book *Vom heutigen Kriege*, which expounded the thesis that war was a biological necessity and a convenient means of ridding the world of the unfit. These views were not confined to a lunatic fringe but won wide acceptance" (Carr, *A History of Germany, 1815–1990* [London: Edward Arnold, 4th ed., 1991], 205). "Bernhardi's *Realpolitik* was not a phenomenon of the lunatic fringe" (T. J. Reed, *Thomas Mann and the Uses of Tradition* [Oxford: Oxford UP, 2nd ed., 1996], 216).

[29] Arden Bucholz, *Moltke, Schlieffen, and Prussian War Planning* (Oxford: Berg, 1991), 215.

[30] Bucholz, *Moltke, Schlieffen*, 214, 219, 220, 223.

[31] Ritter, *Sword & Sceptre*, 113.

[32] Bucholz, *Moltke, Schlieffen*, 214. They also appear to have shared strategic views on the need to emend the Schlieffen Plan — see below in this essay.

[33] Bucholz, *Moltke, Schlieffen*, 223.

[34] Gordon Craig, *Germany, 1866–1945* (1978; repr. Oxford: Oxford UP, 1981), 295.

[35] Ferguson, *Pity of War*, 15.

[36] Fischer, *Krieg der Illusionen*, 343.

[37] Thus Emil Ludwig, remembering Bernhardi from American exile during the Nazi period: *The Germans*, 307.

[38] Wallace, *Image of Germany*, 68.

[39] Wallace, *Image of Germany*, 82. The book of lectures, delivered at Staff College, Camberley, was subtitled "A Reply to Bernhardi." According to Cecil Chesterton (*The Prussian Hath Said in His Heart* [London: Chapman & Hall, 1914], 85) it constituted "a whole-hearted welcome to Bernhardi, an enthusiastic endorsement of Bernhardi, an embracing of Bernhardi's big boots"; see Diane Milburn, *The "Deutschlandbild" of A. R. Orage and the "New Age" Circle* (Frankfurt am Main: Peter Lang, 1996), 148–49, and for British Bernhardi reception in general, 146–51. Bernhardi mentions Roberts's very appreciative foreword to *War and the Arme Blanche*, in which Erskine Childers had argued the Boer case (*Germany and the Next War*, 43).

[40] Strachan, *First World War*, 375–76. Ferguson, *Pity of War*, 11.

[41] "Auch die allgemeine Wehrpflicht trägt zu der Friedensliebe bei; . . . das ganze Volk wird in Mitleidenschaft gezogen" (*Deutschland*, 3); "Zu unserem Unheil sind gerade wir dem Gedanken der allgemeinen Wehrpflicht untreu geworden" (Bernhardi, *Deutschland*, 192).

[42] See the contributions of Martin and Moore to this volume.

[43] Firchow, *Death of the German Cousin*, 161. One bookseller advertised his editions of Nietzsche as explaining "the Euro-Nietzschean" war (Wallace, *Image of Germany*, 50).

[44] A. Wolf, for instance, felt Nietzsche's political views were more reminiscent "of the peace societies and of the Society of Friends rather than Bernhardi and Treitschke" (*The Philosophy of Nietzsche* [1915], 22–23, quoted in Wallace, *Image of Germany*, 254)! A better informed critic, G. M. Wrong, fully appreciated Nietzsche's "aristocratic radicalism" (Georg Brandes's designation, welcomed by Nietzsche) as distinct from "the outlook of the Junker class" conveyed by Bernhardi, recognizing in Nietzsche the "most brilliant exponent" of "the war spirit of Germany" (the title of Wrong's book, London: n.d. [1917/1918 — see the reference on 23 to Bülow as the "last Chancellor but one"], 23), who was nevertheless "no preacher of the greatness of Germany, and no upholder of the fantastic ideals of the German Emperor," but "the apostle of the higher culture in which, as it seemed to him, Germany was wholly lacking." Curiously, he adds: "Probably the great majority of Germans never heard of him" (23–25).

[45] Kennedy, *Anglo-German Antagonism*, 395, drawing on J. Joll, "The English, Friedrich Nietzsche and the First World War," in *Deutschland in der Weltpolitik des 19. und 20. Jahrhunderts*, ed. I. Geiss and B.-J. Wendt (Düsseldorf: Bertelsmann Universitätsverlag, 1974). M. E. Humble, "The breakdown of a consensus: British writers and Anglo-German relations 1900–1920," *Journal of European Studies* 7 (1977): 46–48. Emil Ludwig, writing during the Nazi era, laments that Nietzsche once again finds himself in "company he does not deserve" (*The Germans*, 290), namely Treitschke and Bernhardi, alongside "two eugenic theorizers," "the important Frenchman Gobineau and the trivial Englishman Houston Stewart Chamberlain" (290, 306–7). Thomas Mann's "bemused contempt" for the linking of Bernhardi with Nietzsche is discussed by Nicholas Martin in his essay in this volume.

[46] Wallace, *Image of Germany*, 47, 48–49, 51–53. See John Mander, *Our German Cousins* (London: John Murray, 1974), 197: "In 1844, Jowett met Erdmann, Hegel's chief disciple, at Dresden, and thereafter began the introduction of Hegelian philosophy at Oxford where by the seventies it was to achieve a dominating position."

[47] Strachan, *First World War*, 1131.

[48] Strachan, *First World War*, 463.

[49] Wallace, *Image of Germany*, 26.

[50] Craig, *Germany, 1866–1945*, 204–5.

[51] "It is scarcely possible . . . to go through the memoirs of the Wilhelmine Right without encountering some reference to the impact which Treitschke had made upon their formative thoughts: Bülow, Tirpitz, Monts, Waldersee and Kardorff paid tribute to his noble message, university professors and publicists such as Lamprecht, Schäfer, Schiemann and Meinicke testified their indebtedness to his patriotic ideas, and advocates of Germany's world mission such as Peters, Rohrbach and Houston Stewart Chamberlain all insisted that — in the words of the

Pan-German leader Heinrich Class — 'Treitschke was my master, who determined my life'" (Kennedy, *Anglo-German Antagonism*, 395).

[52] Wallace, *Image of Germany*, 68. A. Dorpalen, *Heinrich von Treitschke* (New Haven: 1957), 298.

[53] J. W. Allen, *Germany and Europe* (London: G. Bell, 1914), 4. Wallace, *Image of Germany*, 68.

[54] See Strachan, *First World War*, 1131–32.

[55] Philip Thody, *The Conservative Imagination* (London: Pinter, 1993), 47.

[56] Strachan, *First World War*, 1127, drawing on Wallace, *Image of Germany*, 38. "Whether Murray read Bernhardi may be doubted" — Strachan's curious gloss — scarcely follows from the fact that Murray "had never studied at a German university. Ignorance, not least of the German language, underpinned many of the portrayals of German ideology." Yet on the same page Strachan himself cites *Germany and the Next War* — the sixth English impression of which, as we have seen, appeared a year earlier. The Murray quotation is taken from "German 'Kultur' — 3. German Scholarship," *Quarterly Review* 223, April 1915 — see Wallace, *Image of Germany*, 252. Strachan appears to have simply extrapolated from Wallace (*Image of Germany*, 105), that "Murray had fewer ties with German culture" and "had never studied in Germany."

[57] Bernhardi, *Denkwürdigkeiten aus meinem Leben* (Berlin: Mittler), 119. See also Fischer, *Krieg der Illusionen*, 78, n. 48. Bernhardi, *Videant consules, ne quid res publica detrimenti capiat* (Kassel: n.p., 1890).

[58] "mit Frankreich abrechnen und sich vergleichen, um danach alle lebendigen Kräfte des Volkes für die großen germanischen Kulturaufgaben gegen Rußland in die Wagschale werfen zu können" — Bernhardi, *Videant consules*, 36–37. Quoted in Fischer, *Krieg der Illusionen*, 78. Bernhardi's language in *Deutschland* is even more forceful: "Frankreich muß so völlig niedergeworfen werden, daß es uns nie wieder in den Weg treten kann" (114; France must be so completely crushed that she can never again cross our path).

[59] "bedeutendste und aufsehenerregendste Schrift" (Fischer, *Krieg der Illusionen*, 78).

[60] "Vorkämpfer des Deutschtums gegen slawische Überhebung" (Kaiser Wilhelm II, *Ereignisse und Gestalten aus den Jahren 1878–1918* [Leipzig and Berlin: K. F. Koehler, 1922], 165). See also Fischer, *Krieg der Illusionen*, 80.

[61] Cited in B. von Bülow, *Denkwürdigkeiten*, vol. 2 (Berlin: Ullstein, 1930), 81, and Fischer, *Krieg der Illusionen*, 81. Bernhardi's 1890 tract was also written in the year of the "New Course" under Caprivi after Bismarck had failed to renew his "Sozialistengesetz" and Social Democrats gained most electoral votes — see Fischer, *Krieg der Illusionen*, 48–49.

[62] "daß Rußland zum Kriege unfähig, bestätigte mir neulich auch Schiemann, der es wissen kann"; "Frankreich seien wir überlegen, und Rußland sei außerstande, Krieg zu führen" — Bernhardi, *Denkwürdigkeiten*, 332, 294. See Fischer, *Krieg der Illusionen*, 81–82. Bethmann Hollweg remained much more apprehensive of Russian power: he told his confidant Kurt Riezler on July 7, 1914: "Die Zukunft gehört Rußland, das wächst und wächst und sich als immer schwererer Alp auf uns

legt" (July 7, 1914; The future belongs to Russia which is growing and growing; like a nightmare it weighs upon us ever more heavily) (Fischer, *Krieg der Illusionen*, 315).

[63] Fischer, *Krieg der Illusionen*, 325.

[64] Fischer, *Krieg der Illusionen*, 83.

[65] "die Machtfrage zwischen Germanen und Slawen" (Bernhardi, *Deutschland*, 81).

[66] Fischer, *Krieg der Illusionen*, 81–82. See Harden on "Herr Professsor Schiemann," in *Die Zukunft* 17 (1896): 383.

[67] See R. Hinton Thomas, *Nietzsche in German Politics and Society, 1890–1918* (Manchester: Manchester UP, 1983), 131, n. 24.

[68] "Bernhardi selbst kam tatsächlich erst durch die Vermittlung Pohls von der *Post* im Oktober 1912 in engere Verbindung mit dem Alldeutschen Verband, dem er vorher ganz ferngestanden hatte" (in fact Bernhardi only associated himself with the Pan-German League in October 1912, thanks to the *Post*, having kept his distance up until then) (Fischer, *Krieg der Illusionen*, 346).

[69] Fischer, *Krieg der Illusionen*, 345.

[70] See Fischer, *Krieg der Illusionen*, 77–78.

[71] In Schiemann, "The United States and the War Cloud in Europe," Mc. Clures Magazine [*sic*], June 1910, cited by Bernhardi in *Deutschland*, 105.

[72] "Immerhin kann die englische Politik . . . statt eines Krieges einen Ausgleich mit Deutschland suchen. Uns wäre diese Lösung jedenfalls die erwünschtere" (*Deutschland*, 105; At all events English policy can seek an accommodation with Germany instead of war. This solution would certainly be preferable to us).

[73] Bernhardi, *Deutschland*, 100–101.

[74] *Deutschland*, 81, 107, 103.

[75] Fischer, *Krieg der Illusionen*, 82–83, 324. This at least was common ground with Hans Delbrück, Treitschke's successor as editor of the most important historical-political monthly, the *Preußische Jahrbücher*, who in 1915 organized a petition (Max Planck, Albert Einstein, and Max Weber were signatories) to stress "the defensive character of the war and the danger that absorption of "politically independent peoples and peoples accustomed to independence" would represent to the integrity of the Reich" — a countermovement to the infamous "Petition of the Intellectuals" (*Intellektuelleneingabe*), which had much wider support and which "called for a programme of annexations" (see Craig, *Germany, 1866–1945*, 361–62).

[76] "The general staff was genuinely surprised that its invasion of Belgium should have become a *casus belli* for Britain" (Strachan, *First World War*, 179). Laurence Lafore gives a cogent explanation of how a German attack on Belgium — long part of German planning — would nevertheless affect Britain's vital interests even more than an attack on France — *The Long Fuse* (Westport, CT: Greenwood Press, 1965), 198. Those with long memories might also have recalled how Palmerston had masterminded (and enforced by naval intervention on the Scheldt) the creation of modern Belgium against Dutch resistance. See James Chambers, *Palmerston* (London: John Murray, 2004), 156–57.

[77] "Der Begriff dauernder Neutralität widerspricht überhaupt dem Wesen des Staates, insofern dieser seine höchsten sittlichen Ziele eben nur im Wettbewerb mit anderen Staaten erreichen kann" (The notion of enduring neutrality completely contradicts the essence of the State insofar as the latter can only achieve its highest moral objectives through competition with other States; Bernhardi, *Deutschland*, 120. See also 109, 119).

[78] See Strachan, *First World War*, 1126. Fischer's chapter "Von Bismarck zu Bethmann: Um die englische Neutralität" (*Krieg der Illusionen*, 85–113) gives a fuller historical account of the guarantee that Bethmann contemptuously dismissed as a mere "Wisch." On Lichnowsky, see *Introduction*, and Williams's paper in this volume (chapter 3).

[79] Bernhardi, *Deutschland*, 120–21.

[80] Schlieffen "expected France to violate Belgium as soon as Germany's deployment at the Belgian frontier revealed her strategy and he therefore planned that Germany should do it first and faster" — Barbara Tuchman, *August 1914* (London: Constable, 1962), 34. Bernhardi equally expected "daß bei einem Kriege Deutschlands gegen Frankreich und England die beiden letztgenannten Staaten gerade in Belgien die Vereinigung ihrer Streitkräfte suchen würden" (that in a German war against France and England, the latter would seek to unite their armies in Belgium). Thus united in Belgium, England and France could outflank the German right, threatening the German fleet from the land side, and launching an invasion of Germany from the coast (Bernhardi, *Deutschland*, 119, 162). The Kaiser had also informed a dumbfounded Leopold in 1904, when his attempted bribe of French territory failed, that, like Napoleon and Frederick the Great, "so should I, in the event of Belgium's not being on my side, be actuated by strategical considerations only" (Tuchman, *August 1914*, 35).

[81] Strachan, *First World War*, 178, 236. This was the second volume, which appeared in English as *How Germany Makes War* (1914), the first having appeared in English as *Cavalry in Future Wars* (1906) — see above.

[82] "Die völlige Vernachlässigung der Kavallerie ferner in ihrem Verhältnis zur Gesamtarmee hat die Heerführung der Mittel beraubt, die gegnerische Operationsfähigkeit zu schädigen und die eigenen Bewegungen wirksam zu verschleiern" (Bernhardi, *Deutschland*, 200; Total neglect of the cavalry in relationship to the army as a whole has furthermore robbed the military leadership of the means to inflict damage on the opposition's operational capacity and to camouflage their own movements successfully). Bernhardi's special pleading for the cavalry incorporates key ideas from his 1906 book (*Cavalry in Future Wars*), including its potentially effective combination with bicycle brigades (*Deutschland*, 228) and airships (*Deutschland*, 255, 269–70), taking the Boer War as a more appropriate model than 1870, when the cavalry had been publicly perceived as too expensive and ineffective (*Deutschland*, 227). Bernhardi's prognosis on the likely role of the machine gun (a purely defensive one — *Deutschland*, 212, 238) is sounder, though he (understandably) did not foresee that of the tank in the "Blitzkrieg" and "Durchbruch" tactics he traces back to Frederick the Great (*Deutschland*, 199).

[83] Strachan, *First World War*, 178–79. It is hardly surprising that "[n]one of the criticisms of Moltke's changes voiced after 1918 were vented before 1914" since the Plan was obviously secret until put into effect. Later accounts of the opening stage of the war leave the reader in little doubt as to the likely impact of the eight divisions Moltke added to the left wing, not the right. Barbara Tuchman wryly observes that "once divinity of doctrine has been questioned there is no return to perfect faith . . . The passionate simplicity of Schlieffen's design for total effort by one wing . . . was broken" (*August 1914*, 237). Tuchman also notes that when an early version of the plan was betrayed to the French by an officer of the German General Staff in 1904, they did not believe it since "to the French logical mind it seemed obvious that the Germans would bring England in against them if they violated Belgium" (52–53).

[84] Bernhardi, *Deutschland*, iii. "Der Krieg und der Mut haben mehr große Dinge getan als die Nächstenliebe. Nicht euer Mitleiden, sondern eure Tapferkeit rettete bisher die Verunglückten. Was ist gut? fragt ihr. Tapfer sein ist gut" (*Also sprach Zarathustra*, I:10). Translations are mine. References in the text are to the German edition of *Deutschland und der nächste Krieg* and are given with the abbreviation *D* and the page number. The fact that the motto is missing from the English edition is a likely indication of the "sympathetic" stance of both publisher and translator towards Bernhardi (see n. 8 above) rather than of a desire not to cite Nietzsche "out of context."

[85] A. J. P. Taylor, characteristically, on "Nietzsche and the Germans," a review — now in *Europe: Grandeur and Decline* (Harmondsworth: Pelican, 1967), 194 — of Walter Kaufmann's *Nietzsche: Philosopher, Psychologist, Antichrist* (1950; 4th ed., Princeton: Princeton UP, 1950). Besides "the Will to Power" and "the Master Race," also, of course, "the Blond Beast" and "the Superman."

[86] "Die Deutschen waren früher das kriegsgewaltigste und kriegslustigste Volk Europas. Lange Zeit haben sie sich durch die Macht der Waffen und den Hochflug ihrer Gedanken als das Herrenvolk des Weltteils erwiesen" (2; The Germans were formerly Europe's most powerful and passionate warriors. For a long time they have proved themselves the dominant people on the Continent by the power of their arms and the loftiness of their ideas). That "formerly" receives attention in later chapters.

[87] "Die Kultur und der Staat — man betrüge sich hierüber nicht — sind Antagonisten: 'Kultur-Staat' ist bloß eine moderne Idee" (Nietzsche, *Götzen-Dämmerung: Was den Deutschen abgeht*, section 4).

[88] Variations on the theme of power in this paragraph: "Ohnmacht" (once), "politischer und kultureller Machtentfaltung" (once), "den größten Kultur- und Machtförderer" (four times), "eine verminderte Machtstellung" (five times), "Machtbedürfnis" (five times).

[89] One is irresistibly reminded of the musical-hall song reflecting similar British resolve when Disraeli sent the fleet into Turkish waters to resist a Russian advance in 1878 — "We don't want to fight, but by Jingo if we do, We've got the guns, we've got the men, and we've got the money too."

[90] See Martin's chapter in this volume (chapter 5).

[91] Nietzsche, *Zur Genealogie der Moral*, II:12: "man hat das Leben selbst als eine immer zweckmäßigere innere Anpassung an äußere Umstände definiert (Herbert Spencer). Damit ist aber das Wesen des Lebens verkannt, sein *Wille zur Macht*; damit ist der prinzipielle Vorrang übersehn, den die spontanen, angreifenden, übergreifenden, neu-auslegenden, neu-richtenden und gestaltenden Kräfte haben, auf deren Wirkung erst die 'Anpassung' folgt"; cited in text from Douglas Smith's translation, *On the Genealogy of Morals* (Oxford: Oxford UP, 1996), 59.

[92] "In keinem Punkte ist aber das gemeine Bewußtsein der Europäer widerwilliger gegen Belehrung als hier . . . Die "Ausbeutung" gehört nicht einer verderbten oder unvollkommnen und primitiven Gesellschaft an: sie gehört ins *Wesen* des lebendigen, als organische Grundfunktion, sie ist eine Folge des eigentlichen Willens zur Macht, der eben der Wille des Lebens ist" (Nietzsche, *Jenseits von Gut und Böse*, section 259).

[93] "eine Aktivität zweiten Ranges, eine bloße Reaktivität," ibid.

[94] "der nach erweiterter Machtsphäre strebende Staat" (Bernhardi, *Deutschland*, 20).

[95] Goethe, *Faust I*, lines 1692, 1676.

[96] "Wie für das Streben des Individuums, so gibt es für die Begehrung der Völker keinen Abschluß und kein Ende" (J. J. Ruedorffer [= Kurt Riezler], *Grundzüge der Weltpolitik in der Gegenwart* [Stuttgart and Berlin, 1914], 102–3). See Imanuel Geiss, "Zur Beurteilung der deutschen Reichspolitik im ersten Weltkrieg," in *Die Erforderlichkeit des Unmöglichen*, ed. H. Pogge v. Strandmann and Imanuel Geiss (Frankfurt am Main: Europäische Verlagsanstalt, 1965), 61. "The need for the impossible" is an allusion to Riezler's own 1912 book of that title that prefigures the argument in more "philosophical" terms (ibid. 55). As Bethmann Hollweg's secretary, Riezler produced the draft program of war aims mentioned above. On this controversial memorandum, see Craig, *Germany, 1866–1945*, 365, esp. n. 69.

[97] "Wie man mit dem Hammer philosophiert," the subtitle of Nietzsche's *Götzen-Dämmerung*. "Du mußt herrschen und gewinnen,/ Oder dienen und verlieren,/ Leiden oder triumphieren,/ Amboß oder Hammer sein" (Goethe's second "Cophtisches Lied" [1787–89]). See "'Verdrängen oder sich verdrängen lassen, ist der Kern des Lebens,' sagt Goethe" ("'Quash or be quashed, that's life,' so says Goethe," cited by Bernhardi, *Deutschland*, 12).

[98] "Der Deutsche selbst *ist* nicht, er *wird*, er 'entwickelt sich,'" Nietzsche, *Jenseits von Gut und Böse*, section 244.

[99] "Wir Deutsche sind Hegelianer, auch wenn es nie einen Hegel gegeben hätte, insofern wir . . . dem Werden, der Entwicklung instinktiv einen tieferen Sinn und reicheren Wert zumessen als dem, was 'ist'" (Nietzsche, *Die fröhliche Wissenschaft*, section 357).

[100] Bernhardi, *Deutschland*; "unsere europäische Machtstellung" (111), "Weltmachtstellung" (112). Further examples of "Macht" in this paragraph: "Gleichgewicht der Macht" (104), "Machtfaktoren" (46, 118–19), "nur durch die lebendige Macht" (4), "uns ist der Staat nicht physische Macht als Selbstzweck, er ist Macht, um die höheren Güter zu schützen und zu befördern" (44–45), "der größte Machterweiterer und Lebenserwecker" (21), "das nach

Machterweiterung aufstrebende Volk" (28), "in fortwährender Machterweiterung begriffen" (82), "die Macht des Goldes" (69).

[101] "Kulturaufgaben" (28).

[102] "nur ein Vorwärts oder ein Zurück" (112).

[103] See Thomas Mann, *Friedrich und die Große Koalition* (Berlin: S. Fischer, 1915).

[104] "die maßgebende Kulturmacht" (41). Further examples of "Macht" in this paragraph: "eine erweiterte Machtsphäre," "eine solche Machterweiterung durch Gebietserwerbungen in Europa selbst . . . so gut wie ausgeschlossen" (113), "ausserhalb der deutschen Machtsphäre" (79), "in unserem Volk den einheitlichen Willen zur Macht . . . zu erwecken" (124).

[105] Bernhardi would undoubtedly have approved of the mass conscription and mass education that helped transform a peasant and merchant economy into Asia's first nation state, but scarcely the slavish imitation of the industrialized West that her cultural revolution ushered in after the Meiji Restoration of 1868.

[106] "So bliebe dann nur noch ein Weg übrig, um die dort sitzenden wertvollen deutschen Volksteile vor dem Untergange zu bewahren: sie längs der preußischen Ostgrenze, etwa in dem früheren Südpreußen, anzusiedeln, dafür einen entsprechenden Teil der slawischen Bevölkerung abzuschieben und die so kolonisierten Landesteile an Preußen anzuschließen." This had happened at least twice to the whole population of Metz, but is now contrary to the "sogenannten Geiste der Zeit" (Bernhardi, *Weltreise*, 19).

[107] Germany "nur ein verstümmelter Torso der alten Kaisermacht" (79). See also Imanuel Geiss, trans. Fred Bridgham, *The Question of German Unification, 1806–1996* (London: Routledge, 1997), 67.

[108] "Wille zur Kultur" (134).

[109] "als Wille zur politischen Macht" (134).

[110] "erst durch den bewußten Menschenwillen" [again quoting Treitschke] (7).

[111] "Wille zum Sieg" (7).

[112] "Willensschwäche" (11).

[113] "der wachsenden Kultur eine kriegüberwindende Macht zugesprochen" (9).

[114] "Die Kraft ist zugleich das höchste Recht" (16).

[115] "Geist" and "geistig" are of course notoriously ambiguous terms. Here, given the proximity to Hegel, "there can be no excuse," as Walter Kaufmann puts it, "for translating Hegel's *Geist* as 'mind' instead of 'spirit'" (*Hegel: A Reinterpretation* [New York: Anchor, 1965], 89).

[116] *Phänomenologie des Geistes*, part 4 — on "Selbstbewußtsein" (self-assurance) — a section greatly admired by Marx.

[117] *Britain as Germany's Vassal* talks in more vivid terms of Germany as "an overheated boiler"; formerly Germans were everywhere, the "manure of civilisation" ("Kulturdünger") [!]. When the hour comes and a great emigration begins, Germans should find new lands ready for them to settle in (*Germany's Vassal*, 83–84, 89).

[118] See "Der Gesichtspunkt der Nützlichkeit ist gerade in bezug auf ein solches heißes Herausquellen oberster rang-ordnender, rang-abhebender Werturteile so fremd und unangemessen wie möglich" (Nietzsche, *Zur Genealogie der Moral* I:2).

[119] Wilhelm von Humboldt, *Ideen zu einem Versuch, die Grenzen der Wirksamkeit des Staates zu bestimmen*, ed. E. Cauer (Breslau: Trewendt, 1851).

[120] From "Wohlfahrtsstaat" to "das Prinzip der Notwendigkeit": Siegfried Kaehler traces these shifts in *Wilhelm von Humboldt und der Staat* (Göttingen: Vandenhoeck & Ruprecht, 1963), 124–50. Indicative of the many incompatibilities in Humboldt's *Ideen* is the fact that Bernhardi can approvingly cite his assessment of the beneficial effect of war on human character a few pages later (*Deutschland*, 22).

[121] "Der Staat ist sich selbst Zweck wie alles Lebendige." See Kaehler, *Wilhelm von Humboldt*, 488.

[122] "Erzieher des Menschengeschlechts zur Freiheit" (*Deutschland*, 19).

[123] "Vor der ernsten Entscheidung, die ein Krieg in sich schließt, verlieren alle kleinlichen Sonderinteressen ihre Bedeutung. Die gemeinsame Gefahr einigt alles" (*Deutschland*, 21).

[124] "Zum ersten Mal seh ich dich aufstehn / hörengesagter fernster unglaublicher Kriegs-Gott . . . und die Ernte beginnt"; "denn immer wars rühmlich, / nicht in der Vorsicht einzelner Sorge zu sein, sondern in *einem* / wagenden Geiste, sondern in herrlich / gefühlter Gefahr, heilig gemeinsam" (Rainer Maria Rilke, *Sämtliche Werke* (Wiesbaden: Insel, 1957), 2:86, 90.

[125] "beständig / nimmt er sich fort und tritt ins veränderte Sternbild/ seiner steten Gefahr" (Rilke, *Sämtliche Werke* 1:707). Even those of the *Duineser Elegien* completed after the War scarcely reflect pacifist tendencies in Rilke, as claimed by Neill Ferguson: "Among the most haunting condemnations of the war in German poetry are Rilke's *Duino Elegies*" (*Pity of War*, 449) — see also *Introduction* in this volume.

[126] Martin Luther, "Ob Kriegsleute auch im seligen Stande sein können." Both Michael Howard, reviewing Strachan's *First World War* (*Times Literary Supplement*, July 20, 2001) and John Keegan pick up Strachan's "arresting idea: that the motivation to war in Germany was religious . . . Teutonic self-righteousness, perhaps deriving from the Lutheran doctrine of justification by faith exclusive of works, underlay the accusation of conspiracy that the Germans trumpeted in the first days of August 1914" (Keegan, *Times Literary Supplement*, April 12, 2004).

[127] A suggestion scarcely in need of refutation ("eine Auffassung, deren Widerlegung wohl überflüßig sein dürfte") from one of our foremost strategic thinkers, according to Friedell, though alas not a comparably gifted biblical scholar ("kein ebenso begabter Bibelleser"; Egon Friedell, *Kulturgeschichte der Neuzeit*, vol. 1 (Munich: Beck, 1929), 334).

[128] Had Prussia supported Austria and Russia then, instead of maintaining her neutrality, Napoleon could certainly have been defeated (*Deutschland*, 40).

[129] Wilson, *Bernhardi and the Germans*, 16, 19.

[130] Wilson, *Bernhardi and the Germans*, 3.

[131] The year, coincidentally, in which the Kaiser and Tirpitz finally abandoned their secret plot to dispatch a huge fleet to invade the USA, with New York as the main target — see *Introduction*.

[132] See chapter 8 of *Deutschland*, "Der nächste Seekrieg." Access to and from the Baltic, according to both Fritz Fischer and John Röhl, was perhaps the decisive factor in persuading the Kaiser and his advisers at a Crown Council meeting on 8 December 1912 not to launch a major war then and there; so completion of the canal can be seen as initiating a premeditated act of aggression in August 1914. See Carr, *A History of Germany*, 206.

[133] This is "eine viel größere und gewichtigere Kulturaufgabe" than that facing the Japanese, already the dominant Asiatic power (*Deutschland*, 297).

[134] In *Britain as Germany's Vassal*, we read that "German language is steadily gaining ground in foreign countries, and partly at the cost of English" (46–47). Moreover, "Germany's export of books is twice as large per year as is the export of books from France, England, and the US combined," proving that "Germany's influence on the intellectual development of mankind is proportionally larger" (46). But if such claims appear implausible, Bernhardi's next claim, that "[the German navy's] strength is exceeded only by the British navy and the navy of the US," (perhaps deliberately) plays down the truth, for the translator notes, "This is an error. The German navy is considerably stronger than that of the US" (47).

[135] "Kein Volk ist so wenig wie das deutsche geeignet, seine Geschicke selbst zu leiten, etwa in einer rein parlamentarischen oder gar republikanischen Verfassung; für keines paßt die landläufige liberale Schablone weniger als für uns" (*Deutschland*, 123).

[136] "Das deutsche Volk ist zu großer gemeinsamer Tat immer nur zu bringen . . . unter der Führung gewaltiger Persönlichkeiten" (*Deutschland*, 123). It is precisely the view that the German people need "powerful personalities" to rule over them that is the main target of Anthony Hope Hawkins's polemic against Bernhardi, *The (New) German Testament* (see Buitenhuis, *Great War of Words*, 31, and note 22 above).

[137] "aus freiem Machtgefühl zu handeln und damit Großes durch und für unser Volk zu erreichen" (*Deutschland*, 123).

[138] E. M. Forster, *Howards End* (1910; repr. Harmondsworth, UK: Penguin, 1986), 42–43.

Academics

8: Peacemaker and Warmonger: Alexander Tille and the Limits of Anglo-German Intercultural Transfer

Stefan Manz

ALEXANDER TILLE (1866–1912) is mentioned in monographs as a key figure in Anglo-German intercultural transfer and late nineteenth-century German intellectual life. Steven E. Aschheim, for example, describes Tille as "the major mediator of Nietzsche in Britain."[1] For Richard Hinton Thomas, he was "the most important of the German Social Darwinists at this time."[2] Despite frequent references of such kind, Tille's academic work and activities have never been thoroughly investigated in a specifically Anglo-German context.[3] The following article, based on Tille's publications and other primary sources, seeks to fill this gap. It will be shown that the clear dichotomy between 'peacemaker' and 'warmonger' does not suffice to categorize figures like Tille. The same can be said about other individuals such as D. H. Lawrence or Kuno Meyer, who are discussed elsewhere in this volume.

Alexander Tille was born in Lauenstein / Saxony into an educated middle-class family, his father being a protestant pastor who introduced his son to Greek, Latin, and classical literature from an early age. After attending the prestigious *Fürstenschule* in Grimma, Tille took up his studies at Leipzig University in German and English philology, as well as philosophy. He received his doctorate in 1890 with a study on the Faust motif in German folk songs.[4] That same year he secured a part-time lectureship in German at Glasgow University. In this position he was highly active, mediating German philosophy and literature in Britain, and, vice versa, British intellectual thought in Germany.

As regards the reception of Nietzsche in the Anglo-Saxon world, Tille's key role is based on the fact that he was the first to translate and edit the philosopher's work in English. In the early 1890s Nietzsche was "very much in the air," not only in London, but also in Dublin and Glasgow.[5] Intellectuals were looking for alternatives to Victorian sentimentality and moralism. As Gertrud Burdett put it: "In judging Nietzsche, it is well to bear in mind that we are living in a time of intellectual unrest, and of social discontents; that we are ripe for new teachings, and longing for new ideas."[6] A differentiated and widespread discussion, however, could not develop, because Nietzsche was only accessible to those who understood German. This is where Tille stepped in: from 1896 onwards he edited translations of some of Nietzsche's works, including his — Tille's — own translation of *Also sprach Zarathustra*. Macmillan in New York acquired the publishing rights for the American market.[7] The editions triggered a wave of reviews and literary reception. W. B. Yeats, for example, had no command of German and, when first reading *Zarathustra* in 1902, relied on Tille's translation. Yeats and other contemporary writers were heavily influenced by Nietzsche, among them Eugene O'Neill, Wyndham Lewis, D. H. Lawrence, and Jack London.[8] Tille's guiding hand, however, had a restricting impact on the reception of Nietzsche in the Anglo-Saxon world, as the selected texts were taken exclusively from Nietzsche's later works. More important, in the foreword to his *Zarathustra* translation, Tille suggests a purely social Darwinist reading of the oeuvre: "Nietzsche had taken up Darwin's whole idea of evolution and made it almost the leading motive of his *Zarathustra*. And it is Nietzsche's undeniable merit to have led this new moral ideal to a complete victory."[9] According to one critic, this reading had lasting consequences for the interpretation of Nietzsche's philosophy.[10]

As for social Darwinism, Tille was part of a philosophical interplay between Britain and Germany. The interpretation of Darwin's theory in social terms was first undertaken in England, but remained basically confined to academic circles. In Germany, however, social Darwinism caught on to a greater extent through a flood of popular scientific works that reached its height in the 1890s. Books like Ernst Haeckel's *Die Welträthsel* (1899) or Wilhelm Bölsche's *Das Liebesleben in der Natur* (1900) were bestsellers at the time.[11] Alexander Tille was a driving force behind this process of intercultural transfer. He was in correspondence with Alfred Russell Wallace and asked him for permission to translate some of his articles into German in order to make his thoughts widely available to the German public. Tille also translated and introduced some of T. E. Huxley's essays into German.[12]

His own concept of "Entwicklungsethik," finally, is based on what C. M. Williams calls "evolutionary ethics."[13] Tille developed this concept in his widely read *Von Darwin bis Nietzsche: Ein Buch Entwicklungsethik*, published in 1895. Here, he postulates:

> [Mit Nietzsches *Zarathustra* ist] der große leitende Gedanke der Entwicklungslehre Darwins zum ersten Male rein und ungetrübt durch herrschende sittliche Vorstellungen auf die heutige Menschheit und die künftige Menschheitsentwicklung angewandt. Mit dem

Augenblick, wo diese Anwendung gefunden ist, tritt die Entwicklungsethik wie die darwinistische Sozialwissenschaft aus der Zeit des Tappens und Tastens heraus und setzt die wissenschaftliche Einzelarbeit ein. Denn noch gilt es die beiden Grundsätze der sozialen Auslese und sozialen Ausscheidung auf alle Gebiete des sittlichen Lebens wie auf das Völkerdasein anzuwenden, die ethischen wie die sozialen Theorien in all ihren Einzelheiten durch sie umzubilden. Der Nationalökonom, der Arzt, der Lehrer, der Gesetzgeber, sie alle haben hier mitzuarbeiten, und dabei wird sich zeigen, daß noch manches sittliche und soziale Dogma von heute fallen und beide Wissenschaften mit ihrem theoretischen Teile ebenso ins Gericht gehen müssen wie mit ihrer praktischen Lehre, ehe eine ausgebaute darwinistische Sozialethik geschaffen ist, deren Einrichtung der Ausdruck der naturgegebenen Verhältnisse der Menschen zu einander sind und die als praktische Wirtschaftskunst des Volksstandes lebendige Früchte trägt.[14]

[(In Nietzsche's *Zarathustra*) we find for the first time the great guiding principle of Darwin's theory of evolution applied to contemporary human society and its future development in a pure form, unadulterated by received notions of morality. From the moment this application was formulated, evolutionary ethics in the shape of Darwinist social science outgrew the stage of groping and hypothesizing and entered the era of scientific study. For we still have to apply the principles of social selection and social elimination in all aspects of the moral life and existence of peoples, and, with their aid, to transform ethical and social theory in every detail. Economists, doctors, teachers, lawyers — all must play their part; and in the process it will come to be seen that many an ethical and social dogma of today will fall, and both sciences will be put to the test as much for their theory as in their practical teaching before a fully developed Darwinist social ethics comes into being — one whose foundation reflects the structure of mankind's nature-given relationships and which bears living fruit as the practical economy of the people.]

Only those acts are deemed ethical that serve the improvement of the fittest race or social class. At the same time, traditional ethics of Christianity and humanism are dismissed. So are equality, socialism, and democracy:

Wenn die Ehe mit einem siechen Weibe sieche Krüppel erzeugt, dann ist sie eine fluchwürdige Handlung, ein unsittlicher Akt, und wenn die herrschende Ethik sie zehnmal als eine heroische That altruistischen Opfermutes preist.[15]

[When marriage to a sick wife produces sick cripples, then that deed deserves condemnation, it is an immoral act — even if conventional ethics praises it as a deed of heroic, altruistic self-sacrifice.]

In another article, entitled "Ostlondon als Nationalheilanstalt," Tille represented slums like the East End as positive for the development of the common good, since they purged society of useless citizens:

> Mit unerbittlicher Strenge scheidet die Natur die zum Tier herab-gesunkenen Menschen aus den Reihen der anderen aus, und so fungiert Ostlondon in einem Maße als Nationalheilanstalt; und alle Versuche, den 'Unglücklichen' zu helfen, mindern nur die enorme Bedeutung, die es als solche hat.[16]

> [Nature, acting ineluctably, eliminates human beings who have de-generated into animals from amongst the ranks of the rest, thus East London operates to an extent as a national sanatorium; any attempt to help the "unfortunate" only reduces Nature's enormous signifi-cance in this regard.]

Scholars like Alfred Kelly have aptly stressed Tille's "dehumanizing brutal-ity"; Fritz Bolle describes him as "den radikalsten und rüdesten der Sozialdarwinisten"[17] (the most radical and primitive of social Darwinists).

Tille's interest in intercultural mediation extended to the literary field. He published in German periodicals on authors such as Robert Louis Ste-venson and William Wordsworth, and claims to have been the first to bring Rudyard Kipling to the attention of the German reader.[18] In Glas-gow, Tille founded the Glasgow Goethe Society, a local branch of the English Goethe Society, which aimed at disseminating Goethe's thought in Britain, but also, on a more general level, "to promote an interest in German Literature by means of meetings, papers, discussions, readings, publications, etc." The society had about 35 members, half of whom were British, the other half Germans living in Glasgow. Two examples of pa-pers read before the society are "Richard Wagner's *Parsifal* and the Baireuth Festival Play," given by Hermann Georg Fiedler, later Professor of German at Oxford,[19] and Tille's "Friedrich Nietzsche, the Herald of Modern Germany." Thus Tille created a platform for intellectual ex-change and regular meetings between British and German *Bildungsbürger* (educated middle-classes). His central position becomes obvious by the fact that, upon his return to Germany in 1900, the Glasgow Goethe Soci-ety ceased to exist.[20]

So Tille can justly be called a major mediator of "intercultural trans-fer."[21] This concept replaces the one-dimensional notion of "influence" by a complex pattern of mutual crisscrossing and adaptation of ideas, knowledge, material, and so on. The phenomena transferred do not nec-essarily have to be expressions of high culture such as literature or science. Consequently, Tille's publications on "Die Glasgower Kabelbahn" or "Der Ausstand der britischen Maschinenbauer" are expressions of inter-cultural transfer just as much as, for example, his article "German Christmas and the Christmas-Tree,"[22] since they each disseminate knowledge of the other culture. Tille's self-assessment regarding his ten years in Glasgow may be exaggerated, but makes the point in principle:

> Ich habe in dieser Zeit für den Austausch wirtschaftlicher und geistiger Erkenntnis zwischen beiden Ländern wohl mehr gethan als irgend ein anderer Deutscher. Drüben habe ich in ununterbrochener Lehrthätigkeit die Teilnahme für deutsche Wissenschaft, Litteratur, Philosophie und deutsches wirtschaftliches Denken zu vertiefen versucht. . . . Vielleicht hat kein Deutscher in allen seinen Arbeiten drüben mehr Wert darauf gelegt, Verständnis für deutsche Art und deutsches Denken zu wecken. In Deutschland habe ich für englische Dinge ähnliches gethan. (*Fl*, ix–x).

> [During this time I did more to explain the two country's economic and spiritual heritage to each other than probably any other German. In England I worked tirelessly as a lecturer to deepen understanding of German science, literature, philosophy and national economy. . . . Perhaps no other German living over there placed such emphasis in all his works on arousing sympathy for our German way of life and thought. In Germany I worked similarly on behalf of things English.]

In the light of this assessment, the circumstances of Tille's return seem all the more paradoxical. He was, as he writes, "mitten im Burenkriege von schottischem Studentenpöbel thätlich beleidigt" (*Fl*, viii; in the middle of the Boer War I was physically abused by Scottish student riff-raff). — I will now turn to his warmongering activities.

In early 1900, Tille published an article in the Berlin weekly *Die Woche* in which he heavily criticized British action in South Africa and ridiculed the state of the British army. In an ironic way, he spoke about "steifbeinige Kahlköpfe mit graugesprenkelten Schnurrbärten und halbe Jungen mit Milchgesichtern" (stifflegged bald-pates with graying moustachios and man-boys with milksop faces), and he continued:

> Aber die Freiwilligen-Ausbildung in Großbritannien ist ein Spiel, kein Dienst. Mit Vorliebe melden sich zu ihr Jünglinge, die das Bedürfnis zu einiger körperlichen Kräftigung durch Bewegung in frischer Luft und Körperübung in sich fühlen und werden auch angenommen, da die physiologischen Anforderungen, die die praktische Handhabung der Aufnahmebedingungen an den Freiwilligen stellt, sehr niedrig sind. . . . Selbst ein paar Wochen Eindrillung kann diese Freiwilligen, trotzdem sie sich aus den intelligenteren Volksschichten zusammensetzen, unmöglich zu einer einigermaßen genügenden Kriegstauglichkeit erheben. Man muß selbst als deutscher Einjährigenfreiwilliger ausgebildet worden sein,

um das beurteilen zu können. . . . Der Burenkrieg ist ein
Eroberungskrieg, wenn je nur ein solcher geführt worden ist, das
wird zwar kaum irgendwo eingestanden, aber mit der liberalen
Phrase, daß unter britischem Regiment die ganze Welt dem
Glückszustande entgegengeführt werde, ist es zu Ende. Ist es doch
allzudeutlich, wie stark die Sehnsucht der Buren nach dieser
britischen Seligkeit ist. . . . Gerade wie Weltbürgertum eine schöne
Sache ist, solange man an seine Mitmenschen verkaufen will, wie sich
aber jedermann auf seine nationale Eigenart besinnt, sobald
dieselben Mitmenschen als Konkurrenten auftreten, so macht sich
auch der demokratische Liberalismus breit, solange man mit
Siebenmeilenstiefeln über halbe Kontinente schreitet (natürlich nur,
um andere zu beglücken), macht aber sofort einem hochgespannten
nationalen Rachegefühl Platz, sobald sich eine Hand voll Holländer
mit dem Mausergewehr gegen die Beglückung sträubt.[23]

[But the training of volunteers in England is no more than a game,
not a serious matter. Generally speaking, those who volunteer are
young men feeling the need to toughen up a bit by means of fresh
air and exercise, and they are accepted because the required physical
attainments are very low. . . . Even several weeks' drill will not raise
them to even a moderately acceptable standard for war service —
despite the fact that these volunteers come from the more intelligent
levels of society. You have to have been trained as a German one-
year volunteer yourself to be able to judge this. . . . The Boer War is
a war of conquest if ever there was, even though this is barely admitted anywhere unless capped with the liberal sentiment that, under
British rule, the whole world is drawing towards a state of happiness.
Yet it is only too clear how little the Boers yearn for this British state
of happiness. . . . Just as the idea of world citizenship is desirable so
long as people want to sell to their fellow-citizens, but everyone sees
to his own country's interests as soon as these fellow-citizens turn
into rivals, so, too, democratic liberalism is extolled whilst people be-
stride the continents in seven-league boots (just introducing a state
of happiness, of course), but this rapidly gives way to highly-charged
feelings of national revenge the moment a bunch of Dutchmen take
up guns to oppose the state of happiness.]

Excerpts from the article appeared in the *Glasgow Herald*, translated by a
Glaswegian studying in Leipzig, "to give my countrymen a sample of the
mental nourishment dealt out to the Germans by those of their nationality who honour us with their presence in the British Isles." This triggered
a wave of public protest in Glasgow. "Ardent patriots and loyal alumni of
our honoured university" were enraged at the "outrageously offensive
phrases of Dr Tille's article," and by the fact that "our eagerly patriotic
Volunteers and our gallant soldiers [were] vilified and held up to the ridi-

cule of our bitterly jealous Continental friends(?)." It was demanded that Tille be removed from his lectureship.[24]

The tension reached its climax on February 23, 1900. Some 500 students gathered in front of the university's German classroom, singing patriotic songs while awaiting the arrival of the German lecturer, Dr Tille. On arriving, he refused to enter the room and made an effort to escape. The students set upon him and threatened to throw him into the River Kelvin. Tille and several other professors were "unceremoniously shoved into a class-room, where they were kept prisoners for some time. Dr Tille suffered somewhat hard usage at the hands of the students, and several of them possessed themselves of portions of his gown." Tille was finally given the opportunity to speak up. He expressed his regret at the consequences of his article, maintained that it had been translated in a misleading way and that it merely encapsulated pro-Boer tendencies in the British press. Further mediating words by a professor defused the situation. "Three cheers were given for the German lecturer, and the students dispersed."[25] Despite the conciliatory outcome, public opinion in Glasgow remained highly critical of Tille. Letters to the editor convincingly dismissed his attempt at playing down the confrontational tone of his article; the student newspaper spoke of a "great patriotic demonstration against the lecturer in German."[26]

The occurrences in Glasgow have to be seen against the background of growing tensions between Britain and Germany around 1900. Wilhelm II's "Kruger Telegram" (1896) had caused a public outcry amongst the British public. Popular invasion novels such as T. W. Offin's *How the Germans Took London* (1900) turned the continental competitor into a lingering threat that was eventually personified by Germans living in Britain.[27] Throughout the country, the minority group had to endure hostile reactions from their host society. In academic circles there were suggestions that Germans teaching at British universities might be required to express their loyalty publicly towards their adopted country.[28] In Aberdeen the German classroom was devastated and the lecturer named Hein was physically attacked. At Edinburgh university there was some agitation against a German-born professor.[29] Pastor Rosenkranz reports from his German evangelical congregation in Liverpool:

> Wenige Monate vorher war der Burenkrieg ausgebrochen. Die Spannung, die sich infolgedessen zwischen dem englischen und dem deutschen Volke offenbarte, zog auch die Liverpooler deutsche Siedelung mehrfach in Mitleidenschaft. Einzelne Gemeindeglieder wurden von der Bevölkerung bedroht. Ein Metzger mußte wegen einer unbedachten Aeußerung nächtlicherweise flüchten.[30]

[The Boer War had broken out just a few months previously. The tension between Britons and Germans that arose in consequence also caused suffering for the German community in Liverpool. Individual members were threatened by the populace. A butcher was obliged to flee by night as a result of an incautious remark.]

In London the home of the Consul General of the Netherlands faced attack. So did the premises of Henry Bish, a German hairdresser, who was described in a Metropolitan Police report as "a German of pro-Boer sympathies who has recently made his opinions known rather widely among his customers." On May 20, 1900 a crowd of 2,000 gathered in front of the shop "and stones being thrown the windows in the upper part of the house were broken and a lighted firework thrown through the broken window, set fire to the lace curtain (*sic*)." On the next day "the place looked like a house about to be pulled down after a fire." Germans traveling on trains were often assaulted and had to seek the protection of the police.[31] The fragile British national consciousness during the Boer war released germanophobic tendencies that were to recur on a larger scale fourteen years later.[32] The occurrences described were merely a prelude to the First World War.

Back to Alexander Tille. He resigned from his lectureship, "[finding] it impossible to remain on the teaching staff of the University, after I have been assaulted by the students of it."[33] Upon his return to Germany he immediately published a highly anti-British book under the title *Aus Englands Flegeljahren* (meaning England's awkward adolescent, or even yobbish, phase) in which he reproduced established stereotypes such as "Händlervolk" or "perfides Albion." A few quotations give an impression of the confrontational tone of the book:

> Der Brite neigt überhaupt nicht dazu, politische Machtverhältnisse mit sicher wägendem Blick ruhig abzuschätzen. Daran verhindert ihn nicht nur seine grenzenlose Unkenntnis von auswärtigen Zuständen, sondern vor allem sein hochgespanntes volkliches Selbstbewußtsein, sein Engländerhochmut, sein Nationalgefühl, eine Kraft, mit der das Ausland stets zu rechnen haben wird, und die heute aller Wahrscheinlichkeit nach durch einen Zusammenstoß mit der Welt der wirklichen Dinge Europa einer schweren Erschütterung zutreibt . . . [Der Engländer] kann nicht verstehen, daß längst die Stunde einer neuen Machtverteilung in Europa geschlagen hat und daß England nicht mehr allein in allen Dingen, die über das Kirchspiel Krähwinkel hinausgehen, das entscheidende Wort zu sprechen hat. (*Fl*, 42–43)..

> [Your Briton is absolutely not inclined to weigh up the balance of political power calmly. What prevents him is not only his limitless ignorance of foreign affairs but above all his over-developed sense of

racial superiority, his English pride, his sense of nationhood, a force that foreign powers will always have to reckon with and that will in all probability drive Europe to a severe crisis in our own day as a result of its coming up against the realities. . . . [Englishmen] are unable to understand that the hour for a new division of power within Europe struck long ago, and that England will no longer be the only power to settle everything that happens beyond their own backyard.]

In allem, was sein Volk betrifft, ist der Brite ebenso anmaßend wie taktlos. Noch immer sieht der Brite auf den Deutschen mit dem Gefühl jener tiefeingewurzelten hochmütigen Geringschätzung herab, die es ihm unmöglich macht, ihn als ebenbürtigen Gegner zu betrachten. Er ist ein Nebenbuhler, aber kein gesellschaftsfähiger, ein Nebenbuhler unter dem eigenen Stande. Man sieht auf ihn herab, wie der Graf auf seinen Winkelbankier herabsieht, dem er verschuldet ist und den er darum zum Gesellschaftsabend in sein Haus einladen muß. Daß wir dem Briten diese Geringschätzung noch austreiben werden, steht ebenso fest, wie daß es noch manchen Hieb brauchen wird, bis sie ausgetrieben ist. (*Fl*, 45–46)

[In all things pertaining to their country the British are as arrogant as they are tactless. . . . The British still look down on Germans with that deeply ingrained attitude of arrogant contempt that renders it impossible for them to regard Germans as equals. The German is a rival, but he is not a socially acceptable one — a rival of lower status. One looks down on him as a Count looks down on a banker to whom he owes money and whom he is thus obliged to invite to parties at home. That we shall drive this contempt out of the British is as certain as the fact that many blows will be required before we succeed.]

Applying his social Darwinist worldview to the relationship between nations, Tille considered war between Britain and Germany a necessity: "Es wird eines Tages in blutigem Kampfe entschieden werden müssen, ob von den europäischen Germanenstaaten Deutschland oder Großbritannien die erste Stelle einzunehmen hat" (*Fl*, xi; The right of Germany or England to take first place amongst Europe's Germanic States will have to be resolved one day in a bloody battle).

According to his brother's biographical account, Tille was obsessed with finding ways of strengthening the German "Volkskraft" as a means of overtaking Britain economically and militarily.[34] His concept of "Entwicklungsethik" had the ultimate purpose of achieving this goal. In his *Flegeljahre*, Tille analyses Britain's social and economic problems with considerable *Schadenfreude*, though still highly competently; and it is with considerable satisfaction that he points to his fatherland's achievements since 1871 and its supposed superiority over Britain. This is in line with his political activities. From 1898 onwards Tille was a member — and later on the board — of the extreme nationalist *Alldeutscher Verband*, which considered German expansion a necessity in its struggle for world power. England, as a colonial power, was one of Germany's major rivals in this struggle.[35] Tille gives expression to his pan-German fantasies in "Das Alldeutsche Lied" (1900):

> . . .
> Wo eines Deutschen Recht man kürzt,
> Wo Deutschen Nachteil sprießt,
> Wo man die deutsche Flagge stürzt
> Und deutsches Blut vergießt, —
> Ob an Marokkos Seegestad
> Und ob am Gelben Fluß:
> Die deutsche Eisenflotte naht
> Mit ihrem groben Gruß.
> Hei, wie dem Feind die Seele graust,
> Wenn niederdonnert schwer
> Die feste deutsche Panzerfaust
> Mit Wucht im fernen Meer!
>
> Wer da von deutschen Eltern stammt
> Und unsre Sprache spricht,
> Wem Deutsch mit uns das Herz entflammt,
> Den lassen wir auch nicht,
> Ob Östreich, Schweiz, ob Frieslands Strand
> Ihm Heimat, gilt uns gleich.
> Die Hand her, großdeutsch Nachbarland
> Am neuen Deutschen Reich!
> Auf! Daß e i n Deutschklang töne bald
> Von Rheines Mündung her
> Bis Mähren und vom Waskenwald
> Zum Adriatschen Meer!
>
> . . .
> Wenn alles, was da deutsch sich hält,
> Zu e i n e m Reich sich eint,
> Wenn ob der ganzen deutschen Welt
> Nur e i n e Krone scheint.
> Da fliegt der Kaiseraar vom Strand,
> Da rauscht sein Fittich schwer:
> "Alldeutschland" brausts vom Meer zum Land,
> "Alldeutsch" vom Land zum Meer![36]

[When a German's rights are restricted and he is everywhere disadvantaged; when the German flag is torn down and German blood spilled, be it on Morocco's strand or on the Yellow River: German ironclads are on their way bringing a rough greeting. Aha! just look at the enemy quail as bazookas rain down their thunderous German fire, blasting foreign waters apart!

All you whose parents are German and who speak our language; whoever's heart, like ours, is set on fire by German, you, too, we shall not desert. Whether from Austria, Switzerland or the Frisian Isles, it's all the same to us. Give us your hand, neighbor in our Greater Germany, our new German *Reich*! Rise up, that soon *one* German tongue may be heard from the mouth of the Rhine to Moravia, from the Vosges to the Adriatic! . . .

When all who feel themselves German unite in *one* Reich, when in the whole German world there is but *one* glittering crown, then the Imperial Eagle flies up from the strand and beats its mighty wings, "Pan-Germany" rings out from sea to land, "pan-German" from land to sea!]

Back in Germany, Tille's initial plan was to write his *Habilitation* and obtain a chair in philosophy at a German university. His writings, however, had attracted the attention of conservative business circles and he accepted the position of deputy business director of the Federation of German Industrialists in Berlin (*Zentralverband Deutscher Industrieller*). He became closely acquainted with the influential industrialist and politician Freiherr Carl Ferdinand von Stumm-Halberg, whose speeches he edited;[37] he also had a brief affair with Germany's foremost suffragette, Helene Stöcker, who shared Tille's passion for Nietzsche and some of his social Darwinist ideas.[38] In 1903 Tille moved to Saarbrücken, where he was appointed a chief representative of several industrial associations, a position he held until his death in 1912. His extensive publications from this latter period are all on business and industrial matters. Here again, his social Darwinist worldview provided a pseudoscientific justification for the social stratification and evils of Wilhelmine capitalist society. For Hans-Ulrich Wehler, Tille was one of the "platten Apologeten" and "plumpen Hagiographen des Wilhelminischen Unternehmertums"[39] (uninspired apologists and clumsy hagiographers of the Wilhelmine entrepreneurial class).

In conclusion, I would like to integrate these findings into a larger framework. Tille's oeuvre and activities present us with a seemingly irreconcilable paradox: on the one hand the cultural mediator with an intimate knowledge of both countries; on the other hand the confrontational warmonger unable to question existing stereotypes. However, Tille was not a unique case. We can point to the Celticist Kuno Meyer, who lived in Britain from 1883 to 1911 but nevertheless went to Germany once a year to do his reservist training exercises and wholeheartedly supported the German cause during World War I;[40] or we can point to Lothar Bucher, who spent 11 years in London as an exile and later wrote his anti-English tirades in close contact with Bismarck.[41] In general, there was a high degree of "Reich"-nationalism among Germans living in Britain before and during the First World War.[42] Residence abroad did not necessarily improve individual intercultural understanding but could lead to increased nationalism intertwined with an Anglophobic attitude. As early as the 18th century Justus Möser had maintained that one could best be healed from Anglomania through a lengthy stay in Britain.[43] This is in line with Tille's statement (which rather inflates his academic standing):

> Als ich im Jahre 1890, als vierundzwanzigjähriger Jüngling als Dozent nach Schottland berufen, zum erstenmale einen britischen Lehrstuhl bestieg, da erstrahlte mir Großbritannien im Lichte vielseitiger jugendlicher Ideale. Als ich 1900 . . . kurzer Hand mein Lehramt niederlegte und trotz aller Versuche mich zu halten in meine Heimat zurückkehrte, da hatten sich jene Ideale jedoch einigermaßen verschoben. . . . Ich hatte die Freude zu sehen, daß sich mein eigenes Vaterland mit ganz anderen Riesenschritten [der Lösung sozialer Probleme] näherte als Großbritannien. Ich war mit dem Gedanken ausgezogen, auf den britischen Inseln vieles verwirklicht zu finden, wovon wir nur erst träumten, und von Jahr zu Jahr mußte ich es als einen bittereren Stachel empfinden lernen, einem fremden Volke zu dienen, das sich dem meinen immer feindlicher gegenüberstellte.[44]

> [When I took up the duties of a British university teacher for the first time, having been offered a lectureship in Scotland in 1890 at the age of 24, Great Britain seemed to me splendid, viewed in the light of manifold youthful ideals. When in 1900 . . . I resigned abruptly and returned home, despite all attempts to keep me, those ideals had shifted somewhat, as you may imagine. . . . I experienced the joy of seeing my own Fatherland approaching the solution of social problems with giant strides that were so different from the ones taken by Great Britain. I had set off with the expectation of finding much already achieved in the British Isles of which we only dreamt, and from year to year I was obliged to feel the bitter pangs of serving a foreign country whose enmity towards mine grew daily worse.]

On a further level, Tille does not seem to have been an unusual case. He both personifies and confirms a paradox recently discussed under the heading "Aneignung und Abwehr."[45] Despite a substantial increase in each country's knowledge of the other during the course of the nineteenth century, Anglo-German relationships did not necessarily improve.

Mutual stereotypes were reinforced rather than dissolved, reaching a climax during the First World War. Intercultural transfer *per se* is not a guarantee for peaceful coexistence but just one factor in a complex historical framework. The case history presented here is a paradigm, rather than an exception.

Notes

[1] Steven E. Aschheim, *The Nietzsche Legacy in Germany, 1890–1990* (Berkeley: U of California P, 1992), 123.

[2] Richard Hinton Thomas, *Nietzsche in German Politics and Society, 1890–1918* (Manchester: Manchester UP, 1983), 113.

[3] Neither of the two short biographies take this aspect into account. Armin Tille is mainly concerned with defending his brother against his critics, whilst Schungel's study concentrates almost exclusively on Tille's social Darwinist ideas. See Armin Tille, *Ein Kämpferleben: Alexander Tille, 1866–1912* (Gotha, Germany: Friedrich Andreas Perthes, 1916); Wilfried Schungel, *Alexander Tille (1866–1912): Leben und Ideen eines Sozialdarwinisten* (Husum: Matthiesen 1980). More recently see Stefan Manz, *Migranten und Internierte: Deutsche in Glasgow, 1864–1918* (Stuttgart: Franz Steiner, 2003), chap. III.3.

[4] Alexander Tille, *Die deutschen Volkslieder vom Doktor Faust* (Halle: Niemeyer, 1890; repr. Wiesbaden: Sändig, 1969 and 1984).

[5] Patrick Bridgwater, *Nietzsche in Anglosaxony: A Study of Nietzsche's Impact on English and American Literature* (Leicester: Leicester UP, 1972), 11.

[6] Bridgwater, *Nietzsche in Anglosaxony*, 15.

[7] Alexander Tille, ed., *The Collected Works of Friedrich Nietzsche*, 11 vols. (London: H. Henry, 1896–1909; New York: Macmillan, 1896–1909; rev. eds. London and Toronto: J. M. Dent, 1933 and 1957). This contained Tille's translation of *Also sprach Zarathustra: Thus spake Zarathustra* (1896). The other works to appear in Tille's edition were *The Case of Wagner; The Twilight of the Idols; Nietzsche contra Wagner; The Anti-Christ* (trans. Alexander Tille and Thomas Common, 1896); *The Dawn of Day* (trans. Johanna Volz, 1903); and *Beyond Good and Evil* (trans. Helen Zimmern, 1907). The first *complete* edition of Nietzsche in English was Oscar Levy, ed., *The Complete Works of Friedrich Nietzsche*, 18 vols. (Edinburgh and London: Foulis, 1909–13; New York: Macmillan, 1909–11).

[8] See Bridgwater, *Nietzsche in Anglo-Saxony*; Eitel Friedrich Timm, *William Butler Yeats und Friedrich Nietzsche* (Würzburg: Königshausen & Neumann, 1980); David S. Thatcher, *Nietzsche in England, 1890–1914* (Toronto: U of Toronto P, 1970); Elmar Schenkel, "Paradoxical Affinities: Chesterton and Nietzsche," in *The Novel in Anglo-German Context: Cultural Cross-Currents and Affinities*, ed. Susanne Stark (Amsterdam and Atlanta: Rodopi, 2000), 241–51; Henning Ottmann, "Englischsprachige Welt," in *Nietzsche-Handbuch: Leben — Werk — Wirkung*, ed. Henning Ottmann (Stuttgart and Weimar: Metzler, 2000), 431–34.

[9] Alexander Tille, Foreword to *Thus spake Zarathustra: A Book for All and None*, trans. Alexander Tille (London: H. Henry, 1896), xxiii.

[10] "[Es] können die nachhaltigen Folgen für die Interpretation von Nietzsches Philosophie kaum als glimpflich bezeichnet werden"; see Hays Alan Steilberg, *Die amerikanische Nietzsche-Rezeption von 1896 bis 1950* (Berlin and New York: de Gruyter, 1996), 3.

[11] Alfred Kelly, *The Descent of Darwin: The Popularization of Darwinism in Germany* (Chapel Hill, NC: U of North Carolina P, 1981), 4–6; Hans-Ulrich Wehler, "Sozialdarwinismus im expandierenden Industriestaat," in *Deutschland in der Weltpolitik des 19. und 20. Jahrhunderts*, ed. Imanuel Geiss and Bernd Jürgen Wendt (Düsseldorf: Bertelsmann Universitätsverlag, 1973), 133–42; Thomas Nipperdey, *Deutsche Geschichte, 1866–1918*, vol. 1 (Munich: C. H. Beck, 1990), chap. 12, 3.

[12] British Library, Department of Manuscripts, Alexander Tille to Alfred Russell Wallace (1894), 46441, 133–34; Thomas E. Huxley, *Soziale Essays: Deutsch mit Einleitung*, trans. Alexander and Lotte Tille (Weimar: Felber, 1897).

[13] C. M. Williams, *A Review of the Systems of Ethics Founded on the Theory of Evolution* (London and Boston: Macmillan, 1893).

[14] Alexander Tille, *Von Darwin bis Nietzsche: Ein Buch Entwicklungsethik* (Leipzig: Naumann, 1895), vii–viii.

[15] Tille, *Von Darwin bis Nietzsche*, 24.

[16] Alexander Tille, "Ostlondon als Nationalheilanstalt," *Die Zukunft* 5 (1893): 268.

[17] See Kelly, *Descent*, 107; Fritz Bolle, "Darwinismus und Zeitgeist," *Zeitschrift für Religions- und Geistesgeschichte* 14 (1962): 173.

[18] Alexander Tille, *Aus Englands Flegeljahren* (Dresden and Leipzig: Reißner 1901), 10: "Ich habe 1893 Rudyard Kipling zuerst in Deutschland bekannt gemacht und seitdem die Aufmerksamkeit Deutschlands auf manches gute Buch gelenkt, das hier nicht die Beachtung gefunden hatte, die es mir zu verdienen schien" (In 1893 I was the first to make Rudyard Kipling known in Germany, and since then I have directed Germany's attention to many a good book that had not received the attention here that I believed it deserved). See Alexander Tille, "Rudyard Kipling," *Die Zukunft* 3 (1893): 165–71; idem, "Robert Louis Stevenson," *Frankfurter Zeitung und Handelsblatt (Feuilleton)*, 39/3, January 3, 1895; idem, "William Wordsworth," *Die Zukunft* 11 (1895): 470.

[19] See Stuart Wallace, *War and the Image of Germany: British Academics, 1914–1918* (Edinburgh: John Donald, 1988), 165.

[20] See the appendices to the two publications of the Glasgow Goethe Society, both edited and introduced by Alexander Tille: *German Songs of Today and Tomorrow* (Glasgow: Friedrich Bauermeister, 1895) and *Goethe's Satyros and Prometheus*, trans. John Gray (Glasgow: Friedrich Bauermeister, 1895). For the English Goethe Society in general, see Günter Hollenberg, "Die English Goethe Society und die deutsch-englischen kulturellen Beziehungen im 19. Jahrhundert," *Zeitschrift für Religions- und Geistesgeschichte* 30 (1978): 36–45; Ann C. Weaver,

ed., *Publications of the English Goethe Society: Index to the Publications, 1886–1986* (Leeds: W. S. Maney, 1987).

[21] See Johannes Paulmann, "Interkultureller Transfer zwischen Deutschland und Großbritannien: Einführung in ein Forschungskonzept," in *Aneignung und Abwehr: Interkultureller Transfer zwischen Deutschland und Großbritannien im 19. Jahrhundert*, ed. Rudolf Muhs, Johannes Paulmann, and Willibald Steinmetz (Bodenheim: Philo, 1998), 21–43.

[22] Alexander Tille, "Die Glasgower Kabelbahn," *Die Zukunft* 23 (1898): 470–78; *idem*, "Der Ausstand der britischen Maschinenbauer," *Zeitschrift für Socialwissenschaft* 1 (1898): 169–81; idem, "German Christmas and the Christmas-Tree," *Folklore* 3 (1892): 166–82.

[23] Alexander Tille, "Die Volksstimmung in England," *Die Woche* February 3, 1900.

[24] *Glasgow Herald*, February 9, 1900, February 19, 1900, February 23, 1900, letters to the editor.

[25] *Glasgow Herald*, February 24, 1900.

[26] *Glasgow University Magazine*, March 14, 1900 (see February 28, 1900); *Glasgow Herald*, February 27, 1900, April 2, 1900.

[27] T. W. Offin, *How the Germans Took London: Forewarned, Forearmed* (Chelmsford: Durrant, 1900).

[28] Wallace, *Image of Germany*, 14.

[29] Tille, *Flegeljahre*, 36.

[30] See Albert E. Rosenkranz, *Geschichte der Deutschen Evangelischen Gemeinde zu Liverpool* (Stuttgart: Ausland & Heimat, 1921), 150.

[31] Panikos Panayi, *German Immigrants in Britain during the Nineteenth Century, 1815–1914* (Oxford-Washington: Berg, 1995), 135–36.

[32] See Panikos Panayi, *The Enemy in Our Midst: Germans in Britain during the First World War* (Providence and Oxford: Berg, 1991); Stefan Manz, "'Our Sworn, Subtle, Savage, Implacable and Perfidious Foe!' — Spy-fever and Germanophobia in Scotland, 1914–1918," *Irish-German Studies* 1/2004, 28–37; Manz, *Migranten und Internierte*, chap. V.

[33] Glasgow University Archives, Glasgow University Court, Supporting Papers, unlisted, February 27, 1900, Tille to University Court, February 24, 1900; ibid., Minute of Meeting of the University Court, February 27, 1900. Tille's part-time position had been turned into a full-time lectureship only a year earlier, in 1899. In 1894, he had already unsuccessfully applied for a lectureship at Edinburgh University; see National Library of Scotland 1694.31(11), *Testimonials in Favour of Alexander Tille*.

[34] Armin Tille, *Kämpferleben*, 19–20.

[35] See e.g. Alexander Tille, "Kampf um den Erdball," *Nord und Süd*, January 1897.

[36] In *Alldeutsches Liederbuch* (Leipzig: Breitkopf & Härtel, 1901); also printed in Armin Tille, *Kämpferleben*, 50–52.

[37] *Die Reden des Freiherrn Carl Ferdinand von Stumm-Halberg,* ed. Alexander Tille, 10 vols. (Berlin: Elsner, 1906–13).

[38] Ernst Nolte, *Nietzsche und der Nietzscheanismus* (Frankfurt and Berlin: Propyläen, 1990), 224, 244–45; Aschheim, *Nietzsche,* 123–25; Hinton Thomas, *Nietzsche,* 92.

[39] Hans-Ulrich Wehler, *Deutsche Gesellschaftsgeschichte,* vol. 3 (Munich: Beck, 1995), 1084.

[40] See Huether on Meyer, chapter 9 in this volume.

[41] Christoph Studt, *Lothar Bucher, 1817–1892: Ein politisches Leben zwischen Revolution und Staatsdienst* (Göttingen: Vandenhoeck & Ruprecht, 1992).

[42] See Stefan Manz, "'Wir stehen fest zusammen / Zu Kaiser und zu Reich!' — Nationalism among Germans in Britain, 1871–1918," *German Life and Letters* 55 (2002): 398–415.

[43] See Rudolf Muhs, "Geisteswehen: Rahmenbedingungen des deutsch-britischen Kulturaustauschs im 19. Jahrhundert," in *Aneignung und Abwehr,* ed. Muhs, Paulmann, and Steinmetz, 67.

[44] Tille, *Flegeljahre,* viii. See also page 55: "Ich habe es in den letzten Jahren wiederholt mit großer Freude bemerkt, daß junge Deutsche, die als Weltbürger und Überdemokraten nach Großbritannien gingen, nach einem halben Jahre als gute, warm empfindende Deutsche heimkamen" (In recent years I have repeatedly noted with joy how young Germans, who had left for Great Britain as citizens of the world and pan-democrats, were returning home after half a year as good, warm-hearted Germans); see also Schungel, *Alexander Tille,* 10, 26, 29.

[45] See Johannes Paulmann, "Interkultureller Transfer zwischen Deutschland und Großbritannien, 21–43.

9: "*In Politik verschieden, in Freundschaft wie immer*": The German Celtic Scholar Kuno Meyer and the First World War

Andreas Huether

1

IN NOVEMBER 1914 THE prominent Celtic scholar Kuno Meyer stated in a letter on the subject of his tour of America: "it is a golden opportunity. I can now do more than merely lecture on Irish literature . . . unless they keep it out of the papers you will soon hear from me."[1] Both predictions came true. The ensuing activities placed him among the plethora of German professors who offered their expertise and social position to the German war cause.[2] While these activities have been examined in their political context in minute detail,[3] a social and cultural examination is still lacking. This, as I will argue, will help to explain why "the nation of Kant and Hegel, Ranke and Dahlmann, had produced a band of professors so ready to justify every action of their government, including the invasion of Belgium."[4] In this respect, Kuno Meyer is a particularly interesting figure: at the outbreak of war he embarked on a propaganda trip to the United State of America, where he lobbied for American neutrality amongst Irish-Americans and German-Americans. He also severed all ties with his numerous friends in England, a country he had been living in for almost half of his life.

According to his own account, Kuno Meyer believed from the summer of 1911 that a war between England and Germany was inevitable.[5] Meyer's vision, written with hindsight in late 1914, points to a radical shift in sentiment — or rather, surfacing of existing sentiment — that is difficult to understand. Born in Hamburg in 1858, Meyer had been appointed lecturer at the University of Liverpool in 1884. He had a successful academic career at Liverpool, and was also accepted and assimilated into English society. After his move to Berlin in 1911 to succeed Heinrich Zimmer to the Chair of Celtic in Berlin, he voiced discomfort about the city and its inhabitants. However, at the outbreak of war in August 1914, Meyer joined in the chorus of enthusiasm in support of the war. In late August 1914 he relished the German victories in the East, but especially those against the English army on the Western front:

> ". . . wir kommen vor Siegesnachrichten gar nicht zur Ruhe. Nun auch dieser großartige Sieg im Osten. Aber am meisten freue ich mich doch, dass die Engländer solche Hiebe bekommen haben; das wird auch politisch die größte Wirkung haben."[6]

> [. . . the news of victories gives us hardly any peace. And now this great victory in the East. But most of all I'm delighted that the English have received these blows; that'll also have the biggest political consequences.]

While this form of enthusiasm sounds like many letters of the time, a second letter indicates that Meyer was to assume a more active role in the German war effort than other professors. Here he writes to his brother Eduard, a prominent ancient historian and leading member of the *Alldeutsche Verband* (Pan-German League):[7]

> "Ich weiß nicht, ob Toni dir schon von dem Gedanken gesprochen hat, der mir gekommen ist, nach meiner Kur nach Amerika zu gehen. Ich könnte der guten Sache nicht besser dienen. . . . Ich würde mich an zwei Kreise wenden: den akademischen u. den irischen."[8]

> [I don't know if Toni mentioned to you my idea of visiting America after I've done with the spa. There's no better way for me to support the good work. . . . I would address two audiences: the academic and the Irish.]

Meyer had also been in contact with Theodor Schiemann, the historian, member of the Pan-German League, publisher of the *Preussische Jahrbücher,* and adviser to Kaiser Wilhelm II. Schiemann was an expert on eastern European history who had had contact with Irish revolutionary circles since the early 1910s. Soon after August 1914, he published a number of articles by Roger Casement in German,[9] a sign that some within the imperial administration were aware of the Irish case and its potential value for German military plans. Schiemann was in favor of Meyer's proposed undertaking — an undertaking that also found support among the Pan-German League, as Eduard Meyer wrote to his colleague Georg Wissowa: "Mein Bruder ist jetzt in Amerika, um unter den Iren für Deutschland zu agitieren. Er hat dort eine große Aufgabe vor sich"[10] (My brother is now in America, agitating amongst the Irish on Germany's behalf. He has a great task ahead of him). This great task was a two-pronged effort to secure American neutrality. Under the guise of a lecture tour on Celtic language and literature, Kuno Meyer attempted to influence German-American and Irish-American circles to support the causes of Germany and Ireland. Embarking in Rotterdam in November 1914, he wrote to a friend: "Don't you feel you have the time of your life, or rather the whole world from creation onwards was not in it? Every day some new surprise, pleasant or unpleasant, but always exciting."[11] His excitement was matched by that he met on his arrival in New York within Irish-American circles. His lecture tour was followed by large articles in relevant papers. While few if any of the contents of these speeches survive, they can be reconstructed from the articles that Meyer wrote, keeping close to his area of expertise — the language and literature of ancient Ireland. Soon, however, the ominous remark quoted at the beginning of the present article cropped up. The undivided interest and fervor about the greatness and value of Irish language and literature, which Meyer conveyed to Irish-American circles, was interspersed with political propaganda targeting England and the English oppression of Ireland. In a rhetorically exquisite manner, Meyer brought together his historic and cultural expertise with current politics: the Golden Age of Irish civilization; the brutal and unlawful oppression of Ireland and its imminent liberation from English chains by armed insurrection; Germany's championship of oppressed small nations; and the Darwinian dimensions of the struggle between Germany and England for economic — and moral — domination.[12]

2

The fusion of ancient tradition with modern politics was a recurring feature of non-sectarian politics from the 1840s. Thomas Davis and Young Ireland agitated in the 1840s for a non-sectarian Ireland that would be rooted in its ancient traditions of Gaelic language and customs. The 1890s saw a major boost to this line of argumentation as some of the leaders of Irish cultural nationalism were language scholars as well — most notably Douglas Hyde and Eoin MacNeill. Kuno Meyer, and with him other German Celtic scholars, were feted by Irish cultural nationalists. The international reputation of German Celtic scholarship dating from the publication of Johann Kaspar Zeuss's *Grammatica Celtica* in 1853 made the German linguists of the 1890s prime witnesses for the greatness of ancient Ireland, which was to be revitalized by re-focusing on these ancient traditions. Language, in a romantic understanding of the nation, played the central part, as it was regarded as the link to the glorious past. Thus by following the well-established pattern — glorious ancient Irish traditions, English suppression, return to the glorious past (by armed resistance with the help of Germany) — Meyer successfully linked his scholarly expertise with the political aspirations of his audience.

Concurrently with his brief success in America, however, Meyer lost his international reputation as a scholar, and also as a trusted friend. While until Christmas 1914 British papers reported Meyer's exploits in relatively neutral terms, Meyer's former Liverpool colleagues reacted differently. In a reaction to a letter — now lost — that Meyer had sent to Vice-Chancellor Alfred Dale, the University Council regarded Meyer's comments as "equivalent to resignation" from his honorary professorship. Dale refused to communicate all of the letter to the public due to its offensive content,[13] but Meyer's remaining ties to his English friends were soon severed publicly. Reminiscing on the Kuno Meyer who had been feted by his Liverpool colleagues and who on his departure from Liverpool had been presented with a portrait painted by the artist Augustus John, Liverpool's *Daily Post* led the deconstruction:

> He was born a German; he could not help it; it was his misfortune, not his fault. . . . He was an officer in the old Kaiser's army, and he looked the part, with his strong, square shoulders, his brown bearded face, his kindly blue eyes, and his great boyish laugh. This was not the Kuno Meyer that crawled to America 'to lie' . . . to spit venom on the hands that fed him.[14]

Meyer's reply came swiftly. It is worth quoting at length as it comprises many of the sentiments that can be traced to the social and cultural context Meyer had been living in:

> I regard all that you say as another indication that England has not even realised what this war means to her and Germany. You talk cheap sentiment and false morality while two mighty empires are engaged in a life and death struggle. In this struggle it behoves every member of the two nations to take an honourable part to the best of his ability; but you say that my indebtedness to England should prevent me from doing so. My answer is that we Germans are not fighting that England which many thousands of us from the Emperor downwards have loved truly and well, but a misguided iniquitous England bent upon destruction of an inconvenient rival. As for myself, I am but continuing what I did while I lived among you, when I fought by the side of some of England's noblest and to me ever dear sons and daughters for freedom, truth, justice against oppression, falsehood, and wrong wherever we encountered it. That is how I served England while eating her bread. As sure as I write these lines the time will come when all honest Englishmen will feel ashamed of this war and abominate it as much as ever they did the Crimean, the Opium, and the Boer wars.[15]

Meyer displayed in this letter commonplaces that many of the self-appointed guides of the German nation brought forward: a morally superior Germany fighting the misled materialist *Krämernation* ("nation of shopkeepers") England. The change in Meyer's attitude towards his host nation of 27 years appeared most radically in the winter 1914/15. Writing in the *Daily Post* on Christmas Eve 1914, Meyer declares: "I am united by ties of long-standing friendship which nothing, not even the present enmity between our two nations, shall sever as far as I am concerned."[16] Towards the end of January 1915, he severed these ties, writing to Richard I. Best: "The English chapter of my life is closed, never to be continued, I am afraid."[17] This seemingly sudden change in attitude towards England and the English has not yet been explained satisfactorily. Lerchenmueller points out that on his arrival in Berlin, Kuno Meyer became immersed in his brother Eduard's Pan-German League circle.[18] In his biography of Kuno Meyer, Seán Ó Lúing — while not hiding Meyer's involvement with the Pan-Germanists — remains extremely vague on this subject.[19] Citing loneliness — Meyer revealed to his trusted friend Richard I. Best that he had "no real friends"[20] — as an explanation for Meyer's joining his older brother's circle of extreme nationalists, whose platforms he adopted, is not a satisfactory explanation. For satisfaction, it is necessary to look at the social and cultural processes that went into the shaping of a German professor and his actions in the late nineteenth century.

3

Professorial involvement in politics in the nineteenth century had a tradition that reached back to Wilhelm von Humboldt and culminated prior to the *Professorenparlament* of 1848 in the expulsion of the *Göttinger Sieben* from Hanover in 1837. After the failed national assembly of 1848, professors stayed out of the political limelight until the 1880s. The two decades before the turn of the century saw the rise of cross-political interest groups, in which academics as well as industrialists and businessmen became leading figures. In the 1890s, the agitation for colonies, both on the fringes of Europe and overseas, increased dramatically, in agreement with Wilhelm II, whose "Neuer Kurs" focused increasingly on territorial expansion.[21] In addition, the demand for an increase in naval production soared in Germany. Similar to the trans-political nature of their associations, professors claimed *Überparteilichkeit* in their numerous publications. Friedrich Paulsen, the historian of Germany's university system, brought it to the fore when he wrote in 1911 that German professors saw themselves as the public consciousness and as non-partisan judges of what was best for the German nation.[22] This elitist feeling of superiority was fostered by an educational system that allowed little social mobility and by an academic selection process that allowed few political and social outsiders to be included.

The educational career of Eduard Meyer took place at a time when the social and cultural elite began to feel themselves under pressure from the new middle class and the erosion of the old social system, but had not yet found a channel to fight these threats. Among the last bastions of the old order were the military and the universities. Kuno Meyer had completed all stages of the educational career of a son of the *Bildungsbür-gertum: Gymnasium, Einjährig-Freiwilliger* military service, university, lectureship, and finally professorship. Following Hans-Ulrich Wehler's *Matrix der autoritären Erziehung*,[23] I will now detail how these stages helped to form Kuno Meyer into an obedient servant of the imperial court and an ardent nationalist, like so many others of his generation.

Kuno Meyer was born in 1858 in Hamburg as the second of four children. His family can be traced back to the seventeenth century, when they had acquired some wealth through commercial enterprises. His father was a teacher at the world-renowned *Johanneum Gymnasium,* where Kuno was enrolled between 1868 and 1879. It can be assumed that the Meyer household was very traditional. Antonia, the only daughter, and intellectually on a par with her two older brothers, was not allowed to attend university. In addition, the paternalistic preschool education was dominated by classical literature.[24] It is documented that Kuno rebelled against the authority of his teachers, but his rebellion was soon quelled when he was sent to Edinburgh for two years, where he became the attendant of a blind German man. This is where he is said to have first come into contact with Celtic languages. Eventually he graduated from the *Johanneum* in 1879. In the late 1870s *Gymnasien* (academically elite high schools) were attended predominantly by middle- and upper-class students. Families below these social strata could seldom muster the financial means required for this education. While a great number of middle-class families were not able to do so either for all their children, their social standing required sending at least their eldest son to a *Gymnasium*. The exclusivity of the *Gymnasium* is reflected in the numbers attending such institutions. From a population of 47 million, with 7.5 million *Volksschüler,* only 238,000 studied at a *Gymnasium*.[25] The *Gymnasium* was possibly the most defining feature of the matrix, as it opened the door to academic education and thus to those who would constitute the future generation of the *Bildungsbürgertum*.[26] History lessons in particular were turned into an "anti-revolutionäres Psychopharmakum zur patri-otischen Gesinnungsbildung" (anti-revolutionary psychiatric drug for the formation of patriotic ideology).[27] This undertaking was ensured by teachers who were civil servants and who had to undergo an inspection of their political allegiance before employment.[28]

A further boost to one's social standing could be achieved by joining the military. After the victorious wars that led to German unification in

1871, military officers were regarded as the epitome of German success and standing in the world. After graduating from the *Gymnasium*, and whilst at university, Meyer attended the *Einjährig-Freiwillige* service. The candidate, attending a one-year voluntary course followed by a number of shorter exercises, gained not only an additional education but also a rise in social prestige. The so-called *Einjährige* or *Einjährig-Freiwillige* service was open to all *Gymnasium* graduates. It was a self-financed — and thus economically limiting — course of one year, from which one would retire as an *Offiziersaspirant zur Reserve*. After a number of annual three-month exercises one was made *Reserveleutnant*, a military rank of high social prestige. The prestige derived from the permission to wear a uniform for public occasions, but even more from the display of discipline and loyalty to state, fatherland, and *Kaiser*.[29] The willingness of the *Bildungsbürger* to embrace state nationalism and bow to the *Staatsdienerverhältnis* in the 1880s had a strong socio-economic reason: fear of the increasingly organized working class, which was being wooed by Bismarck. The memory of being socially sidelined after the revolution of 1848 and the dependence on the state for job security led to a class self-consciousness that was compensated for by *Überpatriotismus*, which welcomed the expansionist policies of the state with "lärmende(m), phrasenhafte(m), bornierte(m) Nationdünkel" (noisy, clichéd, narrow-minded nationalistic arrogance).[30] While Meyer complained of too little time for his private studies during his military service,[31] he certainly enjoyed the social benefits that came with the graduation certificate. The date of his graduation as *Premierleutnant* — December 13, 1892 — even suggests frequent travel between Liverpool and Germany to participate in continuing exercises after the initial one-year course.[32]

The standing of German scholarship in the world led other countries to adopt the German university system. The prestige of having graduated from and of working in this system was only surpassed by being an officer in the German army. Like many others, Meyer combined the two. The social and educational elitism that started with the *Gymnasium* continued and intensified at universities.[33] Of the 230,000 *Gymnasium* graduates, only some 20,000 enrolled at German universities. While this was a rapid increase in absolute terms, and one that fueled the discussion about "the academic proletariat,"[34] it will not have affected the traditional middle-class university of Leipzig at the time Kuno Meyer studied there in the early 1880s.

4

Little is known about his years at Leipzig University. While Meyer studied comparative linguistics, his brother had become an unsalaried assistant in ancient history at the same university. One of Kuno Meyer's teachers,

Ernst Windisch, encouraged him to take up the study of Celtic languages. After graduating in 1884 with a thesis about an Irish version of the legend of Alexander, Meyer seems to have been pressed for a job. He became a private teacher in England for a short while, before succeeding Wilhelm Viëtors as lecturer in German at the newly founded college at Liverpool. Besides teaching German, Meyer soon added Irish and Welsh classes to his curriculum. Despite having only three or four students, he increasingly concentrated on Celtic languages. Meyer became absorbed into the Liverpool academic community but also into British society. He counted Winston Churchill and the poet George Moore among his friends. He also had close contact with British and Irish scholars in his field of interest and frequently traveled to Ireland. With his outspokenness and unlimited energy he was a valuable asset for the newly established college in Liverpool. He not only engaged himself on an academic level but also worked towards upgrading the college to university level. Admiration for his work ethos is reflected in the address given in his honor on his departure for Berlin in 1911, after 27 years in Liverpool:

> You have been a leader here both in the University College and in the University. You have during twenty-seven years spoken and wrought without fear and without remission in the cause of the highest scholarship, and have been a commanding influence in attracting the best scholars to your own Faculty and in pressing their appointment upon your colleagues; thus laying the true foundations of our University, which is still in its infancy. In University Reform of all kinds you have been among the foremost; and those who may not always have agreed with you in particulars are the first to recognize your strength and your sincerity."[35]

The departure from the small university at Liverpool to the much larger university in Berlin, while academically a success, proved to be difficult for Meyer. Soon after his arrival in Berlin he remarked: "I am not very happy here, almost the first time in my life that I feel so. I have left too many good old friends behind and I can take no interest in the affairs of institutions and people here."[36] And even as late as April 1914, he wrote to his colleague Richard I. Best that he had "no real friends in Berlin."[37] While the unfamiliarity of Berlin and its large university can explain Meyer's listlessness in the earlier stages of his residence there, it is surprising that he still felt so in 1914. His main social contact seems to have been with his brother's circle of Pan-German friends.[38] In his obituary for Kuno (1919), his brother Eduard recalled that they shared the same political convictions.[39] While this remark can be regarded as a brotherly gesture, it also contains a vital clue to the connection between the selection process and the political affiliation of professors at German universities.[40] This link ensured that the leading academics spoke with an almost unanimous voice politically and became a self-perpetuating interest group. The political harmony was seldom disturbed and then only by quarrels over details. The group around Eduard Meyer can be counted among the more radical advocates for colonial and naval policies and annexation. Leading academics thus used their position, academic expertise, and access to resources to argue their political position in public.

While the body of students in Germany became more diverse in the late nineteenth century, that of the lecturers remained homogeneous: just over a third of the students came from an academic background, but half of all university teachers between 1890 and 1919 did so.[41] Thus the university became the "breeding ground . . . [and] recruiting pool for both cultural and administrative elites" for the *Bildungsbürgertum*.[42] Indeed, the state "examined" the loyalty of students — the future academics and civil servants — through several measures: through state examinations (*Staatsexamen*), by control over the financial authority of universities, and by intervening in the selection process of professors and other civil servants.[43] Consequently, the *Bildungsbürgertum* occupied the central bureaucratic positions to control the political outlook of university departments,[44] and was able to cultivate the next generation of civil servants. State control over universities was further extended by state exams in all subjects.[45] Hence the education system, the German *Bildungsbürgertum*, and the imperial administration formed an almost perfect symbiosis.

As briefly discussed above, the propaganda tour Meyer had proposed to both his brother and Theodor Schiemann was disguised as a lecture tour. While his lectures were well-received in Irish-American newspapers, his letters to his brother give a detailed account of the American public's feelings regarding the war and his own interpretation of it. The case of the sinking of the *Lusitania* highlights the triangle formed by the Celtic scholar Kuno Meyer, the Pan-German League, and the German imperial administration. On his arrival in New York in November 1914, he not only contacted German-American and Irish-American circles but also President Roosevelt. Roosevelt was known to Meyer as a lay scholar with an interest in Celtic languages. Just over two weeks after the sinking of the *Lusitania* in May 1915, Meyer relayed from Chicago to Germany that public opinion had calmed down again. Taking Woodrow Wilson's election slogan to keep America out of the war for granted, Kuno Meyer wrote to his brother, "dass wir den Ubootkrieg unbekümmert um Amerika mit voller Energie aufnehmen sollen; Amerika werde dem sich fügen"[46] (we should pursue the U-boat war with all dispatch and without being concerned about America; they will play along). Forwarding this information to Georg Wissowa, Eduard Meyer also informed the German Foreign Ministry about his brother's understanding of future American policies.[47]

Despite his failure to incite German-American and Irish-American circles to tip the balance of the American political establishment towards neutrality,[48] Meyer continued to lobby for an inclusion of Ireland in German military plans. In reply to an earlier letter by Kuno Meyer, chief of the general staff Moltke promised to intervene at the German Foreign Ministry and also to ensure that Meyer could lecture to the Kaiser on the situation of Ireland and its value to the German war effort.[49]

5

This brief study of a cosmopolitan scholar who turned into a self-denying propagandist and advocate of the German war effort shows that the social and cultural context of German academics is vital for understanding their beliefs and actions. It also shows that it is worth including literature and language scholars among the canon of academics who contributed to the war effort. Academics with theoretical, and even more so practical, knowledge of cultures and societies other than their own were able to provide their respective governments with inside information. Through his journeys and acquaintances, and also because he lived in Liverpool for 27 years, Kuno Meyer as a Celtic scholar knew of the potential of an Irish uprising. The outbreak of war triggered sentiments towards the fatherland that otherwise might have remained buried while Meyer was living in Liverpool. As we can see from his own self-reflection, the consequences of his activities only dawned on him later. However, when war broke out, he did not hesitate to supply the insights gained through his profession to the German government. His expertise enabled him to judge and draw conclusions, which he readily shared with the appropriate people in the imperial administration and the military. While he could not join the army as an officer due to his age, like so many other men of his standing he contributed to the war effort by lending his expertise on Anglo-Irish antagonism to the German administration.

The study of literary and linguistic academics and their role in the German war effort during the First World War would be an essential addition to current scholarship in this field. Whereas academic historians, economists, sociologists, and theologians attract current research because of their extensive publications and public justification of the war, the role of linguists and literary scholars should not be neglected or underestimated. Their intimate knowledge of the culture, society, history, and politics of other peoples, but especially their long-established private contacts with nationals of other countries, make them an especially interesting group. Of particular interest for future research would be the private reactions of German literary and linguistic scholars with private international links to both academics and non-academics, to the outbreak of the war and to official German rhetoric as expressed in communications with their English counterparts.

Notes

This article is based on the paper given at the "Peacemaker & Warmongers" conference at the University of Leeds. My thanks to the Department for Languages and Cultural Studies, University of Limerick, for financial assistance.

[1] K. Meyer — R. I. Best, Nov. 25, 1914. National Library of Ireland [=NLI] MS 11,002 folder 41. Quoted in Joachim Lerchenmueller, *"Keltischer Sprengstoff": Eine wissenschaftsgeschichtliche Studie über die deutsche Keltologie von 1900 bis 1945* (Tübingen: Niemeyer, 1997), 59.

[2] For the German context see, for example, Bernhard vom Brocke, "Wissenschaft und Militarismus: Der Aufruf der 93 'An die Kulturwelt!' und der Zusammenbruch der internationalen Gelehrtenrepublik im Ersten Weltkrieg," in *Willamowitz nach 50 Jahren*, ed. William M. Calder III, Hellmut Flashar, and Theodor Lindken (Darmstadt: Wissenschaftliche Buchgesellschaft, 1985), 649–719; Klaus Schwabe, *Wissenschaft und Kriegsmoral: Die deutschen Hochschullehrer und die politischen Grundfragen des Ersten Weltkrieges* (Göttingen/Zurich/Frankfurt: Musterschmidt, 1969); and Wolfgang J. Mommsen, "Einleitung: Die deutschen kulturellen Eliten im Ersten Weltkrieg," in *Kultur und Krieg: Die Rolle der Intellektuellen, Künstler und Schriftsteller im Ersten Weltkrieg*, ed. Mommsen (Munich: Oldenbourg, 1996), 1–15.

[3] See especially Lerchenmueller, *"Keltischer Sprengstoff."*

[4] Stuart Wallace, *War and the Image of Germany: British Academics, 1914–1918* (Edinburgh: John Donald, 1988), v.

[5] This statement was made by Meyer on December 6, 1914 during a speech at a Clan na Gael rally.

[6] Kuno Meyer, *Private Papers* (Staatsbibliothek Berlin, Nachlass Kuno Meyer 214, box 1).

[7] For a recent article on the *Alldeutsche Verband* see Michael Peters, "Der 'Alldeutsche Verband,'" in *Handbuch zur "Völkischen Bewegung" 1871–1918*, ed. Uwe Puschner, Walter Schmitz, and Justus H. Ulbricht (Munich: K. G. Saur, 1999), 302–15.

[8] Eduard Meyer, *Private Papers*, K. Meyer — E. Meyer, Sept. 8, 1914 (Berlin-Brandenburgische Akademie der Wissenschaften (=BBAW; formerly Preußische Akademie der Wissenschaften), Nachlass Eduard Meyer, 955).

[9] Lerchenmueller, *"Keltischer Sprengstoff,"* 27.

[10] Eduard Meyer — Georg Wissowa, Berlin, Dec. 4, 1914. Quoted in Gert Audring, ed., *Gelehrtenalltag: Der Briefwechsel zwischen Eduard Meyer and Georg Wissowa, 1890–1927* (Hildesheim: Weidmann, 2000), 407.

[11] Quoted in Anthony Sampson, *The Scholar Gypsy: The Quest for a Family Secret* (London: John Murray, 1997), 116.

[12] The newspaper reports of the speech given at a meeting of the Philo-Celtic Society in Philadelphia on May 8, 1915 provide a good example. Kuno Meyer, *Private Papers* (Staatsbibliothek Berlin, Nachlass Kuno Meyer, 214, box 2).

[13] Quoted in Thomas Kelly, *For Advancement of Learning: The University of Liverpool, 1881–1981* (Liverpool: Liverpool UP, 1981), 174.

[14] *Daily Post*, Jan. 4, 1915. Liverpool University Archive [=LUA] 159.

[15] *Daily Post*, Jan. 7, 1915. LUA 159.

[16] *Daily Post*, Dec. 24, 1914. LUA 159.

[17] Kuno Meyer, *Private Papers*, Meyer-Best, Jan. 21, 1915 (NLI MS 11,002).

[18] Lerchenmueller, *"Keltischer Sprengstoff,"* 23.

[19] Seán Ó Lúing, *Kuno Meyer, 1858–1919: A Biography* (Dublin: Geography Publications, 1991), 153.

[20] Kuno Meyer, *Private Papers*, Kuno Meyer — Richard I. Best, Apr. 12, 1914 (NLI MS 11,002). Quoted in Lerchenmueller, *"Keltischer Sprengstoff,"* 23.

[21] Amongst many others see Volker Ullrich, *Die nervöse Großmacht, 1871–1918: Aufstieg und Untergang des deutschen Kaiserreichs* (2nd ed., Frankfurt am Main: Fischer, 1999), 182–88.

[22] Friedrich Paulsen, *Die deutschen Universitäten und das Universitätsstudium* (1902, 1911; repr. Hildesheim: Olms, 1966).

[23] As outlined in Hans-Ulrich Wehler, *Das deutsche Kaiserreich, 1871–1918* (1973; 7th ed., Göttingen: Vandenhoeck & Ruprecht, 1994), 122–29.

[24] Ó Lúing, *Kuno Meyer*, 1.

[25] Wehler, *Das deutsche Kaiserreich*, 126.

[26] Ulrich Herrmann, "Über 'Bildung' im Gymnasium des wilhelminischen Kaiserreichs," in *Bildungsgüter und Bildungswissen*, ed. Reinhart Koselleck, part 2 of *Bildungsbürgertum im 19. Jahrhundert*, Industrielle Welt, vol. 41, part 2 (Stuttgart: Klett, 1990), 346–68; here, 349.

[27] Wehler, *Das deutsche Kaiserreich*, 125. See also Herrmann, "Über 'Bildung' im Gymnasium des wilhelminischen Kaiserreichs."

[28] Christoph Führ, "Gelehrter Schulmann — Oberlehrer — Studienrat: Zum sozialen Aufstieg der Philologen," in *Bildungssystem und Professionalisierung in internationalen Vergleichen*, vol. 1 of *Bildungsbürgertum im 19. Jahrhundert*, ed. Werner Conze and Jürgen Kocka (Stuttgart: Klett-Cotta, 1992), 417–57; here, 436.

[29] Ullrich, *Nervöse Großmacht*, 289.

[30] Friedrich Paulsen, 1895, in Ullrich, *Nervöse Großmacht*, 288.

[31] Ó Lúing, *Kuno Meyer*, 3.

[32] Graduation certificate in Nachlass Kuno Meyer (Staatsbibliothek Berlin, Nachlass 214, box 1). The archive of the BBAW holds another certificate for a continuation course with the graduation date Mar. 22, 1894 (BBAW, Nachlass Eduard Meyer 955, BBAW 2–3, 35).

[33] Peter Lundgreen, "Zur Konstituierung des 'Bildungsbürgertums': Berufs- und Bildungsauslese der Akademiker in Preußen," in *Bildungsbürgertum im 19. Jahrhundert*, ed. Conze and Jürgen, 1:79–109; here 91 and tables 100–108.

[34] Wehler, *Kaiserreich*, 128.

[35] Nachlass Kuno Meyer (Staatsbibliothek Berlin, Nachlass 214, box 1).

[36] Quoted in Sampson, *Scholar Gypsy*, 115.

[37] Meyer-Best, Apr. 12, 1914 (NLI 11,002). Quoted in Lerchenmueller, *"Keltischer Sprengstoff,"* 23.

[38] Ó Lúing, *Kuno Meyer*, 152.

[39] Eduard Meyer, *Nachruf*, 2.

[40] The regional differences between Prussian selection policies and those elsewhere in Germany are not yet fully clear, as has recently been pointed out — see Sylvia Paletschek, *Die permanente Erfindung einer Tradition: Die Universität Tübingen im Kaiserreich und der Weimarer Republik* (Stuttgart: Franz Steiner, 2001), and also Marita Baumgarten in her unpublished paper "Berufungspolitik im 19. Jahrhundert," delivered at the "Kolloquium zur Geschichte der deutschen Universität im 19. und 20. Jahrhundert," Greifswald March 13–14, 2003.

[41] Hans-Ulrich Wehler, *Deutsche Gesellschaftsgeschichte* (Munich: Beck, 1987), 1212–13 and 1219–20.

[42] Charles E. McClelland, *State, Society, and University in Germany, 1700–1914* (Cambridge: Cambridge UP, 1980), 3, and Klaus Schwabe, "Einführende Bemerkungen: Rahmenbedingungen und Selbstdeutung des beruflichen Wirkens deutscher Gelehrter," in *Deutsche Hochschullehrer als Elite 1815–1945*, ed. Klaus Schwabe (Boppard am Rhein: Harald Boldt, 1988), 9–25; here, 15.

[43] After the failed revolutions of the late 1840s, in which professors played a large part, the state was anxious to prevent political non-conformists from entering the civil service. See for example Wehler, *Deutsche Gesellschaftsgeschichte*, 417–18; and Wolfram Siemann, *Gesellschaft im Aufbruch: Deutschland, 1849–1871* (Frankfurt am Main: Suhrkamp, 1990), 152. Professors were civil servants as well. See Siemann, *Gesellschaft im Aufbruch*, 156; Rüdiger vom Bruch, "Kultur-imperialismus und Kulturwissenschaften," *Berichte zur Wissenschaftsgeschichte* 13 (1990): 83–92; here, 85–86.

[44] Bernhard vom Brocke, "Von der Wissenschaftsverwaltung zur Wissenschafts-politik: Friedrich Althoff," *Berichte zur Wissenschaftsgeschichte* 11 (1988): 1–26; Peter Mast, *Um Freiheit für Kunst und Wissenschaft: Der Streit im Deutschen Reich, 1840–1901* (3rd ed., Rheinfelden and Berlin: Schäuble, 1994).

[45] Lundgreen, "Zur Konstituierung des 'Bildungsbürgertums,'" 80.

[46] Meyer — Meyer, May 23, 1916 (BBAW Nachlass Eduard Meyer 955).

[47] Meyer — Wissowa, Sept. 19, 1916. Quoted in Audring, *Gelehrtenalltag*, 447.

[48] Úna Ní Bhroiméil cites the wish by Irish-Americans "to be assimilated into the multi-ethnic society of the United States, not on sufferance as a debased and de-rided national group, but as civilized and cultured race." See Úna Ní Bhroiméil, *The American Mission: The Gaelic Revival and America, 1870–1915* (Ph.D.

thesis, Lehigh University, Bethlehem, PA, 1998). I am indebted to Úna for lend-ing me her facsimile of the thesis.

[49] Moltke — Meyer, Oct. 31, 1917 (BBAW Nachlass Kuno Meyer 11). Moltke also wrote that Julius Pokorny had contacted him about the Irish situation. Pokorny was another Celtic scholar who became politically active. See Lerchenmueller, *"Keltischer Sprengstoff,"* passim.

10: Austrian (and Some German) Scholars of English and the First World War

Holger Klein

LET ME BEGIN WITH a remarkable document: the report of the extraordinary session of the Imperial Academy of Sciences in Vienna held on July 1, 1914. It must be one of the shortest and most colorless reports in that august institution's history.

> Der Präsident macht Mitteilung von dem am 28. Juni 1914 erfolgten Ableben Seiner k. und k. Hoheit des durchlauchtigsten Herrn Kurators der Akademie der Wissenschaften Erzherzog Franz Ferdinand.[1]

> [The President begs to inform of the decease on 28th June, 1914 of His Serene Imperial & Royal Highness, Curator of the Academy of Sciences, Archduke Franz Ferdinand.]

I doubt whether anyone could still find out what was actually said. As it stands, this statement is a classic instance of reserve. One does not need to go to the first scenes of Karl Kraus's *Die letzten Tage der Menschheit* to know that at the time such reserve was a rarity. On first reading "Serbien muß sterbien" (Serbia must bite the dust) and all the other jingoist slogans,[2] I admired the author's ingenuity without realizing that it was stark realism, as some contemporary posters and descriptions setting them in their historical context make abundantly clear.[3] Nor was the world of learning always proceeding *sine ira et studio* (without wrath and heat) in those trying years.

Coming to look more closely at just one branch of learning, English studies in Austria (American studies we may disregard here, they were introduced much later),[4] the first thing to be said is that we are talking about very few people indeed. There were four professorships in what is nowadays Austria: Vienna, of course (one since 1872, two from 1908 onwards), Graz (since 1892), and Innsbruck (since 1896). In addition, there was one professorship in Prague (since 1874), and one in Czernowitz (since 1904).[5] In 1914 Karl Luick was the only professor in Vienna (Jakob Schipper having retired in 1912/1913, the other post remained unfilled until 1927). Albert Eichler was the professor in Graz (after a longish vacancy following the retirement of Alois Pogatscher in 1911). Rudolf Fischer, the first professor in Innsbruck, filled this post from 1896 until his death in 1923. In addition, Rudolf Brotanek was the professor at the German university of Prague from 1909 (to 1911 as a locum) until 1918, when he moved to Dresden and was replaced in Prague by Otto Funke (qualified as a professor in 1914), and Leon Kellner was in Czernowitz until dismissed in 1919 by the Romanians, who had acquired the Bukovina after the end of the First World War.[6] Finally, there was an Austrian Pole, Roman Dyboski, who left Vienna in 1908, having acquired his qualifications as a professor (*Habilitation*) with Schipper, to teach English at the University of Cracow, where he was given a professorship in 1911. As for *Privatdozenten* (outside lecturers), they were also sparse: Francis Pughe had left Vienna for Halle in 1913, Karl Brunner was only qualified in the winter of 1914/15, and Friedrich Wild in 1918. In Prague there was Otto Funke, no one in Innsbruck (Rudolf Hittmair, who had taken his doctorate with Fischer in 1912, obtained his qualification in 1925 with Brunner, Fischer's successor), and no one in Czernowitz. In Graz three younger people were on the road to the *venia legendi* (the right to give lectures): Robert von Fleischhacker (qualified in 1922), Leo von Hibler-Lebmansport (qualified in 1925) and Fritz Karpf (qualified in 1930). Whereas there were thus just six professors of English active in 1914 in the Austrian half of the Dual Monarchy, there were thirty-two of them in Germany.[7] Two of those came from Austria: Alois Brandl, who moved from Prague to Göttingen in 1888, thence to Strassburg and in 1895 to the prestigious chair in Berlin, where he taught until his retirement in 1925; and Arnold Schröer, who had left Vienna in 1886 for a professorship in Freiburg and in 1900 in Cologne, where he remained until his retirement in 1926. In addition, the departments had native speakers as lectors.

Two factors somewhat enlarge our field of study. The first is the closeness in situation and outlook of German and German-Austrian scholars. According to Hermann Bahr, who in his student days had been an ardent advocate of a voluntary *Anschluß* (and was wisely checked in this bent by Bismarck), there was a universally growing sense of a separate, specifically Austrian identity in the two decades framing the turn of the century.[8] And yet, at practically the same time, Bahr jubilantly exclaimed: "wir haben uns wieder, nun sind wir nichts als deutsch"[9] (Now we're together again, now we're all just German). That seems also to have generally been the way that Austrian scholars tended to feel at the time. (After all, the two countries had been separate states for only half a century, after forming parts of one, however loosely organized, for about nine hundred years.) To give just one concrete example: in his capacity as President of the Shakespeare-Gesellschaft, the German Shakespeare Society, Alois Brandl welcomed the new Austrian Emperor, Charles I, who had joined in 1917, as a member with the words: "solange alle Deutschen zusammenhalten, haben wir keine Feindesrotte zu fürchten"[10] (As long as all Germans stick together, we need fear no enemy gangs). Corresponding utterances stem from other Austrians who had remained in the Habsburg monarchy.[11] This feeling was also general in contemporary publications, as Eberhard Sauermann has noted,[12] and coincided after the end of the war with the fairly universal wish for unification with Germany, a wish that in the academic world was notably promoted — as underlined by Gerhard Oberkofler and Eduard Rabofsky[13] — by the Academy of Sciences, no longer called "Imperial" and not yet, as after the Second World War, "Austrian."

Furthermore, we must remember that there existed no Austrian university association for the study of English; there were far too few people for that (indeed, there was no such society in Germany at the time either). Austrian academics were (like their Swiss colleagues) members of the *Shakespeare-Gesellschaft* (in addition to Brandl, Rudolf Fischer of Innsbruck was a member of its board), or else members of the *Neuphilologenverband*, the German Modern Language Association (which had held its 1898 conference in Vienna, organized by Schipper). If one looks into *Englische Studien*, which in its rubric "Kleine Mitteilungen" charted *Habilitationen* (the occasion of qualifying as a university teacher) as well as appointments, moves, and deaths, Austrians were regularly included — while similar news from the Dutch, Scandinavian, and British universities and world of letters were apparently listed only if felt to be particularly important.[14] Moreover, scholars moved between the two countries: Brandl and Schröer have already been mentioned; Schipper was born near Oldenburg and had originally taught in Königsberg before coming to Vienna;[15] Fischer (born in Vienna) had taken his *Habilitation* in Strassburg with Brandl, then moved to Innsbruck, while Brotanek (born in Troppau) did not stay in Dresden but moved to Erlangen, refusing an invitation to teach at Innsbruck in 1923. Considering their close links, one cannot exclude German scholars from the picture, though, of course, I shall look more closely at the Austrians and try to highlight what appears as their specific response to the Great War.

The second factor enlarging the field may surprise in view of the relationships of secondary schools and universities in our world today. Until 1918 and even beyond, the links between secondary and tertiary education were very close indeed. I remember my own surprise when, preparing my doctoral thesis in the late 1960s, I came across a substantial book on symbols and appellations of the Virgin Mary in German and Latin medieval hymns, which an Austrian teacher had dedicated to the annual meeting of German Philologists and School Teachers in 1893.[16] But this was no exception. If one looks at the proceedings of the German *Neuphilologenverband*, one notices the active participation of university professors as well as teachers from various types of secondary schools.[17] *Englische Studien* bore the subtitle: *Organ für englische Philologie unter Mitberücksichtigung des englischen Unterrichts auf höheren Schulen* [until 1919 set in lower case], *Anglia* had a *Beiblatt* for reviews and information that included [school] teaching in its subtitle: *Mitteilungen über englische Sprache und Literatur und über englischen Unterricht;* conversely, at least one important Austrian school periodical, the *Zeitschrift für das Realschulwesen*,[18] regularly reviewed scores of scholarly books as well as, besides school-teaching periodicals, journals such as *Imago, Euphorion*, and the *Germanisch-Romanische Monatsschrift*. More: the *Zeitschrift für das Realschulwesen* also printed, in addition to language materials and contributions to didactics, learned articles. What is more: not a few of the English scholars in the universities concurrently taught English in schools for shorter or longer periods.[19] Thus there was also a personal link between the two levels.[20] One should not overlook, of course, that this dual teaching role was motivated by something far less happy: namely, the diminutive remuneration to be had in the university system unless one was lucky enough to obtain a chair or at least a non-tenured professorship. In other words: scholarship in English Studies cannot, for the period under consideration, be limited to the university departments but must include secondary-school teachers. In my view this closeness of school and university, with the university as the guiding force, was a very happy state of affairs (whereas we ourselves are nowadays frequently admonished to gear our academic teaching more to the — apparently quite unacademic — needs of school teachers . . .).

Nevertheless, my main object of investigation remains a small circle. And — that is the upshot of fairly extensive though perhaps not exhaustive searches — only three of these men[21] were engaged in what has come to be called "The Professors' War,"[22] and two of those three, Alois Brandl and Arnold Schröer, had many years earlier moved permanently to chairs in Germany. Within Austria apparently only Albert Eichler participated in the battle of the pens. Brandl's and Eichler's very emphatic nationalism later led them into the orbit of National Socialism — Brandl (who died in 1940) relatively mildly so, Eichler in a more determined and active manner.[23] However, that lies beyond my present brief.[24]

The general response to the outbreak of hostilities in August 1914 was patriotic, enthusiastically so, on the part of the universities.[25] Histories of the Austrian *almae matres* are curiously reticent on the war period, either simply leaving it out, or merely offering a brief mention.[26] However, Gerhard Oberkofler and Peter Goller give us a little more and reprint the proclamation by the *Rektor* of Innsbruck, put on the university's notice boards on 1 August 1914, which may be taken as representative. The opening sentences include the following:

Kommilitonen!

Eine ernste Stunde für Österreich ist angebrochen, der Kampf um sein Recht, lange zurückgehalten von den Rücksichten unserer friedlichen Gesinnung, ist unaufschiebbar geworden. Die alte Aufgabe Österreichs, Vorkämpfer deutscher Kultur gegen den halbbarbarischen Osten zu sein, nötigt uns zu einem harten Waffengang. Das Ansehen unseres Staates, das Wohl unserer geliebten Heimat, unsere[r] und unseres Volkes Ehre hängt von der Kraft ab, die wir jetzt beweisen.

Innsbrucks akademische Bürger sind [,] so oft das Vaterland rief, mutig ins Feld gezogen. . . . Die Universität vertraut darauf, liebe Kommilitonen, daß Ihr dessen eingedenk auch jetzt mit ganzem Herzen Eure Pflicht erfüllt.[27](*GUI*, 198).

[Colleagues —

A solemn moment has arrived in the destiny of Austria. The battle for her rights, so long held back because of her desire for peace, is now unavoidable. Austria's ancient duty to promote German culture in the conflict with a half-barbarian East obliges us to take up arms. Respect for our State, the well-being of our beloved country, our individual honor and that of our people depend on the strength which we show now.

Innsbruck's academic citizens have joined the fray courageously whenever the Fatherland called. The university counts on you, dear colleagues, to remember this again, as you carry out your duty now with all your hearts.]

And they did. Of Innsbruck's male students and staff, 186 men, that is, about 12%, died in the Great War (*GUI*, 199);[28] again one may assume this to be representative for the country's university system. The senior scholars of English were luckier on the whole. Six of the round dozen with whom we are concerned served in the war: Dyboski (born 1883), Brunner (born 1887) Funke (born 1885), Hittmair (born 1889), Karpf (born 1887), and Wild (born 1888) — the war generation. All six survived and were able to resume their careers.[29]

The lector at Graz 1913–14 was Edward Arthur Parker. He did not return, obviously, from the long summer vacation — nor did he ever send a message. His position was only temporarily filled until 1919. In 1920 he returned out of the blue, resubmitted his thesis, which he had already finished in 1914, and obtained his doctorate, after which he left Graz to take up a job in Bombay.[30] In Innsbruck, Peter Denholm Haworth had left after serving for two years; a new man, Ralph Leonard George had been appointed for the academic year 1914–15, but could not take up his post because of the war; it was left unfilled until 1918, when Anna Grisse-mann, an Austrian (who had already served as departmental librarian), obtained it and kept it until 1932.[31] Vienna had two lectors at the time. Thomas Watson McCallum did not return in the autumn of 1914,[32] but showed up again in 1927 and resumed his duties, staying until early in 1939. The second lector, Sidney Frederic Hooper, did not return either. He served as a subaltern with the Wiltshires in France and fell in the battle of Neuve Chapelle on 12 March 1915. Professor Karl Luick learned of his death through a letter from Otto Jespersen in Copenhagen — and in his turn wrote to inform the Austrian Ministry, warmly describing the young man in terms of high praise — an admirably humane document in a mad, inhuman period.[33]

Apart from the reduction in staff, there was, it appears, no change in the work of the departments — certainly no curtailment of teaching. With exemplary steadfastness, the professors, now largely on their own, carried on and did not, at least in their choice of topics, let the war interfere. In the summer semester of 1916, for instance, Luick in Vienna offered Historical Grammar, Chaucer, and Romanticism, in the winter semester of 1916/17 Fischer in Innsbruck offered Old English Literature, Shakespeare's Sonnets, and Victorian Poetry, and in the winter semester 1917/18 Eichler in Graz offered Historical Grammar, Old English Literature, and *The Merchant of Venice*. This continuation of the usual teaching parallels what Peter Firchow found happening in Oxford at the time, though teachers and the teaching of German seem to have come under much more severe strain in England.[34] We cannot know, of course, with what remarks, exhortations, imprecations, sighs, or other emotional utterances these lectures and seminars were accompanied in Austria, but the bets are that the university teaching of English and the teachers' convictions remained separate, and politics were kept out of the departments' classrooms. In both countries the number of students was, of course, drastically diminished.[35] In Innsbruck, for example, Fischer was left with fewer than 6 students, compared to 13 in 1913/14 and 38 in 1919.[36] Not surprisingly, fewer students took their final examinations, and in Graz there were no doctoral theses presented in English in the war years — but that was, one may assume, because the young men were occupied elsewhere and the women not yet ready. In 1919 two theses were accepted, and they were the first to be offered by women students.[37] Innsbruck shows a similar pattern: only two theses were accepted in the war years, and they were again the first to be offered by women.[38] I have not come by comparable information relating to Vienna, but it is reasonable to suppose that things were not very different there, though numbers would be higher in absolute terms.

In *War and the Image of Germany: British Academics 1914–1918*, Stuart Wallace has taken a comprehensive, thorough look at the role of university teachers during the Great War itself. Peter Firchow's book *The Death of the German Cousin* has given us a fascinating wider conspectus of changes in British public opinion, particularly as expressed in journalistic and literary writings as they reflect — to use Paul Kennedy's expression — *The Rise of the Anglo-German Antagonism*.[39] Insofar as the outbreak of hostilities in 1914 led to coordinated propaganda campaigns in Britain,[40] Firchow could build, apart from Wallace, on Peter Buitenhuis's book *The Great War of Words*; and there are other relevant studies, too. What emerges from their investigations is a dismal picture of nearly universal, systematic hatred being preached against anything and everything German (Austria-Hungary apparently not figuring in this, perhaps just trailing along as the archfiend's ally). The culmination of this hate campaign was unleashed by the publication, early in 1915, of the Bryce Report on alleged German atrocities, a document about which Buitenhuis (27) rightly quotes Peterson, who in 1939 had called it "one of the worst atrocities of the war."[41] I am stressing the aspect of British propaganda, because, as we shall see, this is what particularly infuriated German and Austrian scholars of English.

Before looking at their publications, however, a brief glance at what other quarters brought forward against England (the usual term for Britain). It is by and large everywhere the same *repertoire* of accusations and reproaches, if one disregards such absurd squirtings as *Händler und Helden* by the Berlin economist Werner Sombart, who — to convey just a whiff, an inkling of his method — coins sentences like "Die Grundlage alles Engländertums ist ja wohl die unermeßliche geistige Beschränktheit dieses Volks"[42] (Fundamental to all Englishness is assuredly this people's limitless spiritual poverty).[43] The Socialist Max Schippel in his pamphlet *England und Wir* of 1917 has a fairly complete list.[44] England engineered the encirclement of Germany, the notorious *Einkreisung*,[45] against which Germany had to defend itself (8); due to its island position, England looked seawards, acquired territories overseas, and created a dominating fleet to protect them, arranging affairs on the Continent in such a way as to unite alliances against whoever happened to be the strongest rival (11); it also used a "halo" of fighting for the liberty of conscience in religion and for free thinking; a reputation not quite undeserved perhaps, but always splendidly compatible with England's basic, if needs be brutally asserted, material interests (13). The first target of this continuous line of policy was Spain (14), the next Holland (14), followed by France (15). The *Endziel* (18), to wit, world domination, was never lost sight of. The last of these rivals is Germany (21–33). Austria's treatment of Serbia after 28 June and Germany's breach of Belgium's neutrality were merely pretexts to start the war sooner rather than later in order to achieve the downfall of Germany (35). With these theses, Schippel is absolutely typical. He is rather exceptional among German authors writing on the war in that he adds a separate chapter on England's "Wühlarbeit gegen Österreich-Ungarn" (63–79; subversive activities against Austria-Hungary) with the more and more openly avowed aim of dismantling the Habsburg Monarchy (75).

The same arguments, though not always in the same sequence, were advanced in Austria itself by Leopold von Jedina-Palombini, "Der Krieg und die Engländer" early in 1915:[46] England started the war out of rivalry with Germany, having dealt with Spain, Holland, and France in like manner before (1; compare Schippel 9), Germany and Austria-Hungary merely defend themselves (1; compare 10); England is not particular in its choice of means to realize its consistent aim of domination (2, 4), and so on. The main points of difference are, first, the thesis that no one should have been surprised at the English declaration of war; it was foreseeable, a position that implicitly denies the universally leveled charge of "perfidy" (3). Second, the stressing of contrasts in England, both among individuals and between individual behavior, often gentlemanly, and collective behavior, mostly brutal (4). Third, Jedina-Palombini maintains that, while one should stop indulging in the prewar fashionable Anglomania, one should not fall into the other extreme either: "in ein Vorurteil gegen alles Englische sollen wir trotz allem auch nicht verfallen" (we should not, however, descend into prejudice against all things English) — and exclaims:

> Unterlassen wir überhaupt, den Krieg auf das Gebiet der Wissenschaft, der Kunst und der Literatur zu übertragen. Diese sind gemeinschaftliche Güter der Menschheit, welche nur durch Zusammenwirken aller Völker eine entsprechende Förderung erfahren können. Und niemand wird bestreiten, daß England daran ganz hervorragend teilgenommen hat. (10)

> [By no means should we transfer war into the realms of Science, Art, and Literature. These are spiritual goods common to all mankind and can only be advanced by the joint endeavor of all peoples. And nobody will deny that England has made an outstanding contribution in this.]

One would wish that others, in particular in England but also in Germany, had taken up the same stance.

Similar in basic attitude is Georg Landauer, who published his pamphlet also in 1915, calling it a "preliminary investigation."[47] He realizes that national characteristics are unlikely to be clearly perceived in war (2–3) and looks forward to clearer views, a "Wiederherstellung" and "Weiterentwicklung des ethisch-kulturellen Wechselverkehrs zwischen den heute feindlichen Nationen"[48] (a restoration and further development of the ethical and cultural exchanges between the nations currently at war) on the basis of a peace without exactions and annexations (4) — the poor, benighted idealist! Then he presents a review of the principal accusations against England (6–13), cautiously underwriting them, but insisting that the English used to be different (thus Jedina-Palombini's concept of contrasts here implicitly becomes a model of two Englands),[49] and giving high praise to the kind of people they were (14–16), before mentioning some inherent weaknesses, among them a superiority complex (16). With Landauer, then, there is a second fairly reasonable voice. Ottokar Weber, a historian teaching at Prague university, also published a pamphlet in 1915, *Österreich und England*, which opens with the observation that there had been few conflicts between Austria-Hungary and England in the past, and that the declaration of war by England was simply a logical consequence of the overall political constellation.[50] The English policies with regard to the Continent are reviewed under the auspices of the country's egoism (7 — conceding that every country needs to be egoistical), but calmly highlighting in particular the contrary development of the two countries after the Napoleonic wars, England developing towards democracy (however faulty), Austria instituting absolutist repression (15). Then Weber comes to the anti-German attitudes of Edward VII (22), the encirclement (23), the charge of hypocrisy (25; compare Schippel, 30) and the English campaign to destabilize the Habsburg Empire (27). He also mentions English arrogance and the Englishmen's general lack of knowledge about European countries (29), while still upholding some good qualities in them (30).

The harsh title of a long book by Karl Rausch, another Austrian historian, *Die angelsächsische Verschwörung*, which appeared two years later, speaks for itself;[51] the conspiracy is to achieve world domination by the Anglo-Saxon race. Among the usual accusations he adds the tendency towards self-deception to that of hypocrisy (8). Remarkably, while of course supporting the war of self-defense, he advocates mainly persuasion of the rest of the world as a weapon against the Anglo-Saxons, observing that they have produced far more effective propaganda (12; compare Schippel, 66).

Finally, a word about the famous Otto Loewi (after his emigration: Loewy), a pharmacologist at Graz, who in his turn, like so many others, felt moved to contribute his views about the war: *Unsere Stimmung gegen England*.[52] What surprises here is that, under the guise of a careful, cautious, scientific procedure, Loewi expounds very radical views. War and culture are compatible (6), war is a necessity in nature (7), albeit only as an *ultima ratio* (8). The usual charges against England are echoed (9–12), bitterly exposing its campaign of lies and slander (12; compare

Schippel, 14), but all this is nothing compared to the gradually developed theory that England lacks culture and indeed both the will and the capacity to become a cultured nation (13) — touching the supposed gulf between "civilization" and "culture" which, among others, Thomas Mann has made notorious. And Loewi discusses the now widespread hatred of England in the country (without referring to Ernst Lissauer's *Haßgesang*), though he insists that Germans cannot deliver themselves over to this base emotion to the extent of the French and the English, by way of illustration quoting a poem which was published in the *Daily Graphic* on 30 August 1914:

> Down with the Germans, down with them all!
> O Army and Navy be sure of their fall!
> Spare not one of them[,] those deceitful spies,
> Cut [out] their tongues, pull out their eyes,
> Down, down with them all![53]

Of this poem he proceeds to offer a prosodically improved, eloquent verse translation. To Loewi, "Gott strafe England" seems, in the light of such cannibalistic emotions, a justifiable wish (24). English arrogance here meets a claim of superiority on the part of the Germans (29). Moreover, learning English, Loewi opines, may well be confined to the needs of people in special occupations; for the rest it is not necessary — not even to read the English classics — many people have got a great deal out of Shakespeare even in translation (27). This is definitely a minority view, others — most emphatically Hans Borbein[54] — stress the need for an increase rather than retrenchment of language teaching, be it even only under the motto "know thine enemies."[55]

With these notions, which are of course anathema to *Anglisten*, we have reached a convenient point of transition from general contributions to those specific to English studies. What has emerged so far has gone to show, I hope, the practical identity of German and Austro-German feelings and arguments as reflected in book and pamphlet literature of the war years. By and large what emerges corresponds to the findings of Klaus Schwabe's *Wissenschaft und Kriegsmoral*, confirming them with material which, with the exception of Sombart's tract, does not figure in his enormous list of such publications; Hans-Joachim Lang also adds some titles to this list, towards the end of an article mainly dealing with German poems of hatred against England.[56] This, then was the intellectual environment in which scholars of English produced their own reactions to the war.

Among the contributions by German Anglicists, the public lecture Wilhelm Dibelius delivered on 2 October 1914[57] is both very early and, it seems, very typical, containing all the notions we have already met in others.[58] The "Erzfeind" (archenemy) note to which Lang has rightly given prominence informs his opening paragraphs and eventually leads to the question of what explanations for the surprising and un-cousinly behavior of England may be offered by people like himself, scholars who have made the country and its culture their special study (6). The answer is the standard one — the drive of English imperialism (6–10), but it is fleshed out with the postulate that England stagnated spiritually in the nineteenth century (14), has not absorbed the impulses of German literature (15), and has seen the urge for freedom and individuality (16–17) lose out against a uniform mass culture and the ubiquitous forces of commercialism (20). What seems especially strange, not to say ominous, in Dibelius, who, according to Finkenstaedt (127) worked in the Presseamt (press office) during the war, together with Rudolf Immelmann and Wolfgang Keller, is the tendency to identify this individualism — and with it the highest achievement of the English spirit in Shakespeare, Burns, Wordsworth, and others — as specifically Germanic (25). And it is in this common heritage of the two countries, according to Dibelius, that German *Anglisten*, however fervently and patriotically they hope for German victory,[59] perceive the possibility of future reconciliation and renewed efforts at understanding. This will also depend on England's renunciation, not just of its drive for economic domination, but of its Puritan sense of cultural domination and world mission (26). The basic tenets in the 1914 lecture, in particular the consistent English drive for economic and even cultural domination, entered Dibelius's two-volume book on England, which appeared in 1924 and became for long a standard work on British civilization.[60] By comparison, a similar book by Karl Brunner (Fischer's successor to the chair at Innsbruck) which appeared in 1929 impresses me as far less biased.[61]

Friedrich Brie's famous — or notorious — study "Imperialistische Strömungen in der englischen Literatur" (1916) starts quite soberly by stating that all nations have an imperialist orientation (2), the implication being that the English just have it more persistently — and successfully.[62] Brie then picks up all kinds of literary manifestations that answer to his rather comprehensive definition of imperialism (1).[63] Wading through history with steady scholarly gait, his remarks only become somewhat abrasive regarding the later nineteenth century, his thesis being that the meager power the English have of seeing themselves as they really are prevented them from realizing that only the utilitarian coloring of their brand of imperialism distinguished it from those of other countries (164). Just as he does not resent the existence of imperialism in England, he has no objection to the thought of a divine mission of the English people (165); what he does resent is the puritanical hypocrisy (171) and above all the blind fury of chauvinism unleashed against Germany at the outbreak of the war and the propagation of lies about atrocities (164). As a whole, this is a reasonably sober and industrious survey which presents material much of which modern British contributions have also discussed and partly deplored, to say nothing of post-colonial studies.[64] Brie was preceded by Gregor Sarrazin, as he handsomely acknowledges (2, note) — and the subject of English imperialism continued to be treated later — also in Austria.[65]

Levin Schücking's *Der englische Volkscharakter* (1915) begins by enumerating many good and lovable qualities of the English, but adds that the war has made one more sharply aware of others that are less admirable (9).[66] The bad ones include the ignorance of the masses (9), the university education that forms gentlemen instead of critically thinking and independent scholars (10), laziness in many fields (10–17), ignorance leading to belief in the slanderous propaganda about atrocities (14), an absurd idea of a world mission (15; he conveniently forgets Geibel and his *Genesung* [recovery], which the world will enjoy through *deutsches Wesen* [German nature], an idea which also features, for instance, within our specific context, in Borbein's contribution, 17), the lack of *Innigkeit* (warmth and inwardness; 21) and the suppression of the emotions (24), the assertion of utility over morals (29), hypocrisy, particularly that shown in 1914 (31), arrogance (32) — and brutality (16), leading again up to the notion of two Englands, this time called two faces, underpinned with reference to Stevenson's *Dr. Jekyll and Mr. Hyde* (20). Yet good qualities keep popping up (17, 23), and this eminent *Anglist* thinks that after a new *modus vivendi* has been found,[67] those qualities will come to the fore again (32).

Most of Arnold Schröer's writings on the war issue, as collected in *Zur Charakterisierung der Engländer* in 1915,[68] first appeared in the form of articles in his local newspaper, the *Kölnische Zeitung*,[69] and represents the shrillest contribution from a scholar of English that I have so far found. Perhaps the very fact that he was an immigrant from Austria made him more than one hundred percent patriotic.

The English are "unsere[r] gefährlichsten Feinde" (*Zur Charakterisierung*, 5; compare 37, 78); while individual egoism is bad, national egoism is normal and good (9); English nationalism, arising from a feeling of belonging to a cultural community, is linked to the notion of services to mankind — the sense of a world mission (11 — see also, among others, Schücking), which is quite mad (12; compare 65–66). Their indolence and phlegm (15; compare, for example, 86) makes the English a nation of born *Rentner* (pensioners; 15 — though Sombart with his notion of *Händler* is wrong, 77), caught up in complete ignorance of, and indifference to, other nations (16). The perfidious policies of England (including the encirclement of Germany, 91) began with Edward VII (18; compare 37, 57, 76, and so on), English education strengthens egoism

(23), and arrogance and bigotry are the nation's dominant traits (28; compare 48). The English have made great contributions to cultural progress (30), but now they are, in their majority, so lazy, demoralized, and blinkered that they simply cannot understand the nature of the Germans (34). German militarism is a wonderful thing (36–38), so is the German "kategorische Imperativ der Arbeit" (categorical imperative of work, 38), heightened to "Evangelium der Arbeit" (gospel of work, 39). The diabolical English government of the day, which he distinguishes from the native and uneducated masses, caused the war in order to divert attention from the explosive situation in Ireland, other internal difficulties (an allusion to industrial strife), and their inability to deal effectively with the "tollen Wahlweiber[n]," as Schröer is pleased to dub the suffragettes (38). Schröer repeats his arguments with variations; just two notions need to be added for our purposes: the present war needs to be a fight to the finish (60; compare 67, 70), the Germans must beat some sense into the English (81) — and yet the war is really a pity, because, united, England and Germany could have divided up the world between them and given it the stamp of their cultures (61) — imperialism of the purest water.

Brandl, likewise from Austria and also permanently settled in Germany, is of much greater importance and also more balanced in his views. As he retrospectively describes it his autobiography, *Zwischen Inn und Themse* (303–16), he became increasingly aware, during the last decade of peace, of the cooling of relationships with people in England, a development which he rightly saw within the context of the rising antagonism and which filled him with great sorrow and anxiety.[70] This is not a recollection colored by later events; his early concern is documented. In the winter of 1914 he had presented, in article form, a number of English appreciations of famous Germans ("Deutsche Charakterköpfe") with the express aim of contributing to a preservation, or rather reestablishment, of understanding and appreciation between the two nations.[71] Brandl also shows the dilemma of his academic discipline and its students: "Sie hatten ihr Leben der Verbreitung der englischen Sprache und Dichtung gewidmet und sahen sich auf einmal vor britischen Kanonen" (320; They had devoted their lives to the spread of English language and literature and now saw themselves suddenly confronted by British cannons). His disappointment was shared, among many others, by the aged Jakob Schipper in Vienna (as reported in Friedwanger's obituary), and his wrath after war was declared was most acute. Remembering the many words of praise and admiration showered by representatives of other nations on the Shakespeare-Gesellschaft when its fiftieth anniversary was being celebrated in Weimar in April, 1914,[72] he exclaimed in his presidential address of April, 1916: "Heute klingt uns von denselben Völkern ein Chor der Unmenschlichkeit entgegen, den wir nicht für möglich gehalten hätten. Sind wir nicht mehr dieselben?"[73] (Today those selfsame peoples greet us with a chorus of inhumanity that we would not have thought possible. Are we no longer the same?)

And he did join the fray, notably with a public lecture, delivered in February 1915, on Byron's struggles with the establishment — Byron serving to attack England's rapacity, puritanical hypocrisy (6), and plutocracy (14). The lecture's second part discusses, after a bold transition (19), English war poems of 1914, of which he clearly had at his elbow a goodly number of anthologies (duly documented, of course). Like others, Brandl starts from the assumption that the war was forced on Germany (19), he deplores the atrocities campaign against Germany (21–22), and in passing he even notes the attack on the German professors in a poem by one R. H. Forster (26). What he selects from the mass of English war poems is truly lamentable — and remarkably poor poetry. And he is sad as well as angry at this "Meer von Gift" (32; ocean of poison), concluding by adapting Wordsworth's sonnet and wishing that indeed Milton were living at this hour (31–32) — incautiously assuming that Milton as well as Byron would have understood and supported "deutsche Freiheitsverteidigung und Rechtsempfindung und Wahrheitsliebe" (32; German defense of freedom, sense of justice, and love of truth].

A second significant contribution by Brandl is an article on England and Austria-Hungary, written at about the same time. This is much harsher, talking of the declaration of war against the Habsburg monarchy as understandable only in the wider context of England's dream of world domination, which necessitated a measure of accommodation with Russia (193), accusing England of exploiting others (195), and having them fight its wars (196 — which certainly did not apply to the First World War), and so on. Brandl calls for better public relations on the part of the central powers (197, 198) and for school reforms, giving more room to technical subjects, civic education, modern languages — and Islamic studies (198 — clearly thinking of links with Turkey and beyond, countervailing the influence of England and its plutocracy). The article shows how attached Brandl still was to his native country. Reading it is not particularly gratifying, but not revolting either.

Albert Eichler's best-known contribution to the war debate started as a newspaper article early in December 1914, which was rewritten, without changing the tenor of anger and fury at England's behavior, for publication in the *Zeitschrift für das Realschulwesen* of 1915.[74] Here is a key passage from the *Grazer Tagespost* of December 6, 1914:

> Wie steht aber der Anglist deutscher Zunge zu diesem Kriege da?
> Selbstverständlich denkt er über die Berechtigung der rücksichtslosesten Abwehr dieses überraschenden Angriffs durch England, der

gerade uns Anglisten die Röte der Scham und der Entrüstung ins Gesicht trieb, nicht um ein Haar anders als jeder brave Deutsche, innerhalb und außerhalb der schwarz-weiß-roten Pfähle. Viele, die Englands Sprache und Art daheim und im fremden Land eifrig erforscht haben, stehen im Felde und helfen mit, deutschem Wesen nachdrücklich und allen Lügenmeldungen einer skrupellosen Presse zum Trotz mit vornehmer Wahrung der Gesittung Achtung zu verschaffen. . . . (10th sheet, no page)

[But what is the attitude of native German scholars of English towards this war? Naturally we reflect on the rightness of a most vigorous defense against this surprising attack by England that causes us *Anglisten* to blush with shame and indignation — no whit differently from any other honest German within or without the black-red-white camp. Many who have diligently studied England's language and character at home and abroad are now on active service and, nobly preserving the highest standards, assist in achieving respect for all that is German despite the worst lies of an unscrupulous press.]

The "rücksichtsloseste[n] Abwehr" [most vigorous defense] I take to be a veiled reference to the invasion of Belgium, which, remarkably enough for us at any rate, not one of the publications I have read found objectionable. And the "Wahrung der Gesittung" (preserving the highest standards) upholds, in unison with all others, the view that German troops behaved impeccably, which is in its turn an exaggeration, though someone writing at home might well believe it.

Eichler goes on to praise the pronouncements of colleagues who had already taken up the pen and written about England, underscoring their objectivity, which was not even impaired by the "zuweilen durchzitternde Empörung über den letzten Streich dieses 'perfiden Albions'" (indignation at the latest deed of this "perfidious Albion" occasionally breaking through). He asks whether one should stop discussing contemporary English literature, concentrating only on the great achievements of the English spirit from *Beowulf* to Thackeray, for the appreciation of which German scholarship has done so much, particularly in the fields of Old and Middle English. Eichler argues against this option, saying that a great deal may be learned also from less worthy products, and the task of the *Anglist* is to convey an all-round picture of England so that people may justly assess it and be prepared. The article is not free of snide remarks, such as the one about the "gleichgültig-träge Menge der ungebildeten Durchschnittsengländer" (the lazy, indifferent mass of average, uneducated Englishmen), but there are not many.[75] Hopes of reconciliation are vain, according to Eichler; the dreams of universal goodwill and fraternal understanding such as were proclaimed by many sides at the last peacetime *Neuphilologentag* (held in Bremen in early June 1914)[76] have been thoroughly destroyed.[77]

As well as slightly reworking the article for publication in the organ of the *Realschulen*, Eichler reused its opening again in 1917 when he reviewed an extremely successful work, the *Britenspiegel* assembled by Erwin Rosen.[78] While understanding and sharing the general "aufflammen der maßlosen gerechten empörung und wut" (173; outburst of wholly justified wrath and indignation at the actions of "unseres gefährlichsten gegners" (173; our most dangerous enemy), and while agreeing that England's democracy is rather a sham, and rejecting English boastfulness and hypocrisy (174), Eichler for one thing raises scholarly objections at the haphazard selection Rosen made, ignoring the work of specialists. And he objects, moreover, to the inclusion of German material from the war years, like Lissauer's *Haßgesang*, which cannot, he rightly argues, throw any light on the character of the English (173). Most interesting perhaps, he stresses that the genuine German warrior of the gun or the pen does not fight simply because he hates England, but primarily out of love of Germany and its "positive ideale" (173; positive ideals).

Also in 1917 Eichler took the opportunity of a review of the German edition of essays by Sir Roger Casement[79] to launch a general historical survey of England's subjugation of Ireland, homing in with gusto on one of the dark aspects of Britain's policies;[80] yet even here the scholar is not lost: he dutifully notes slips and anglicisms of the translator (464, n. 5).

Eichler's principal work continued unabated. A staunch enemy to the Baconians, especially as organized in the Österreichische Shakespeare-Bacon Gesellschaft, his principal book of literary criticism in the war period is given to upholding Shakespeare's authorship of the plays,[81] while in the field of philology — at the time, professors of English were both historical linguists and literary critics — he helped Jakob Schipper (his father-in-law) prepare a new edition of the famous Zupitza-Schipper Old and Middle English Reader, later editions of which he prepared alone.[82]

It is significant where Eichler published the articles I have been dealing with here. Taking a hint from Firchow, who in "Goethe, Shakespeare, and the War of the Professors" presents items from the war-years volumes of the *Jahrbuch der deutschen Shakespeare-Gesellschaft*, I have looked around in other German-language English Studies periodicals. And my findings are both interesting and, in a way, reassuring. *Anglia* yields only the article by Brie in 1916, otherwise there is nothing to distinguish the war-years volumes from those preceding and those following them. They steadily contain the fruits of philological and literary research. Eichler's review of Rosen appeared in the *Beiblatt zur Anglia*.[83] Also the *Archiv* continued as it was, save for a very few items. Volume 69/133 (1915) contains a poem in praise of Germany and another in praise of Austria-

Hungary from the pen of an American, W. P. Trent (265–67). Volume 70/134 (1916) contains "Sitzungsberichte der Gesellschaft für das Studium der neueren Sprachen für das Jahr 1915," which in one session condemned the British press campaign with the words: "Selten ist die englische Brutalität neben englischer Scheinheiligkeit so in Erscheinung getreten" (395; rarely has English brutality manifested itself so plainly alongside English hypocrisy), while stressing that not all neutrals have fallen for those lies. Another session was given to a survey of French war diaries — done, it appears, in a very reasonable manner (404). I have found nothing else. *Englische Studien* contains nothing of topical reference, as far as I can see, during those years save for the notices about chairs and so on already mentioned.[84] Nor does the *Germanisch-Romanische Monatsschrift*; indeed, that periodical printed nothing to do with the war at all in its few wartime issues. It would be highly useful to analyze British scholarly journals during those years.

The picture is totally different when we look at the *Zeitschrift für das Realschulwesen* that, while published in Vienna and concentrating on the Habsburg Empire in school reports and similar items, also contains much from and about Germany. And this very bulky organ geared up to the war quite fast and with enormous energy. Volume 38 (1913) could never be mistaken for a later volume — the journal mournfully folded up halfway through volume 44 (1919). It is in the later issues of vol. 39 (1914) that the first war items appear: a discussion by one of the three editors, Adolf Bechtel, entitled "Die Stellung der Neuphilologen zu Frankreich und England" (710–15), which contains most of the usual strictures of the "Kaufmannsinsel" but energetically rejects calls for a retrenchment of language teaching, as did, among others, Fritz Karpf in 1916.[85] Most of the contents of this volume, however, had been written before war broke out.

It is with vol. 40 (1915) that the war really shows its enormous impact on schools and the thinking of teachers at all levels. Under "Schulnachrichten" (school news) it reprints the message of "Die Universitäten des Deutschen Reiches an die Universitäten des Auslandes" (universities of the German *Reich* to universities abroad) which protests against the anti-German press campaigns and places responsibility for the war and for any destruction of valuable cultural monuments (one immediately thinks of Louvain/Loewen and Rheims) on those who caused the war — that is, the Allies (26–27). And it contains articles on the war from every imaginable angle — Eichler's "Der Krieg und die Anglistik" (The War and English Studies), which was clearly unsuitable for the purely academic periodicals, is here in the company of "Die Wirkungen des Weltkrieges auf den neusprachlichen Unterricht" (The Effects of the World War on the Teaching of Modern Languages) by Rudolf Richter (Vienna), "Krieg und Schule" (The War and the School) by E. Zellwecker (Triest), "Der

Krieg, die Sprache und die Sprachen" (The War, Language, and Languages) by Franz Kemény (Budapest), "Krieg und Erdkunde" (The War and Geography) by Otto Leitgeb (Vienna), "Der Krieg im Geschichtsunterricht" (The War in History Lessons) by Hugo Pöpperl (Vienna), as well as "Schulnachrichten," a reprint of a Prussian ministerial order called "Der Krieg und die höheren Lehranstalten Preußens" (the War and Prussia's Institutions of Higher Education). Moreover, the volume contains, apart from individual reviews of topical books such as Karl Strecker's *England im Spiegel der Kulturmenschheit*, of which Adolf Bechtel remarks that it will "auch den verblendeten Anglomanen die Augen öffnen" (283; will even open the eyes of blinded anglophiles), collective notices like "Gute Kriegsbücher für die Jugend" (161–62; good war-books for young people), while continuing to review all kinds of books for use in schools and acquisition for school libraries.[86] Later war volumes of this journal go on along these lines while also printing learned disquisitions of the type appearing in 1915: for instance, "Orbiforme Kurven" (Orbiform Curves), and pedagogical articles such as "Beiträge zur Durchführung der praktischen Übungen im chemischen Laboratorium" (Contributions on the Carrying Out of Practical Training in the Chemistry Laboratory).[87] *Die neueren Sprachen*, also devoted to school teaching, follows the same pattern, but it took a little longer to get going on the war, so many peacetime articles obviously being in the pipeline and having to be printed, and took a little longer to stop talking about it — but that would be matter for a separate paper.

In "Goethe, Shakespeare and the War of the Professors" Firchow went through the *Jahrbuch der deutschen Shakespeare-Gesellschaft*, in particular Brandl's presidential addresses, with discernment and verve (esp. 469–78), noting their patriotism, indeed defiant nationalism, and the way in which Shakespeare is being claimed as by now belonging to Germany as well as to England and mankind in general.[88] And he notes that, while the English Goethe Society folded up and scholarly work on Goethe was practically suspended (479–81), the *Shakespeare-Gesellschaft* continued throughout the war. However, some points may well be added to Firchow's account.

Most articles published in the war years of the *Shakespeare-Jahrbuch* show nothing that would not or could not have appeared earlier or later; that is, in this respect the journal remains on a par with the learned periodicals like *Englische Studien*. Yet not only the personality of its president but the composition of its membership and the nature of its functions tended to draw the *Shakespeare-Gesellschaft* more deeply into the struggle, albeit only at the margins of its activities. This becomes evident in vol. 51 (1915). Straight after Brandl's address the *Jahrbuch* prints a letter that was sent from the front line by Professor Hans Hecht, and that contains a number of the points already amply presented (6).[89] Then follows the speech Gerhart Hauptmann had given at the annual meeting in April 1915: "Deutschland und Shakespeare,"[90] which — while unjustifiably claiming that Shakespeare is best understood in, and spiritually belongs to, Germany,[91] is still a nobler and at the same time more sensible contribution than Max Förster's article three years after the end of the war on "Shakespeare und Deutschland."[92] Hauptmann begins by asking: "Ist der Kultus des Dichters, den eine englische Mutter geboren hat, in Deutschland fortan noch erlaubt?" (Is the culture of a poet whose mother was English still permissible henceforth in Germany?) — and immediately answers: "Ja! Er ist erlaubt. Und nicht nur erlaubt: er ist geboten." (7; Of course it is permissible! And not just permissible: it is obligatory). The reason is obvious to the great German dramatist: "Auch im Kriege also verbleibt ein ewiger Friedens- und Kulturbestand. . . . In diesem Bereiche liegt nun auch ein ideeller Allgemeinbesitz, ein Schatz der Menschheit" (8; Thus even in wartime there exists a treasury of peace and culture. . . . Within this sphere there also exists a body of ideas common to all, a treasury of mankind). This question crops up again in the same volume in Carl Grabau's "Zeitschriftenschau," which devotes a separate section to the war (240–44).[93] It reproduces from the *Tägliche Rundschau* of September 27, 1914 the question "Darf ein Theater, daß sich in diesen Tagen der allgemeinen nationalen Erhebung seiner ernsten nationalen Aufgabe im tiefsten Sinn bewußt ist, Shakespeare spielen oder nicht?" (In these times of general national mobilization, may a theater that is truly conscious of its duty perform Shakespeare or not?) and gives a selection of the resoundingly affirmative replies gathered in from people such as Chancellor von Bethmann-Hollweg and the painter Max Liebermann.[94]

Of particular interest in this connection are performances of Shakespeare on German-language stages during the war, which are fully recorded in the journal's "Theaterschau" section — and are truly stunning.[95] Moreover, volume 52 (1916) contains a particularly thorough review of Shakespeare performances in Vienna by H. Richter, which once more deals with the question of what one can and cannot play during the war.[96] Richter concludes that contemporary British and French authors tended to be shelved — though not systematically — but that classics, and in particular Shakespeare, were played as a matter of course. "Der Wiener trägt im allgemeinen seinen Feindeshaß nicht in die Kunst hinein" (160; the Viennese do not generally carry their hatred of the enemy into the Arts). In Eichler's analysis of a *Hamlet* production in Graz (188–89) this is exemplified — the review turns exclusively on the quality of the staging and acting.[97]

One further volume of the *Shakespeare-Jahrbuch* contains some material to do with the war. Volume 52 (1916) prints, apart from a rather silly

poem by Ernst Hardt that was spoken at various Shakespeare performances in 1914,[98] the speech given by Rudolf Brotanek (Prague) at the
annual meeting, entitled "Shakespeare über den Krieg"; it collects innu-
merable references and presents the thesis that, although he presents the
evils of war, Shakespeare did allow it under certain circumstances. (By implication: Germany's situation in 1914 was one of those).[99] The same volume contains Franz Kaibel's "Dichter und Patriotismus," which — in
parts erupting into near-hymnic prose — demands that poets (and drama-
tists) worthy of Germany's present heroic struggle should arise to celebrate it as Shakespeare had celebrated other struggles.[100] After this, no
more articles of the kind appear in the *Jahrbuch* — and wisely so.

In his presidential address to the *Shakespeare-Gesellschaft* in April 1916
Brandl argued with reference to the hate campaign against Germany:

> Wir können an dieser Stätte unserem herrlichen Vaterlande nicht
> besser dienen, als indem wir Ruhe und Würde bewahren. Hier wird
> kein Wort gesprochen, dessen sich einmal unsere Nachkommen in
> hundert Jahren, wenn sich die Lage auf dem politischen Schachbrett
> vielleicht gründlich verändert hat, schämen müßten. (*SJ* 52, 1916: 5).

> [In this place we cannot serve our great country better than by hold-
> ing our peace and retaining our dignity. Here no word will be spo-
> ken of which our successors a century hence need feel the least bit
> ashamed, when the situation on the political chess-board may per-
> haps have altered completely.]

A noble resolution. One may well believe that it was kept on the occasion
in Weimar itself. However, what was written during the war by German
Shakespeareans and scholars generally did not always live up to these intentions, as we have seen. Yet what I have found was not, for the most
part, despicable, though it strikes one as often biased, somewhat con-
ceited, and at times downright silly. If my assessment may sound kinder
than that of other Austrian and German critics writing after the Second
World War with its unforgettable crimes committed by Germans and Austrians in those years, it is for the following reasons.

For one thing, long years of comparative studies of the literature
connected with the First World War have taught me to put into the right
perspective the findings in one particular quarter. First, the nationalism
that was rampant in those days was something as thoroughly English and
French as it was Austrian and German and Italian, and so on. Second, one
must remember the state of information of most people. As, among other
things, Brandl's tale of how he tried in vain to warn the German government of the impending danger of Britain joining forces with Germany's
foes makes very clear,[101] these scholars were not connected to the rulers of
either Germany or Austria and were not privy to their secret counsels.

Neither they nor anyone else, one might sum up this point, had read Fritz Fischer, Volker Berghahn, or Imanuel Geiss. That Germany, if I have understood these modern German historians rightly, actively prepared for war and forced Austria-Hungary's hand was unknown at the time. Nor had anyone at his of her disposal the insights about both Britain and Germany that Paul Kennedy could use for his authoritative study of the rivalry between the no longer very cousinly cousins. These scholars, and with them their entire nations, were told that the fatherland was being threatened and had to defend itself — and they believed this and rallied to the flag, as did the nationals of other countries, in each case with some exceptions.

The exponents of English scholarship in Austria and Germany may have been misguided in their pronouncements at the time — indeed I fear they were so to a large extent — but they were not evil either; on the contrary, they were filled with goodwill and, subsequently, filled with the bitterness that disappointment and rebuffs can provoke. In view of the fact that there had been no rivalry between England and Austria-Hungary, this may not be all that surprising, but it gives me particular pleasure nevertheless to add that the Austrian voices in Austria that I have come across were, with few exceptions, on the milder side of a wide spectrum of lament, accusation, and recrimination.[102]

Notes

An earlier version of this essay appeared as "Austrian (and Some German) Scholars of English and the First World War," in *Krieg und Literatur/War and Literature* 8 (2002, pub. 2003): 5–34.

The subject proved difficult to handle, and I am indebted to many people for their friendly assistance. Brigitte Reiffenstein (Vienna) selflessly made available to me fruits of research concerning Vienna University that she herself had long conducted, and moreover continued to supply information and materials while my work was in progress. Without her I would have had a much slower start, and I gladly record my profound gratitude to her. Cordial thanks for various kinds of valuable help are also due: in Vienna to Eva-Maria Csáky and Agnes Lössl; in Graz to Josef Huber-Grabenwarter, and especially to Isolde Müller and Gertraud Schober, in Innsbruck especially to Heidi Ganner, but also to Peter Goller, Werner Haas, and Wolfgang Zach; in Salzburg to Hildemar Holl and especially Sieglinde Reschen; in Berlin to Günther Walch, in Cologne to Heidrun Beckers; and in Szeged to György E. Szönyi.

[1] Kaiserliche Akademie der Wissenschaften in Wien, Philosophisch-historische Klasse, *Sitzungsberichte*, vol. 176, 1914/15 (Vienna: in Kommission bei Alfred Hölder, 1916), 22.

[2] Karl Kraus, *Die letzten Tage der Menschheit* (1915–19; repr. in 2 vols. after the 1926 ed., Munich: dtv, 1957), 1:43. Kraus is the most weighty exception to the war hysteria in Austria, to which so many succumbed, albeit several only temporarily; and thus he is the obvious darling of post-1945 critics like Denscher, Sauermann, Weigel/Lukan/Peyfuss, and many others — and rightly so. For a more balanced account, interestingly enriched by a comparison with Hašek, see Paul Pynsent, "The Last Days of Austria: Hasek and Kraus" in *The First World War in Fiction*, ed. Holger Klein (London: Macmillan, 1976), 136–48; Kraus and his unique contribution also gain additional profile from being embedded in the literary environment of the time better and more dispassionately than in many of the other accounts collected by Kann — see Robert A. Kann, "Trends in Austro-German Literature During World War 1: War Hysteria and Patriotism," in *The Habsburg Empire in World War 1*, ed. Robert A. Kann (1977), 159–83; here, 162.

[3] See especially Bernhard Denscher, *Gold gab ich für Eisen* (Vienna, Munich: Jugend und Volk Verlagsgesellschaft, 1987), and Hans Weigel, Walter Lukan, and Max D. Peyfuss, *Jeder Schuss ein Russ* (Vienna: Brandstätter, 1983).

[4] See Thomas Finkenstaedt, *Kleine Geschichte der Anglistik*, (1983), esp. 147–51; see also, rather less well informed, Sigmund Skard, *American Studies in Europe: Their History and Present Organization*, 2 vols. (Philadelphia: Pennsylvania UP, 1958), 1:407–9.

[5] See Finkenstaedt, *Kleine Geschichte der Anglistik*, 56–57; in addition, for Vienna, Brigitte Reiffenstein "Zu den Anfängen des Englischunterrichts an der Universität Wien und zur frühen wissenschaftlichen Anglistik in Wien," in *Wiener Beiträge zur Englischen Philologie, 80: A Yearbook of Studies in English Language and Literature, 1985/86: FS Siegfried Korninger*, ed. Otto Rauchbauer (Vienna: Braumüller, 1986), 163–85; for Graz, Peter Feldhofer, *Geschichte der Anglistik an der Universität Graz von den Anfängen bis zur Berufung Albert Eichlers*, Hausarbeit [equivalent to M.A. thesis], University of Graz, 1981, and Alwin Fill and Alois Kernbauer, eds., *100 Jahre Anglistik an der Universität Graz* (Graz: Akademische Druck- u. Verlagsanstalt, 1993); and for Innsbruck, Christoph Zecha, *Lehrkanzel und Institut für englische Philologie an der philosophischen Fakultät Innsbruck (1894–1938)*, Zulassungsarbeit [Equivalent to M.A. thesis], Innsbruck, 1966.

[6] See Gunta Haenicke, *Zur Geschichte der Anglistik an deutschsprachigen Universitäten, 1850–1925*, Augsburger I & I-Schriften, 8 (Augsburg: Universität Augsburg, 1979), 188–95, Karl Baschiera, "Zur Geschichte des Englischunterrichtes in Österreich und der Kulturbeziehungen zu den englischsprechenden Ländern," vol. 2 (1968): 69–86, in Otto Hietsch, *Österreich und die angelsächsische Welt: Kulturbegegnungen und Vergleiche*, ed. Otto Hietsch, vol. 2 (Vienna: Braumüller, 1968), 73–74, and Manfred Markus, "English University Studies in Austria: An In(n)sider's Report," in *European English Studies: Contributions Towards the History of a Discipline*, ed. Balz Engler and Renate Haas (London: The English Association, 2000), 143–60; here, 146 (dates among these sources vary somewhat, but not substantially). For practical reasons I was unable to include in this little survey the Hungarian universities of Austro-Hungary; György Szönyi kindly informed

me that there was only one chair of English at the time, the one at Budapest, established in the 1880s.

[7] See Finkenstaedt, *Kleine Geschichte*, 123.

[8] See Hermann Bahr, "Österreich," *Die Tat* 6 (1914–15), 584–90. The question of whether Austrians at large felt German and if so, in what ways, is very problematic. I was disappointed in my hopes of finding elucidation in *Österreich und die deutsche Nation*, ed. Andreas Mölzer (Graz: Aula-Verlag, 1985), though Nikolaus von Prevadovich in that volume touches on the issue, see: "Österreichs nationales Lager, 1882–1938," 169–85, especially 172–73; nor did I find information relevant to my specific angle in Friedrich Heer, *Der Kampf um Österreichs Identität* (Vienna, Cologne, Graz: Böhlau, 1981), where chaps. 1, 8, and 9 might have been supposed to yield it.

[9] Quoted by Hans Weigel in Weigel/Lukan/Peyfuss, *Jeder Schuss*, 10–11. Succinctly to the point about Bahr's oscillations of attitude, see Kann in Kann, *The Habsburg Empire*, 178–79.

[10] *Jahrbuch der deutschen Shakespeare-Gesellschaft* 54 [1918]: 9. Further references to this journal will be made in the text using the abbreviation *SJ*.

[11] See e.g. Alois Brandl, who began his Berlin lecture of 1915 on Byron and English war poetry with the words: "Verehrte Landsleute" (Brandl, *Byron im Kampf mit der englischen Politik und die englische Kriegslyrik von heute*, lecture given February 12, 1915 in Berlin [Carl Heymans Verlag, 1915], 3); by then, he would have acquired German nationality; we find the same identification in Otto Loewi, who must have acquired Austrian nationality, in *Unsere Stimmung gegen England und ihre Bedeutung für später*, lecture given June 19, 1915 in Graz (Leipzig: Leuscher & Lobensky's k.k. Universitätsbuchhandlung, 1915), esp. 15, 17, 21; and in Albert Eichler, especially in his article "Der Krieg und die Anglistik," sheet 10 of no. 325 of *Grazer Tagespost*, December 6, 1914, expanded in *Zeitschrift für das Realschulwesen* (Henceforth *ZsfdR*) 40 (1914): 193–201; Georg Landauer is more careful, stating in a footnote: "Die Worte 'uns,' 'unser' sind in den folgenden Ausführungen als Kollektivbezeichnung für Deutsche und Angehörige der österr.-ung. Monarchie zu verstehen; wo sich die Notwendigkeit ergibt, zwischen den Verbündeten zu differenzieren [I have found no such case in his lecture], wird dies ausdrücklich hervorgehoben werden." (*England: Eine Voruntersuchung* [Vienna: Manz'sche k.u.k. Hof-, Verlags- und Universitätsbuchhandlung, 1915], 5).

[12] Eberhard Sauermann, *Literarische Kriegsfürsorge: Österreichische Dichter und Publizisten im Ersten Weltkrieg* (Vienna, Cologne, Weimar: Böhlau, 2000), 356–57, also 352. His book is a highly useful contribution. By contrast, Kurt Koszyk's *Deutsche Pressepolitik im Ersten Weltkrieg* (Düsseldorf: Droste, 1968) disappoints, and his section "Von der Rußlandfeindschaft zum Englandhaß" (126–30) is not only confusing but actually itself confused.

[13] See Gerhard Oberkofler and Eduard Rabofsky, *Studien zur Geschichte der österreichischen Wissenschaft zwischen Krieg und Frieden* (Vienna: Edition Fortschrittliche Wissenschaft, 1987), 19–40, esp. 20.

[14] See, for example, *Englische Studien* (henceforth: *ES*) 48 (1914–15), 192: *Habilitation* of Charles Macpherson at Greifswald, move of Bernhard Fehr from St. Gallen to the chair at Dresden; 480: death of the Vienna chair, Jakob Schipper "der Altmeister der österreichischen Anglisten"; *ES* 50 (1916–17), 197: *Habilitation* of Karl Jost at Basel, of Marie de Meester at Groningen; *ES* 51 (1917–18), 480: the deportation to Siberia of Roman Dyboski (who served as officer in the Austro-Hungarian army and became a prisoner of war); *ES* 52 (1918), 144: the promotion of Albert Eichler (until then an *außerordentlicher Professor*) to a chair at Graz, etc. It is quite in keeping with the general spirit as well as policy of this journal that the death of Sir Walter Raleigh, who had so strongly written about his contempt for the Germans during the war was honored with such a notice (see Firchow, "Shakespeare, Goethe, and the War of the Professors, 1914–1919," in *Intimate Enemies: English and German Literary Reactions to the Great War 1914–1918*, ed. Franz Karl Stanzel and Martin Löschnigg [Heidelberg: Winter, 1993], 465–92; here, 472–74), and *The Death of the German Cousin: Variations on a Literary Stereotype, 1890–1920* [London and Toronto: Associated UP, 1986; Lewisburg: Bucknell UP, 1986], 45); to this notice was added: "Mit ihm ist einer der ersten englischen Literaturhistoriker dahingeschieden, der Verfasser bekannter Werke über den englischen Roman, über R. L. Stevenson, Milton, Wordsworth, Shakespeare und Johnson" (*ES* 57 [1923], 480; with him has passed away one of the foremost historians of English literature, author of well-known works on the English novel, on R. L. Stevenson, Milton, Wordsworth, Shakespeare, and Johnson).

[15] Earlier moves had been Julius Zupitza, the first incumbent of the Vienna chair, who had come from Breslau in 1872, and Matthias Konrath, who had moved from Vienna to Greifswald in 1882. Another case of interest in our context is Otto Loewi (later: Loewy), who was born in Frankfurt and took a medical chair (pharmacology) in Graz in 1909; he was awarded the Nobel Prize in 1936 — to be hounded out of Austria after the *Anschluß* in 1938.

[16] Anselm Salzer, *Die Sinnbilder und Beiwörter Mariens in der deutschen Literatur und der lateinischen Hymnenpoesie des Mittelalters.* Der 42. Versammlung deutscher Philologen und Schulmänner gewidmet von dem k.k. Obergymnasium der Benediktiner, Seitenstetten, (N[ieder]-Österreich: Linz, 1893).

[17] E.g., at the famous sixteenth meeting in Bremen (June 1914) speakers included school men from Berlin, Bochum and Elberfeld, to say nothing of a British guest: the London County Council divisional inspector of schools, Cloudesley, M.A. (first name illegible because of a splotch on the copy consulted at the Technical University, Graz). See Neuphilologenverband, *Bericht über die Verhandlungen der XVI. Tagung des Allgemeinen Deutschen Neuphilologenverbandes (ADNV) Bremen, 1–4 Juni 1914* (Heidelberg: Carl Winter, 1915), 6–7.

[18] I would have liked to extend my reading to the *Jahrbuch des höheren Unterrichtswesens in Österreich* and to *Sokrates: Zeitschrift für das Gymnasialwesen* and the *Zeitschrift für österreichische Gymnasien*, all promising fields of studies such as the present one, but there was no opportunity; I have more than enough material as it is.

[19] This applies notably to Karl Brunner (in Vienna, 1914), Albert Eichler (in Vienna, 1908–12), Otto Funke (in Prague, 1911–14), Leo von Hibler-Lebmannsport (in Graz, 1911–27), Rudolf Hittmair (in Vienna, 1913–14), Leon Kellner (Troppau and Vienna, in the 1890s), Karl Luick (in Vienna, 1890–91), Alois Pogatscher (Salzburg and Graz, from 1875 until 1889, when he obtained a professorship in Prague), Arnold Schröer (in Vienna in the early 1880s), and Friedrich Wild (in Vienna, 1912–13, 1918–27). All such information is drawn from the largely overlapping reference works by Gunta Haenicke, partly written in cooperation with Thomas Finkenstaedt: *Zur Geschichte der Anglistik and deutschsprachigen Universitäten, 1850–1925,* Augsburger I & I — Schriften, 8 (Augsburg: Universität, 1979); *Biographisches und bibliographisches Lexikon zur Geschichte der Anglistik, 1850–1925 (Mit einem Anhang bis 1945),* Augsburger I & I — Schriften, 13 (Augsburg: Universität Augsburg, 1981); *Anglistenlexikon 1929–1990: Biographische und bibliographische Angaben zu 318 Anglisten,* Augsburger I & I — Schriften, 64 (Augsburg: Universität Augsburg, 1992). For Pogatscher see in addition Ludwig Schuch, "Alois Pogatscher zum 70. Wiegenfest," *ES* 56 (1922), 177–84, esp. 178.

[20] This is still common practice at the five full English and American Studies departments in present-day Austria (Graz, Innsbruck, Klagenfurt, Salzburg, and Vienna) — with one huge difference: present-day so-called *Lektoren* or *Lektorinnen* who are schoolteachers and teach language and/or literature or linguistics at the university do no research (there may be the odd exception, but I know of none), nor are they required to under their contracts; neither are those language teachers fully integrated into the departmental staff as *Bundeslehrer* or *Bundeslehrerinnen* (though among them there are a few exceptions — I know of two). More's the pity — this is a grave structural defect of our departments.

[21] The Innsbruck department of English holds two piously hand-made little volumes of Rudolf Fischer's *Kleinere Schriften,* which yield nothing. He did translate into English, Peter Goller has kindly informed me, a memoir and appeal, written by leading scholars of Innsbruck University and published by the university, against the splitting off and giving to Italy of the southern portions of the Tyrol after the War: see Oberkofler, "Der Kampf der Universität Innsbruck um die Einheit des Landes Tirol (1918–1920)," *Tiroler Heimatblätter* 55 (1980), 78–89; here, 80; I have not been able to lay hands on this publication itself. In any case, it would be of only marginal relevance to my present concern. Perhaps a search in the archives of newspapers in Innsbruck for Fischer and in Vienna for Luick and the others might yield something, but I doubt it. On the other hand, Fritz Karpf contributed some articles connected with the war, but not specifically with England.

[22] See, e.g., Peter Firchow's "Shakespeare, Goethe."

[23] See Brandl's memoirs, *Zwischen Inn und Themse: Lebensbeobachtungen eines Anglisten — Alt-Tirol/England/Berlin* (Berlin: G. Grote'sche Verlagsbuchhandlung, 1936), just the last two pages ("Schluß"), and in particular the concluding sentence: "Vor allem, wir haben einen Führer, der jeden Keim der alten Zwiste und Parteiungen mit starkem Arme ausrottet und neuen Bruderkriegen gründlich vorbeugen will" (342). I heartily hope and indeed suppose that Brandl was not

aware of the horrible literalness of this *Ausrottung*, but the phrase sticks in one's gullet. And perhaps in 1936 Hitler could still appear as someone not wanting wars. Yet the anodyne and blandly laudatory description of Brandl in Scheler cries out for revision (Manfred Scheler, ed., *Berliner Anglistik in Vergangenheit und Gegenwart, 1810–1985* [Berlin: Colloquium, 1987], 19–34, esp. 32–34). For Eichler, who became PVC (*Prorektor*) of the renamed Reichsuniversität Graz from 1938–44, one must in this connection point to his hardly digestible book on the *Gentleman* (Albert Eichler, *Der Gentleman: Wesen — Wachsen — Verwesen* (Graz: Steirische Verlagsanstalt, 1943). Friedrich Wild's long obituary is much too reserved and kind ("Albert Eichler," in *Almanach für das Jahr 1953*, 103. Jahrgang, ed. Österreichische Akademie der Wissenschaften [Vienna: in Kommission bei Rudolf M. Rohrer, 1954], 437–49); to suppose no worse of him, he must have abided by the well-known Latin maxim, but would have served Austria better had be been more forthright. Schröer died in Cologne in 1935; I have been unable to ascertain his political line after 1915.

[24] It is worth adding that — much later than German and Romance studies in Germany — the *Anglisten* recently decided to explore the attitudes, utterances, and actions of their guild during the Third Reich, devoting a fascinating section of the 2001 Anglistentag (held in Vienna) to that subject. The papers delivered on that occasion appeared in *Anglistik*, the organ of the German Anglistenverband, in 2002.

[25] The same applies to Germany; see Fritz F. F. Ringer, *The Decline of the German Mandarins* (Cambridge, MA: Harvard UP, 1989) 180–83, and Willis Rudy, *Total War and Twentieth-Century Higher Learning* (Rutherford, NJ: Farleigh Dickinson UP, 1991), 13, who also discusses Britain and France, but unfortunately not Austria-Hungary.

[26] This is the policy of Gall for Vienna, 27–28: "In dieser zweiten nachmärzlichen Blüteperiode bis zum Ersten Weltkrieg errang die Wiener Universität . . . Weltruf" (In this second pre-First World War period of flowering in the wake of the March Revolution of 1848 the University of Vienna achieved worldwide renown), followed by a list of renowned teachers, and then on page 28 by: "Der Zusammenbruch der östereichisch-ungarischen Monarchie hat naturgemäß auch die Wiener Universität schwer betroffen" (As a matter of course the collapse of the Austro-Hungariian monarchy also heavily affected the University of Vienna) (Franz Gall, *Alma Mater Rudolphina 1365–1965: Die Wiener Universität und ihre Studenten*, 3rd ed., herausgegeben von der Österreichischen Hochschülerschaft an der Universität Wien [Vienna: Verlag Austria Press, 1965]). See similarly Richard Georg Plaschka, "Universität 1884 — Neues Haus mit neuen Weichenstellungen: Die Universität Wien in den Herausforderungen der zweiten Hälfte des 19. Jahrhunderts," in Günter Hamann, Kurt Mühlberger, and Franz Skacel, eds., *100 Jahre Universität am Ring: Wissenschaft und Forschung an der Universität Wien seit 1884* (Vienna: Universitätsverlag der österreichischen Hochschülerschaft für Wissenschaft und Forschung, 1986), 9–26; here, 20. All we learn from Oswald Redlich, "Geschichte der Universität Wien," in *Die Universität Wien: Ihre Geschichte, ihre Institute und Einrichtungen*, ed. Robert Wettstein (Vienna, Düsseldorf: Lindner, 1929), 1–11; here, 11, is that the university was in part

turned into a hospital, housing some 1,000 wounded soldiers (see Kurt Mühlberger in Hermann Fillitz, ed., *Die Universität am Ring* [Vienna: Brandstätter, 1984], 12), and that many students and teachers died. Some more information, accompanied by several photographs, is given about the main building and its function as a hospital in Mühlberger/Maisel, *Rundgang durch die Geschichte der Universität Wien* (Vienna: Archiv der Universität Wien, 1999), 65–66. Smekal (Ferdinand G. Smekal, *Alma universitas: Geschichte der Grazer Universität in vier Jahrhunderten* [Vienna: Verlag der Vereinten Nationen, 1967], 115) touches in half a paragraph on the events and their grave consequences for the University of Graz. Hölbing/Stratowa (Franz Hölbing und Wulf Stratowa, *300 Jahre Universitas Oenipontana: Die Leopold-Franzens Universität zu Innsbruck und ihre Studenten* [Innsbruck: Verlag der *Tiroler Nachrichten*, 1970], 69–70), leave a complete blank regarding the war years for Innsbruck, while Oberkofler/Goller are somewhat more informative about the period in the case of the University of Innsbruck (Gerhard Oberkofler and Peter Goller, *Geschichte der Universität Innsbruck (1669–1945)* [Frankfurt: Lang, 1995], 198–200). Further references to this work will be made in the text using the abbreviation *GUI* and the page number.

[27] Oberkofler/Goller, *Geschichte der Universität Innsbruck*, 198.

[28] According to information kindly sent me by Peter Goller, Innsbruck had 1480 students in 1914, plus probably 134 members of staff. 77 of the students were women, thus we are left with 1537 men.

[29] There must have been students and former students of English who were less lucky, but I have been unable to follow up that line of investigation. In Germany, even some professors of English went to the front to fight, see Finkenstaedt, *Kleine Geschichte*, 127.

[30] See Fill/Kernbauer, *100 Jahre Anglistik*, 120–21.

[31] See Zecha, *Lehrkanzel und Institut*, 65–67.

[32] I have been unable to ascertain what he did during the war (he may have served with the British armed forces) and from 1918 to 1927.

[33] Luick on Hooper, dated 23 June, 1915: "Durch den Hingang Hoopers ist ein verheißungsvoller Anfang jäh zum Abschluss gekommen. Er hat sich während der kurzen Zeit seiner Wirksamkeit als ein begabter und eifriger Lehrer erwiesen, dessen Tätigkeit bei längerer Dauer die schönsten Früchte erwarten ließ. Ich bedauere aufrichtig sein Ausscheiden aus dem Lehrkörper unserer Universität." [Hooper's death has brought a promising start to an abrupt end. During his short life he proved himself to be a gifted and assiduous teacher; there was the promise of fine fruits to come, had he but lived longer. I deeply regret his loss to our Faculty.] There is a note in the margin of this letter in which a civil servant coldly if logically remarks that, as Hooper had served on the enemy side, he would have had to leave the staff of Vienna University anyway. I would never have found this story without Brigitte Reiffenstein, who had herself only mentioned the bare facts in her article, see "Zu den Anfängen . . ." in the *FS Korninger*; she handed me a copy of the letter, which she had unearthed. Apparently Hooper was still owed some money, which his mother claimed and was sent in 1921 (see Reiffenstein, "Zu den Anfängen . . . ," 180, and 183 note 45.).

[34] See Firchow, "Shakespeare, Goethe," 481–82. See also Stuart Wallace, *War and the Image of Germany: British Academics 1914–1918* (Edinburgh: John Donald, 1988), as the most thorough study of British professors' involvement, a pendant to Klaus Schwabe's *Wissenschaft und Kriegsmoral: Die deutschen Hochschullehrer und die politischen Grundfragen des Ersten Weltkrieges* (Göttingen, Zürich, Frankfurt: Musterschmidt, 1969), but even more useful on account of its appendices with lists of names and functions, etc. In addition, Hans Borbein states that the teaching of German has been stopped in many parts of the enemy countries, but cites no specific examples (*Auslandsstudien und neusprachlicher Unterricht im Lichte des Weltkriegs* [Leipzig: Quelle & Meyer, 1917], 5). He also mentions the fact that the German-born professors of German in Britain publicly proclaimed their total adherence to the British cause; their statement was reprinted from the *Frankfurter Zeitung* of 27 May 1915 (which had taken the item over from *The Times* of 14 May) under the heading "Die Deutsch-Engländer gegen Deutschland" in *Die neueren Sprachen* 23 (1915–16): 176.

[35] The same applies to Germany, Britain, and France — see Rudy, *Total War*, 17.

[36] Zecha, *Lehrkanzel und Institut*, 37.

[37] See Fill/Kernbauer, *100 Jahre Anglistik*, 216–17, the table of final examinations taken — which had included women since 1905 — and 196–97, the table of doctorates awarded.

[38] Zecha, *Lehrkanzel und Institut*, 74.

[39] In an earlier contribution, Kennedy had already given an outline of developments in public opinion regarding Germany, including the literary response; see Paul Kennedy, "British Views of Germany, 1864–1938," *Transactions of the Royal Historical Society*, 5th series, 25 (1975): 137–56. See also his book, *The Rise of Anglo-German Antagonism 1860–1914* (London: Allen & Unwin, 1980). For the literary voices, see, apart from Firchow's *Death of the German Cousin* (1986), also Günther Blaicher, *Das Deutschlandbild in der englischen Literatur* (Darmstadt: Wissenschaftliche Buchgesellschaft, 1992, 19–25, not very systematic or thorough); Peter Buitenhuis, *Great War of Words: Literature as Propaganda, 1914–18 and After* (Vancouver, Canada: UBCP, 1987); M. E. Humble, "The Breakdown of a Consensus: British Writers and Anglo-German Relations, 1900–1920," *Journal of European Studies* 7 (1977): 41–68; and Holger Klein, "Distorting Mirror? Images of Prussia-Germany in English Prose, 1890–1914," in *The Artistry of Political Literature: Essays on War, Commitment and Criticism* (Lewiston, Queenston, Lampeter: Edwin Mellen, 1994), 21–24; furthermore of course I. F. Clarke, *Voices Prophesying War: Future Wars 1763–3749* (1966; 2nd ed., Oxford & New York: Oxford UP, 1992), chap. 4, 107–61, from his specific angle; and, specifically about the academy, Wallace, *War and the Image of Germany*, chap. 10, 167–90.

[40] See Wallace, *War and the Image of Germany*, chap. 10, and Firchow, *The Death of the German Cousin*, chap. 6.

[41] On British and Allied propaganda see, in addition to Peterson, other early works, esp. Harold D. Lasswell, *Propaganda Technique in the World War* (London: Kegan Paul; New York: Knopf, 1923); James Read, *Atrocity Propaganda 1914–1919* (New Haven: Yale UP, 1941); and George Viereck, *Spreading Germs*

of Hate (London: Duckworth, 1931); and, concentrating on Britain alone, Cate Haste, *Keep the Home Fires Burning: Propaganda in the First World War* (London: Allen Lane, 1977). Read's summary (285–86) is still valuable; he underestimates, however, the fact that the British campaign was concerted and "masterminded" (in the main by C. F. G. Masterman) in a uniquely efficient way. Concentrating on university teachers and also comparative, though more brief, is Rudy's chapter 8, "Professors as Propagandists" (*Total War*, 42–51) — its very brevity, of course, entailing considerable problems of foreshortening and imbalanced selectivity. By comparison, Austria's efforts to guide the press and the work of writers for propaganda purposes were not as successful; see Peter Broucek's short article "Das Kriegspressequartier und die literarischen Gruppen im Kriegsarchiv, 1914–1918," in *Österreich und der Große Krieg, 1914–1918: Die andere Seite der Geschichte*, ed. Klaus Amann & Hubert Lengauer (Vienna: Brandstätter, 1989), 132–39.

[42] Sombart, *Händler und Helden: Patriotische Besinnungen* (Munich, Leipzig: Duncker & Humblot, 1915).

[43] On Sombart see also Ringer, *The Decline of the German Mandarins*, esp. 183–85.

[44] Max Schippel, *England und Wir: Kriegsbetrachtungen eines Sozialisten* (Berlin: Fischer, 1917).

[45] This concept was, as far as I am aware, decisively dismantled by Hermann Kantorowicz in 1929, whom I read in the 1970s, though I must admit to not having followed up the matter in recent years.

[46] Leopold von Jedina-Palombini, "Der Krieg und die Engländer," *Österreichische Rundschau* 42 (January–March 1915): 1–10.

[47] Georg Landauer, *England: Eine Voruntersuchung*. I have not found out what Landauer's profession was. A year later, in 1916, he was less careful, publishing another pamphlet — which I have not seen or found described anywhere — with the title: *Der Verrat des Freundes: Gott strafe England; Die Wacht am Rhein* (Vienna: Manz'sche Buchhandlung, 1916).

[48] Landauer, *England: Eine Voruntersuchung*, 5; compare 15.

[49] This corresponds to the notion, widespread in France and Britain, of "two Germanies" — one the cultured nation of poets and thinkers, the other the jackbooted junkers and adherents of Bismarck's *Realpolitik*. See Holger Klein, "Distorting Mirror?" 38–40.

[50] Ottokar Weber, *Österreich und England*, Flugschriften für Österreich-Ungarns Erwachen, 2nd ed., ed. Robert Strache and Ferdinand Gruner (Warnsdorf, Bohemia: Ed. Strache, 1915), 5.

[51] Otto Loewi, *Unsere Stimmung gegen England*.

[51] Karl Rausch, *Die angelsächsische Verschwörung: Eine zeitgeschichtliche Untersuchung* (Vienna: Manzsche k.u.k. Hof -, Verlags- und Universitätsbuchhandlung, 1917).

[52] Otto Loewi, *Unsere Stimmung gegen England*.

[53] I have not been able to check this, but think it unlikely that he could have invented both poem and source. The poem is not in any anthology I could lay my

hands on, though some do come near it. For hate poems see, for example, Klein "Comrades? The Enemy as Individual in First World War Poetry," in *Intimate Enemies: English and German Literary Reactions to the Great War 1914–1918*, ed. Franz Karl Stanzel and Martin Löschnigg (Heidelberg: Winter, 1993), 181–99, esp. 183–85, reprinted in Klein, *The Artistry*, 241–51, esp. 242–44; in general, see also Elizabeth Marsland, *The Nation's Cause: French, English and German Poetry of the First World War* (London, New York: Routledge, 1991).

[54] Hans Borbein, *Auslandsstudien*, 5–7.

[55] Much later in his book Borbein adds a somewhat different idea, namely, the possibility of teaching French and English a little less and increasing the teaching of other modern languages (92) — presumably of those countries that were allies or remained neutral.

[56] Lang, like Weigel/Lukan/Peyfuss and so many other critics writing about German-language literature in the First World War, including notably Klaus Schroeter ("Chauvinism and Its Tradition: German Writers at the Outbreak of the First World War," *Germanic Review* 43 [1968]: 120–35) would have done well to consider the other side (e.g., Bernard Bergonzi's article ""Before 1914: Writers and the Threat of War," *Critical Quarterly* 6 (1964): 126–34, to say nothing of Clarke's book). As I have argued for the last twenty-five years, starting with my introduction to *The First World War in Fiction*, this kind of literature can only satisfactorily be dealt with on a comparative basis. (See for the same opinion also Baltz Engler's "Shakespeare in the Trenches," *Shakespeare Survey* 44 [1992]: 105–11) — not to excuse any verbal excesses that did happen, but to help put each individual nation's voices into perspective.

[57] Wilhelm Dibelius, "England und Wir," lecture given October 2, 1914 (Hamburg: Friedrichsen, 1914).

[58] Encirclement (2, 9), the war forced upon Germany (6, 29), odiousness of the English press campaign against Germany (5, 22) and the existence of two Englands (29).

[59] "Gewiß steht selbstverständlich auch der deutsche Anglist heute mit all seinem Denken und Wollen im deutschen Feldlager und erhofft mit aller Kraft seines Gemüts den Sieg der deutschen Waffen" (25; Today, of course, German scholars of English take their place too in Germany's camp with uncompromised mind and will, yearning with heart and soul for the victory of German arms.) This sums up the general position — and not just in the early stages of the war.

[60] Wilhelm Dibelius, *England*, 2 vols. (Stuttgart, Leipzig, and Berlin: Deutsche Verlagsanstalt, 1922) is held by the libraries at Graz, Innsbruck, and Vienna — the three universities of present-day Austria that had English departments before 1945. I have not checked German libraries, but am convinced that most of them had and still have it. Thousands of students must have read it over the years. For passages corresponding to the 1914 lecture see, for example, 1:26, 87, 92, 200, 2:191, 226. A veiled admission in 1914 of German shortcomings and diplomatic errors ("England und Wir," 6) has become stronger and more open (1, 11).

[61] Karl Brunner, *Großbritannien: Land — Volk — Staat* (Bielefeld, Leipzig: Velhagen & Klasing, 1929).

[62] Friedrich Brie, "Imperialistische Strömungen in der englischen Literatur," *Anglia* 40 (1916): 1–200.

[63] "ist der begriff des imperialismus so weit als möglich gefaßt worden, so daß er nicht nur das streben nach erweiterung der landesgrenzen, nach erwerb überseeischen besitzes, nach beherrschung der meere und nach zusammenschluß von mutterland und kolonien umfaßt, sondern auch das streben nach ausbreitung von rasse, religion, sprache, recht oder sonstiger nationaler ideen überhaupt; auch die mittel und voraussetzungen derartiger bestrebungen wie die lehren von der machtidee des staates, vom nutzen des krieges oder von der allgemeinen wehrpflicht mußten, ebenso wie die äußerungen übertriebener verherrlichung der eigenen nation und übertriebenen hasses gegenüber einer fremden, vielfach in den kreis der betrachtungen eingezogen werden" (*Anglia* 40 (1916): 1; thus the concept of imperialism has been defined as broadly as possible to include not only a country's attempts to widen its boundaries, to acquire overseas territories, to rule the waves, and to bind together motherland and colonies, but also its attempts to spread race, religion, language, law, and every other such national idea; but also the means and the presuppositions of such attempts — such as teaching about the power of the state, the value of war or of general conscription, along with expressions of an exaggerated notion of one's country's importance and exaggerated hatred towards other countries — had to be included frequently in our considerations).

[64] See, for example, Robert Giddings, ed., *Literature and Imperialism* (Basingstoke: Macmillan, 1991).

[65] Sarrazin's article, "Der Imperialismus in der neueren englischen Literatur," which I could not obtain, appeared in 1915 (in the *Internationale Monatsschrift für Wissenschaft und Technik* 9 [June 1915]: 11). Dibelius's book on English civilization has already been mentioned. "Imperialism" also fills the entire first volume, *Imperialismus: Das Britische Grundproblem; Englands weltpolitische 'Sendung,' beleuchtet durch sein Schrifttum aus drei Jahrhunderten* (Bamberg: C. C. Buchner, 1930), of the series *Grundzüge britischer Kultur*, by Josef Bausenwein et al. in 1930 (note the "British" rather than English). For Austria we have already met the phenomenon treated under another name, but using the precise term; see further, for example, K. Woynar (Vienna), "Über den britischen Imperialismus," *ZsfdR* 42 (1917), 199–204, an extended, highly laudatory review of the work of the Leipzig historian Felix Salomon, and also Eichler (discussed below).

[66] Levin L. Schücking, *Der englische Volkscharakter*, booklet no. 53 of Der Deutsche Krieg: Politische Flugschriften, ed. Ernst Jäckh (Stuttgart, Berlin: Deutsche Verlags-Anstalt, 1915).

[67] Schücking does not say how — but it appears that he has a compromise peace in mind rather than, as so many others, German victory.

[68] M. M. Arnold Schröer, *Zur Charakterisierung der Engländer* (Bonn: A Marcus & E. Webers, 1915).

[69] Schröer details, without giving sections or page numbers, that chap. 1 (now called "Ein Amerikaner über England und die Engländer, fünf Jahre vor dem

Weltkrieg") appeared before the war, on April 9, 1912, in the *Kölnische Zeitung*, chaps. 2–7 on September 13 and 15, October 26, December 16, 1914, January 10, February 27, and March 28, 1915 of the same newspaper. Chap. 8 first appeared in the *Süddeutsche Monatshefte*, November 1914. Apart from the *Kölnische Zeitung* of September 7 (not mentioned by Schröer in the book) and October 26, 1914, of which I obtained copies, unfortunately without page numbers, I have been unable to obtain these separate sources to check the exact extent of his "gerinfügige[n] Änderungen und Zusätze[n]." In the following synopsis I can therefore only refer to the book. On Morsbach, who, according to Eichler's article in the *Grazer Tagespost*, also wrote in the *Kölner Zeitung*, I have had to give up for the time being.

[70] This antagonism also impressed the young Heinrich Spies; when he first visited England he saw a variety show with a song in it turning on the refrain: "The world for England/ And a rasher for Germany" — see the opening pages of his *Deutschlands Feind* (1915).

[71] See also Brandl's report on Lord Haldane's speech at Oxford on the occasion of his being given an honorary doctorate in 1911, in which speech the Secretary of State for War had found words of praise for Germany and applauded in particular the German university system and its impact on the German economy as well as life in general — not withholding some slight criticisms of present conditions, however. Brandl faithfully reports these also, and the article clearly aims to prove the possibility of understanding between the two nations.

[72] Already in his article "Englische Philologie" in *Die deutschen Universitäten: Für die Universitätsausstellung in Chicago 1893* . . . , ed. Wilhelm Lexis (Berlin: Asher, 1893), 482–96, he had had occasion to be glad at such praise — in those days from Furnivall, Sweet, and Child (482).

[73] *SJ* 52, (1916): 6; see Brandl, *Zwischen Inn und Themse*, 320–21.

[74] Albert Eichler, "Der Krieg und die Anglistik," *Grazer Tagespost*, December 6, 1914; repr. in expanded form in *ZsfdR* 40 (1914): 193–201.

[75] Other examples are the statements about the Englishmen's lack of understanding of *deutsche Bildung* and the frequent immaturity of their judgment.

[76] For this conference, see also, for example, the detailed report by Max Lederer (Vienna), "XVI, Allgemeiner Neuphilologentag zu Bremen (1.–4. Juni 1914)," in *ZsfdR* 39 (1914): 577–92 and 641–50.

[77] The proceedings of that *Neuphilologentag* (Neuphilologenverband, *Bericht über die Verhandlungen der 16. Tagung*), bear him out. It was the apogee of European scholarly and pedagogic unity and cooperation. Eichler's argument that this unity was destroyed rests in particular on the Allies' bringing into battle Asian and African troops — but such racialist views were pretty common at the time on all sides. Words of praise for the native troops in Harmsworth's *War Illustrated* (e.g. September 19, 1914, 103, September 26, 1914, 140, October 10, 1914, 172–73) are clearly geared to the situation.

[78] Albert Eichler, Review of Erwin Rosen, *England: Ein Britenspiegel, Beiblatt zur Anglia: Mitteilungen über englische Sprache und Literatur und über englischen Unterricht* 28 (1917): 171–76.

[79] Sir Roger Casement, *Gesammelte Schriften: Irland, Deutschland und die Freiheit der Meere, und andere Aufsätze* (Diessen nr Munich: J. H. Huber, 1916).

[80] Albert Eichler, Review of Sir Roger Casement, *Gesammelte Schriften, Beiblatt zur Anglia: Mitteilungen über englische Sprache und Literatur und über englishen Unterricht,* 28 (1917), 176–84.

[81] Culminating in the publication of a book that was ready for the press in the spring of 1918 but could, because of the unquiet mood of the times, only appear in 1919: Albert Eichler, *Antibaconianus* (Vienna, Leipzig: Karl Harbauer, 1919), which bears the ironic (but irrelevant and confusing) subtitle *Shakespeare-Bacon? Zur Aufklärung seines Anteils an der Erneuerung Österreichs.* Earlier articles on the subject had appeared during the war in the *ZsfdR* 42 (1917): 577–91 and 649–66.

[82] *Alt- und mittelenglisches Übungsbuch . . . mit einem Wörterbuche von Julius Zupitza,* 11, unter Mitwirkung von Rudolf Brotanek und Albert Eichler verbesserte Auflage, ed. Jakob Schipper (Vienna: Braumüller, 1915). Compare the 12th ed., which Eichler prepared alone (Vienna: Braumüller, 1922).

[83] There may have been in the *Beiblatt* some other reviews of books concerned with the war; I did not check systematically, but doubt whether much is to be found.

[84] Firchow states that Johannes Hoops, the editor of *ES,* though not engaging in propaganda himself, "published propagandistic criticism written by others" ("Shakespeare, Goethe," 489, n. 9). I have found no evidence for this.

[85] See Fritz Karpf, "Die neueren sprachen nach dem krieg," *Die Neueren Sprachen* 24 (1916–17): 385–93.

[86] See Fritz Karpf, "Die k. und k. feldbücherei," *Die Neueren Sprachen* 24 (1916–17): 623–24, which vaunts the ongoing acquisition of English and French books and asks whether the same applies on the other side.

[87] This *Zeitschrift* would really warrant a special, separate study — preferably alongside *Die neueren Sprachen* and similar British and French publications such as *Modern Language Teaching* (and those in still other languages). It is amazing that Barbara Holzer did not consult it at all; it does not invalidate her findings on patriotic education in Austria during the war, gained from other sources, but would have substantially enriched and helped to consolidate them. All I can do here is to convey some impressions of *ZsfdR:* vol. 41 (1916) contains amongst other items: "Ein Beitrag zur militärischen Erziehung der Jugend," "Humanismus und Weltfrieden," "Unsere turnunterrichtlichen und militärischen Vorschriften," and "Der Weltkrieg und die Naturwissenschaften"; vol. 42 (1917) amongst others "Die deutsche Schule und die deutsche Zukunft," "Kriegspädagogik," and the items already mentioned by Woynar on British Imperialism, and by Eichler on Ireland; in vol. 43 (1918) see especially once more Adolf Bechtel (who was a school administration official and teacher of French but had, I assume, also studied English) with an accusatory article on English exactions in eighteenth-century India: "Die englische Verwaltung Ostindiens und die Ausplünderung der eingeborenen Bevölkerung im 18. Jahrhundert," *ZsfdR* 42 (1917): 641–48. A very interesting angle on the subject of school teaching and

the war is treated by Thomas Winkelbauer ("Krieg in deutschen Lesebüchern der Habsburgermonarchie [1880–1918]," in *Österreich und der Große Krieg, 1914– 1918: Die andere Seite der Geschichte,* ed. Klaus Amann and Hubert Lengauer [Vienna: Brandstätter, 1989], 37–47), where one can also find an article by Sigurd Paul Scheichl on journalism, who takes a single important publication as his example ("Journalisten leisten Kriegsdienst," in *Österreich und der Große Krieg 1914–1918,* 104–9), and another ("Das Kriegspressequartier") on the war archive and the armed forces press center by Peter Broucek.

[88] Peter Firchow, "Shakespeare, Goethe."

[89] Finkenstaedt quotes a passage as an example of the "Pathos des geradezu persönlich beleidigten Anglisten" (*Kleine Geschichte der Anglistik,* 127). Firchow shows rather more empathy with the situation of the German Anglicists at the time. It is a tragic irony that Hecht, along with other non-Aryans, was excluded from the Shakespeare Society to conform with new Nazi legislation in 1936.

[90] Gerhart Hauptmann, "Deutschland und Shakespeare," *SJ* 51 (1915): 7–12.

[91] For this speech by Hauptmann and an angry riposte to it by Henry Arthur Jones, see Pfister in the *Shakespeare-Jahrbuch* (Bochum), 1992, 17.

[92] Max Förster, "Shakespeare und Deutschland," *SJ* 57 (1921): 7–27. Among other things, Förster (using some interesting but many more specious arguments) claims that Shakespeare is more easily understood by speakers of German and hence better appreciated by them than by native speakers of English; and he does not omit to point to England's black war record (11); and, not content to state the fact that there were more Shakespeare productions in Germany than in England, he asserts that also the quality of the German productions was superior (12). While quite a few utterances of *Anglisten* during the war may be explained and even excused to some extent, this 1921 address makes one wonder and turn away in sadness. Ruth von Ledebur's book has only just appeared (*Der Mythos vom deutschen Shakespeare: Die Deutsche Shakespeare-Gesellschaft zwischen Politik und Wissenschaft (1918–1945)* [Cologne, Weimar: Böhlau, 2002]), and I have not been able to read it, but I imagine that Förster plays an important part in it for the first phase of the interwar years. For earlier phases of what is often called the German "appropriation" of Shakespeare, see Manfred Pfister's article in *New Comparison* ("Germany is Hamlet: The History of a Political Interpretation," *New Comparison* 2 [1986]: 106–26) and the earlier portions of his second article on the subject ("Hamlet und der Deutsche Geist: Die Geschichte einer politischen Interpretation," *Jahrbuch der Deutschen Shakespeare-Gesellschaft West* [Bochum] [1992]: 13–38).

[93] Carl Grabau, "Zeitschriftenschau," *SJ* 51 (1915): 240–44.

[94] Firchow ("Goethe, Shakespeare," 489, n. 12) also mentions this, but by a small slip gives *Englische Studien* 50 (1916/17): 140–41 as the source. One will seek there in vain; it is really as given in note 96. See also Engler, "Shakespeare in the Trenches," 108.

[95] *SJ* 50 (1914), 107–41 — including in the list of theatres from that in Aachen to that in Zürich, also the Michael-Theater in St. Petersburg (perhaps it was a German-language theatre?) — shows that 24 plays were performed in 1913 in 1133 per-

formances by 190 companies, *A Midsummer Night's Dream* leading with 133 performances by 37 companies, *Cymbeline* trailing at the end with one performance only. *SJ* 51 (1915): 214–17 (much shorter, just giving the statistical tables), shows that, in 1914, 25 plays were given in 983 performances (thus a big drop) by 155 companies, *Twelfth Night* proving the most popular with 129 performances by 33 companies, and *Love's Labours Lost* finding itself at the bottom of the list with just one performance. *SJ* 52 (1916): 159–92 (back to full-scale reviews before the statistical table), shows for 1915 that 21 plays were given in 675 performances by 94 companies — an even more marked drop than in 1914; *The Merchant of Venice* leads the table with 98 performances by 23 companies, and *Measure for Measure* is the least popular, with one performance. *SJ* 53 (1917): 139–87 shows for 1916 that 25 plays were played in 1179 performances (thus: more than in 1913!) by 108 companies, *Hamlet* being the leader this time with 141 performances by 42 companies, and *Coriolanus* the last, with 2 performances by 2 companies; *SJ* 54 (1918): 94–108 shows for 1917 that again 25 plays were given, but in only 990 performances, *As You Like It* leading with 122 performances by 18 companies, *Cymbeline* being the least popular: just one performance; *SJ* 55 (1919): 214–36 for 1918 again shows 25 plays performed by 123 companies in 1035 performances, the lead again being taken by *As You Like It* with 122 performances by 18 companies, while *Cymbeline* again is bottom of the list with one performance only. *SJ* 56 (1920): 137–52 shows that in 1919 there were 23 plays given in 1349 performances by 283 companies, *As You Like It* still outstripping all others with a total of 204 performances by 15 companies, while this time *Pericles* came last with only two performances by one company. In view of these figures, can one really wonder that the German-speaking lovers of Shakespeare were proud of their record? He really had become one of the nation's classics — in the sense that he formed a part and parcel — indeed a mainstay — of its theatrical life. It would be interesting to assemble the statistics for Britain in the same period.

[96] Hans Richter, "Shakespeare im Zeichen des Krieges: Eindrücke aus Wiener Theatern," *SJ* 52 (1916): 159–80.

[97] See also Wilhelm Widmann "Der Engländer im Spiegel der Bühne," in *Der Merkur* 9:4 (15 February 1918), 117–26, which points out that, while England is perfidious, there have always been Englishmen who attacked their compatriots and chid them for their faults — naming above all Shakespeare before concentrating on the subject of *Inkle and Yariko* from the *Spectator*, nr. 11 (March 13, 1711; in the standard edition by Donald F. Bond, 5 vols. [Oxford: Blackwell, 1965], 1:49–51) to very recent theatrical productions. One must add that Widmann is not always well informed, as appears from a comparison of his article with the corresponding entry in Elisabeth Frenzel, *Stoffe der Weltliteratur* (Stuttgart: Kröner, 1962, rev. ed. 1963), 292–94.

[98] Ernst Hardt, "Prolog zu einer Shakespeare-Aufführung [of *Twelfth Night*] im Herbst des Jahres 1914. Gesprochen [by the actor playing Feste] am Stadttheater in Leipzig und anderen Bühnen," *SJ* 2 (1916): 2.

[99] See on this lecture also Engler, "Shakespeare in the Trenches," 107.

[100] Franz Kaibel, "Dichter und Patriotismus: Die Betrachtung eines Deutschen zum dreihundertjährigen Todestag eines Engländers," *SJ* 52 (1916): 36–63.

[101] Brandl, *Zwischen Inn und Themse*, 314–16.

[102] Yet the relationship with Britain was deeply disturbed beyond the war years, not least owing to the continuation of the blockade and the deprivations it caused. See — rather too apologetically — Leo Kober's article "Das Englandbild in der Ersten Republik" in Hietsch, *Österreich und die angelsächsische Welt*, 1:110–24 (esp. 110–11).

Works Cited

Primary Literature / Sources

Abel, Othenio, ed. *Wien: Sein Boden und seine Geschichte*. Vienna: Wolfrum-Verlag, 1924.

Akademie der Wissenschaften, Philosophisch-Historische Klasse. *Sitzungs-berichte* 173 (1914).

——. *Sitzungsberichte* 187 (1919).

Alldeutsches Liederbuch. Leipzig: Breitkopf & Härtel, 1901.

Allen, J. W. *Germany and Europe*. London: G. Bell, 1914.

Angell, Sir Norman. *Prussianism and Its Destruction: With Which Is Reprinted Part II of "The Great Illusion."* London: William Heinemann, 1914.

Anglia: Zeitschrift für englische Philologie. Vols. 28 (1914) through 42 (1918).

Anon. *Einiges über das vornehme England*. Munich: Carl Haushalter, 1902.

Anon. *Luftschiff 13: Ein Zukunftsroman*. Leipzig: A. F. Schloffel, 1908.

Anon. *The English Invasion of Germany*. By a French Staff Officer. London: David Nutt, 1910.

Anon. *Der fliegende Tod*, von einem deutschen Offizier. Wiesbaden: Westdeutsche Verlagsgesellschaft, 1911.

Anon. "Musings Without Method." *Blackwood's Magazine* 196 (July–December 1914): 694–705.

Anon. *Karl Luick zu seinem 70. Geburtstag: Ein Verzeichnis seiner Schriften dargebracht von seinen Freunden, Kollegen und Schülern*. Vienna: Universität, 27 Jänner 1935.

Archer, William. *Fighting a Philosophy*. Oxford Pamphlets 1914–15, 65. Oxford: Oxford UP; London: Humphrey Milford, 1915.

Archiv für das Studium der neueren Sprachen und Literaturen [*Archiv*]. Vols. 48 (1914) through 73 (1919).

Argus [pseud.]. *Die Englander kommen! Der Überfall Hamburgs durch die englische Flotte*. Hamburg: C. H. A. Kloss, 1908.

Arnim, Elizabeth von. *The Pastor's Wife*. 1914. Reprint: London: Virago, 1987.

Bahr, Hermann. "Englisches Gespräch." *Die Neue Rundschau* 22 (1911): 845–49.

———. "Österreich." In *Die Tat: Eine Monatsschrift*, edited by Eugen Diederichs and Karl Hoffmann [Jena]. Vol. 6 (1914–1915): 584–90.

Barker, Ernest. . *Nietzsche and Treitschke: The Worship of Power in Modern Germany.* Oxford Pamphlets 1914, 20. Oxford: Oxford UP; London: Humphrey Milford, 1914.

Bausenwein, Josef, and Otto Schnellenberger. *Grundzüge britischer Kultur.* Vol. 1., *Imperialismus: Das Britische Grundproblem: Englands weltpolitische "Sendung,"' beleuchtet durch sein Schrifttum aus drei Jahrhunderten.* Bamberg: C. C. Buchner, 1930.

Bausenwein, Josef, and Friedrich Henner. *Grundzüge britischer Kultur.* Vol. 2., *Die soziale Frage in der neueren englischen Literatur.* Bamberg: C. C. Buchner, 1931.

Bechtel, Adolf. "Die englische Verwaltung Ostindiens und die Ausplünderung der eingeborenen Bevölkerung im 18. Jahrhundert." *Zeitschrift für das Realschulwesen* 42 (1917): 641–48.

Bennett, Arnold. *Liberty: A Statement of the British Case.* London: Hodder and Stoughton, 1914.

Bentley, E. C. "The German State of Mind." *Fortnightly Review* 97 (1915): 42–53.

Beowulf [pseud.]. *Der deutsch-englische Krieg: Visionen eines Seefahrers.* Berlin: H. Walther, 1906.

Bernhardi, Friedrich von. *Videant consules, ne quid res publica detrimenti capiat.* Kassel: n.p., 1890.

———. *Cavalry in Future Wars.* Translated by C. S. Goldman. London: John Murray, 1906.

———. *Deutschland und der nächste Krieg.* Stuttgart and Berlin: J. G. Cotta'sche Buchhandlung Nachfolger, 1912. In English, *Germany and the Next War.* Translated by Allen H. Powles. London: Edward Arnold, 1914.

———. *Unsere Zukunft: Ein Mahnwort an das deutsche Volk.* Stuttgart-Berlin, 1913. In English, *Britain as Germany's Vassal.* Translated by J. Ellis Barker. Bream Buildings, [London] E.C.: Wm. Dawson & Sons, 1914.

———. *Eine Weltreise 1911/1912 und der Zusammenbruch Deutschlands.* Leipzig: S. Hirzel, 1920.

Bernstorff, Hans Nikolaus Ernst. *Unsere blauen Jungen.* Berlin: W. Paulis Nachfolger, 1899.

———. *Deutschlands Flotte im Kampf.* Minden: W. Kohler, 1909.

———. *Ran an den Feind!* Leipzig: Amelings Verlag, 1913.

Blaicher, Gunther. "Zur Entstehung und Verbreitung nationaler Stereotypen in und über England." *Deutsche Vierteljahrsschrift fur Literaturwissenschaft und Geistesgeschichte* 51, no. 4 (1977): 549–74.

Bleibtreu, Karl. *Geschichte der englischen Litteratur in der Renaissance und Klassicität.* Leipzig: Wilhelm Friedrich, 1887.

———. *Bur und Lord.* Heilbronn: Eugen Salzer, 1900.

———. *Der Militarismus im 19. Jahrhundert.* Berlin: Verlag Aufklärung, 1901.

———. *Die "Offensiv-Invasion" gegen England.* Berlin: Verlag von Schall und Rentel, 1908.

———. *Deutschland und England.* Berlin: Carl Curtius, 1909.

———. *Weltbrand.* Berlin: Schwetschke & Sohn, 1912.

———. "Die englische Flotte." *Hochland* 12, no. 2 (November 1914): 129–41.

"Blond Beast," A. "Nietzsche." *English Review* 18 (August–November1914): 392–96.

Bohme, Klaus, ed. *Aufrufe und Reden deutscher Professoren im Ersten Weltkrieg.* Stuttgart: Reclam, 1975.

Borbein, Hans. *Auslandsstudien und neusprachlicher Unterricht im Lichte des Weltkriegs.* Leipzig: Quelle & Meyer, 1917.

Brandl, Alois. "Englische Philologie." In *Die deutschen Universitäten: Für die Universitätsausstellung in Chicago 1893,* edited by Wilhelm Lexis, 482–96. Berlin: Asher, 1893.

———. "Der englische Kriegsminister und die deutschen Universitäten." *InternationaleMonatsschrift für Wissenschaft und Kunst* 6:3 (December 1911): 259–60.

———. "Deutsche Charakterköpfe in englischer Beleuchtung." *Deutsche Rundschau* 158 (January–March 1914): 358–68.

———. *Byron im Kampf mit der englischen Politik und die englische Kriegslyrik von heute.* Lecture given on February 12, 1915. Berlin: Carl Heymans Verlag, 1915.

———. "England und Österreich-Ungarn." *Österreichische Rundschau* 42 (January–March 1915): 193–99.

———. "Rudolf Fischer (December 31, 1860–December 13, 1923)." *Jahrbuch der Deutschen Shakespeare-Gesellschaft* 60 (1924): 162–65.

———. *Zwischen Inn und Themse: Lebensbeobachtungen eines Anglisten — Alt-Tirol/England/Berlin.* Berlin: G. Grote'sche Verlagsbuchhandlung, 1936.

Brie, Friedrich. "Imperialistische Strömungen in der englischen Literatur." *Anglia* 40 (1916): 1–200.

Brooke, Rupert. *The Poetical Works.* London: Faber & Faber, 1950.

Bruchhausen, Karl von. *Der kommende Krieg: Eine Studie uber die militarische Lage Deutschlands.* Berlin: Pan-Verlag, 1906.

Brunner, Karl. *Großbritannien: Land — Volk — Staat.* Bielefeld, Leipzig: Velhagen & Klasing, 1929.

Bundschuh. *Die Revolution von 1912.* Leipzig: Friedrich Rothbarth, 1907.

Butler, Sir W. F. *The Invasion of England: Told Twenty Years After by an Old Soldier.* London: Sampson Low, 1882.

Cairns, D. S. *An Answer to Bernhardi.* Papers for War Time, 12. London: Humphrey Milford, Oxford UP, 1914.

Campbell, Harry. *The Biological Aspects of Warfare.* London: Baillière, 1918.

Casement, Sir Roger. *Gesammelte Schriften: Irland, Deutschland und die Freiheit der Meere, und andere Aufsätze.* Diessen nr. Munich: J. H. Huber, 1916.

Chapple, W. A. "German Culture." *Contemporary Review* 107 (1915): 355–60.

Chesney, George Tomkyns. *The Battle of Dorking.* Edinburgh: Blackwood & Sons, 1871. In German, "Die Schlacht bei Dorking," *Grenzboten* 30 (1871): 870–79; 910–24; 936–47.

Chesney, Sir George Tomkyns. *Englands Ende in der Schlacht bei Dorking. Erinnerungen eines alten Britten im nächsten Jahrhundert. Eine Studie* [by G. T. Chesney], aus dem Englischen übertragen vom Verfasser des Ethiopien [W. Huebbe-Schleiden]. Hamburg, 1879.

———. "The Battle of Dorking: Reminiscences of a Volunteer." In *The Tale of the Next Great War, 1871–1914: Fictions of Future Warfare and Battles Still-To-Come,* edited by I. F. Clarke, 27–73. Liverpool: Liverpool UP, 1995.

Chesterton, Cecil Edward. *The Prussian Hath Said in His Heart.* London: Chapman & Hall, 1914.

Chesterton, G. K. *The Crimes of England.* London: Palmer & Hayward, 1915.

Childers, Erskine. *The Riddle of the Sands.* London: Smith & Elder, 1903.

Clutton-Brock, A. *Bernhardism in England.* Papers for War Time, 26. London: Humphrey Milford, Oxford UP, 1915.

Cole, Robert William. *The Struggle for Empire: A Story of the Year 2236.* London: Eliot Stock, 1900.

———. *The Death Trap.* London: Greening, 1907.

Colles, W. Morris, and A. D. McLaren. "The War of Ideas." *Nineteenth Century* 86 (1919): 1114–24.

Colomb, Rear-Admiral P., Colonel J. F. Maurice, R. A., Captain F. N. Maude, Archibald Forbes, Charles Lowe, D. Christie Murray, and F. Scudamore. *The Great War of 189–: A Forecast*. With illustrations from sketches specially made for "Black and White" by F. Villiers. London: Heinemann, 1892.

Cramb, J. A. *Germany and England*. London: John Murray, 1914.

Crichton-Browne, James. *Bernhardi and Creation: A New Theory of Evolution*. Glasgow: James Maclehose & Sons, 1916.

Darwin, Charles. *The Descent of Man, and Selection in Relation to Sex*. 2nd ed. 2 vols. London: Murray, 1877.

Dehmel, Richard. "An meine Kinder." *Berliner Tageblatt*, October 9, 1914.

Delbrück, Hans. "Zukunftskrieg und Zukunftsfriede." *Preußische Jahrbücher* 96, no. 11 (May 1899): 228–29.

———. "Deutschland in der Weltpolitik: Der Krieg." *Preußische Jahrbücher* 116 (April–June 1904): 375–83.

———. "Regierung und Sozialdemokratie; Innere Politik: Deutschland und England." *Preußische Jahrbücher* 119 (January–March 1905): 183–91.

———. "Weshalb baut Deutschland Kriegsschiffe? Beantwortung der Frage eines Engländers." *Preußische Jahrbücher* 138 (October–December 1909): 149–61.

Dibelius, Wilhelm. "England und Wir." Lecture, given on October 2, 1914. Hamburg: Friedrichsen, 1914.

———. *England*. 2 vols. Stuttgart, Leipzig, and Berlin: Deutsche Verlags-Anstalt, 1922.

Diederich, Benno. "Ernst Lissauer, ein Lyriker unserer Zeit." *Preußische Jahrbücher* 157 (July–September 1914): 193–224.

Dietz, Carl. "Deutsche Kultur im Spiegel englischer Urteile." *Preußische Jahrbücher* 160 (April–June 1915): 100–124.

Doyle, Sir Arthur Conan. *The German War*. London: Hodder & Stoughton, 1914.

———. "Danger." *Strand Magazine*, July 1914. In German, *Der Tauchbootkrieg: Wie Kapitän Sirius England niederzwang*. Translated by Sta. Schanzer. Stuttgart: R. Lutz, c.1914.

———. *Danger and Other Stories*. London: John Murray, 1918.

Eichler, Albert. "Der Krieg und die Anglistik." Bogen 10 zu Nr. 325 der *Grazer Tagespost*, December 6, 1914. [Expanded in *Zeitschrift für das Realschulwesen* 40 (1914): 193–201].

———. "Hamlet am Grazer Stadttheater." *Jahrbuch der deutschen Shakespeare-Gesellschaft* 42 (1916): 187–88.

———. Review of Erwin Rosen, *England: Ein Britenspiegel*. In *Beiblatt zur Anglia: Mitteilungen über englische Sprache und Literatur und über englischen Unterricht* 28 (1917): 171–76.

———. "Irlands Stellung in der inneren und äußeren Politik Großbritanniens in Vergangenheit und Gegenwart." *Zeitschrift für das Realschulwesen* 42 (1917): 449–64.

———. *Der Gentleman: Wesen — Wachsen — Verwesen*. Graz: Steirische Verlagsanstalt, 1943.

Eisenhart, Karl. *Die Abrechnung mit England*. Munich: J. F. Lehmann, 1900.

Ellis, Havelock. *Essays in War-Time: Further Studies in the Task of Social Hygiene*. London, 1917. Reprint, Freeport, NY: Books for Libraries Press, 1969.

Elwell-Sutton, A. S. *Humanity vs. Un-Humanity: A Criticism of the German Idea in Its Political and Philosophical Development*. London: Unwin, 1916.

Englische Studien [ES]. Vols. 47 (1913–14) through 58 (1924).

Erdmann, Gustav Adolf. *Wehrlos zur See: Eine Flottenphantasie an der Jahrhundertwende*. N.p., 1900.

———. *Zwei Grundfragen der deutschen Flottenpolitik*. Oldenburg: Gerhard Stalling, 1910.

Escott, T. H. S. "German Culture in the Crucible." *British Review* 9 (1915): 321–43.

Excubitor. "Sea and Air Command: Germany's New Policy." *The Fortnightly Review*, new series, 1007 (May 1, 1913): 869–89.

Flew, R. Newton. "Kant and Modern Prussianism." *London Quarterly Review* 13 (1917): 264–68.

Forster, E. M. Recollections of Nassenheide." *The Listener*, January 1, 1959: 12–14.

———. *Howards End*. 1910; reprint, Harmondsworth, UK: Penguin, 1986.

Förster, Max. "Shakespeare und Deutschland." *Jahrbuch der deutschen Shakespeare-Gesellschaft* 57 (1921): 7–27.

Friedwanger, M. "Jakob Schipper †." Obituary. *Die neueren Sprachen* 23 (1915–16): 65–69.

Frobenius, Leo. *Die Zukunft Englands: Eine kulturpolitische Studie*. Minden: J. C. C. Bruns, 1900.

General Staff [pseud.]. *Mene, mene tekel upharsin! Überwältigung durch Deutschland: Von einem Generalstabsoffizier; Autorisierte Übersetzung von einem deutschen Stabsoffizier*. Hanover: A. Sponholtz, 1906.

Germanisch-Romanische Monatsschrift. Vols. 6 (1914) through 8 (1920). [Vol. 7 covers 1915–1919].

Glaser, Friedrich. "Season in London." *Die Neue Rundschau* 23 (1912, 2): 1039–40.

Grabau, Carl. "Zeitschriftenschau." *Jahrbuch der Shakespearegesellschaft* 51 (1915): 240–44.

Graves, Robert. *Good-bye to All That: An Autobiography.* London: Jonathan Cape, 1929; Harmondsworth, UK: Penguin, 1982.

Graz University. *Verzeichnis der Vorlesungen an der kais. kön. Karl-Franzens-Universität zu Graz für das Sommer-Semester 1916.* Graz: Verlag des Akademischen Senats, 1916.

Groeper, Richard. "Nietzsche und der Krieg." *Die Tat* 8/1 (April 1916): 25–38.

Gruber, Max von. *Krieg, Frieden und Biologie.* [no pub.] 1915.

Haeckel, Ernst. *Generelle Morphologie der Organismen.* Berlin: Reimer, 1866.

Hansa [pseudo. Otto Hoepner, Kapt. A.D.] *Hamburg und Bremen in Gefahr!* Altona: J. Harder, 1906.

Hansen, Wilhelm. *Die vierte Waffe: Zukunfts-Roman.* Leipzig: Dieterich'sche Verlagsbuchhandlung, 1913.

Hardy, Thomas. Letter to the editor. *Manchester Guardian,* October 9, 1914.

———. Letter to the editor. *Manchester Guardian,* October 13, 1914.

Harrison, Austin. *England and Germany.* London: Macmillan, 1907.

Hartmann, Eduard von. *Wahrheit und Irrthum im Darwinismus: Eine kritische Darstellung der organischen Entwickelungstheorie.* Berlin, Leipzig: Duncker, 1875.

Hauptmann, Gerhart. "Deutschland und Shakespeare." *Jahrbuch der deutschen Shakespeare-Gesellschaft* 51 (1915): 7–12.

Hawke, Napier. *The Invasion That Did Not Come Off.* London: Henry J. Drane, 1909.

Hessen, Robert. "Fortschritt und Sport." *Die Neue Rundschau* 24 (1913, 2): 1308–13.

Hirschfeld, Magnus. *Warum hassen uns die Völker? Eine kriegspsychologische Betrachtung.* Bonn: Marcus & Webers, 1915.

Hobhouse, L. T. *Morals in Evolution.* [n.p.] Chapman & Hall, 1906.

Hoppenstedt, Julius. *Die Schlacht der Zukunft.* Berlin: E. S. Mittler & Sohn, 1907.

———. *Ein Neues Wörth: Ein Schlachtenbild der Zukunft*. Berlin: E. S. Mittler & Sohn, 1909.

———. *Deutschlands Heer in der Entscheidungsschlacht*. Berlin: E. S. Mittler & Sohn, 1913.

———. *Die Millionenschlacht an der Saar: Ein Beispiel moderner Kriegskunst*. Berlin: E. S. Mittler & Sohn, 1913.

Hueffer, Ford Madox. "High Germany — 1: How It Feels to Be Members of Subject Races." *The Saturday Review* 112 (September 30, 1911): 421–22; "High Germany — 2: Utopia." *The Saturday Review* 112 (October 7, 1911): 454–56.

———. *Between St Dennis and St George*. London: Hodder & Stoughton, 1915.

Hügel, Friedrich von. *The German Soul*. London, Paris: Dent, 1916.

Humboldt, Wilhelm von. *Ideen zu einem Versuch, die Grenzen der Wirksamkeit des Staates zu bestimmen*. Edited by E. Cauer. Breslau: E. Trewendt, 1851.

Hunt, Violet, and Ford Madox Hueffer. *Zeppelin Nights*. London: John Lane, 1916.

Huxley, Thomas E. *Soziale Essays: Deutsch mit Einleitung*. Translated by Alexander and Lotte Tille. Weimar: Felber, 1897.

Innsbruck University. *Vorlese-Ordnung an der K. K. Leopold-Franzens-Universität zu Innsbruck im Sommer-Semester 1916*. Innsbruck: Verlag des Akademischen Senats, 1916.

Jahrbuch der Deutschen Shakespeare-Gesellschaft [SJ]. Vols. 50 (1914) through 57 (1921).

James, William. *The Varieties of Religious Experience*. 1902. Reprint, London: Longmans, Green, 1912.

———. *The Moral Equivalent of War* [1906]. See: http://www.constitution.org/wj/meow.htm.

Jedina-Palombini, Leopold von. "Der Krieg und die Engländer." *Österreichische Rundschau* 42 (January–March 1915): 1–10.

Jerome, Jerome K. *Three Men on the Bummel*. Harmondsworth, UK: Penguin, 1983.

Joël, Karl. *Neue Weltkultur*. Leipzig: Wolff, 1915.

Jones, Dora M. "Nietzsche, Germany, and the War." *London Quarterly Review* 245 (January 1915): 80–94.

Kaibel, Franz. "Dichter und Patriotismus: Die Betrachtung eines Deutschen zum dreihundertjährigen Todestag eines Engländers." *Jahrbuch der deutschen Shakespeare-Gesellschaft* 52 (1916): 36–63.

Kaiser Wilhelm II. *Ereignisse und Gestalten aus den Jahren 1878–1918.* Leipzig & Berlin: K. F. Koehler, 1922.

Kantorowicz, Hermann. *The Spirit of British Policy and the Myth of the Encirclement of Germany.* Translated by W. H. Johnston. London: Allen & Unwin, 1931. [German original: *Der Geist der englischen Politik und der Mythos der Einkreisung Deutschlands.* Berlin: Rowohlt, 1929].

Karpf, Fritz. "Die k. und k. feldbücherei." *Die Neueren Sprachen* 24 (1916–17): 623–24.

———. "Die neueren sprachen nach dem krieg." *Die Neueren Sprachen* 24 (1916–17): 385–93.

———. "Zur Methodik des englischen Unterrichts." Review of *Praktische Methode des Unterrichts in der englischen Sprache,* by E. Nader. *Zeitschrift für das Realschulwesen* 42 (1917): 518–27.

Kellermann, Hermann. *Der Krieg der Geister.* Weimar: A. Duncker, 1915.

Kellner, Anna. *Leon Kellner: Sein Leben und sein Werk.* Vienna: Carl Gerold's Sohn, 1936.

Kessler, Harry, Graf. *Tagebücher, 1918–1937.* Edited by Wolfgang Pfeiffer-Belli. Frankfurt am Main: Insel, 1961.

Kipling, Arthur Wellesley. *The Shadow of Glory, Being a History of the Great War of 1910–1911.* London: Alston Rivers, 1910.

Koziol, Herbert. *Friedrich Wild.* Obituary. Sonderdruck aus dem *Almanach* der Österreichischen Akademie der Wissenschaften 116 (1966). Vienna: Adolf Holzhausen, 1967.

Kraus, Karl. *Die letzten Tage der Menschheit.* 1915–1919. Reprint, Vienna: Verlag "Die Fackel," 1922.

———. *Die letzten Tage der Menschheit.* 1915–1919. Reprinted in 2 vols. after the 1926 ed., Munich: dtv, 1957.

Kretzmann, Edwin M. J. "German Technological Utopias of the Pre-War Period." *Annals of Science 3* (vol. 4, 1938): 417–30.

Landauer, Georg. *England: Eine Voruntersuchung.* Vienna: Manz'sche k. u. k. Hof-, Verlags- und Universitätsbuchhandlung, 1915.

———. *Der Verrat des Freundes: Gott strafe England; Die Wacht am Rhein.* Vienna: Manz'sche Buchhandlung, 1916.

Langbehn, Julius. *Rembrandt als Erzieher: Von einem Deutschen.* 1893. Reprint, Weimar: Duncker, 1922.

Lasswell, Harold D. *Propaganda Technique in the World War.* London: Kegan Paul; New York: Knopf, 1923.

Laßwitz, Kurd. *Auf zwei Planeten.* Edited by Rudi Schweikert. 1897. Reprint, Munich: Wilhelm Heyne, 1998.

———. "Über Zukunftsträume." 1899. In Kurd Laßwitz, *Homchen und andere Erzählungen*, 450–70.

———. *Homchen und andere Erzählungen*. Heyne Science Fiction Classics 4309. Munich: Heyne, 1986.

———. *Auf zwei Planeten*. Revidierte, ungekürzte Jubiläumsausgabe. Edited by Rudi Schweikert. Munich: Heyne, 1998. In English, *Two Planets*, abridged by Erich Laßwitz and translated by Hans Rudnick. Carbondale, ILL: Southern Illinois UP, 1971.

Lawrence, D. H. *The Cambridge Edition of the Letters and Works of D. H. Lawrence*. Edited by James T. Boulton et al. Cambridge: Cambridge UP, various dates.

———. *The Prussian Officer and Other Stories*. Edited by John Worthen. In *The Cambridge Edition*. Cambridge: Cambridge UP, 1983.

———. *Mr Noon*. Edited by Lindeth Vasey. In *The Cambridge Edition*. Cambridge: Cambridge UP, 1984.

———. *Mr Noon*. London: Grafton Books, 1986.

———. *The Mortal Coil and Other Stories*. Harmondsworth, UK: Penguin, 1988.

———. *England, my England and Other Stories*. Edited by Bruce Steele. In *The Cambridge Edition*.

———. *Twilight in Italy and Other Essays*. Edited by Paul Eggert. In *The Cambridge Edition*.

Le Queux, William. *The Great War in England in 1897*. London: Tower Publishing, 1894.

———. *England's Peril*. London: F. V. White, 1899.

———. *The Invasion of 1910*. London: Eveleigh Nash, 1906. In German, *Die Invasion von 1910*. Translated by Traugott Tamm. Berlin: Concordia Deutsche Verlags-Anstalt, 1906.

———. *Spies of the Kaiser: Plotting the Downfall of England*. London: Hurst & Blackett, 1909. Reprint, London: Frank Cass, 1996.

Lehmann-Russbuldt, O. *Die Schöpfung der Vereinigten Staaten von Europa: Eine Luftphantasie von 1910*. Berlin: Neues Vaterland, 1914.

Leighton, Sir Baldwyn. *The Lull before Dorking*. London: R. Bentley & Son, 1871.

Lenschau, Thomas, ed. *England in deutscher Beleuchtung*. Halle: Gebauer-Schwetschke, 1906.

Levy, Oscar, ed. "The Nietzsche Movement in England (A Retrospect — A Confession — A Prospect)." In Levy, *The Complete Works of Friedrich Nietzsche*, 18:ix–xxxvi.

———. "Nietzsche im Krieg: Eine Erinnerung und eine Warnung." *Die weissen Blätter* 6 (1919): 277–84.

———. "Thomas Hardy and Friedrich Nietzsche." *New Outlook* 61 (1928): 217–18.

Lichnowsky, Karl Max, Prince. *My Mission to London, 1912–1914.* London: Heinemann, 1918.

Loewi, Otto. *Unsere Stimmung gegen England und ihre Bedeutung für später.* Lecture given on 19 June 1915 in Graz. Graz and Leipzig: Leuschner & Lobensky's k. k. Universitätsbuchhandlung, 1915.

Ludwig, Emil. *The Germans.* Translated by Heinz and Ruth Norden. London: Hamish Hamilton, 1942.

MacClure, Canon E. *Germany's War-Inspirers: Nietzsche and Treitschke.* London: Society for Promoting Christian Knowledge, 1914.

Mann, Thomas. "Gedanken im Kriege." *Die neue Rundschau* 25 (1914): 1471–84. Reprinted in Thomas Mann, *Gesammelte Werke,* 13 vols., 13: 527–45. Frankfurt am Main: Fischer, 1974.

———. *Friedrich und die Große Koalition.* Berlin: S. Fischer, 1915.

———. "German Letter." *The Dial,* 74 (January–June 1923): 609–14.

———. *Thomas Mann an Ernst Bertram: Briefe aus den Jahren 1910–1955.* Edited by Inge Jens. Pfullingen: Neske, 1960.

Mansfield, Katherine. *In a German Pension.* Harmondsworth, UK: Penguin, 1985.

Marshall, Beatrice. Letter to the editor. *Daily News,* October 12, 1914.

Martin, Rudolf. *Stehen wir vor einem Weltkrieg?* Leipzig: F. Engelmann, 1900.

———. *Berlin-Bagdad: Das deutsche Weltreich im Zeitalter der Luftschiffahrt, 1910–1931.* Stuttgart and Leipzig: Deutsche Verlags-Anstalt, 1907.

———. *Kaiser Wilhelm II und König Eduard VII.* Berlin: Verlag Dr. Wedekind, 1907.

———. *Das Zeitalter der Motorluftschiffahrt.* Leipzig: Theod. Thomas, 1907.

———. *Deutschland und England: Ein offenes Wort an den Kaiser.* Hanover: A. Sponholtz, 1908.

———. *Luftpiraten und andere Fluggeschichten.* Berlin: Wertheim, 1910.

Maurier, Guy du. *An Englishman's Home: A Play; By a Patriot.* London: Edward Arnold, 1909.

Maurus [pseud.]. *Ave Caesar! Deutsche Luftschiffe im Kampfe um Marokko.* Leipzig: Dieterich'sche Verlagsbuchhandlung, 1909.

McClellan, C. M. S. Letter to the editor. *Daily Chronicle,* October 8, 1914.

Meinecke, Friedrich. *Erlebtes, 1862–1919.* Stuttgart: Verlag, 1964.

Members of the Oxford Faculty of Modern History. *Why We Are at War: Great Britain's Case.* Oxford: Clarendon Press, 1914.

Meyer, Eduard. *Private Papers.* Berlin-Brandenburgische Akademie der Wissenschaften [formerly Preussische Akademie der Wissenschaften]. Nachlass Eduard Meyer, 955.

Meyer, Kuno. *Private Papers.* Liverpool University Archives.

———. *Private Papers.* Staatsbibliothek Berlin. Nachlass Kuno Meyer, 214.

Mitchell, Peter Chalmers. *Evolution and the War.* London: Murray, 1915.

More, Paul. "Lust of Empire — The Responsibility for the Present War — Nietzsche and Bernhardi." *Nation* [New York] 99 (1914): 493–95.

Moritorus [pseud.]. *Mit deutschen Waffen über Paris nach London: Eine sachliche Antwort auf Seestern, Hansa, Beowulf.* Hanau: Claus & Federsen, 1906.

Muirhead, J. H. *German Philosophy and the War.* Oxford Pamphlets 1914–1915, 62. Oxford: Oxford UP; London: Humphrey Milford, 1915, 19–26.

———. *German Philosophy in Relation to the War.* London: Murray, 1915.

Munch, Paul Georg. *Hindenburgs Einmarsch in London: Von einem deutschen Dichter.* Leipzig: Grethlein, 1915.

Munro, H. H. *When William Came.* 1913. In *The Complete Stories of Saki.* Ware: Wordsworth Editions, 1993.

Munro, Robert. *From Darwinism to Kaiserism: Being a Review of the Origin, Effects, and Collapse of Germany's Attempt at World-Dominion by Methods of Barbarism.* Glasgow: J. Maclehose & Sons, 1919.

Murray, Gilbert. "German 'Kultur' — III: German Scholarship." *Quarterly Review* 223 (April 1915).

Neueren Sprachen, Die. Vols. 21 (1913–14) through 27 (1920).

Neuphilologenverband. *Bericht über die Verhandlungen der XVI. Tagung des Allgemeinen Deutschen Neuphilologenverbandes (ADNV) Bremen, 1–4 Juni 1914.* Heidelberg: Carl Winter, 1915.

Nicolai, G. F. *Die Biologie des Krieges.* Zurich: Füssli, 1917.

Niemann, August. *Der Weltkrieg — Deutsche Träume.* Berlin and Leipzig: W. Vobach, 1904.

Nietzsche, Friedrich. *The Works of Friedrich Nietzsche.* Edited by Alexander Tille. 4 vols. London: T. Fisher Unwin, 1899–1903.

———. *The Collected Works of Friedrich Nietzsche.* Edited by Alexander Tille. 11 vols. London: H. Henry & Co.; New York: Macmillan, 1896–1909.

————. *The Complete Works of Friedrich Nietzsche*. Edited by Oscar Levy. 18 vols. Edinburgh and London: T. N. Foulis, 1909–13.

————. *Nietzsche-Worte: Weggenossen in grosser Zeit*. Edited by Hermann Itschner. Leipzig: Kröner, 1915.

————. *Werke: Kritische Gesamtausgabe* [*KGW*]. Edited by Giorgio Colli, Mazzino Montinari and others. Berlin and New York: de Gruyter, 1967–.

————. *Briefwechsel: Kritische Gesamtausgabe*. Edited by Giorgio Colli, Mazzino Montinari and others. Berlin and New York, 1975–.

————. *Sämtliche Werke: Kritische Studienausgabe in 15 Bänden*. Edited by Giorgio Colli und Mazzino Montinari. Munich: Deutscher Taschenbuch Verlag; Berlin: Mouton de Gruyter, 1980.

————. "An die deutschen Esel." In *Friedrich Nietzsche, Sämtliche Werke: Kritische Studienausgabe*, vol. 9.

————. *Die fröhliche Wissenschaft*. In *Friedrich Nietzsche, Sämtliche Werke: Kritische Studienausgabe*, vol. 3.

————. *On the Genealogy of Morals*. Translated by Douglas Smith. Oxford: Oxford UP, 1996.

Offin, T. W. *How the Germans Took London: Forewarned, Forearmed*. Chelmsford, UK: Durrant, 1900.

Parabellum [Pseudo. Grautoff, F. H.]. *Banzai!* Leipzig: Dieterich'sche Verlagsbuchhandlung, 1908.

Peddie, James Anderson. *Capture of London*. London: General Publishing, 1887.

Peetz, Alexander von. *England und der Kontinent*. Vienna and Leipzig: Carl Fromme, 1909.

Pemberton, Sir Max. *Pro Patria*. London: Ward Lock, 1901.

Powys, John Cowper. *The War and Culture*. New York: G. Arnold Shaw, 1914. Reprint, London: Village Press, 1975.

————. *The Menace of German Culture*. London: William Rider & Son, 1915.

Rádl, Emanuel. *The History of Biological Theories*. London: Humphrey Milford, 1930.

Raleigh, Sir Walter. *The War of Ideas*. Oxford: Oxford UP, 1917.

Rausch, Karl. *Die angelsächsische Verschwörung: Eine zeitgeschichtliche Untersuchung*. Vienna: Manzsche k. u. k. Hof-, Verlags- und Universitäts-buchhandlung, 1917.

Richards, Alfred Bate. *The Invasion of England*. Privately printed in August 1870.

Richter, Hans. "Shakespeare im Zeichen des Krieges: Eindrücke aus Wiener Theatern." *Jahrbuch der deutschen Shakespeare-Gesellschaft* 52 (1916): 159–80.

Riezler, Kurt. *Tagebücher, Aufsätze, Dokumente.* Edited by Karl Dietrich Erdmann. Göttingen: Vandenhoeck und Ruprecht, 1972.

Rilke, Rainer Maria. *Sämtliche Werke.* Vol. 2: *Gedichte: Zweiter Teil.* Wiesbaden: Insel, 1957.

Roeder, Fritz, ed. *Englischer Kulturunterricht: Leitgedanken für seine Gestaltung; Vorträge, gehalten auf der Göttinger Tagung der Lehrer und Lehrerinnen des Englischen an Höheren und Mittelschulen vom 2.–4. Juli 1923.* 2nd ed. Berlin: Teubner, 1925.

Rolffs, Ernst. "Treitschke, Nietzsche, Bernhardi." *Die christliche Welt* 30 (1916): 857–65, 882–88.

Rosen, Erwin [Pseud. Erwin Carlé]. *England: Ein Britenspiegel: Schlaglichter aus der Kriegs-, Kultur- und Sittengeschichte.* Stuttgart: Robert Lutz, 1916.

Rosenkranz, Albert E. *Geschichte der Deutschen Evangelischen Gemeinde zu Liverpool.* Stuttgart: Ausland und Heimat, 1921.

Ruedorffer, J. J. [Pseud. Kurt Riezler]. *Grundzüge der Weltpolitik in der Gegenwart.* Stuttgart and Berlin: Deutsche Verlagsanstalt, 1914.

Saenger, S. "Das englische Vorbild." *Die Neue Rundschau* 19, no. 8 (August 1908): 1228–36.

Saki [Pseud. Munro, H. H.]. *When William Came: A Story of London under the Hohenzollerns.* London: John Lane, 1914.

Salomon, Felix. *Der britische Imperialismus: Ein geschichtlicher Überblick über den Werdegang des britischen Reiches vom Mittelalter bis zur Gegenwart.* Leipzig, Berlin: Teubner, 1916.

Sarolea, Charles. *The Anglo-German Problem.* London and Edinburgh: Thomas Nelson, 1912.

Sarrazin, Gregor. "Der Imperialismus in der neueren englischen Literatur." *Internationale Monatsschrift für Wissenschaft und Technik* 9 (June 1915): 11.

Scheler, Max. *Ressentiment im Aufbau der Moralen.* 1914. In *Gesammelte Werke*, vol. 3.

———. *Der Genius des Krieges und der Deutsche Krieg.* 1915. In *Gesammelte Werke*, vol. 4.

———. *Gesammelte Werke.* 15 vols. Berne: Francke, 1954–97.

Schiller, Friedrich. *Über die ästhetische Erziehung des Menschen.* 1795. Reprint, Stuttgart: Reclam, 1965.

Schippel, Max. *England und Wir: Kriegsbetrachtungen eines Sozialisten.* Berlin: Fischer, 1917.

Schröer, M. M. Arnold. *Zur Charakterisierung der Engländer.* Bonn: A Marcus & E. Webers Verlag, 1915.

Schücking, Levin L. *Der englische Volkscharakter.* Booklet no. 53 of *Der Deutsche Krieg: Politische Flugschriften.* Edited by Ernst Jäckh. Stuttgart, Berlin: Deutsche Verlags-Anstalt, 1915.

Searchlight [Pseud. Rear-Admiral Arthur Parry Eardley-Wilmot]. *The Battle of the North Sea in 1914.* London: Hugh Rees, 1912.

Seeliger, Ewald Gerhard. *Englands Feind: Der Herr der Luft.* Wiesbaden: Westdeutsche Verlagsgesellschaft, 1910.

Seestern [Pseud. Ferdinand Grautoff]. *"1906" — Der Zusammenbruch der alten Welt.* Leipzig: Dieterich'sche Verlagsbuchhandlung, 1906. In English, *Armageddon 190–.* Translated by G. Herring. London: Kegan Paul, Trench, Trubner, 1907.

Sombart, Werner. *Händler und Helden: Patriotische Besinnungen.* Munich, Leipzig: Duncker & Humblot, 1915.

Sommerfeld, Adolf. *Frankreichs Ende im Jahre 19??: Ein Zukunftsbild.* Berlin: Continent, 1912. In English, *How Germany Crushed France (the Story of the Greatest Conspiracy in History).* London: Everett, 1914.

Spies, Heinrich. *Das moderne England: Einführung in das Studium seiner Kultur; Mit besonderem Hinblick auf einen Aufenthalt im Lande.* Strassburg: Trübner, 1911.

————. *Deutschlands Feind: England und die Vorgeschichte des Weltkriegs.* Berlin: Carl Heymanns Verlag, 1915.

Spottiswoode, Sybil. *Marcia in Germany: An Indiscrete Chronicle.* London: Heinemann, 1908.

————. *Hedwig in England.* London: Heinemann, 1909.

————. *Her Husband's Country.* London: Heinemann, 1911.

Sternheim, Carl. *Carl Sternheim: Gesammelte Werke.* Edited by Wilhelm Emrich and Manfred Linke. 10 vols. Neuwied and Darmstadt: Luchterhand, 1963–76.

————. *Carl Sternheim: Briefe.* Edited by Wolfgang Wendler. 2 vols. Darmstadt: Luchterhand, 1988.

Stevenson, P. L. *How the Jubilee Fleet Escaped Destruction, and the Battle of Ushant.* London: Simpkin & Marshall, 1899.

Stewart, Herbert Leslie. *Nietzsche and the Ideals of Modern Germany.* London: Edward Arnold, 1915.

Straß, Rudolf. *Seine englische Frau.* Stuttgart and Berlin: J. Cotta'sche Buchhandlung, 1913.

Suttner, Bertha von. *Die Waffen nieder!* Dresden: E. Pierson, 1889.

The Times, August 27, 1900; August 20, 1914; August 29, 1914; September 1, 1914; September 2, 1914; September 10, 1914; September 13, 1914.

The Times Literary Supplement, August 13, 1914.

Thirlmere, Roland. *The Clash of Empires.* London: Heinemann, 1907. In German, *Der Zusammenprall der Weltmächte.* Berlin: Verlag von Karl Curtius, 1907.

Tille, Alexander. *Die deutschen Volkslieder vom Doktor Faust.* Halle: Niemeyer, 1890. Reprint, Wiesbaden: Sändig, 1969 and 1984.

——. "German Christmas and the Christmas-Tree." *Folklore* 3 (1892): 166–82.

——. "Rudyard Kipling." *Die Zukunft* 3 (1893): 165–71.

——. "Ostlondon als Nationalheilanstalt." *Die Zukunft* 5 (1893): 268.

——. "Robert Louis Stevenson." *Frankfurter Zeitung und Handelsblatt (Feuilleton)* 39/3, January 3, 1895.

——. *German Songs of Today and Tomorrow.* Glasgow: Friedrich Bauermeister, 1895.

——. *Goethe's Satyros and Prometheus.* Translated by John Gray. Glasgow: Friedrich Bauermeister, 1895.

——. *Von Darwin bis Nietzsche: Ein Buch Entwicklungsethik.* Leipzig: Naumann, 1895.

——. "William Wordsworth." *Die Zukunft* 11 (1895): 470–72.

——. Foreword to *Thus spake Zarathustra: A Book for All and None.* Translated by Alexander Tille. London: H. Henry, 1896.

——. "Kampf um den Erdball." *Nord und Süd,* January 1897.

——. "Der Ausstand der britischen Maschinenbauer." *Zeitschrift für Socialwissenschaft* 1 (1898): 169–81.

——. "Die Glasgower Kabelbahn." *Die Zukunft* 23 (1898): 470–78.

——. "Die Volksstimmung in England." *Die Woche,* February 3, 1900.

——. *Aus Englands Flegeljahren.* Dresden and Leipzig: Reißner, 1901, ix–x.

——, ed. *The Collected Works of Friedrich Nietzsche.* 11 vols. London: H. Henry & Co.; New York: Macmillan, 1896–1909.

——, ed. *Die Reden des Freiherrn Carl Ferdinand von Stumm-Halberg.* 10 vols. Berlin: Elsner, 1906–13.

Tille, Armin. *Ein Kämpferleben: Alexander Tille, 1866–1912.* Gotha: Friedrich Andreas Perthes, 1916.

Tönnies, Ferdinand. "Glückliches England." *Die Neue Rundschau* 19, no. 3 (March 1908): 457–58.

Uexküll, Jakob von. "Darwin und die englische Moral." *Deutsche Rundschau* 173 (1917): 215–42.

———. "Biologie und Wahlrecht." *Deutsche Rundschau* 174 (1918): 183–203.

Vance, John. "Nietzsche: A Study in Paganism." *British Review* 9 (January 1915): 13–28.

Vienna University. *Öffentliche Vorlesungen an der K. K. Universität zu Wien im Sommer-Semester 1916.* Vienna: Holzmann, 1916.

Viëtor, Wilhelm. "Krieg und Unterricht in Österreich." *Die neueren Sprachen* 23 (1915–16): 303–4.

Waechter, Max. "England, Germany and the Peace of Europe." *The Fortnightly Review* 93 (May 1, 1913): 829–41.

Wagebald, Michael. *Europa in Flammen: Der deutsche Zukunftskrieg von 1909.* Berlin: Concordia Deutsche Verlags-Anstalt, 1908.

Waldeyer, W., and R. v. Erdberg, eds. *Deutsche Reden in schwerer Zeit.* 3 vols. Berlin: Carl Heymanns Verlag, 1915.

Wallace, Edgar. *Private Selby.* London: Ward Lock, 1912.

———. *"1925": The story of a Fatal Peace.* London: George Newnes, 1915.

The War Illustrated: A Weekly Picture-Record of Events by Land, Sea and Air. Edited by J. A. Hammerton. London: The Amalgamated Press [Harmsworth], August 22, 1914–1918.

Weber, Ottokar. *Österreich und England.* Flugschriften für Österreich-Ungarns Erwachen, 2nd ed. Edited by Robert Strache und Ferdinand Gruner. Warnsdorf (Bohemia): Verlag Ed. Strache, 1915.

Wells, Herbert George. *The War of the Worlds,* [serialized 1897, book 1898]. London: Heinemann, 1968; Harmondsworth, UK: Penguin, 1974.

———. *Anticipations of the Reaction of Mechanical and Scientific Progress upon Human Life and Thought.* London: Chapman & Hall, 1902.

———. *The War in the Air.* London: George Bell, 1908; Harmondsworth, UK: Penguin, 1967.

———. "The Sword of Peace." *Daily Chronicle*, Aug 7, 1914.

———. "The War of the Mind." *Daily Chronicle*, August 29, 1914.

———. *The World Set Free.* London: Macmillan, 1914.

———. *Outline of History.* London: Cassell, 1920.

———. *Apropros of Dolores.* London: Jonathan Cape, 1938.

Widmann, Wilhelm. "Der Englander im Spiegel der Bühne." *Der Merkur* 9:4 (15 February 1918), 117–26.

Wild, Friedrich. *Karl Luick († 20. September 1935): Ein Lebensbild und ein Verzeichnis seiner Schriften.* [Off-print of the "Festschrift-Luick" of *English Studies* 35:1 (1935)]. Vienna: Zellmayer, 1936.

——. "Albert Eichler." Obituary. In Österreichische Akademie der Wissen- schaften, *Almanach für das Jahr 1953*, 103. Jahrgang. Vienna: in Kommission bei Rudolf M. Rohrer (1954): 437–49.

Williams, C. M. *A Review of the Systems of Ethics founded on the Theory of Evo- lution.* London and Boston: Macmillan, 1893.

Williams, Lloyd. *The Great Raid.* London: Black & White Publishing, 1909.

Willis, Irene Cooper. *England's Holy War.* New York: Knopf, 1928.

Wilson, David Alec. *Bernhardi and the Germans.* Manchester: National La- bour Press, 1915.

Wodehouse, P. G. *The Swoop! or How Clarence Saved England.* London: Alston Rivers, 1909.

Woynar, K. "Über den britischen Imperialismus." *Zeitschrift für das Realschulwesen* 42 (1917): 199–204.

Wrong, G. M. *The War Spirit of Germany.* London: n.d. [1917/1918].

Wylie, I. A. R. *My German Year.* London: Mills & Boon, 1910.

——. *Dividing Waters.* London: Mills & Boon, 1911.

——. *Eight Years in Germany.* London: Mills and Boon, 1914.

——. *Towards Morning.* London: Cassell, 1918.

Zabeltitz, M. Zobel von. "Englands Bild in den Augen der deutschen Klassiker." *Die Grenzboten* [Berlin] 77:3 (1918): 199–202, 228–31, 252–54.

Zapp, Arthur. *Standesehre: Sittenbilder aus den deutschen Offiziersleben.* Leipzig: n.p., 1897.

Zeitschrift für das Realschulwesen [*ZsfdR*]. Vols. 28 (1913) through 44 (1919).

Zweig, Stefan. *Die Welt von Gestern.* Stockholm: Bermann-Fischer Verlag, 1944.

Secondary Literature

Aldiss, Brian W. *Trillion Year Spree: The History of Science Fiction*. London: Gollancz, 1986.

Amann, Klaus, und Hubert Lengauer, eds. *Österreich und der Große Krieg, 1914–1918: Die andere Seite der Geschichte*. Vienna: Brandstätter, 1989.

Annan, Noel. *Our Age*. London: Weidenfeld and Nicolson, 1990.

————. *The Dons*. London: Harper Collins, 1999.

Anz, Thomas, and Michael Stark, eds. *Expressionismus: Manifeste und Dokumente zur deutschen Literatur, 1910–1920*. Stuttgart: Metzler, 1982.

Aschheim, Steven E. *The Nietzsche Legacy in Germany, 1890–1990*. Berkeley, Los Angeles and London: U of California P, 1992.

Audring, Gert, ed. *Gelehrtenalltag: Der Briefwechsel zwischen Eduard Meyer and Georg Wissowa, 1890–1927*. Hildesheim: Weidmann, 2000.

Baschiera, Karl. "Zur Geschichte des Englischunterrichtes in Österreich und der Kulturbeziehungen zu den englischsprechenden Ländern." In Hietsch, *Österreich und die angelsächsische Welt*, 2:69–86.

Baumgarten, Marita. "Berufungspolitik im 19. Jahrhundert." Unpublished lecture delivered at the "Kolloquium zur Geschichte der deutschen Universität im 19. und 20. Jahrhundert." Greifswald, March 13–14, 2003.

Beal, Anthony, ed. *D. H. Lawrence: Selected Literary Criticism*. London: Mercury, 1961.

Bentley, Eric. *The Cult of the Superman: A Study of the Idea of Heroism in Carlyle and Nietzsche, with Notes on Other Hero-Worshippers of Modern Times*. London: Robert Hale, 1947.

Berghahn, Volker. *Germany and the Approach of War in 1914*. London: Macmillan, 1973.

Bergonzi, Bernard. *The Early H. G. Wells: A Study of the Scientific Romances*. Manchester: Manchester UP, 1961.

————. "Before 1914: Writers and the Threat of War." *Critical Quarterly* 6 (1964): 126–34.

Billetta, Rudolf. "Carl Sternheim." Ph.D. thesis, University of Vienna, 1950.

Blaicher, Günther. *Das Deutschlandbild in der englischen Literatur*. Darmstadt: Wissenschaftliche Buchgesellschaft, 1992.

Bolle, Fritz. "Darwinismus und Zeitgeist." *Zeitschrift für Religions- und Geistesgeschichte* 14 (1962): 173.

Bölsche, Wilhelm. "Das Märchen vom Mars." In *Vom Bazillus zum Affenmenschen*, 319–41. Leipzig: Diederichs, 1900.

Bowler, Peter. *The Non-Darwinian Revolution: Reinterpreting a Historical Myth.* Baltimore: Johns Hopkins UP, 1992.

Brennecke, Detlef. "Die blonde Bestie." *Germanisch-Romanische Monatsschrift* 20 (1970): 467–69.

Bridgwater, Patrick. *Nietzsche in Anglosaxony: A Study of Nietzsche's Impact on English and American Literature.* Leicester: Leicester UP, 1972.

———. "English Writers and Nietzsche." In Pasley, ed. *Nietzsche: Imagery and Thought,* 220–58.

———. *H. G. Wells and Nietzsche.* H. G. Wells Society Occasional Papers, No. 3, 1980.

Brinton, Crane. "The National Socialists' Use of Nietzsche." *Journal of the History of Ideas* 1 (1940): 131–50.

———. *Nietzsche.* Cambridge, MA: Harvard UP, 1941.

Brock, Michael. "Britain Enters the War," in *The Coming of the First World War,* edited by R. J. W. Evans and Hartmut Pogge von Strandmann, 145–78. Oxford: Oxford UP, 1988.

Brocke, Bernhard vom. "Wissenschaft und Militarismus: Der Aufruf der 93 'An die Kulturwelt!' und der Zusammenbruch der internationalen Gelehrtenrepublik im Ersten Weltkrieg." In *Willamowitz nach 50 Jahren,* edited by William M. Calder III, Hellmut Flashar, and Theodor Lindken. Darmstadt: Wissenschaftliche Buchgesellschaft, 1985.

———. "Von der Wissenschaftsverwaltung zur Wissenschaftspolitik: Friedrich Althoff." *Berichte zur Wissenschaftsgeschichte* 11 (1988): 1–26.

Broucek, Peter. "Das Kriegspressequartier und die literarischen Gruppen im Kriegsarchiv, 1914–1918. In Amann and Lengauer, *Österreich und der Große Krieg 1914–1918,* 132–39.

Bruch, Rüdiger vom. "Kulturimperialismus und Kulturwissenschaften." *Berichte zur Wissenschaftsgeschichte* 13 (1990): 83–92.

Bucholz, Arden. *Moltke, Schlieffen, and Prussian War Planning.* Oxford: Berg, 1991.

Buitenhuis, Peter. *The Great War of Words: Literature as Propaganda, 1914–18 and After.* Vancouver: UBCP, 1987. London: Batsford, 1987, 1989.

Carey, John. *The Intellectuals and the Masses: Pride and Prejudice among the Literary Intelligentsia, 1880–1939.* London: Faber and Faber, 1992.

Carr, William. *A History of Germany, 1815–1990.* 4th ed. London: Edward Arnold, 1991.

Chambers, James. *Palmerston.* London: John Murray, 2004.

Clarke, Arthur C. *The Making of a Moon.* London: Frederick Muller, 1957.

Clarke, I. F. *Voices Prophesying War, 1763–1984.* London: Oxford UP, 1966.

————. *Voices Prophesying War: Future Wars, 1763–3749.* 2nd ed. Oxford and New York: Oxford UP, 1992.

————. *The Great War with Germany, 1890–1914.* Liverpool: Liverpool UP, 1997.

Cockburn, Claud, *Bestseller: The Books That Everyone Read, 1900–1939.* Harmondsworth, UK: Penguin, 1975.

Coldham, James D. *German Cricket: A Brief History.* Limited ed. of 125 copies. London: 1983.

Conze, Werner, and Jürgen Kocka, eds. *Bildungsbürgertum im 19. Jahrhundert.* Vol. 1: "Bildungssystem und Professionalisierung in internationalen Vergleichen." Series Industrielle Welt, vol. 38. Stuttgart: Klett-Cotta, 1992.

Craig, Gordon A. *Germany, 1866–1945.* Oxford: Clarendon Press, 1978. Oxford: Oxford UP, 1981.

Crook, Paul. *Darwinism, War and History: The Debate over the Biology of War from "The Origin of Species" to the First World War.* Cambridge: Cambridge UP, 1994.

Dachs, Herbert. *Österreichische Geschichtswissenschaft und Anschluß, 1918–1930.* Vienna, Salzburg: Geyer-Edition, 1974.

Darracot, Joseph, and Belinda Luftus. *Imperial War Museum: First World War Posters.* London: Imperial War Museum, 1972.

Dedijer, Vladimir. *The Road to Sarajevo.* London: MacGibbon & Kee, 1967.

Deiritz, Karl. *Geschichtsbewußtsein, Satire, Zensur: Eine Studie zu Carl Sternheim.* Königstein im Taunus: Forum Academicum in der Verlagsgruppe Athenäum, Hain, Scriptor, Hanstein, 1979.

Denscher, Bernhard. *Gold gab ich für Eisen: Österreichische Kriegsplakate, 1914–1918.* Vienna, Munich: Jugend und Volk Verlagsgesellschaft, 1987.

Dockhorn, Klaus. *Der Einsatz der englischen Wissenschaft im Weltkrieg.* Berlin: Junker & Dünnhaupt, 1940.

Dorpalen, Andreas. *Heinrich von Treitschke.* New Haven: Yale UP, 1957.

Eley, Geoff. *Reshaping the German Right: Radical Nationalism and Political Change after Bismarck.* New Haven and London: Yale UP, 1980.

Engler, Baltz. "Shakespeare in the Trenches." *Shakespeare Survey* 44 (1992): 105–11.

Evans, R. J. *The Feminist Movement in Germany, 1894–1933.* London and Beverly Hills: Sage Publications, 1976.

Falk, Walter. *Der kollektive Traum vom Krieg: Epochale Stukturen der deutschen Literatur zwischen "Naturalismus" und "Expressionismus."* Heidelberg: Carl Winter, 1977.

Faulenbach, Bernd. *Ideologie des deutschen Weges.* Munich: C. H. Beck, 1980.

Feldhofer, Peter. *Die Geschichte der Anglistik an der Universität Graz von den Anfängen bis zur Berufung Albert Eichlers.* Hausarbeit [equivalent to M.A. thesis], 1981.

Ferguson, Niall. *The Pity of War.* Harmondsworth, UK: Allen Lane, Penguin, 1998.

Fill, Alwin, und Alois Kernbauer, eds. *100 Jahre Anglistik an der Universität Graz.* Graz: Akademische Druck- u. Verlagsanstalt, 1993.

Fillitz, Hermann, ed. *Die Universität am Ring.* Vienna: Brandstätter, 1984.

Finkenstaedt, Thomas. *Kleine Geschichte der Anglistik in Deutschland: Eine Einführung.* Darmstadt: Wissenschaftliche Buchgesellschaft, 1983.

Firchow, Peter Edgerly. *The Death of the German Cousin: Variations on a Literary Stereotype, 1890–1920.* London and Toronto: Associated UP, 1986. Lewisburg: Bucknell UP, 1986.

———. "Shakespeare, Goethe, and the War of the Professors, 1914–1919." In *Intimate Enemies: English and German Literary Reactions to the Great War, 1914–1918,* edited by Franz Karl Stanzel and Martin Löschnigg, 465–92. Heidelberg: Winter, 1993.

Fischer, Fritz. *Griff nach der Weltmacht.* Düsseldorf: Droste, 1961, 1964, 1967.

———. *Germany's Aims in the First World War.* London: Chatto & Windus, 1967.

———. *Krieg der Illusionen: Die deutsche Politik von 1911 bis 1914.* Düsseldorf: Droste, 1970.

———. *War of Illusions: German Policies from 1911 to 1914.* London: Chatto & Windus, 1971.

———. *Hitler war kein Betriebsunfall: Aufsätze.* Munich: C. H. Beck, 1992.

Fischer, William B. *The Empire Strikes Out: Kurd Laßwitz, Hans Dominik, and the Development of German Science Fiction.* Bowling Green, OH: Bowling Green U Popular P, 1984.

Foster, Richard. "Criticism as Rage: D. H. Lawrence." In *D. H. Lawrence: A Collection of Critical Essays,* edited by Mark Spilka, 151–61. Englewood Cliffs, NJ: Prentice-Hall, 1963.

Frank, Richard. *Krummel, Nietzsche und der deutsche Geist.* 3 vols. Berlin and New York: de Gruyter, 1974–98), vol. 2 (1983), 571–84.

Frenzel, Elisabeth. *Stoffe der Weltliteratur.* Stuttgart: Kröner, 1962; rev. ed. 1963.

Friedell, Egon. *Kulturgeschichte der Neuzeit.* Vol 1. Munich: Beck, 1929.

Friedrich, Hans-Edwin. *Science Fiction in der deutschsprachigen Literatur: Ein Referat zur Forschung bis 1993. 7.* Sonderheft, Internationales Archiv für Sozialgeschichte der deutschen Literatur. Tübingen: Niemeyer, 1995.

Führ, Christoph. "Gelehrter Schulmann — Oberlehrer — Studienrat: Zum sozialen Aufstieg der Philologen." In Conze and Kocka, *Bildungsbürgertum im 19. Jahrhundert,* vol. 1, "Bildungssystem und Professionalisierung in internationalen Vergleichen," 417–57.

Fussell, Paul. *The Great War and Modern Memory.* Oxford: Oxford UP, 1975.

Gabel, Gernot U. *Friedrich Nietzsche: Ein Verzeichnis westeuropäischer und nordamerikanischer Hochschulschriften, 1900–1980.* Cologne: Gemini, 1985.

Gall, Franz. *Alma Mater Rudolphina, 1365–1965: Die Wiener Universität und ihre Studenten.* 3rd ed. Herausgegeben von der Österreichischen Hochschülerschaft an der Universität Wien. Vienna: Austria Press, 1965.

Gannon, Charles E. "'One Swift, Conclusive Smashing and an End.' Wells, War and the Collapse of Civilisation." *Foundation* 28, no. 77 (1999): 35–46.

Geiss, Imanuel, ed. *Julikrise und Kriegsausbruch, 1914: Eeine Dokumentensammlung.* 2 vols. Hannover: Verlag für Literatur und Zeitgeschehen, 1963/1964.

———. "Zur Beurteilung der deutschen Reichspolitik im ersten Weltkrieg." In *Die Erforderlichkeit des Unmöglichen,* edited by H. Pogge von Strandmann and Imanuel Geiss. Frankfurt am Main: Europäische Verlagsanstalt, 1965.

———. *Das Deutsche Reich und der Erste Weltkrieg.* Munich: Hanser, 1978.

———. *Der lange Weg in die Katastrophe: Die Vorgeschichte des Ersten Weltkrieges, 1815–1914.* Munich, Zurich: Piper, 1990.

———. *The Question of German Unification, 1806–1996.* [*Die deutsche Frage 1806–1990.* Mannheim: Brockhaus, 1992]. Translated by Fred Bridgham. London: Routledge, 1997.

———. "Alt-Neues Licht auf Gerhard Ritter." *Historische Mitteilungen der Ranke-Gesellschaft* 16 (Stuttgart: Steiner, 2003): 230–50. Repr. in *Gerhard Ritter: Geschichtswissenschaft und Politik im 20. Jahrhundert,* edited by Christoph Cornelison. Düsseldorf: Droste Verlag, 2001.

Geiss, Imanuel, and Bernd-Jürgen Wendt, eds. *Deutschland in der Weltpolitik des 19. und 20. Jahrhunderts.* Düsseldorf: Bertelsmann Universitätsverlag, 1974.

Giddings, Robert, ed. *Literature and Imperialism.* Basingstoke: Macmillan, 1991.

Glatzer, Diether and Ruth Glatzer. *Berliner Leben, 1914–1918.* Berlin: Rutten & Loening, 1983.

Goch, Klaus. "Elisabeth Förster-Nietzsche: Ein biographisches Portrait." In *Schwestern berühmter Männer,* edited by Luise F. Pusch, 353–413. Frankfurt am Main: Suhrkamp, 1995.

Goldhagen, Daniel. *Hitler's Willing Executioners.* London: Little, Brown, 1996.

Gray, Ronald. *The German Tradition in Literature, 1871–1945.* Cambridge UP, 1965.

Green, Martin. *The von Richthofen Sisters.* New York: Basic Books, 1974.

Gunn, James. "The Man Who Invented Tomorrow," electronic edition, http://falcon.cc.ukans.edu/~sfcenter/tomorrow.htm.

Guthke, Karl S. *Der Mythos der Neuzeit: Das Thema der Mehrheit der Welten in der Literatur- und Geistesgeschichte von der kopernikanischen Wende bis zur Science Fiction.* Bern, Munich: Francke, 1983.

———. "Are We Alone? The Idea of Extra-terrestrial Intelligence in Literature and Philosophy from the Scientific Revolution to Modern Science Fiction." In *Trails in No-Man's Land: Essays in Literary and Cultural History.* Columbia, SC: Camden House, 1993, 152–71, 240–41.

Haenicke, Gunta. *Zur Geschichte der Anglistik an deutschsprachigen Universitäten, 1850–1925.* Augsburger I & I-Schriften 8. Augsburg: Universität Augsburg, 1979.

———. *Biographisches und bibliographisches Lexikon zur Geschichte der Anglistik, 1850–1925. (Mit einem Anhang bis 1945).* Augsburger I & I-Schriften 13. Augsburg: Universität Augsburg, 1981.

Haenicke, Gunta, and Thomas Finkenstaedt. *Anglistenlexikon, 1929–1990: Biographische und bibliographische Angaben zu 318 Anglisten.* Augsburger I & I-Schriften 64. Augsburg: Universität Augsburg, 1992.

Hamann, Brigitte. *Bertha von Suttner: Ein Leben für den Frieden.* Munich: Piper, 1986.

Hamann, Günther, Kurt Mühlberger, and Franz Skacel, eds. *100 Jahre Universität am Ring: Wissenschaft und Forschung an der Universität Wien seit 1884.* Vienna: Universitätsverlag der österreichischen Hochschüler-schaft für Wissenschaft und Forschung, 1986.

Harrington, Anne. *Reenchanted Science: Holism and German Culture from Wilhelm II to Hitler.* Princeton: Princeton UP, 1996.

Hart, Sir Basil Henry Liddell. *A History of the World War, 1914–1918.* 2nd ed. London: Faber & Faber, 1934.

Haste, Cate. *Keep the Home Fires Burning: Propaganda in the First World War.* London: Allen Lane, 1977.

Heiß, Gernot, Siegfried Mattl, Sebastian Meissl, Edith Saurer, and Karl Stuhlpfarrer, eds. *Willfährige Wissenschaft: Die Universität Wien, 1938–1945.* Vienna: Verlag für Gesellschaftskritik, 1989.

Herrmann, Ulrich. "Über 'Bildung' im Gymnasium des wilhelminischen Kaiserreichs." In *Bildungsbürgertum im 19. Jahrhundert,* part 2: *Bildungsgüter und Bildungswissen,* edited by Reinhart Koselleck. Series Industrielle Welt, vol. 41, part 2, 346–68. Stuttgart: Klett, 1990.

Hietsch, Otto. *Österreich und die angelsächsische Welt: Kulturbegegnungen und Vergleiche.* 2 vols. Vienna: Braumüller, vol. 1, 1961; vol. 2, 1968.

Hillegas, Mark R. "Martians and Mythmakers: 1877–1938." In *Challenges in American Culture,* edited by Ray B. Browne, Larry N. Landrum, and William K. Bottorff, 150–77. Bowling Green, OH: Bowling Green U Popular P, 1970.

Hinton Thomas, R. *Nietzsche in German Politics and Society, 1890–1918.* Manchester: Manchester UP, 1983.

Hölbing, Franz, and Wulf Stratowa. *300 Jahre Universitas Oenipontana: Die Leopold-Franzens Universität zu Innsbruck und ihre Studenten.* Zur 300-Jahr-Feier herausgegeben von der Österreichischen Hochschülerschaft an der Universität Innsbruck. Innsbruck: Verlag der *Tiroler Nachrichten,* 1970.

Hollenberg, Günter. "Die English Goethe Society und die deutsch-englischen kulturellen Beziehungen im 19. Jahrhundert." *Zeitschrift für Religions- und Geistesgeschichte* 30 (1978): 36–45.

Holzer, Barbara. *Die politische Erziehung und der vaterländische Unterricht in Österreich zur Zeit des Ersten Weltkrieges.* MA. Thesis, University of Vienna, 1987.

Horne, John, and Alan Kramer. *German Atrocities, 1914: A History of Denial.* New Haven and London: Yale UP, 2001.

Howard, Michael. "Europe on the Eve of the First World War." In *The Coming of the First World War,* edited by R. J. W. Evans and Hartmut Pogge von Strandmann, 1–17. Oxford: Oxford UP, 1988.

———. Review of Hew Strachan, *First World War.* In *Times Literary Supplement,* July 20, 2001.

Humble, M. E. "Early British Interest in Nietzsche." *German Life and Letters* 24 (1970/71): 327–35.

———. "The Breakdown of a Consensus: British Writers and Anglo-German Relations, 1900–1920." *Journal of European Studies* 7 (1977): 41–68.

Hynes, Samuel. *The Edwardian Turn of Mind.* Princeton, NJ and London: Princeton UP, Oxford UP, 1968.

James, Harold. *A German Identity, 1770–1990.* London: Weidenfeld & Nicolson, 1989.

Joll, James. *The Unspoken Assumptions: An Inaugural Lecture delivered 25 April 1968.* London: Weidenfeld & Nicolson, 1968.

———. *1914.* "The English, Friedrich Nietzsche and the First World War." In *Deutschland in der Weltpolitik des 19. und 20. Jahrhunderts,* edited by Imanuel Geiss and Bernd Jürgen Wendt, 287–305. Düsseldorf: Bertelsmann Universitätsverlag, 1973.

———. "War Guilt 1914: A Continuing Controversy." In Kluke and Alter, *Aspekte der deutsch-britischen Beziehungen im Laufe der Jahrhunderte.*

Kaehler, Siegfried. *Wilhelm von Humboldt und der Staat.* Göttingen: Vandenhoeck & Ruprecht, 1963.

Kann, Robert A., ed. *The Habsburg Empire in World War I.* Boulder, CO: East European Quarterly; New York: Columbia UP, 1977.

Kaufmann, Walter. *Hegel: A Reinterpretation.* New York: Anchor, 1965.

———. *Nietzsche: Philosopher, Psychologist, Antichrist.* 1950. 4th ed. Princeton: Princeton UP, 1974.

Kelly, Alfred. *The Descent of Darwin: The Popularization of Darwinism in Germany.* Chapel Hill, NC: U of North Carolina P, 1981.

Kelly, Thomas. *For Advancement of Learning: The University of Liverpool, 1881–1981.* Liverpool: Liverpool UP, 1981.

Kennedy, Paul M. "British Views of Germany, 1864–1938." *Transactions of the Royal Historical Society,* 5th series, 25 (1975): 137–56.

———. *The Rise of the Anglo-German Antagonism, 1860–1914.* London: George Allen & Unwin, 1980.

Kettenacher, Lothar, Manfred Schlenke, and Helmut Seier. *Studien zur Geschichte Englands und der deutsch-britischen Beziehungen.* Munich: Wilhelm Fink Verlag, 1981.

Kinkead-Weekes, Mark. *D. H. Lawrence: Triumph to Exile, 1912–1922.* Cambridge: Cambridge UP, 1996.

Klein, Holger, ed. *The First World War in Fiction.* London: Macmillan, 1976.

———. "Distorting Mirror? Images of Prussia-Germany in English Prose, 1890–1914." 1989. In Klein, *The Artistry of Political Literature,* 21–43.

———. "Comrades? The Enemy as Individual in First World War Poetry," in Stanzel and Löschnigg, *Intimate Enemies: English and German Literary Reactions to the Great War, 1914–1918,* 181–99, reprinted in Klein, *The Artistry of Political Literature,* 241–51.

———,. *The Artistry of Political Literature: Essays on War, Commitment and Criticism.* Lewiston, Queenston, Lampeter, Wales: Edwin Mellen, 1994.

Kluke, Paul. *Außenpolitik und Zeitgeschichte: Ausgewählte Aufsätze zur englischen und deutschen Geschichte des 19. und 20. Jahrhunderts.* Wiesbaden: Steiner, 1974.

Kluke, Paul, and Peter Alter, eds. *Aspekte der deutsch-britischen Beziehungen im Laufe der Jahrhunderte.* Stuttgart: Klett-Cotta, 1978.

Kober, Leo. "Das Englandbild in der Literatur der Ersten Republik." In Hietsch, *Österreich und die angelsächsische Welt,* 1:110–25.

Kolinsky, Eva. *Engagierter Expressionismus: Politik und Literatur zwischen Weltkrieg und Weimarer Republik.* Stuttgart: Metzler, 1970.

Koss, Stephen. *The Rise and Fall of the Political Press in Britain.* London: Fontana, 1984.

Koszyk, Kurt. *Deutsche Pressepolitik im Ersten Weltkrieg.* Düsseldorf: Droste Verlag, 1968.

Krummel, Richard Frank. *Nietzsche und der deutsche Geist.* 3 vols. Berlin and New York: de Gruyter, 1974–98.

Kurzke, Hermann. "Die politische Essayistik." In *Thomas-Mann-Handbuch,* edited by Helmut Koopmann, 697–98. Stuttgart: Kröner, 1990).

Lafore, Laurence. *The Long Fuse.* Westport Connecticut: Greenwood Press, 1965.

Lang, Hans-Joachim. "England als Erzfeind in der deutschen Kriegsdichtung, 1914–1915." In Stanzel and Löschnigg, *Intimate Enemies: English and German Literary Reactions to the Great War 1914–1918,* 201–21.

Laqueur, Walter. *Young Germany: A History of the German Youth Movement.* London: Routledge & Kegan Paul, 1962.

Lasswell, Harold D. *Propaganda Techniques in the World War.* New York: Knopf; London: Kegan Paul, 1923.

Ledebur, Ruth von. *Der Mythos vom deutschen Shakespeare: Die Deutsche Shakespeare-Gesellschaft zwischen Politik und Wissenschaft (1918–1945).* Cologne, Weimar: Böhlau, 2002.

Lerchenmueller, Joachim. *"Keltischer Sprengstoff": Eine wissenschaftsgeschichtliche Studie über die deutsche Keltologie von 1900 bis 1945.* Tübingen: Niemeyer, 1997.

Lexikon der Science Fiction Literatur. Edited by Hans-Joachim Alpers, Werner Fuchs, Ronald M. Hahn and Wolfgang Jeschke. Munich: Heyne, 1980–88.

Lundgreen, Peter. "Zur Konstituierung des 'Bildungsbürgertums:' Berufs- und Bildungsauslese der Akademiker in Preußen." In Conze and Kocka, *Bildungsbürgertum im 19. Jahrhundert,* vol. 1: "Bildungssystem und Professionalisierung in internationalen Vergleichen," 79–108.

Macintyre, Ben. *Forgotten Fatherland: The Search for Elisabeth Förster-Nietzsche.* London: Macmillan, 1992.

MacKenzie, Norman, and Jeanne MacKenzie. *The Time-Traveller: The Life of H. G. Wells.* London: Weidenfeld & Nicolson, 1973.

Maddox, Brenda. *The Married Man: A Life of D. H. Lawrence.* London: Minerva, 1994.

Mander, John. "Must we love the Germans?" *Encounter* 33 (December 1969): 36–44.

———. *Our German Cousins.* London: John Murray, 1974.

Manz, Stefan. "'Wir stehen fest zusammen / Zu Kaiser und zu Reich!' — Nationalism among Germans in Britain, 1871–1918." *German Life and Letters* 55 (2002): 398–415.

———. "'Our sworn, subtle, savage, implacable and perfidious foe!' — Spy-fever and Germanophobia in Scotland, 1914–1918." *Irish-German Studies* 1 (2004): 28–37.

Markus, Manfred. "English University Studies in Austria: An In(n)sider's Report." In *European English Studies: Contributions Towards the History of a Discipline,* edited by Balz Engler and Renate Haas, 143–60. London: Published for the European Society for the Study of English by The English Association, 2000.

Marsiske, Hans-Arthur. "Der Traum vom Mars." *Spiegel* online series, December 22–30, 2000, http://www.spiegel.de/kultur/gesellschaft/0,1518,109283,00.html.

Marsland, Elizabeth. *The Nation's Cause: French, English and German Poetry of the First World War.* London, New York: Routledge, 1991.

Mast, Peter. *Um Freiheit für Kunst und Wissenschaft: Der Streit im Deutschen Reich, 1840–1901.* 3rd ed. Rheinfelden and Berlin: Schäuble, 1994.

McClelland, Charles E. *State, Society, and University in Germany, 1700–1914.* Cambridge: Cambridge UP, 1980.

McConnell, Frank. *The Science Fiction of H. G. Wells.* New York: Oxford UP, 1981.

Mecenseffy, Grete. *Evangelische Lehrer an der Universität Wien.* Graz: Böhlau, 1967.

Meyers, Jeffrey. *D. H. Lawrence: A Biography.* London: Macmillan, 1990.

Milburn, Diane. *The "Deutschlandbild" of A. R. Orage and the "New Age" Circle.* Frankfurt am Main: Peter Lang, 1996.

Mommsen, Wolfgang J. *Bürgerliche Kultur und politische Ordnung: Künstler, Schriftsteller und Intellektuelle in der deutschen Geschichte 1830–1933.* Frankfurt am Main: Fischer, 2000.

———. "Einleitung: Die deutschen kulturellen Eliten im Ersten Weltkrieg." In *Kultur und Krieg: Die Rolle der Intellektuellen, Künstler und Schriftsteller im Ersten Weltkrieg*, edited by Wolfgang S. Mommsen, 1–16. Munich: Oldenbourg, 1996.

———. "Zur Entwicklung des Englandbildes der Deutschen seit dem Ende des 18. Jahrhunderts." In *Studien zur Geschichte Englands und der deutschbritischen Beziehungen*, edited by Kettenacker, Schlenke, and Seier.

Moore, Gregory. "The Super-Hun and the Super-State: Allied Propaganda and German Philosophy during the First World War." *German Life and Letters* 65 (2001): 310–30.

———. *Nietzsche, Biology and Metaphor*. Cambridge: Cambridge UP, 2002.

Moore, Harry T. *The Priest of Love: A Life of D. H. Lawrence*. Harmondsworth, UK: Penguin, 1980.

Mühlberger, Kurt, und Thomas Maisel. *Rundgang durch die Geschichte der Universität Wien*. Vienna: Archiv der Universität Wien, 1999.

Muhs, Rudolf, Johannes Paulmann, and Willibald Steinmetz, eds. *Aneignung und Abwehr: Interkultureller Transfer zwischen Deutschland und Großbritannien im 19. Jahrhundert*. Bodenheim: Philo, 1998.

———. "Geisteswehen. Rahmenbedingungen des deutsch-britischen Kulturaustauschs im 19. Jahrhundert." In Muhs, Paulmann, and Steinmetz, *Aneignung und Abwehr*, 44–70.

Müller, Götz. *Gegenwelten: Die Utopie in der deutschen Literatur*. Stuttgart: Metzler, 1989.

Ní Bhroiméil, Úna. *The American Mission: The Gaelic Revival and America, 1870–1915*. Ph.D. thesis, Lehigh University, Bethlehem, PA, 1998.

Nipperdey, Thomas. *Deutsche Geschichte, 1866–1918*. Vol. 1. Munich: C. H. Beck, 1990.

Nolte, Ernst. *Nietzsche und der Nietzscheanismus*. Frankfurt and Berlin: Propyläen, 1990.

Ó Lúing, Seán. *Kuno Meyer, 1858–1919: A Biography*. Dublin: Geography Publications, 1991.

Oberkofler, Gerhard, and Eduard Rabofsky. *Studien zur Geschichte der österreichischen Wissenschaft zwischen Krieg und Frieden*. Vienna: Edition Fortschrittliche Wissenschaft, 1987.

Oberkofler, Gerhard, and Peter Goller. *Geschichte der Universität Innsbruck (1669–1945)*. Frankfurt: Lang, 1995.

Oppel, Horst. *Englisch-deutsche Literaturbeziehungen*. 2 vols. Berlin: Erich Schmidt Verlag, 1971.

Ottmann, Henning. "Englischsprachige Welt." In Ottmann, *Nietzsche-Handbuch: Leben — Werk — Wirkung*, 431–34.

———, ed. *Nietzsche-Handbuch: Leben — Werk — Wirkung*. Stuttgart-Weimar: Metzler, 2000.

Paletschek, Sylvia. *Die permanente Erfindung einer Tradition: Die Universität Tübingen im Kaiserreich und der Weimarer Republik*. Stuttgart: Franz Steiner, 2001.

Panayi, Panikos. *The Enemy in our Midst: Germans in Britain during the First World War*. Providence, RI and Oxford: Berg, 1991.

———. *German Immigrants in Britain during the Nineteenth Century, 1815–1914*. Oxford and Washington, DC: Berg, 1995.

Parrinder, Patrick. "How Far Can We Trust the Narrator of *The War of the Worlds?*" *Foundation* 28, No. 77 (1999): 15–24.

Pasley, Malcolm, ed. *Nietzsche, Imagery and Thought: A Collection of Essays*. London: Methuen, 1978.

Paulmann, Johannes. "Interkultureller Transfer zwischen Deutschland und Großbritannien: Einführung in ein Forschungskonzept." In Muhs, Paulmann, and Steinmetz, *Aneignung und Abwehr*, 21–43.

Paulsen, Friedrich. *Die deutschen Universitäten und das Universitätsstudium*. Berlin: 1902, 1911. Reprint, Hildesheim: Olms, 1966.

Peters, Michael. "Der 'Alldeutsche Verband.'" In *Handbuch zur "Völkischen Bewegung," 1871–1918*, edited by Uwe Puschner, Walter Schmitz, and Justus H. Ulbricht, 302–15. Munich: K. G. Saur, 1999.

Pfister, Manfred. "Germany Is Hamlet: The History of a Political Interpretation." *New Comparison* 2 (1986): 106–26.

———. "Hamlet und der Deutsche Geist: Die Geschichte einer politischen Interpretation." *Jahrbuch der Deutschen Shakespeare-Gesellschaft West* [Bochum] (1992): 13–38.

Pomerin, Reiner. *Der Kaiser und Amerika: Die USA in der Politik der Reichsleitung 1890–1917*. Cologne: Böhlau Verlag, 1986.

Preglau-Hämmerle, Susanne. *Die politische und soziale Funktion der österreichischen Universität: Von den Anfängen bis zur Gegenwart*. Innsbruck: Inn-Verlag, 1986.

Pynsent, Paul. "The Last Days of Austria: Hasek and Kraus." In Klein, *The First World War in Fiction*, 136–48.

Ramm, Agatha. *Germany, 1789–1919*. London: Methuen, 1967.

Rauchbauer, Otto, ed. *Wiener Beiträge zur Englischen Philologie*, no. 80: *A Yearbook of Studies in English Language and Literature, 1985/86: Festschrift Siegfried Korninger*. Vienna: Braumüller, 1986.

Read, Herbert. *The Contrary Experience: Autobiographies.* London: Faber, 1963.

Read, James Morgan. *Atrocity Propaganda, 1914–1919.* New Haven: Yale UP, 1941.

Redlich, Oswald. "Über die Geschichte der Universität Wien." In *Wien: Sein Boden und seine Geschichte,* edited by Othenio Abel, 195–96. Vienna: Wolfrum-Verlag, 1924.

———. "Geschichte der Universität Wien." In Wettstein, *Die Universität Wien: Ihre Geschichte, ihre Institute und Einrichtungen,* 1–11.

Reed, T. J. "Nietzsche's Animals: Idea, Image, and Influence." In Pasley, *Nietzsche, Imagery and Thought: A Collection of Essays,* 159–219. London: Methuen, 1978.

———. *Thomas Mann and the Uses of Tradition.* 1974. 2nd ed. Oxford: Oxford UP, 1996.

Reiffenstein, Brigitte. "Zu den Anfängen des Englischunterrichts an der Universität Wien und zur frühen wissenschaftlichen Anglistik in Wien." In Rauchbauer, *Wiener Beiträge zur Englischen Philologie,* no. 80: *A Yearbook of Studies in English Language and Literature,* 163–85. Vienna: Braumüller, 1986.

Richards, Robert J. *Darwin and the Emergence of Evolutionary Theories of Mind and Behavior.* Chicago: U of Chicago P, 1987.

Ringer, Fritz F. F. *The Decline of the German Mandarins.* Cambridge, MA: Harvard UP, 1989.

Ritter, Gerhard. *The Sword and the Sceptre: The Problem of Militarism in Germany.* Translated by Heinz Norden. Coral Gables, FL: U of Miami P, 1972.

Rohl, C. F. *Kaiser, Hof und Staat: Wilhelm II. und die deutsche Politik.* Munich: C. H. Beck, 1987.

Rose, Mark. *Alien Encounters: Anatomy of Science Fiction.* Cambridge, MA: Harvard UP, 1981.

Rottensteiner, Franz. "Kurd Laßwitz, a German Pioneer of Science Fiction." In *Science Fiction: The Other Side of Realism,* edited by Thomas D. Clareson, 289–306. Bowling Green UP: 1971.

———. "Kurd Laßwitz — Erkenntnis und Ethik dazu," in Kurd Laßwitz, *Homchen und andere Erzählungen.* Heyne Science Fiction Classics 4309. Munich: Heyne, 1986.

Rudy, Willis. *Total War and Twentieth-Century Higher Learning.* Rutherford: Farleigh Dickinson UP, 1991.

Rumold, Rainer, and O. K. Werckmeister, eds. *The Ideological Crisis of Expressionism: The Literary and Artistic German War Colony in Belgium, 1914–1918.* Columbia, SC: Camden House, 1990.

Sampson, Anthony. *The Scholar Gypsy: The Quest for a Family Secret.* London: John Murray, 1997.

Sanders, M. L., and Philip M. Taylor. *British Propaganda during the First World War, 1914–18.* London: Macmillan, 1982.

Sauermann, Eberhard. *Literarische Kriegsfürsorge: Österreichische Dichter und Publizisten im Ersten Weltkrieg.* Vienna, Cologne, and Weimar: Böhlau, 2000.

Scheichl, Sigurd Paul. "Journalisten leisten Kriegsdienst." In Amann und Lengauer, *Österreich und der Große Krieg 1914–1918*, 104–9.

Scheler, Manfred, ed. *Berliner Anglistik in Vergangenheit und Gegenwart, 1810–1985.* Berlin: Colloquium Verlag, 1987.

Schenkel, Elmar. "Paradoxical Affinities. Chesterton and Nietzsche." In *The Novel in Anglo-German Context: Cultural Cross-Currents and Affinities,* edited by Susanne Stark, 241–51. Amsterdam and Atlanta: Rodopi, 2000.

Schröter, Klaus. "Chauvinism and its Tradition: German Writers at the Outbreak of the First World War." *Germanic Review* 43 (1968): 120–35.

———. *Literatur und Zeitgeschichte.* Mainz: von Hase u. Koehler, 1970.

Schungel, Wilfried. *Alexander Tille (1866–1912): Leben und Ideen eines Sozialdarwinisten.* Husum: Matthiesen 1980.

Schwabe, Klaus. *Wissenschaft und Kriegsmoral: Die deutschen Hochschullehrer und die politischen Grundfragen des Ersten Weltkrieges.* Göttingen, Zürich, and Frankfurt: Musterschmidt, 1969.

———. "Einführende Bemerkungen: Rahmenbedingungen und Selbstdeutung des beruflichen Wirkens deutscher Gelehrter." In *Deutsche Hochschullehrer als Elite, 1815–1945,* edited by Klaus Schwabe, 9–25. Boppard am Rhein: Harald Boldt, 1988,.

Schweikert, Rudi, "Von Martiern und Menschen, oder: Die Welt, durch Vernunft dividiert, geht nicht auf." In *Kurd Laßwitz: Auf zwei Planeten,* edited by Rudi Schweikert, 847–912. Munich: Heyne, 1998.

Schwonke, Martin. "Naturwissenschaft und Technik im utopischen Denken der Neuzeit." In *Science Fiction,* edited by Eike Barmeyer, 57–75. Munich: UTB, 1972.

Siemann, Wolfram. *Gesellschaft im Aufbruch: Deutschland, 1849–1871.* Frankfurt am Main: Suhrkamp, 1990.

Smekal, Ferdinand G. *Alma universitas: Geschichte der Grazer Universität in vier Jahrhunderten.* Vienna: Verlag der Vereinten Nationen, 1967.

Snider, Nancy V. *An Annotated Bibliography of English Works on Friedrich Nietzsche.* Ph.D. diss., U of Michigan, 1962. Ann Arbor, MI: University Films International, 1984.

Spilka, Mark, ed. *D. H. Lawrence: A Collection of Critical Essays.* Englewood Cliffs, NJ: Prentice-Hall, 1963.

Stanzel, Franz Karl, and Martin Löschnigg, eds. *Intimate Enemies: English and German Literary Reactions to the Great War, 1914–1918.* Heidelberg: Winter, 1993.

Steilberg, Hays Alan. *Die amerikanische Nietzsche-Rezeption von 1896 bis 1950.* Berlin and New York: de Gruyter, 1996.

Steinmüller, Angela, und Karlheinz Steinmüller. *Visionen 1900 2000 2100: Eine Chronik der Zukunft.* Hamburg: Rogner & Bernhard, 1999.

Strachan, Hew. *The First World War.* Vol. 1: *To Arms.* Oxford: Oxford UP, 2001.

Stromberg, Roland N. "The Intellectuals and the Coming of War, 1914." *Journal of European Studies* 3:2 (1973): 109–22.

———. *Redemption by War: The Intellectuals and 1914.* Lawrence, KS: The Regents Press of Kansas, 1982.

Studt, Christoph. *Lothar Bucher, 1817–1892: Ein politisches Leben zwischen Revolution und Staatsdienst.* Göttingen: Vandenhoeck & Ruprecht, 1992.

Taylor, A. J. P. *The First World War: An Illustrated History.* London: Hamish Hamilton, 1963.

———. "Nietzsche and the Germans." In A. J. P. Taylor, *Europe: Grandeur and Decline,* 194–98. Harmondsworth, UK: Pelican, 1967.

———. *War by Timetable: How the First World War Began.* London: Macdonald, 1969.

———. *A Personal History.* London: Hamish Hamilton, 1983.

Thatcher, David S. *Nietzsche in England, 1890–1914: The Growth of a Reputation.* Toronto: U of Toronto P, 1970.

Thody, Philip. *The Conservative Imagination.* London: Pinter, 1993.

Timm, Eitel Friedrich. *William Butler Yeats und Friedrich Nietzsche.* Würzburg: Königshausen & Neumann, 1980.

Timms, Edward. *Karl Kraus, Apocalyptic Satirist.* New Haven and London: Yale UP, 1986.

Tomalin, Claire. *Katherine Mansfield: A Secret Life.* New York: Viking, 1987.

Tuchman, Barbara W. *August 1914.* London: Constable, 1962.

Ullrich, Volker. *Die nervöse Großmacht, 1871–1918: Aufstieg und Untergang des deutschen Kaiserreichs.* 2nd ed. Frankfurt am Main: Fischer, 1999.

Viereck, George Sylvester. *Spreading Germs of Hate*. London: Duckworth, 1931.

Wallace, Stuart. *War and the Image of Germany: British Academics 1914–1918*. Edinburgh: John Donald, 1988.

Weaver, Ann C., ed. *Publications of the English Goethe Society: Index to the Publications, 1886–1986*. Leeds: W. S. Maney, 1987.

Wehler, Hans-Ulrich. "Sozialdarwinismus im expandierenden Industriestaat." In Geiss and Wendt, *Deutschland in der Weltpolitik des 19. und 20. Jahrhunderts*, 133–42.

———. *Das deutsche Kaiserreich, 1871–1918*, 1973. 7th ed. Göttingen: Vandenhoeck & Ruprecht, 1994.

———. *Deutsche Gesellschaftsgeschichte*. Vol. 3. Munich: Beck, 1995.

Weigel, Hans, Walter Lukan, und Max D. Peyfuss. *Jeder Schuss ein Russ/Jeder Stoss ein Franzos: Literarische und graphische Kriegspropaganda in Deutschland und Österreich, 1914–1918*. Vienna: Brandstätter, 1983.

Weilen, Alexander von. "Jakob Schipper †." In *Wiener Abendpost*, "Feuilleton," Beilage zur *Wiener Zeitung*, January 22, 1915, 1–2.

Weintraub, Stanley. *Journey to Heartbreak: The Crucible Years of Bernard Shaw, 1914–1918*. New York: Weybright & Talley, 1971.

Weisstein, Ulrich. "Der letzte Zivilist? Carl Sternheim at La Hulpe." In Rumold and Werckmeister, *The Ideological Crisis of Expressionism: The Literary and Artistic German War Colony in Belgium 1914–1918*, 115–31.

Wenzel, Dietmar, ed. *Kurd Laßwitz, Lehrer, Philosoph, Zukunftsträumer: Die ethische Kraft des Technischen*. Meitingen: Corian, 1987.

Wessels, Dieter. *Welt im Chaos: Struktur und Funktion des Weltkatastrophenmotivs in der neueren Science Fiction*. Frankfurt am Main: Akademische Verlagsgesellschaft, 1974.

Wettstein, Robert, ed. *Die Universität Wien: Ihre Geschichte, ihre Institute und Einrichtungen*. Vienna, Düsseldorf: Lindner-Verlag, 1929.

Winkelbauer, Thomas. "Krieg in deutschen Lesebüchern der Habsburgermonarchie (1880–1918)." In Amann and Lengauer, *Österreich und der Große Krieg, 1914–1918*, 37–47.

Wolfe, Gary K. *The Known and the Unknown: The Iconography of Science Fiction*. Kent, OH: Kent State UP, 1979.

Young, Harry F. *Prinz Lichnowsky and the Great War*. Athens: U of Georgia P, 1977.

Zecha, Christoph. *Lehrkanzel und Institut für englische Philologie an der philosophischen Fakultät Innsbruck (1894–1938)*. Zulassungsarbeit [equivalent to M.A. thesis], Innsbruck, 1966.

Contributors

IAIN BOYD WHYTE is Professor of Architectural History at the University of Edinburgh. He has written extensively on architectural modernism in Germany, Austria, and the Netherlands; his most recent work is *Modernity and the Spirit of the City* (2003). He has served as a Trustee of the National Galleries of Scotland, is a Fellow of the Royal Society of Edinburgh, and from 2002 to 2005 was Visiting Senior Program Officer at the Getty Foundation, Los Angeles.

FRED BRIDGHAM is a Senior Lecturer at the University of Leeds. He has published variously on Rilke, Kafka, Benn, Kleist, and on German history and language, notably *The Friendly German-English Dictionary: A Guide to German Language, Culture and Society through Faux Amis, Literary Illustration and Other Diversions* (1996). He translated Hans Werner Henze's *Der Prinz von Homburg* for performance by the English National Opera in 1995 and is currently completing a book on Wagner.

INGO CORNILS is a Senior Lecturer in the Department of German at The University of Leeds. His research focuses on the complex relationship between political, utopian, and fantastic thought. He has special interests in German science fiction, Hesse (he is coeditor of *Hermann Hesse Today*, 2005), Thomas Mann, and Uwe Timm. He is currently writing a book on the literary representation of the German Student Movement.

ANDREAS HUETHER currently teaches cultural studies courses on twentieth-century Ireland and the Northern Ireland conflict in the English Department at Freiburg University. He previously worked in the German Department at the University of Limerick, where he began his PhD research on "Regional Identity, Federal Nationalism and Celtic Studies in Germany, 1840s-1890s."

HOLGER KLEIN recently retired from the Chair of English at Salzburg, having previously taught at Cologne, Norwich, and Poitiers. His research interests have led to publications on Renaissance Literature (for example, an edition and translation of *Hamlet* and *Much Ado About Nothing*), Restoration and eighteenth-century comedy, translation studies, J. B. Priestley, and committed literature. In the latter field he edited *The First World War in Fiction* (1976) and coedited *The Second World War in Fiction* (1984). At present he is engaged on an edition and translation of *Henry IV*.

STEFAN MANZ is Senior Lecturer in German and International Studies at the University of Greenwich, London. He is a Fellow of the Royal Historical Society. His Research interests include migration studies,

Anglo-German relations, German history and politics, and European area studies. Relevant publications include *Migranten und Internierte: Deutsche in Glasgow, 1864-1918* (2003) and, as coeditor, *Discourses of Intercultural Identity in Britain, Germany and Eastern Europe* (2004).

NICHOLAS MARTIN is Senior Lecturer in European Intellectual History and Director of the Graduate Centre for Europe at the University of Birmingham. His publications include *Nietzsche and Schiller: Untimely Aesthetics* (1996) and, as editor, *Nietzsche and the German Tradition* (2003). He has recently edited a special issue of *Forum for Modern Language Studies* on literary reflections of modern war. He is currently researching German literary responses to the First World War during the 1920s and early 1930s.

GREGORY MOORE is currently Lecturer in German at St Andrews, having taught previously at Cambridge and Aberystwyth Universities. He is secretary of the Friedrich Nietzsche Society, author of *Nietzsche, Biology and Metaphor* (2002), and editor of *Nietzsche and Science* (2004). He is also the translator of Johann Gottfried Herder's *Selected Writings on Aesthetics* (2006) and is preparing a study of Oswald Spengler.

HELENA RAGG-KIRKBY has been working as a freelance writer since 2004, having previously held lecturing posts at the universities of Sheffield and Leeds. An eighteenth- and nineteenth-century specialist, her study *Adalbert Stifter's Late Prose: The Mania for Moderation* was published by Camden House in 2000. Her translation, *Sigmund Freud, An Outline of Psychoanalysis,* for Penguin appeared in 2003.

RHYS W. WILLIAMS is Professor of German and Pro-Vice-Chancellor at the University of Wales, Swansea, and recent Chair of the Conference of University Teachers of German in Britain and Ireland. He has published substantially on German Expressionism and postwar German literature. Currently he is general editor of the "Contemporary German Writers" series, to which he has contributed articles for the volumes on Sarah Kirsch, Peter Schneider, Jurek Becker, Uwe Timm, and Hans-Ulrich Treichel.

Index